MUSTER ROLLS

OF THE

PENNSYLVANIA VOLUNTEERS

IN THE

WAR OF 1812-1814,

WITH COTEMPORARY

PAPERS AND DOCUMENTS.

VOLUME I.

Southern Historical Press, Inc.
Greenville, South Carolina

This volume was reproduced
from a personal copy located in
the Publishers private library

Please direct all correspondence and book orders to:
SOUTHERN HISTORICAL PRESS, Inc.
1071 Park West Blvd.
Greenville, SC   29611

Originally Printed Harrisburg, PA 1880
ISBN #978-1-63914-619-2
Printed in the United States of America

ROLL OF PENNSYLVANIA VOLUNTEERS.

GENERAL OFFICERS, WAR OF 1812–14.

Commander-in-Chief.

SNYDER, SIMON, Governor of the Commonwealth of Pennsylvania; born at Lancaster, November 5, 1759; member of the convention of 1790; member of the Pennsylvania House of Representatives 1797 to 1808, and speaker thereof; Governor of the State, 1808 to 1817; subsequently a member of the Senate; died November 9, 1819.

Adjutants General.

Reed, William, of Adams county; died in office, June 15, 1813.
Irvine, William N., *acting*.
Duncan, William, October, 1813.
Hyneman, John M., 1814; died in office, May 8, 1816.

Quarter-master General.

Smith, Wilson, of Erie county, 1812–14.

Commissary General.

Irvine, Callender.

Aids to the Commander-in-Chief.

Boileau, Nathaniel B.
Gibson, John Bannister.
Binns, John.
Duane, William.

Major Generals.

[The numbers refer to divisions.]

I. Worrell, Isaac, Philadelphia, 1812–14.
II. Sheetz, Henry, Montgomery, 1812–14.
III. Pearce, Cromwell, Chester, 1812.
IV. Whitehill, James, Lancaster, 1812.
V. Gilliland, William, Adams, 1812–14.
VI. Udree, Daniel, Berks, 1812–14.
VII. Rea, John, Franklin, 1812–14.

VIII. Craig, Thomas, Northampton, 1812-14.
IX. Montgomery, Daniel, Northumberland, 1812-14.
X. Borrows, John, Lycoming, 1812-13.
XI. Banks, James, Mifflin, 1812-13.
XII. Ogle, Alexander, Somerset, 1812-14.
XIII. Merchant, David, Westmoreland, 1812-14.
XIV. Stevenson, James, Washington, 1812.
XV. Tannehill, Adamson, Pittsburgh, 1812-13.
XVI. Mead, David, Crawford, 1812-13.
III. Steel, James, Chester, 1813-14.
IV. Watson, Nathaniel, Lancaster, 1813-14.
XIV. Atcheson, Thomas, Washington, 1813-14.
X. Steel, William, Huntingdon, 1814.
XV. Wilson, John, Allegheny, 1814.
XVI. Phillips, John, Erie, 1814.

Brigadier Generals.

I. 1. Bright, Michael, Philadelphia, 1812-13.
   2. Duncan, William, Philadelphia, 1812-13; promoted adjutant general, 1814.
II. 1. Wells, Isaiah, Montgomery, 1812.
   2. Smith, Samuel, Bucks, 1812.
III. 1. Cunningham, John W., Chester, 1812.
   2. Harris, William, Chester, 1812-13.
IV. 1. Hibshman, Jacob, Lancaster, 1812.
   2. Miller, Robert, Lancaster, 1812.
V. 1. Hetrick, Christian, York, 1812.
   2. Gettys, James, Adams, 1812.
VI. 1. Bower, Jacob, Dauphin, 1812-13.
   2. Hottenstine, David, Berks, 1812.
VII. 1. Boden, John, Cumberland, 1812.
   2. Young, William, Franklin, 1812.
VIII. 1. Kreider, Conrad, Jr., Northampton, 1812.
   2. Spering, Henry, Easton, 1812.
IX. 1. Light, Adam, Northumberland, 1812.
   2. Ross, William, Luzerne, 1812.
X. 1. Cummings, John, Lycoming, 1812.
XI. 1. Doty, Ezra, Mifflin, 1812.
   2. Steel, William, Huntingdon, 1812; promoted major general, 1814.
XII. 1. Saylor, Jacob, Somerset, 1812.
   2. Noble, John, Bedford, 1812.
XIII. 1. Craig, Alexander, Westmoreland, 1812.
XIV. 1. Atcheson, Thomas, Washington, 1812; promoted major general, 1813.
   2. Crooks, Richard, Greene, 1812.

XV. 1. Wilson, John, Pittsburgh, 1812; promoted major general, 1814.
 2. McComb, James, Armstrong, 1812; died 1814.
XVI. 1. Kelso, John, Erie, 1812-14.
 2. Graham, Thomas, Butler, 1812.
I. 1. Wharton, Robert, Philadelphia, *vice* Bright, dec'd, 1813.
III. 2. Brooke, William, Delaware, 1813.
VI. 1. Harrison, John, Dauphin, 1813.
XIII. 2. Mason, Thomas, Fayette, 1813.
XIV. 1. Patterson, Thomas, Washington, *vice* Atcheson, promoted, 1813.
I. 1. Bartram, George, Philadelphia, *vice* Wharton, 1814.
 2. Snyder, Thomas, Philadelphia, *vice* Duncan, promoted, 1814.
IV. 2. Dicks, John, Lancaster, *vice* Miller, 1814.
V. 2. Eyster, Jacob, Adams, *vice* Gettys, 1814.
VI. 1. Forster, John, Dauphin, *vice* Harrison, 1814.
 2. Addams, John, Berks, *vice* Hottenstine, 1814.
VII. 2. Waddell, Thomas, Franklin, *vice* Young, 1814.
VIII. 1. Mertz, Henry, Lehigh, *vice* Kreider, 1814.
X. 2. Wells, Henry, Bradford, 1814.
XI. 1. Evans, Lewis, Mifflin, *vice* Doty, 1814.
 2. Moore, Arthur, Huntingdon, *vice* Steel, promoted, 1814.
XII. 2. Philson, Robert, *vice* Saylor, 1814.
XIII. 1. Murray, James, Westmoreland, *vice* Craig, 1814.
 2. McClelland, Alexander, Fayette, 1814.
XIV. 2. Brown, John, Greene, *vice* Crooks, 1814.
XV. 1. Marks, William, Jr., Allegheny, *vice* Wilson, promoted, 1814.
XVI. 2. Hurst, Henry, Crawford, *vice* Kelso, 1814.

Brigade Inspectors.

I. 1. Sharp, Daniel, Philadelphia, 1812.
 2. Etris, William, Philadelphia county, 1812.
II. 1. Snyder, Christian, Montgomery, 1812.
 2. Vansant, Harman, Bucks, 1812-14.
III. 1. Steel, James, Chester, 1812, promoted brigadier general.
 2. Brooke, William, Delaware, 1812.
IV. 1. Light, John, Lancaster, 1812.
 2. Sample, Nathaniel W., Lancaster county, 1812.
V. 1. Jordan, Archibald S., York, 1812.
 2. Welsh, George, Adams, 1812-14.
VI. 1. Doebler, Abraham, Lebanon, 1812.
 2. Shoemaker, Peter, Reading, 1812.

VII. 1. Lamberton, James, Carlisle, 1812.
  2. McClelland, William, Franklin, 1812.
VIII. 1. Saeger, Nicholas, Northampton, 1812.
  2. Brodhead, Richard, Wayne, 1812.
IX. 1. Smith, Robert, Northumberland, 1812.
  2. Fruit, John, Northumberland, 1812.
X. 1. Stewart, Samuel, Lycoming, 1812.
XI. 1. Young, John, Centre, 1812.
  2. Moore, William, Huntingdon, 1812.
XII. 1. Graham, George, Somerset, 1812.
  2. Mann, Andrew, Bedford, 1812.
XIII. 1. Armstrong, George, Westmoreland, 1812.
  2. Springer, Uriah, Fayette, 1812–13.
XIV. 1. Dunlap, James, Washington, 1812–14.
  2. Huston, Samuel, Greene, 182.
XV. 1. Cochran, Samuel, Pittsburgh, 1812.
  2. Beatty, Robert, Kittanning, 1812.
XVI. 1. Clark, William, Meadville, 1812.
  2. Powers, Samuel, Beaver, 1812.
III. 1. Park, James, Chester, 1813.
VIII. 2. Post, Isaac, 1814.
XV. 1. Johnston William, 1814.
XIII. 1. Kirkpatrick, John, 1814.
VI. 1. Spayd, Christian, Dauphin, 1814.
VIII. 2. Fogel, John, 1814.
XIII. 2. Dearth, George, 1814.
XIV. 2. Mitchell, Thomas, 1814.
VIII. 1. Jones, John, 1814.
XII. 2. Hanna, James, 1814.
VIII. 1. Gress, Matthias, 1814.
III. 2. Stanley, Matthew, 1814.
  1. Snyder, Casper, 1814.
I. 2. Tryon, Jacob, G., 1814.

Hospital Surgeons.

Agnew, Samuel.
Bemus, Daniel.

Hospital Surgeon's Mates.

Reily, Luther.
Watson, David.

Deputy Quarter-Masters General.

Foering, Frederick, 1812.
Hay, John, 1812.
Linnard, William, 1812.
Moore, William, 1813.
Sergeant, Henry, September 24, 1814.

Judges Advocate.

Fullerton, ———.
Smith, William S.

Superintendents of Military Stores.

Duncan, William.
Duane, William.
Johnston, Lieutenant.

Contractors.

Denny, Ebenezer, Pittsburgh.
Parker, Richard, Carlisle.

Aides-de-Camp.

Biddle, John G., to General Cadwalader.
Ellmaker, Amos, to General John Forster.
Franks, Samuel D., to General Addams.
Farrelly, Patrick.
McCall, Richard, to General Cadwalader.
Martin, Charles.
Patterson, James, to General N. Watson.
Shippen, Benjamin, Jr., to General N. Watson.

Brigade Majors.

Badgers, William C.
Forster, John M., from sergeant.
Hiester, Gabriel, Jr.
Hunter, ———, promoted Assistant Adjutant General.
Junkin, John.
McCall, Richard.
Powell, John Hare.
Rodgers, Thomas J.

Commissaries.

Beall, Thomas.
McCannum, Robert.
Moore, William.
Reed, Rufus S.
Rawle, George.
Stewart, Nathaniel.
Wolverton, Stephen.

Forage Masters.

Dempsey, David.
Greenfield, H.
McClean, William.
Smith, G. W.

Wagon Masters.

Boyd, David.
Coryell, Lewis.
Himrod, Moses.
Johnson, Fergus.
McComb, William.
Martin, John.
Rigler, Stephen.
Woodside, Archibald.

REGIMENTAL OFFICERS.

Colonels.

Bache, Louis, from lieutenant colonel.
Ball, James M., from lieutenant colonel.
Biddle, Clement C.
Cochran, John.
Fenton, James.
Ferguson, E.
Ferree, Joel, from lieutenant colonel.
Findlay, John.
Freeman, ———.
Gilkeyson, Andrew, from lieutenant colonel.
Hamilton, William, from lieutenant colonel.
Hill, Rees, promoted brigadier general.
Humphreys, Thomas, from lieutenant colonel.
Irwin, Jared.
Kennedy, Maxwell.
Krickbaum, Conrad, from lieutenant colonel.
Lefever, ———.
Marlin, Ralph, from lieutenant colonel.
Nelson, David, from lieutenant colonel.
Patterson, Robert.
Pearce, Cromwell; promoted major general, 1812.
Pearson, John L.
Procter, ———.
Rush, Lewis.
Schappel, Jeremiah, from lieutenant colonel.
Snider, Jeremiah.
Sloan, John.

Lieutenant Colonels.

Bache, Louis, promoted colonel.
Berry, Peter L.

WAR OF 1812-14.

Ball, James M., promoted colonel.
Bull, Robert.
Christy, Andrew.
Cochran, ———.
Dale, Samuel.
Ferree, Joel, promoted colonel.
Gilkeyson, Andrew, promoted colonel.
Gowdy, Samuel.
Hamilton, William, from major; promoted colonel.
Horn, Abraham.
Hosack, Thomas.
Humphrey, Thomas, promoted colonel.
Hutter, Christian J.
Krickbaum, Conrad, promoted colonel.
Lutz, John.
Marlin, Ralph, promoted colonel.
Miller. James.
Miller, Robert.
Montgomery, James.
Neligh, Nicholas.
Nelson, David, from major; promoted colonel.
Phillips, John.
Prevost, Andrew M., from major.
Purviance, John.
Raguet, Condy.
Ritscher, Adam.
Schappel, Jeremiah, promoted colonel.
Sutherland, Joel B.
Smith John.
Thompson, Andrew.
Wallace, John C., from major.
Weirick, George.

Majors.

Alexander, John B.
Allison, William.
Andrews, John.
Benezet, ———.
Bennett, Anthony.
Brawley, Francis.
Boyer, Philip.
Bozorth, William.
Burke, ———.
Clemson, Jehu.
Cossett, Epaphroditus.
Duffield, Thomas W.
Fisher, Thomas.

Fisher, George.
Forster, James.
Fullerton, David.
Galloway, Samuel.
Ganet, James.
Griffith, Isaac.
Hall, James.
Hamilton, William, from captain; promoted lieutenant colonel.
Harvenal, Jonathan.
Hellick, Jacob.
Herkimer, John.
Hyner, Robert.
Ingersoll, Joseph R.
Jacoby, ———.
Jenkins, Andrew.
Jones, Samuel.
Kepner, A.
McCoy, John.
McClure, John.
McCullough, Hugh.
McFarlane, James.
McFarland, William.
Martin, Charles.
Moore, George.
Nelson, David, promoted lieutenant colonel.
Porter, George B.
Prevost, Andrew M., promoted lieutenant colonel.
Price, Edward.
Rogers, W. C.
Rumble, Peter.
Scott, John.
Scott, William.
Shaffer, Jacob.
Sims, John.
Sparks, Samuel.
Speese, William.
Sproat, James W.
Stevenson, Cornelius.
Stewart, John.
Terrill, Jehiel.
Uhle, John.
Wallace, John C., promoted lieutenant colonel.
Warner, James.
Waters, William.
Wood, James.
Voorhees, Samuel S.
Vodges, Jacob.

Surgeons.

Beard, John M.
Bemus, Daniel.
Clark, David.
Cossit, Epaphroditus.
Culbertson, Samuel D., promoted brigade surgeon.
Dawson, G.
Eberle, John.
Gilfillan, Alexander.
Humes, Samuel.
McClelland, John.
McCullough, William.
Otto, John B.
Parsons, Usher.
Patton, William.
Rogers, John J.
Scull, Edward.
Smith, Thomas.
Spencer, ——.
Stephenson, Josiah E., from surgeon's mate.
Stewart, Samuel.
Wallace, John C.
Wilson, Martin.

Surgeons' Mates.

Blossom, Ira A.
Boggs, John.
Clark, David.
Cossett, James S.
Denig, George.
Duherhitz, Charles.
Erb, John.
Fahnestock, Derrick.
Farr, Eliel.
Ferguson, James G.
Ingram, John.
Johnston, William.
Logan, James.
McClymons, John.
Magaw, Jesse.
Pratt, Zaccheus.
Stephenson, Josiah E., promoted surgeon.
Stewart, Samuel.
Terrill, ——.

Quarter-Masters.

Allee, John.
Arthur, William.

Bishop, Moses.
Bowman, Andrew.
Boyd, S.
Chambers, John.
Curray, William K.
Doran, John.
Fox, John.
Gibson, James.
Goodman, Joseph.
Hurst, George.
Kennedy, William.
Leidich, John.
Love, Thomas.
Lowry, ———.
McClany, William.
McCullough, Thomas G.
Murray, Robert, from quarter-master sergeant.
Noblit, ———.
Patterson, James.
Peters, Jacob.
Porter, John.
Powers, Ebenezer.
Quigley, John.
Rahm, Melchior.
Russell, Hamlin.
Swartz, John.
Wade, Noah T.
Weber, Michael.
Wharton, Francis R.
Williamson, Samuel.
Wolff, Bernard.
Uhler, John.

Paymasters.

Bingham, Hugh.
Clark, George.
Clark, William.
Dennison, George.
Gleim, Christian, from ensign.
Gher, John.
Harris, Robert.
Hosack, Henry.
Hull, Basherer.
Noble, Andrew.
Porter, James M.
Prevost, Lewis M.

Peters, Thomas R.
Rawle, ———.
Witman, Charles.
Scull, Jasper.

Chaplains.

Eaton, Johnston.
Montany, ———.
Rossel, Robert.
Sample, Robert.
Tait, Samuel.

Adjutants.

Ash, Michael W.
Aston, Owen.
Backus, Joseph.
Baily, Joel.
Compton, David.
Courtney, David.
Forster, Thomas.
Gill, Robert.
Glasgow, John.
Harriott, Sidney.
Hart, William.
Home, Daniel.
Hutton, John G.
Irwin, Ninian.
Irwin, Robert, Jr.
Kirkner, ———.
Levan, Abraham.
Lockart, Robert.
McCombs, Daniel.
McDowell, James.
Myers, Isaac.
Poe, Thomas.
Scott, Francis.
Selin, Anthony C.
Swift, ———.
Trump, Isaac.
Williamson, William.
Wright, Edward.
Youse, William.

Sergeants Major.

Aiken, Alexander.
Allee, John.
Brawley, James.
Brown, John.

Byrnes, Patrick.
Colt, Henry.
Dempsey, David.
Gilliland, Robert.
Levis, Joseph.
Lindsay, Andrew.
Kirkpatrick, William.
O'Neill, Robert.
Patterson, Robert.
Scott, William.
Smith, John.
Stewart, Andrew.
Stewart, Thomas.
Wallace, Robert.
Wilson, John.
Wilcocks, Samuel.

Quarter-Master Sergeants.

Beans, James A.
Brown, John G.
Carson, William.
Chenowith, Arthur.
Hall, Joseph.
Hamilton, James.
Hull, Gersham.
Johnson, Ephraim.
McGrady, William.
Maxwell, Robert.
Miller, Alexander.
Murray, Robert, promoted quarter-master.
Newell, ———.
Pearson, George.
Power, Ebenezer.
Shelmire, Abraham.
Sperry, Frederick W.
Stewart, James.
Sutley, George.
Swan, John.
Taylor, Henry.
Winters, Josiah.

Drum Majors.

Claar, Jacob.
Clingensmith, Peter.
Fryer, John.
Glazier, Ira.
Hoffman, Powel.

Martin, Armand.
Person, Jacob.
Shannon, Samuel.
Shoop, Michael.

Fife Majors.

Brode, Joseph D.
Clough, Rufus.
Everhart, Frederick.
Johnston, Samuel.
Levan, Daniel.
McCloskey, Daniel.
McClure, Thomas.
Morrell, Thomas.

VOLUNTEERS ON THE DELAWARE—1814.

ADVANCE LIGHT BRIGADE.

Brigadier General.

Cadwalader, Thomas.

Brigade Majors.

Hunter, ———, promoted Assistant Adjutant General.
Powel, John Hare.

Aids.

McCall, Richard.
Biddle, John G.

Assistant Quarter-Master General.

Sergeant, Henry.

Assistant Deputy Quarter-Master General.

Conney, David.

FIRST REGIMENT VOLUNTEER ARTILLERY.

Lieutenant Colonel.

Prevost, Andrew M.

Majors.

Stevenson, Cornelius.
Duffield, Thomas W.

WAR OF 1812–14.

Adjutant.

Hutton, John G.

Quarter-Master.

Peters, Jacob.

Pay-Master.

Prevost, Lewis M.

Surgeon.

Smith, James.

Sergeant Major.

O'Neil, Robert.

FIRST REGIMENT VOLUNTEER INFANTRY.

Colonel.

Biddle, Clement C.

Lieutenant Colonel.

Raguet, Condy.

Majors.

Ingersoll, Joseph R.
Voorhees, Samuel S.

Adjutant.

Ash, Michael W.

Quarter-Master.

Wharton, Francis R.

Pay-Master.

Peters, Thomas R.

Surgeon.

Stewart, Samuel.

Surgeon's Mate.

Ferguson, James G.

Sergeant Major.

Wilcocks, Samuel.

Quarter-Master Sergeant.

Sperry, Fred. W.

Drum Major.

Fryer, John.

Fife Major.

Brode, Joseph D.

WAR OF 1812-14.

FIRST REGIMENT VOLUNTEER RIFLEMEN.

Colonel.

Humphreys, Thomas.

Lieutenant Colonel.

Horn, Abraham.

Majors.

Waters, William.
Speese, William.
Boyer, ———.

Adjutant.

Hart, William.

Quarter-Masters.

Goodwin, Joseph.
Shelmire, Abraham.

Surgeon.

Spencer, ———.

Surgeon's Mate.

Rawle, ———.

Sergeant Major.

Patterson, Robert.

BATTALION VOLUNTEER RIFLEMEN.

Major.

Uhle, John.

Adjutant.

Selin, Anthony C.

Quarter-Master.

Love, Thomas.

Quarter-Master Sergeant.

Hall, Joseph.

DETACHMENT OF MILITIA.

Lieutenant Colonel.

Berry, Peter L.

Majors.

Vodges, Jacob.
Bozorth, William.

Adjutant.

Trump, Isaac.

Quarter-Master.

Gibson, James.

B—VOL. XII.

Sergeant Major.

Byrnes, Patrick.

Quarter-Master Sergeant.

Hamilton, James.

VOLUNTEERS AT BALTIMORE, 1814.

GENERAL ORDERS.

HEAD QUARTERS, YORK, *September 16, 1814.*

The detachment of Penna. Militia ordered to rendesvous at York are organized into four regiments and one battalion, forming two brigades, under the command of the following officers:

Major General.

Watson, Nathaniel.

Aids-de-Camp.

Shippen, Henry.
Patterson, James.

Hospital Surgeon.

Agnew, Samuel.

Surgeon's Mates.

Watson, David.
Reily, Luther.

FIRST BRIGADE.

Brigadier General.

Forster, John.

Aid-de-Camp.

Ellmaker, Amos.

Brigade Major.

Forster, John M.

FIRST REGIMENT.

Colonel.

Kennedy, Maxwell.

Lieutenant Colonel.

Cochran, William.

Major.

Porter, George B.

Adjutant.

Bailey, Joel.

Quarter-Master.

Rahn, Melchior.

WAR OF 1812–14.

Paymaster.

Gleim, Christian.

Surgeon.

Patton, William.

Captains.

Walker, Thomas.
Achey, Jacob.
Crain, Richard M.
Knight, Richard.
Morehead, John B.
Elder, John.
Doebler, Henry.
Carothers, John.
Lesher, Benjamin.
Henry, Gawin.

Lieutenants.

Still, Charles.
Wilson, Hugh.
Piper, H.
Kline, Philip.
Manley, John.
Reed, William.
Embich, Jacob.
Henning, John.
Thomas, William.
Carothers, George.

Ensigns.

Gleim, Christian.
Steger, Adam.
Roberts, George.
Habble, David.
Conrad, Henry W.
Fasnacht, Frederick.
Orr, Thomas.
Ross, Adam.

SECOND REGIMENT.

Lieutenant Colonel.

Ritscher, Adam.

Majors.

Allison, William.
Fisher, George.

Adjutant.

Youse, William.

Quarter-Master.
Uhler, John.

Paymaster.
Noble, Andrew.

Surgeon.
Eberle, John.

Captains.
Graham, John.
Neal, Thomas.
Snyder, Peter.
Todd, James.
Fetterhoff, Philip.
Dietrich, Jacob.
McElhenny, Thomas.
Hehn, William.
Smith, Isaac.
Peter, Michael.

Lieutenants.
Porter, James.
Milligan, Robert.
Bonnewitz, Benjamin.
Ward, John.
Woodsides, Thomas.
Hoffman, Daniel.
Finley, Thomas.
Sallada, George.
Lentz, Michael.
Sallada, Jacob.

Ensigns.
Turner, John.
Noble, Andrew.
Moody, Robert.
Winter, John.
Shive, John.
Kinsel, Christian.
Berry, John.
McClure, Abraham.
Buchanan, Nathan.
Garman, John.

FIFTH BATTALION.

Major.
McFarland, William.

WAR OF 1812-14.

Quarter-Master.

Curray, William K.

Adjutant.

Lochart, Robert.

Captains.

Stuart, William.
Wilson, Fobert.
Robinson, John.
McCullough, James.
Fisher, Philip.
Rees, Jeremiah.
Steel, William.
Holmes, John.

Lieutenants.

Potts, James W.
Williamson, David.
Robinson, William.
King, Robert.
Brook, John.
Knepley, Conrad.
Weiley, David.
Downing, John.

Ensigns.

Bailey, Israel.
Miller, Joseph.
Pendell, Benjamin.
Dayton, John.
Shay, Thomas.
Dill, James.
Lefevre, Samuel.
Wilson, James.

SECOND BRIGADE.

Brigadier General.

Addams, John.

Aid-de-Camp.

Franks, Samuel D.

Brigade Major.

Hiester, Gabriel, Jr.

WAR OF 1812–14.

FIRST REGIMENT.

Lieutenant Colonel.

Schappel, Jer.

First Major.

Jones, Samuel.

Second Major.

Kepner, A.

Adjutant.

Myers, Isaac.

Quarter-Master.

Swartz, John.

Paymaster.

Witman, Charles.

Surgeon.

Otto, John B.

Captains First Battalion.

Hamilton, William.
Zieber, George.
Maugre, John.
Willotts, Henry.
Marx, George.

Captains Second Battalion.

Hambright, George.
Jones, Jonathan.
Ritter, George.
Marshall, Jacob.
Hughes, Theophilus.

First Lieutenants.

Musser, George.
Griesemer, Isaac C.
Fisher, Jacob.
Herman, William.
Boyer, George.
Jordan, Thomas R.
Morrow, Samuel.
Barto, John.
Burkhart, Henry.
Lefevre, John C.

Second Lieutenants.

Hill, Frederick.
Witman, Charles.

WAR OF 1812–14.

Hiester, Gabriel.
Musser, Mathias.
Franks, S. D.
Myers, Isaac.
Heister, William.
Dreibelbeis, Jacob.

Ensigns.

Wein, George.
Fuhrman, Jacob.
Greiner, Samuel.
Heberling, John.
Christian, Michael.
Hambright, Frederick.
Groves, Samuel.
Slottman, Daniel.
Alston, Samuel.
Looser, Christopher.

SECOND REGIMENT.

Lieutenant Colonel.

Lutz, John.

First Major.

McClure, John.

Second Major.

Clemson, Jehu.

Adjutant.

McClure, Samuel.

Quarter-Master.

Patterson, James.

Paymaster.

Scull, Jasper.

Surgeon.

Humes, Samuel.

Captains First Battalion.

Moore, Thomas.
Snyder, Jacob.
Good, Henry.
Hetselberger, George.
Christian, John.

Captains Second Battalion.

Schriver, Thomas.
Diller, Adam.

Huston, Thomas.
May, John.
Old, Gabriel.

First Lieutenants.

Tilton, William.
Singer, Abraham.
McMillan, Robert.
Crider, Samuel.
Alspach, Mathias.
Musser, William.
Kerr, David.
Gartner, Israel.
Coheen, Edward.
Fister, John.

Second Lieutenants.

Swarts, John.
Boyer, Henry.
McClellan, Samuel.
Scull, Jasper.

Ensigns.

Baum, George.
Scott, John E.
Dietrich, Michael.
Welsh, George.
Zimmerman, Abra.
Small, Joseph.
McKee, Christian.
Shimp, John.
Reigle, George.
Shook, William.

By order, Major General NATHANIEL WATSON.

H. SHIPPEN,
First Aid-de-Camp.

MUSTER ROLLS

OF THE

WAR OF 1812-14.

1—Vol. XII

ROLLS OF THE WAR OF 1812-14.

ROLL OF CAPT. JACOB ACHEY'S COMPANY.

Muster-roll of Capt. Jacob Achey's company, in the First regiment, First brigade, Pennsylvania militia, under the command of Col. Maxwell Kennedy, at York, Pennsylvania, September 5, 1814. (In service from September 1, 1814, to March 1, 1815. From Lebanon county.)

Captain.

Achey, Jacob.

Lieutenant.

Wilson, Hugh.

Ensign.

Steger Adam.

Sergeants.

Hartman, Joseph.
Coil, William.
Steitzer, Christian.
Hubley, William.

Corporals.

Welsh, David.
Bechtell, Isaac.
Mitchell, Thomas.
Atkins, Samuel.

Fifer.

Drumens, Alexander.

Drummer.

Marr, Peter.

Privates.

Achey, George.
Achey, Peter.
Biship, Thomas.
Bleirstine, Abraham.
Boger, Paul.
Bowman, Samuel.

Boyer, Henry.
Daub, Jacob.
Daub, Peter.
Day, Francis.
Deitrich, Christian.
Deitrich, Henry.
Dimmy, Alexander.
Felty, Henry.
Fland, Joshua.
Fogle, Samuel.
Fox, Peter.
Hamuth, Jacob.
Hawer, John.
Johnson, Charles.
Kershling, Henry.
Kolp, Lewis.
Kreider, Tobias.
Lewis, Cyrus.
Loeb, Henry.
Loeb, John.
Lowry, James.
Martin, James.
McKarhan, David.
Miller, Jacob.
Ott, Henry.
Reed, Samuel.
Smith, John.
Steger, Jacob.
Thomas, Jacob.
Uhler, Jacob.
Weiss, Peter.
Zweil, Anthony.

ROLL OF CAPT. WM. ALEXANDER'S COMPANY.

Muster-roll of Capt. Wm. Alexander's company of volunteers, belonging to the Fifth detachment Pennsylvania militia, under the command of Col. James Fenton, at Carlisle.

Captain.

Alexander, William.

WAR OF 1812–14.

Lieutenant.

Spotswood, Lindsey.

Ensign.

Right, William.

Sergeants.

Hutton, James H.
Hays, John L.
Alexander, William.
McManus, Francis.

Corporals.

Bowyer, Frederick.
Wyncoop, John.
Hoffman, Christian.
Spotwood, James.

Musicians.

Johnston, Edward.
Stine, George.
Barclay, James.

Privates.

Armor, Samuel.
Armor, Edward.
Armor, John.
Armstrong, James.
Alexander, William.
Bollinder, Conrod.
Bell, Isaac.
Bullock, William.
Boyd, James.
Brown, Joseph.
Butler, John.
Borland, Joseph.
Biggs, William.
Brumbaugh, Samuel.
Craven, William.
Doyle, Elisha.
Dawson, James.
Davidson, John.
Domling, Daniel.
Ellison, Andrew.
Eaken, Andrew.
Fagon, Enoch.
Fagan, Charles.

Foulke, John.
William, Graham.
Gilmore, William.
Gibson, John.
Hoffer, Isaac.
Holcomb, Michael.
Kline, George.
Laird, William.
Magee, Alexander.
McKean, John.
McKean, Joseph.
Miller, Daniel.
Mahmor, Henry.
Miller, John.
Moore, John.
Morrice, John.
Jacob, Mull.
McClure, James.
James, McCartney.
Otto, John.
Parkinson, Robert.
Philips, Emanuel.
Roney, William.
Ramsey, John.
Rine, George D.
Richardson, John.
Smith, Samuel.
Scott, John.
Sullivan, Thomas.
Smith, William H.
Steele, John.
Thompson, William.
Wyncoop, Cornelius.
Walker, Thompson.
Weibley, Martin.
Witsell, John.
Wheeler, William.
Walker, William.

I do certify, that the above and forgoing is a true and correct muster-roll of my company. Given under my hand, at Carlilse, this 14th day of September, Anno Domini 1814.

WM. ALEXANDER,
Captain of Carlisle Infantry.
JAMES FENTON,
Colonel.

ROLL OF CAPTAIN DAVID ALTEMUS' COMPANY.

Pay-roll of Captain David Altemus' company of light infantry of the Second brigade, First division, Pennsylvania Militia, late in the service of the United States, under the command of Brigadier General Thomas Snyder.

Sergeants.

Hallowell, Joseph.
Vanharn, Samuel.
McNelly, John.
Clayton, Zephaniah.

Corporals.

Foster, Striclen S.
Vandegrift, Joseph.
Clark, Caleb.
Reed, John.

Musician.

Adair, William.

Privates.

Altemus, Jonathan.
Scuff, Samuel.
Britton, Thomas.
Bodine, James.
Beish, George, never mustered.
Burk, William.
Cuckle, John.
Crewson, John J.
Crewson, Jesse.
Curtis, Benjamin C.
Crewson, William.
Deprefontaine, John.
Engle, Charles.
Edwards, Robert, appointed sergeant major.
Farr, George.
Fritz, George.
Hamilton, John.
Hendricks, Josiah.
Henderson, John.
Johnson, Elias.
Kelly, William.

Lyons, Aaron W.
McNelly, Bernard.
Mooney, John.
Miller, John.
Murvine, John.
Mann, Charles.
Merkle, Solomon.
Otterson, John.
Owen, Owen.
Senin, Rodey.
Thomson, Robert.
Vandegrift, Benjamin.
Watton, William.
Wybrant, Hugh.
Walton, Britton.
Whartenby, John.

I certify, on honor, that the aforegoing is a true list of the men's names who were late in the service of the United States from the 11th day of September, 1814, to the 2d day of January, 1815.

(Signed) JOHN FOULKROD,
Late Lieutenant Commanding in service of United States.

OXFORD TOWNSHIP, PHILADELPHIA COUNTY,
February 7, 1815.

JOHN THOMPSON,
Colonel Commanding.

ROLL OF CAPT. BENJAMIN ANDERSON'S COMPANY.

Pay-roll of Capt. Benjamin Anderson's company of drafted militia, attached to the First regiment, commanded by Col. Joel Feree, in the service of the United States, from the State of Pennsylvania, Brig. Gen. Richard Brooks commanding, commencing the ——— and ending the ———.

Captain.

Anderson, Benjn, volunteered fifteen days.

Lieutenant.

White, James.

Ensign.

Lindsey, William, volunteered fifteen days.

WAR OF 1812-14.

Sergeants.

Gordon, John, volunteered fifteen days.
Anderson, John.
Rankin, John, volunteered fifteen days.
Post, Ephraim.

Corporals.

Parker, James, volunteered fifteen days.
Stoolfire, Christopher.
Fowler, Sylvester.
Thompson, James.

Privates.

Anderson, Abra^m, volunteered fifteen days.
Anderson, James.
Bedilon, Philip.
Cook, Jacob.
Craige, William.
Cummins, Samuel.
Dunlap, Alexander, volunteered fifteen days.
Drake, Daniel.
Delong, Abra^m, volunteered fifteen days.
Elliott, Jacob.
Fauner, John.
Griffey, John.
Harris, William.
Hawthorn, John.
Hallowday, Andrew.
Harvey, James.
Hazley, Joshua, volunteered fifteen days.
Huffman, Benjamin.
Huffman, James, discharged November 26, 1812.
Hoge, William.
Jamison, George.
Jenkins, Alexander, volunteered fifteen days.
Kelley, William.
Kuntz, George.
Laughlin, John.
Linn, William, discharged January 9, 1813.
Linn, Moses, volunteered fifteen days.
Loid, Eli.
McMillen, John.
Miller, Henry.
Munnel, Hugh.
McCarty, John, volunteered fifteen days.
McMiken, Hance, volunteered fifteen days.

Morris, Jessey, volunteered fifteen days.
McVay, Jacob.
Moser, Henry, discharged November 26, 1812.
McConnel, Alexander.
Officer, James.
Ostler, George.
Pensel, Lenard.
Rodgers, Andrew.
Ritner, Joseph.
Rolston, Robert.
Rolston, John.
Ramsey, George, died at Upper Sandusky, February 7, 1813.
Ross, Kennet.
Shearn, John.
Simpson, William, discharged November 4, 1812.
Simpson, David.
Scott, Robert, discharged October 19, 1812.
Suven, Reuben.
Urie, Thomas.
White, John, Sr.
White, John, Jr.
Wire, Edward.
Waters, Arcable.
Walker, James.

I do certify, upon honor, that this pay-roll exhibits a true statement of my company of the First regiment of Pennsylvania Militia, for the period therein mentioned, and that the remarks set opposite the names of men are accurate and just.

BENJ'N ANDERSON,
Captain.

ROLL OF CAPT. SAMUEL ANDERSON'S COMPANY.

Muster-roll of a company of Mifflin guards, under the command of Capt. S. Anderson, in the service of the United States, First regiment, Pennsylvania Volunteers, commanded by Col. Clement C. Biddle, from the 6th September, when last mustered, to the 26th September, 1814.

Captain.

Anderson, S.

First Lieutenant.

Shull, F.

Second Lieutenant.

Marshall, D.

Ensign.

Biggart, William.

Sergeants.

Caldwell, John.
Haskins, Benjamin.
Evans, William.
Thorn, Henry.

Corporals.

Thomson, John.
Hawkins, George.
Marshall, John.
Derrick, Joseph.
Rowan, John.

Privates.

Kille, Thomas.
Edwards, Samuel.
Lambert, John.
Hall, Joseph.
Martin, Joseph.
Hawkins, John.
Broomall, Daniel.
Pedrick, Tho.
Burns, James.
Beatty, William.
Beatty, Robert.
Martin, Lazarus.
Stevenson, John.
Minshall, Edward.
Garrett, John.
Lloyd, John.
Fisher, David.
Martin, Levi B.
Parsons, Thomas.
Brown, Jeremiah.
Painter, Tho.
Smith, Tho. P.
Evans, James.
Lear, Charles.
Pywell, John.
Geary, William.
Marshall, William H.

Locke, John.
Mitchell, Daniel.
McKee, John.
Wilkerson, Joseph.
Hook, John Martin.
Cole, Leonard.
Cummins, William.
Bowers, Thomas.
Barnard, T. D.
Justus, Charles.
Dunant, John.
Cleary, James.
Martin, Richard G.
Snowden, Charles G.
Pyle, Joseph.
Lindsey, William.
Caldwell, George.
Cummins, David.
Brattin, James.
Chester, John Martin.
Martin, Aaron.
Hibbart, Joseph.
Hansal, John.
Johns, Joseph T.
Tawrence, William.
Dermontt, John.
Grubb, William.
Bradford, John.

The following persons have joined since the 26th September, the date of last muster:
Johns, Townsend T., September 28.
Tawrence, William, September 28.
McDermott, John, September 28.
Grubb, William, October 1.
Bradford, John, October 2.

J. Bradford was a member, previous to the date of our marching orders; was taken sick about the time the company marched.

I certify that the Mifflin Guards, commanded by Captain S. Anderson, is in the service of the United States, under orders of the general commanding the Fourth military district.

THOMAS CADWALADER,
Brigadier General Commanding.

CAMP DUPONT, *7th October, 1814.*

We certify, on honor, that this muster-roll exhibits a true state of the company of Mifflin Guards, First Regiment, Pennsylvania

Volunteers, for the period therein mentioned, and that the remarks set opposite the names of the men are accurate and just.

S. ANDERSON,
Captain.

I believe the above muster-roll to be correct.

CONDY. RAGULT,
Lieutentenant Colonel, First regiment, P. V.

ROLL OF CAPTAIN THOMAS ATKINSON'S COMPANY.

Roll and muster of Capt. Thomas Atkinson's company of volunteers, attached to the One Hundred and Thirty-seventh regiment, Pennsylvania militia, Ralph Martin, lieutenant colonel commandant, from the 26th of August, to the 10th of September, 1812, (both days inclusive,) on duty at Erie.

Captain.

Atkinson, Thomas.

Lieutenant.

McClanahan, Robert.

Ensign.

Sinclair, Brad.

Sergeants.

Shannon, William.
Daniels, John.
Daniels, Casper C.
Sinclair, John.

Corporals.

Brown, Nathan.
Townly, William.
Clark, Samuel.
Lowrey, Hugh.

Privates.

Heights, Jacob.
Alle, James.
Dunn, Simeon.
David, Owen.
Bell, Alexander.

Buckley, William.
McClanahan, Eli, (Elisha.)
Mitchel, Peter.
McBride, Jacob.
Hains, Albert.
Bloomfield, Thomas.
Straight, Stephen.
Holman, Alexander.
Hights, David.
Carrol, Samuel.
Vancort, John.
Ryan, Edward.
Martin, Samuel.
Gibson, Thomas.
Clark, Robert.
Phillips, Daniel.
Skelton, William.
Adams, Joseph.
Duprey, Thomas.
Rodgers, John.
Dunn, John.
Foster, William.
Lowrey, James.
McGuire, John.
Williams, Daniel
Williams, John.
Randolph, James.
Henderson, Robert.
Steel, Samuel.
Anderson, James.
Johnston, John.
Larber, Philip, waiter.

I do certify that the above roll and muster is just and true.

THOS. ATKINSON,
Captain.

September 13, 1812.
Examined:

R. MARTIN,
Lieutenant Colonel Commandant.

ROLL OF CAPT. RICHARD BACHE'S COMPANY.

Muster-roll of a company of "Franklin Flying Artilley," under the command of Capt. Richard Bache, of the First brigade, first division Pennsylvania militia in the service of the United States, commanded by Gen. Thomas Cadwalader from September 15, 1814, to December 25, 1814.

Captain.

Bache, Richard.

First Lieutenant.

Chew, B., Jr.

Second Lieutenant.

Bryne, John.

Cornet.

McLean, Thomas.

Sergeants.

Carson, John.
Darnel, Henry.
Wallace, John, promoted from corporal, November 20.
Smith, Thomas, promoted from corporal, November 20.

Corporal.

Borland, John.
Earley, John, appointed from private, November 20.
Reese, Martin, appointed from private, November 20.
Lubins, Isaac, September 25, 1814; appointed from private November 20.
Conner, Bernard.

Quarter-master.

McLaughlin, Charles.

Private.

Duff, Patrick, reduced from sergeant.
Kennedy, Patrick, reduced from sergeant.
Taylor, Robert, reduced from corporal.
Agnew, Andrew.
Bloomfield, John.
Boyle, Patrick.
Boyle, Bartholomew.

Biddle, David.
Campbell, James.
Clark, Robert.
Cronory, Henry.
Campbell, Anthony.
Cronier, Stephen.
Campbell, Michael.
Cassady, Edward, received no State pay.
Dunwoody, Robert.
Graham, Charles.
Hardy, Patrick.
Harvy, James.
Huston, James.
Jones, Evan.
Kirby, Edward.
Kelly, John.
Linden, Hugh.
Lynch, Edward.
McCafferty, Patrick.
Cormick, William.
McKinley, Thomas.
McCurdy, Daniel.
McClaskey, Michael, died December 20, 1815.
Muntzer, Joseph.
McDonough, William.
McCrury, Samuel.
O'Brian, Lawrence.
Patton, William.
Todd, William.
Wrench, Henry.
Wray, William.
Ward, Thomas.
Warr, John.
Wall, John.
Yurbley, George.
Yournson, Giles,
Laughton, John.
Little, William, September 25, 1814.
Lubins, Al., October 2, 1814; no State pay.
Monaghan, Henry.

I certify, on honor, that this muster-roll exhibits a true state of the company of "Franklin Flying Artillery," in the service of the United States for the period herein mentioned, and that the remarks set opposite the names of the men are accurate and just.

RICHARD BACHE,
Captain.

ROLL OF CAPTAIN BELA BADGER'S COMPANY.

Muster and pay-roll of the company of Frankford volunteer artillery, Bela Badger, captain, late in the service of the United States, attached to the light brigade, under the command of Gen. T. Cadwalader. Date of service, September 13, 1814; discharged, January 3, 1815.

Captain.

Badger, Bela.

First Lieutenant.

Whitaker, Robert.

Second Lieutenant.

Doak, Washington.

Third Lieutenant.

Shallcross, John.

Quarter-Master.

Lee, William A.

Sergeants.

Thomas, James F.
Fulton, Gardner.
Clark, John.
Tees, Daniel.
Gilbert, John T.

Corporals.

Tyler, Rufus.
Neff, Robert.
Dover, Levi Th.
Linton, James.
Baldwin, Joseph.

Privates.

Denny, Samuel.
Jones, Isaa.
Bodine, Jacob.
Burk, John.
Burger, William.
Botner, Joseph.
Bordman, John.
Buckius, Rudolph.
Courtney, Samuel P.
Coucker, George.

Chute, Thomas.
Coon, Jacob.
Coon, Christopher.
Clark, Daniel.
Doran, Francis.
Delaney, Jacob.
Erbin, Adam.
Fisher, George.
Friese, Conrad.
Frazer, David.
Gray, John.
Hamilton, Benjamin.
Harper, Jacob.
Haines, George.
Hamilton, James.
Hart, Oliver.
Jenkins, Benjamin.
Landenberger, Samuel.
Landenberger, William.
Lear, James.
Merkle, George.
Marshall, Joseph.
Miller, James.
Matlack, Benjamin.
McMullen, John.
Newcamp, John.
Potts, Thomas.
Pennell, Joseph.
Phillips, Henry.
Palmer, Aaron.
Peters, John.
Quicksill, Charles.
Rorar, George.
Rorar, Joseph.
Rorar, John.
Retzer, Michael.
Restine, Charles.
Robinson, George.
Reese, James.
Soley, Robert.
Sparks, Henry D.
Shetzline, Michael.
Sanderson, Joseph M.
Shallcross, William.
. Scates, Lawrance.
Sparks, Isaac W.

Schoch, Henry.
Scott, Benjamin.
Schoch, Jonathan.
Schoch, Joseph.
Cumberland, Shepherd.
Thomas, Moses.
Thomas, William.
Vannaken, Paul.
Worrell, Stephen.
Worrell, Isaiah.
Worrell, Rudolph.
Worrell, Hawley.
Williams, Giles.
Thomas, Martin.

Artillery Drivers.

Clendening, John.
Hetherington, Arthur.
Rimal, Jacob.
Uber, Nicholas.

I do hereby certify that the above muster-roll and date of service is correct.

BELA BADGER,
Captain.

July 24, 1816.

ROLL OF CAPT. J. BAKEOVEN'S COMPANY.

Pay-roll of Capt. J. Bakeoven's company, Second brigade, ——— division Pennsylvania militia, in the service of the United States, under command of Col. John Thompson.

First Lieutenant.

Neveling, Daniel.

Second Lieutenant.

Pate, Peter H.

Ensign.

Pate, Peter M.

Sergeants.

Moser, Jacob.
Baker, Samuel.
Sheppard, William.
Fordam, Richard.

Corporals.

Henderson, David.
Mood, John.
Mood, Jacob.
Faunce, Isaac.

Privates.

Keffer, Anthony.
Hoffman, Jacob.
Morris, John.
Cornwell, James.
Hoffman, Adam.
Morgan, Luke.
Baker, Peter.
Boat, Jacob H.
Upperman, George.
Cramer, Rudolph.
Toy, Isaac.
Shillingforth, James.
Grissim, Adam.
Wright, William.
Smith, Jacob.
Wall, Henry.
Sheetz, John.
Creely, Michael.
Gardy, John.
Bennet, John.
Vance, John.
Croud, John.
Johnston, William.
Sickfrit, John.
Alexander, Nicholas.
Montgomery, John.
Kinsey, Conrad.
Smith, John.
Denny, John.
Forster, John.
Crist, Joseph.
Stockbine, or Storkpine, Henry.
Crist, Michael.
Bault, Frederick.
Shipe, John.
Peterson, Jere.
Causor, George.
Nasor, Jacob.
Arons, James.

WAR OF 1812-14.

Williams, Theopilus.
Walters, Mitchel.
Dickerson, William.
Gahn, John.
Elliot, John.
Fox, Lewis.
Erle, John.
Penik, James.
Parker, George.
Riffit, Joseph.
Redek, Adam.
Giger, George.
Campbell, James.
Knox, Nehemiah.
Newton, John.
Fitzell, Lewis.
Cantreel George.
North, Josiah.
Thorp, John.
Willis, Ebenezer.
Harman, (or Harmer,) Jessy.
Tees, Peter.
Mahon, Thomas.
McClary, Alexander.
Seeker, Philip.
Kepler, (or Kepple,) Christian.
Gill, Thomas.
Abraham, Henry.
Weaver, Henry.
Fields, John.
Wallow, (or Wallace,) William.
Wagner, John.
Price, William.
Chilcot, George.
Christ, Henry.
Afflerbauch, George.
Erhard, Frederick.
Tull, Richard.
Duffy, James.
Sheppard, John.
Stinceman, Caspar.
Moser, Jacob.
Crist, John, Jr.,

We do certify, on honor, that the within roll contains a true state of the company of non-commissioned officers and privates, commanded by Capt. Bakeoven, Second brigade, First division, Pennsylvania militia, under command of Col. John Thompson.

JOHN BAKEOVEN,
Captain.
JOHN THOMPSON,
Colonel.

CAMP MARCUS HOOK, *October 17, 1814.*

I certify, that the company commanded by Capt. J. Bakeoven, is in the service of the United States, under order of the general commanding the Fourth military district.

THOMAS SNYDER,
Brigadier General commanding.

CAMP MARCUS HOOK, *October 17, 1814.*

ROLL OF CAPTAIN JOHN BANICKMAN'S COMPANY.

Pay-roll of a company of infantry, under the command of Capt. John Banickman, of the First regiment, Second brigade, of Pennsylvania militia, commanded by Brig. Gen. Richard Crooks, in the service of the United States, on the 29th day of March, 1813, in the northwestern army under Gen. William H. Harrison.

Sergeants.

Keen, Greenberry.
Chapman, Samuel.
Middleton, William H. B.
Shannon, Samuel.

Corporals.

Calhoon, Alexander C.
Reed, Thomas.
Armstrong, John.
Hunter, Samuel.

Privates.

Carrel, James B.
Burns, John.
Baily, James.
Carnahan, George.
Crozier, William.
Downing, John.
Furgeson, John.
Gamble, William.
Heiny, Charles.
Gilbreath, Hugh.
James, Joseph.

Jones, Elisha.
McCrum, John.
McFarland, John.
Peters, John B.
McClelland, John.
McSpenen, James.
Miller, Horace.
McDonald, John.
McCoy, Alexander.
McCorland, James.
McCullough, Samuel.
McMillin, John.
Robison, James.
Reed, James.
Rereigh, George.
Shell, Flora.
Thompson, James.
Wilson, Joseph.
Peck, Edward C.
Allen, Aaron.
Dunlap, James.
Drinnen, William.
Hammett, Hanse.
Hammett, Jacob.
Harrison, John L.
Kennedy, David.
Kennedy, James.
MuMullen, David.
McAfee, William.
McKinsey, Alexander.
McMun, David.
Such, James.
Whigham, John.
Ebbert, Frederick.
Franklin, Thomas.
Niman, James.
Wilson, James.
Irwin, William.

We certify, on honor, that this pay-roll exhibits a true statement of Capt. John Banickman's company of Pennsylvania militia for the period therein mentioned.

J. BANICKMAN,
Captain.
JOSHUA LOGAN,
Lieutenant.

September 14, 1813.

ROLL OF CAPT. THOMAS BARD'S COMPANY.

Roll of Capt. Thomas Bard's company, Mercersburg September, 1814.

Captain.

Bard, Thomas.

First Lieutenant.

McDowell, James.

Second Lieutenant.

Johnston, John.

Ensign.

Bowers, Joseph.

Sergeants.

Dean, A. T.
Duffield, G.
Smith, Thomas.
Spangler, G.

Corporals.

Smith, William.
Grubb, Thomas.
McDowell, William.
Johnston, Thomas.

Fifer.

Mull, John.

Privates.

Abbott, John.
Brown, John.
Bard, Archibald.
Carson, Robert.
Coxe, John.
Campbell, John.
Craig, Samuel.
Cox, John, Jr.
Donnyhon, John.
Dick, Joseph.
Dunlap, Joseph.
Elliott, Peter.
Evans, Jeremiah.
Furley, John.
Gaff, Leonard.
Glaze, John.
Garvin, Joseph.
Garver, James.

Glass, William.
Garner, Henry.
Hart, William.
Harrington, Joseph.
Hamilton, James.
Harrison, James.
Henchy, Frederick.
Harrer, John.
Houston, William.
Johnston, Samuel.
King, John.
Liddy, John.
McDowell, James.
McClelland, John.
McDowell, Thomas, C.
McDowell, William, Sr.
McFerren, George.
Montgomery, James.
McNeal, James.
McNeal, Augustus.
Markle, Samuel.
McCurdy, John.
McCoy, Robert.
McCulloch, John.
Maxwell, John.
McKinstry, William.
Patton, Matthew.
Pike, Charles.
Robston, David.
Stewart, William.
Speer, Thomas.
Sheilds, James.
Smith, David.
Stevens, George.
Sybert, John.
Squire, Thomas.
Stinger, Conrad.
Witherow, Samuel.
Williamson, Thomas.
Wilson, William.
Werlby, John.
Witherow, John.
Walker, James.
Rankin, William.
Waddle, Thomas.
Wise, Christopher.

ROLL OF CAPT. JOHN BERGSTRESSER'S COMPANY.

Pay-roll of the company of infantry, under the command of Capt. John Bergstresser, attached and organized by Adjutant General ――――, of the ―――― brigade Pennsylvania militia, in the service of the United States, commanded by Lieut. Col. George Weirick, October 31, 1814.

Captain.

Bergstresser, John.

Lieutenant.

Fisher, Thomas.

Ensign.

Nule, Henry.

Sergeants.

Setsbay, Urias.
Reedy, Philip.
Gillaspie, John.
Rangles, Daniel.

Corporals.

Neyveus, William.
Vartz, John.
McUrley, Jacob.
Lutz, John.

Privates.

Shaffer, Daniel.
Joden, Benjamin.
Struble, Peter.
Hewsel, Joshua.
Irwin, William.
Shekler, Jonas.
Flickinger, Charles.
Irwin, John.
Sheekler, Simon.
Clark, Joseph.
Mingle, George.
Frederick, Peter.
Huffert, John.
Egbert, Jesse.
Rose, Adam.
Ikey, Lewis.
Dimpsey, Jonathan.
Mizner, John.

Kimmell, Adam.
Caufman, Jacob.
McGee, James.
Kline, Abraham.
Sargant, John.
Wilson, Samuel.
Moyer, Peter.
Walters, John.
Rorabaugh, Christopher.
McClare, Richard.
Clark, William.
Rorabaugh, Philip.
Wilson, Thomas.
Jamison, John.
Mowry, Peter.
Stricklin, Samuel.
Starner, Daniel.
Moyer, Henry.
Baldy, Benjamin.
Wilmingson, Gideon.
Bennet, John.
Clark, Flavel.
Bowar, George.
McGlaughlin, James.
Cipher, Jacob.
Welch, Nicholas.
Bennage, Samuel.
Deffendorfer, Philip.
McKinley, Hugh.
Darsham, Ludwig.
Gudlenger, Paul.
Jodan, William.
Wallas, James.
Steel, Richard.
Belman, George.
Lutz, Samuel.
Merwin, Samuel.
Rauck, Jonathan.
Bowar, William.
Kline, George.
Clark, Fransus.
Campbell, William.
Smith, Adam.
Campbel, Joseph.
Bower, John.
Johnson, Thomas.

Zarphaus, George.
Young, Abraham.
Kountz, Daniel.
Bidelman, Abraham.
Rees, John.
Darrah, John.
Fredrick, Jacob.
Vanhorn, William.
Steel, David.
Haringdon, William.
Maughimer, Daniel.
Quin, Michael.
Vanderhoof, Henry.
Vanhorn, Abraham.
Hoobler, Jacob.
Campbel, John.
Frederick, Samuel.
Vanderhoof, William.
Anderson, James.
Shaffer, Henry.
Smith, Jonathan.
Gilman, Jacob.
Johnes, John.
Kelley, Andrew, discharged October 28, 1814, on account of sickness.
Clingan, George.
Lilley, Peter, discharged October 8, 1814, on account of sickness.
Heiser, Frederick, discharged October 2, 1814, on account of sickness.

 I do certify, on honor, that this pay-roll exhibits a true state of the Union county company of militia, under my command, attached to the ——— regiment, under the command of Lieut. Col. George Weirick, Pennsylvania militia, John Bergstresser, captain Union county militia.

 I believe the above to be a correct pay-roll.

GEO. WEIRICK,
Lieutenant General commanding.

 I certify, that the militia company commanded by Capt. John Bergstresser, is now in the service of the United States, under orders of the general commandant the Fourth military district.

THOS. J. ROGERS,
Brigade Major.

ROLL OF CAPT. NICHOLAS BECKWITH'S COMPANY.

Pay-Roll of a company of volunteer riflemen, commanded by Capt. Nicholas Beckwith, of the Fifth battalion, Pennsylvania militia, commanded by Major D. Nelson, of the United States, under the command of Brig. Gen. Richard Crooke, in the service of the United States, under the command of General W. H. Harrison. Commencement of service, October 2, 1812; expiration of service, April 2, 1813.

Captain.

Beckwith, Nicholas.

Lieutenant.

Metzler, David.

Ensign.

Alexander, Thomas.

Sergeants.

Mulwits, V. Michael.
Gibson, Robert.
Smith, T. John.
Dryden, David.

Corporals.

Wilson, Alexander.
Metzler, Daniel.
Brown, Thomas.
Bowers, Adam.

Musician.

Suck, M. Henry.

Privates.

Rinedollar, George.
Rinedollar, Christopher.
Stephens, William.
Nobel, Robert.
Bender, John.
Gaff, William.
Lynn, John.
Martin, Samuel.
Wilson, Hance.
Smith, Joseph.
Bender, Henry.
Forsythe, David.
Whitstone, David.
Isor, Henry.

Snider, Michael.
Fordney, Daniel.
Irwin, Jerret.
Brown, David.
Humbert, John.
Isor, John.
McCorcle, Joseph.
Glass, John.
McClain, Robert.
Full, John.
Duffield, William.
Sirley, Samuel.
　Witness present.

JACOB BONNETT.

September 27, 1813.

I do certify, on honor, that the within pay-roll is correct, and that the remarks set opposite the men's names are accurate and just.

NICHOLAS BECKWITH,
Captain.

ROLL OF CAPT. JOHN BEEUHLER'S COMPANY.

Receipt-roll of a Company of militia, commanded by Capt. John Beeuhler, of the Third regiment, First brigade, performing a tour of duty under the command of Col. Lefever, who rendezvoused at Hanover, under the general order of the Governor, dated October 15 and 22, 1814. Commencement of service, October 25, 1814; expiration of service, December 5, 1814.

Captain.

Beeuhler, John.

Lieutenant.

Blake, M. Walter.

Ensign.

Campbell, Thomas.

Sergeants.

Smith, Jacob.
White, David.
Durdorff, Daniel.
Coughnour, Jacob.

Corporals.

Butt, William.
Neeley, James.
Newman, Alexander.
Tate, Israel.

Privates.

Beachler, Jacob.
Booner, Francis.
Boak, Lewis.
Booner, David.
Cavenough, Matthew.
Draver, George.
Decker, Lewis.
Davis, David.
Decker, Joseph.
Evans, Peter.
Eckert, Jacob.
Fisher, Samuel.
Fickle, John.
Grubb, Michael.
Hartsell, Frederick.
Himes, Charles.
Hinckle, George.
Hykes, John.
Hykes, Henry.
James, David.
Joyce, William.
Jones, Thomas.
Krider, Henry.
Kennedy, Joseph.
McCafferty, Benjamin.
Myers, Daniel.
Martin, John.
McMarrow, Joseph.
McNight, John.
Martin, Christian.
McGaw, James.
Neeley, James.
Nelson, William.
Nickle, David.
Nailer, S. James.
Pew, Benjamin.
Raumer, George.
Ross, John.
Steel, John.

Smith, C. John.
Sands, Robert.
Smith, Peter.
Sutton, John.
Smith, C. James.
Tanny, Thomas.
Uncle, Christopher.
Vanasdall, William.
Walls, Samuel.
Williams, John.
White, Thomas.
Blake, James.
Shedrick, Melonee.
Kittlewell, Thomas.

I certify the foregoing to be a correct pay-roll of my company of Pennsylvania militia.

JOHN BEEUHLER,
Captain.

Test:

JNO. FORSTER,
Brigadier General.

ROLL OF CAPT. DANIEL BENEZET'S COMPANY.

Pay-roll of the First corps, Bucks county militia, under the command of Captain Benezet, attached to the —— regiment Pennsylvania militia, now in the service of the United States.

Privates.

Harrison, Joseph.
Milnor, Joseph.
Bowman, David.
Vanzant, Joseph, on furlough.
Graham, Henry.
Bailey, Daniel.
Morton, Hugh.
West, Joseph.
Copeland, Samuel.
Gosline, William.
Leech, Johnston.
Scott, Benjamin.
Vandegrift, Cornelius.
Branson, John.

Green, John.
Cabeen, Samuel.
Lawrence, Joseph.
Renzhaw, William.
Shafer, John.
Weasel, Peter.
Calihan, John.
Haines, Joshua.
Sipler, David.
Sanderson, Robert.
Mood, Samuel.
Doan, Moses.
Titus, Ira.
Gregg, James.
Brown, Joseph.
Morris, Amos.
Carigan, Thomas.
Allen, Joel.
Crozier, Andrew.
Ceetleow, Jacob.
Hunter, James.
Armstrong, Alexander.
Snyder, Charles.
Brodnax, Aaron.
Brutton. Joseph.
Winder, William.
Slack, Jacob.
Capple, Joseph, on furlough.
Napphas, William.
Johnston, Christopher.
Winship, Richard C.
Northrop, George.
Booze, William.
Rue, Adam.
Stackhouse, Ebenezer.
Tomlinson, Henry.
Slack, Joseph.
Riley, Charles.
Boozer, Henry.
Vernon, Jesse.
Tombz. David.
Wright, Mitchel.
Rue, Richard.
Cox, Moses.
Lawrence Benjamin.
Sutton, John.

3—VOL. XII.

Davis, Thomas.
Harrison, John.
Gibbs, John.
Carigan, Daniel, on furlough.
Bloomsbury, Charles.
Vandegrift, John.
Cummings, John.
Ritchison, Clement.
Scattergood, Thomas.
Vandegrift, William T.
Wells, Valentine.
States, Peter.
Douglas, James.
Barnhile, James.
Wilkinson, W. H.
Wise, Joseph.
Woolard, John.
Winkoop, Joshua.
Rich, John D.
Sisco, Benjamin.
States, Zachariah.
Wright, Benjamin.
Molesburry, Joel.
Stackhouse, Mahlon.
Evans, Thomas.
Sipler, George.
Paterson, Charles.
Francis, White.
Murdoch, Abraham.
Jackson, Jonathan.
Allen, William.
Sutton, Benjamin.
Schaffer, Jacob.
Bowman, Henry, on furlough.
White, Malachi.
Coxe, John.
Dobble, John.
Carson, Jacob.
Woodington, James.
Hutchinson, Edward C.
McMasters, Robert.
Brelsford, Joseph.
Guyon, John.
Sopus, James.
Hunter, Amos.
Boyd, Joseph, on furlough.

Tomlinson, Nathan.
Wink, Samuel, on furlough from the surgeon.
Nelson, William.
Hanna, William R.
Babcock, William.

We do certify, on honor, that the within muster-roll exhibits a true state of the company, and that the remarks set opposite the men's names are correct and just.

DANIEL BENEZET,
Captain.
CONRAD KRICHBAUM,
Colonel.

CAMP MARCUS HOOK, *October 28, 1814.*

I do certify, on honor, that the company commanded by Capt. Benezet, of Bucks county, is in the service of the United States, under command of the general commanding the Fourth military district.

By order,

W. C. RADGERS,
Brigade Major.

CAMP MARCUS HOOK, *October 28, 1814.*

ROLL OF CAPTAIN SAMUEL BORDEN'S COMPANY.

Muster-roll of a company of infantry, under the command of Capt. Samuel Borden, in the Fourth detachment, Pennsylvania militia, in the service of the United States, commanded by Col. Lewis Rush, from May 13, 1813, when last mustered, to June 18, 1813.

Captain.

Borden, Samuel.

Lieutenant.

Oldenburg, Daniel.

Second Lieutenant.

Howel, John.

Third Lieutenant.

Wright, George G.

Ensign.

Snyder, John.

Quartermaster Sergeant.

Stimmel, Philip.

Sergeants.

Knorr, Henry.
Allison, Walter.
Clinton, John.

Corporals.

Springer, Benjamin.
McClure, Robert.
Chalfant, Jacob.
Aitkins, Robert.

Drummer.

Witherstene, Samuel.

Fifer.

Ouram, Thomas.

Privates.

Apple, Jacob.
Alexander, Joseph.
Bayly, John.
Butcher, John.
Bastian, Charles.
Bates, William.
Baxter, Samuel.
Brent, John.
Beale, William C.
Buckingham, Edward.
Burke, Jacob.
Buckart, Thomas.
Burden, Benjamin C.
Chappel, John.
Bowles, John.
Butler, George.
Course, William.
Clement, Arthur H.
Colliday, Charles.
Cline, Henry.
Cain, Dennis.
Cain, Aaron.
Danniker, George, entered the United States army.
Dubse, John.
Strahan, Paul.
Daly, Edward.
Davis, Russel G., discharged by surgeon; served one month.
Dollman, John.
Debeust, John.
Dowdell, John.

WAR OF 1812–14.

Ebling, John.
Faukes, Richard.
Frowert, John.
Fortescue, Thomas.
Goggins, William.
Gould, Walter.
Germon, Greenbuy D.
Henry, John.
Hassel, Daniel.
Hall, Benjamin.
Hansel, Jacob, served one month.
Houran, Daniel.
Hooton, Andrew.
Hoff, George.
Hardinbrook, Peter
Hannah, William.
Hardy, Thomas.
Johnson, William.
Kettering, Jacob.
Keck, John.
Kritz, Peter.
King, Joseph.
Keller, John.
Lindsay, John, discharged by surgeon.
Layland, John.
Lynd, William.
Larer, Henry.
Lieutier, Lawrence.
McCoy, Kenneth.
McElwee, Thomas, entered the United States army.
McKadge, John.
McKaraher, Daniel.
Masker, Philip.
Katz, John.
Meeser, Henry.
Matson, James.
Murphy, John.
Merrick, John.
Millhouse John.
Meiniker, Christian.
Nice, Matthias.
Olwine, Samuel.
Patterson, George.
Rushae, Joseph.
Raivly, John.
Ritchy, James.

Snyder, David.
Savoy, Francis.
Smith, John.
Spotts, George.
Scrimenger, John.
Smith, Joseph.
Simpson, John.
Swartz, Joseph.
Shaw, Robert.
Spreigle, John R.
Steele, William H.
St. Clair, Samuel.
Sutherland, John.
Stine, Adam.
Sturges, Stokely.
Sproneyburg, John.
Sears, John.
Trainer, John.
Viant, Samuel.
Willis, Joseph.
Wile, John.
Wood, Edward.
McDonaugh, William.
Ward, William P.

We certify, on honor, that the muster-roll exhibits a true state of Capt. Samuel Borden's company of the Fourth detachment of Pennsylvania Militia, for the period therein mentioned, and that the remarks set opposite the names of the men are accurate and just.

DAN'L OLDENBERG,
Lieutenant Commanding.

Upon the return of the detachment to the city the muster-roll had undergone no alteration since the above period.

DAN'L OLDENBERG,
Lieutenant Commanding.

I do certify, upon honor, that I believe the above return and remarks to be accurate and just.

LEWIS RUSH,
Colonel Fourth Detachment, Pennsylvania Militia.

August 6, 1813.

WAR OF 1812-14.

ROLL OF CAPT. JAMES BOWNER'S COMPANY.

A pay-roll of Capt. James Bowner's company of Pennsylvania militia, attached to the Fifth battalion, Second detachment, Pennsylvania militia, under the command of Brig. Gen. Richard Crooks, in the service of the United States. Commencement of services, October 2, 1812.

Captain.
Bowner, James, volunteered for fifteen days.

Lieutenant.
Ross, Richard, volunteered for fifteen days.

Ensign.
Coil, Patrick.

Sergeants.
Brown, John.
McCombs, William.
Godwin, Joseph, volunteered for fifteen days.
Carter, Francis.

Corporals.
Gilson, Thomas.
Bowman, Henry.
Camp, John.
Robinson, Arthur, volunteered for fifteen days.

Privates.
Kerr, Samuel.
Kerr, William.
Kerr, David.
Elder, John.
Littlefield, John.
Wilson, Samuel.
Hair, William.
Green, James.
Frew, James.
Sims, Jesse.
Miles, Robert.
Frampton, John, died the —th day of March, 1813.
Wasson, James, volunteered for fifteen days.
Wasson, William, volunteered for fifteen days.
McCool, Alexander.
Dunwoody, Robert.
Porter, Hugh.
Ridgway, Samuel.
Martin, John.

Martin, William.
Foster, John.
Whitmer, Jonathan.
Duffield, William.
Hason, John.
Hannah, William.
Beaty, John.
Runinger, Jacob.
Russel, Thomas.
McFaden, Eijah.
Sedorus, John.
Cooper, Samuel.
Sutley, Jacob.
Sutley, Henry.
Clifford, Hugh, furloughed October 25, 1812, and did not return.
Elder, James, discharged October 26, 1812.
Dotey, Samuel.
Simons, Samuel, volunteered for fifteen days.
Mengar, Joseph, volunteered for fifteen days.
Lee, Jared, volunteered for fifteen days.
Ingram, John, volunteered for fifteen days.
McClure, Mathew, volunteered for fifteen days.
Portman, James, volunteered for fifteen days.
Russel, John, volunteered for fifteen days.
Crane, Ira, volunteered for fifteen days.
Harris, Nathan, volunteered for fifteen days.
Cole, Benjamin.
Scaddon, James B.
Stewart, William.
Dempsey, David, volunteered for fifteen days.

I do hereby certify, on honor, that the within pay-roll is correct, and that the remarks set opposite the men's names are accurate and just.

RICHARD ROSS,
Lieutenant.

ROLL OF CAPT. JOHN BROWN'S COMPANY.

Pay-roll of a company of volunteer infantry, commanded by Capt. John Brown, of the First regiment, Pennsylvania militia, under the command of Gen. Richard Crooks.

Sergeants.

Wood, Micajah.
Lewis, Willmauth.

WAR OF 1812–14.

Rinehart, Joseph, taken sick at Mansfield, and hired a substitute for the remainder of the term.
Patterson, John.

Corporals.

Smith, Thomas.
Dawson, William.
Hamler, Adam.
Yeater, Andrew.

Privates.

Bulger, Samuel.
Hicks, Joseph.
Ayres, Silas.
Armor, John W., appointed on the staff, March 29.
Baker, Anthony, died after discharged.
Cather, Robert.
Conkling, Henry, volunteered for fifteen days.
Dawson, Moses.
Echelberger, George.
Echelberger, Abraham.
Foredyce, Abraham.
Headley, Elias.
Hughs, Thomas.
Hickethorn, George.
Hair, John.
Hays, Adam, appointed in the staff; served in company.
Ingram, William.
Jewel, Aaron.
Kirkpatrick, Thomas.
Archer, James.
Lantz, Alexander, volunteered for fifteen days.
Lapping, Robert.
Maple, William.
Mitchel, Thomas.
Moor, Carl.
Mickle, Reuben.
Poland, Jonathan.
Pettit, John, volunteered for fifteen days.
Parker, James, volunteered for fifteen days.
Pechtel, Henry.
Robison, Thomas.
Reese, John.
Reed, Edward.
Reynolds, John.
Sayres, William, volunteered for fifteen days.
Sharp, William.

Stockdale, William.
Seals, Vincent.
Smith, James, died at Upper Sandusky, February 24, 1813.
Stockdail, John.
Stattoo, Henry, furloughed December 8, 1812; taken sick on return, and never joined company.
Stiegers, David.
Cyphers, Peter.
Smith, Thomas.
Tuston, Andrew.
Winget, Luther.
Yeager, Peter.
Peirce, Samuel.
Tuston, Abraham.
Young, Andrey.
White, Samuel.
Isminger, John.
Taif, James.

I do certify, upon honor, that this pay-roll exhibits a true statement of my company, of the First regiment, Pennsylvania militia, for the period therein mentioned, and the remarks set opposite the names of men are accurate and just.

JOHN BROWN,
Captain.

ROLL OF CAPT. PETER A. BROWN'S COMPANY.

Pay-roll of a company of volunteer infantry commanded by Capt. Peter A. Brown, of the First Regiment of Pennsylvania Volunteers, under the command of Col. Clement C. Biddle, late in the service of the United States.

Captain.

Brown, P. A.

First Lieutenant.

Campbell, James.

Second Lieutenant.

Tempest, William.

Third Lieutenant.

Rayfield, William I.

Ensign.

Taylor, Thomas.

Sergeants.

Patterson, Thomas, August 26, 1814—January 4, 1815.
Ballentine, Joseph.
McKay, John.
Murphey, Alexander.
Leidy, Jacob.

Corporals.

Knox, John.
Magill, Henry.
Ware, Stephen.
Kinney, James.
Ross, Samuel.
Kugler, Henry.

Drummer.

Densill, Frederick.

Fifer.

Roy, Thomas.

Quarter-Master.

Brock, Thomas.

Privates.

Buchanan, George.
Bolton, Henry.
Bingham, Bingham.
Brouster, Charles.
Buckious, Aaron.
Bowers, Jesse.
Best, John.
Brown, Alexander.
Claytor, John.
Cassiday, Hugh.
Cress, John H.
Caldwell, William.
Caldwell, John.
Cornwill, Daniel.
Cochran, Charles.
Cunningham, John.
Dougherty, Charles.
Dicks, Henry.
Egenton, William.
Flanigan, Henry.
Fox, John.
Finn, John.
Gibbons, James.
Gouldey, Casper.
Gilmore, Patrick.

Henderson, David.
Hanna, John.
Hagan, James.
Holland, James.
Hemphill, Alexander.
Houke, Frederick.
Hubermill, Henry.
Hulings, Ab^m.
Henry, Alexander.
Hilton, William.
Irwin, Jared.
Jones, George W.
Jameson, Andrew.
Kerrick, Andrew.
Louge, James.
Lott, Thomas.
Lehn, George.
Little, John.
Little, Charles.
Lloyd, Joseph.
Lemmine, Samuel.
McNeill, Alexander.
McLaughlin, James.
McGeaugh, Thomas, October 2, 1814—January 4, 1815.
McCormick, Francis, August 26, 1814—January 4, 1815.
Murdock, George D.
Miller, Hugh.
McKinley, Nathan.
Maley, Peter.
McCartney, John.
Monaghan, Henry, transferred to Capt. Bache's troop, November 7, 1814.
McMichael, John.
Moore, Joseph.
McNally, John.
McNulty, John.
McFaden, Stephen.
McKnight, George.
McKee, Thomas.
McAlonan, Hugh.
Nickles, Simon.
North, James, September 21, 1814—January 4, 1815.
Odenheimer, John, August 26, 1814—January 4, 1815.
Priest, George.
Park, William.
Reese, Morris.

Robert, Daniel.
Rutherford, John.
Roney, Bernard.
Reilly, Michael.
Ryan, William.
Snyder, Aaron.
Siscoe, James.
Shannon, James.
Slatter, Peter.
Sloan, Hugh.
Smith, Jacob.
Savidge, William.
Thomas, David.
Trimble, W. H.
Triedy, Henry G.
Wineburner, David.
Wester, Samuel.
Wilson, Joseph, August 26, 1814—January 4, 1816.
Wagoner, Jacob.
Wise, Thomas.
Warnick, William.
Ware, John B.
Young, Matthew.
Yohe, Samuel.
Fletcher, Edward.

We, the subscribers, certify that this is a correct and true copy.

A. P. BROWN,
Late Captain.
CLEMENT C. BIDDLE,
Colonel First Regiment Pennsylvania Volunteers.

ROLL OF CAPT. THOMAS BUCHANAN'S COMPANY.

Muster-roll of Capt. Thomas Buchanan's company of rangers, under the command of Lieut. Col. Shappell, (in service from September 26, 1814, to December 4, 1814, from Lancaster county.)

Captain.
Buchanan, Thomas.

First Lieutenant.
Miller, John.

Second Lieutenant.
Gipp, Henry.

Ensign.
Garner, Jacob.

Sergeants.

Brown, John.
Albright, Joseph.
Sink, Henry.
Cochran, John.

Corporals.

Gilman, Matthias.
Mockert, John.
Gorner, George.
Miller, Peter.

Drummer.

Hugey, John.

Fifer.

Parker, Alexander.

Privates.

Albright, Conrad.
Anderson, Jurden.
Barnes, David.
Betts, Frederick.
Bundle, Jesse.
Clinton, Joseph.
Clinton, Robert.
Clipper, Jacob.
Clipper, John.
Cunning, Alexander.
Daily, William.
Elliot, John.
Fisher, George.
Fitch, John.
Fitsgerald, ———.
Foster, Joshua.
Fulck, George.
Galbaugh, Frederick.
Galligher, Thomas.
Gorner, John.
Grant, Benjamin.
Hawk, Abner.
Inloes, Samuel.
Miller, Barney.
Morrison, John.
Mourer, Samuel.
Murry, John.
Nicholas, Frederick.
Nicholas, John.
Norris, John.

Reppard, John.
Shaffner, Philip.
Sharer, Jacob.
Shiff, Jacob.
Smith, Samuel.
Stape, Barney.
Swords, Smith.
Swords, William.
Vastine, John.
Witmer, Boston.

ROLL OF CAPT. JOHN M. BUCKIUS' COMPANY.

Pay-roll of a volunteer company, called the Union Riflemen, under the command of Capt. John M. Buckius, attached to the Second brigade, Pennsylvania militia, in the service of the United States, commanded by Lieut. Col. Joel B. Sunderland.

CAMP, NEAR MARCUS HOOK, *October 15, 1814.*

Captain.

Buckius, John M.

First Lieutenant.

Smith, Henry.

Second Lieutenant.

Rex, Christopher.

Third Lieutenant.

Weise, Jesse.

Sergeants.

Norton, Jesse.
Lentz, Charles.
Wintercast, William.
Engle, Samuel.

Corporals.

Colody, Charles.
Scattergood, Charles.
Gouldson, George.
Weiss, Samuel.

Privates.

Navin, Mitchel.
Armbrister, John.
Conover, Cornelius.
Stout, John.

Coston, George W.
Stout, Peter.
Dannehower, Charles.
Stout, John S.
Costor, Benton.
Smith, James.
Gouldson, William.
Haines, John.
Venner, Ab^m.
Street, Thomas.
Barrow, John.
Myers, Henry.
Snyder, George.
Pressler, William.
Ennis, John.
Weiss, Ab^m.
Tripler, Jacob.
Shope, Henry.
Griffith, Isaac.
Lowden, Isaac.
Wolf, Christopher.
Zink, Jacob.
Dickerson, John.
Arnach, Christian.
Haines, Joseph.
Ross, Thomas.
Pifer, Jacob.
Adams, Bernard.
Venner, Henry.
Narigong, Peter.
Miller, John.
Dake, John.
Johnston, Samuel.
Pressler, Henry.
Hornboch, Isaac.
Coffman, David.
Coston, Eleven M.
Wintercast, George.

We certify, on honor, that this pay-roll exhibits a true state of the rifle company attached to the Second brigade, Pennsylvania militia, and that the remarks set opposite the names of the men are accurate and just.

HENRY SMITH,
Lieutenant Commandant.
JOEL B. SUTHERLAND,
Lieutenant Colonel Commandant.

WAR OF 1812-14. 49

I certify that the rifle company commanded by John M. Buckius, is in the service of the United States, under the orders of the general commanding the Fourth military district.

THOMAS SNYDER,
Brigadier General.

ROLL OF CAPT. JUSTUS P. BULLARD'S COMPANY.

Muster-roll of a company of drafted militia under the command of Capt. Justus P. Bullard, in the service of the United States, First brigade, First division, Pennsylvania militia, the detachment commanded by Lieut. Col. Peter L. Berry, from the 26th August, 1814, to the 26th September, 1814, inclusive.

Captain.
Bullard, Justus P.

First Lieutenant.
Sexton, Silas W.

Second Lieutenant.
Fimple, Philip.

Sergeants.
Fimple, Jacob.
Forsithe, James.
Mace, Joseph.
Cost, George.

Corporals.
Hutchinson, Ephraim.
Howard, William.
Rickets, George.
Haines, Joseph.

Privates.
Archer, Samuel.
Askins, Hugh.
Andress, George.
Bruce, Thomas.
Boyd, Alexander.
Brown, Adam.
Brady, James.
Buckanan, Alexander.
Buckley, George.
Bosworth, Samuel.
Crilley, John.
Chatham, Ezekiel.

4—VOL. XII.

Casiday, Patrick.
Carlin, Patrick.
Dubenaud, Thomas.
Davis, Samuel E.
Daniels, William.
Diamond, John J.
Desaby, Lewis.
Elton, Thomas.
Edwards, Thomas.
Fimple, John.
Fry, Peter.
Gilbert, Michael.
Girton, Barzilla.
Gray, Robert.
Hughs, Albert.
Hill, Charles.
Howard, Robert.
Humphreys, James.
Harden, George.
Hamilton, Thomas, joined volunteers; transferred.
Isburn, Samuel.
Kinsley, Samuel.
Kitlar, Charles.
Keel, Baltus.
Lynch, James.
Lowrey, William.
Laughton, John, joined volunteers; transferred.
Leatherbury, Perrygrin.
McElhany, John.
McKirnan, Charles.
Massol, Augustus.
McGaha, Terrence.
McKinley, Nathan, transferred to volunteers.
Moore, Joseph, transferred to volunteers.
McNight, George, transferred to volunteers.
McFlanigan, Henry, transferred to volunteers.
Nagle, William.
Northrop, Eanoch.
Peck, Joseph.
Randall, Robert.
Sapp, James.
Sharp, Patrick.
Trout, David.
Timmings, Uriah.
Troll, Jacob.
Taney, Jacob.

Wilson, John.
Wentling, David.
Weaver, Conrad.
White, John.
Wardell, Philip.

We certify, on honor, that this muster-roll exhibits a true state of the Fourth company of the drafted militia of Pennsylvania for the period therein mentioned, and that the remarks set opposite the names of the men are accurate and just.

(Signed,)   JUSTUS P. BULLARD,
Captain.
SILAS W. SEXTON,
First Lieutenant.
PHILIP FIMPLE,
Second Lieutenant.

I believe the above to be correct.

PETER A. BERRY,
Lieutenant Colonel.

I certify, that the Fourth company of drafted militia, under command of Capt. Justus P. Bullard, is in the service of the United States, under orders of the general commanding the Fourth military district.

THOMAS CADWALADER,
Brigadier General Commanding.

CAMP DUPONT, *October, 1814.*

ROLL OF CAPT. JAMES R. BUTLER'S COMPANY.

Pay-roll of a company of United States volunteer infantry commanded by Capt. James R. Butler, of the independent battalion of twelve months volunteers, lately commanded by Major John B. Alexander, in the service of the United States.

Sergeants.

Travillo, Elijah.
Williams, Isaac.
Willock, John.
Haven, George.

Corporals.

Patterson, Nathaniel.
Benny, John.
Elliott, Samuel.
Reed, Israel.

Privates.

Allison, Robert.
Boss, Daniel C.
Chess, Isaac.
Deal, John.
Davis, John, absent, taking care of sick.
Deemer, Andrew, absent, taking care of sick.
Dodd, Joseph, died June 16, 1813.
Davis, John D.
Dobbins, Thomas.
Eliott, John.
English, Oliver.
Fairfield, Enoch.
Lousong, John Francis, killed December 18, 1812.
Graham, Samuel.
Hull, Nathaniel.
Jones, Samuel.
Lewis, Jessee.
Orton, Peter B.
McFall, George.
McClarnen, Thomas.
McNeal, Robert.
Mathews, Norris.
Maxwell, John.
McKee, Oliver, died May 28, 1813.
McGiffen, Nathaniel, sick, absent; discharged.
Newman, James, killed May 5, 1813.
Park, John.
Parker, Mathew.
Pentland, Charles.
Pollard, John.
Pratt, Edward F.
Robinson, George.
Richardson, William, killed May 5, 1813.
Swift, Samuel.
Thompson, Henry.
Vernon, Nathaniel.
Watt, David, left sick at Cleveland on return.
Weidner, Charles.
Wahrendorf, Charles.
Nevill, Presley, promoted to sergeant; absent.
Wilkins, George, promoted May, 1813.
Marcy, John, discharged; absent; not deducted as unpaid on the statement of June, 1816.
Mors, Moses.
McMasters, Joseph.

I certify, on honor, the above pay-roll to be correct.

JAMES R. BUTLER,
Captain Pittsburg Blues.

ROLL OF CAPTAIN WILLIAM F. BUYERS' COMPANY.

Pay-roll of the company of volunteers, under the command of Capt. William F. Buyers, attached and organized by adjutant general of the First brigade, Pennsylvania militia, in the service of the United States, commanded by Lieut. Col. George Weirick, of the Seventy-seventh regiment, Pennsylvania militia.

Captain.
Buyers, William F.

First Lieutenant.
Jenkins, Thomas S.

Second Lieutenant.
Scott, Samuel H.

Ensign.
Hepburn, John.

Sergeants.
Wilson, Samuel H.
Walles, Joseph T.
Sweney, A. M.

Corporal.
Kiehl, John.

Fifer.
Armor, William.

Drummer.
DeLong, Samuel.

Privates.
Haunes, John S.
Lyan, John, (Sun.)
Cook, Adam.
Bonham, Thomas.
Ross, John.
Weitzel, George.
Rochell, Theodore I.
Oliphant, James.
Buyers, George P.
Prune, George.
Huffman, Joseph.
Cremer, Joseph B.

Maus, Charles.
Black, David.
Frazier, Charles.
Leatherland, William.
Gray, William.
Lebo, Daniel.
Lyon, Robert.
McCord, Isaac.
Gale, William.
Grant, Mac^t.
Peninger, Henry.
Wilson, Samuel.
Jones, William.
Jones, John.
Lyon, John, (Nor.)
Kreamer, Abraham.
Quin, John.
Cook, William.
Watson, William.
Hopher, Jacob.
Chapman, Edward.
Dougle, James.
McPherson, John.
Cameron, William.
Weimer, John.
Dale, Henry.
Harris, Thomas.
Lealand, William.
Hendershot, Isaac.
Armstrong, Jacob.
Martin, John.
Campbell, Robert.
Dirus, William.
Grant, William.
Grant, Thomas, Jr., discharged 23d October.

Jacob Armstrong, John Martin, Robert Campbell, and William Dirus, drafts in Capt. Humel's company, joined my company on the 29th instant. They have been in service the same time that our company has.

ROLL OF CAPT. JACOB CAMPBELL'S COMPANY.

Pay-roll for the Third company, Sixty-fifth regiment, commanded by Capt. Jacob Campbell.

Sergeants.

Buzzard, John.
Davis, Samuel.
Davis, Shannon.
Staler, John.
Hagers, John.

Corporals.

Kurtz, Jacob.
Williams, James.
Hawk, Jacob.
Christopher, John.

Privates.

Weaver, Christian.
Shriver, John.
Griffeth, John.
Young, John.
Miller, John.
Vanderslice, Edward R.
Adams, Davis.
Ewing, John.
Turner, Samuel.
Himes, Charles.
Morgan, Lewis.
O'Neill, Francis.
Wertz, John.
Hampton, David.
Hartman, Peter.
McCowan, Samuel.
King, George.
Glandy, John Davis.
Mcentire, Daniel.
Abraham, Philips.
Hampton, Thomas.
Hardy, John.
Kelly, John.
Knowles, Samuel.
Jones, Isaiah.
Clair, John.
Horner, Adam.

Golder, John.
Sowersworth, Isaac.
Jones, John.
Wiles, John.
Neily, John.
Williams, Charles.
Williams, Daniel.
Hawk, Benjamin.
Keiter, George.
Parker, Ralph.
James, Matthias.
Youngblood, John.
Isaac, Anderson.
Hawk, John.
Fox, Joseph.
Baits, Jonathan.
Rossiter, Thomas.
Buckwalter, Jacob.
Pennypacker, Samuel.
Smith, John A.
Huston. James.
McCarrahen, Alexander.
Grub, Emanuel.
Davis, John.
Stall, Daniel.
Kourtney, James.
Steward, William.
Bankus, Adam.
Reynolds, Henry.
Crosier, Morris.
Heck, Peter.
Shingle, Jacob.
Price, George.
Rembey, Jacob.
Remly, Henry.
March, Jesse.
Rembey, Valentine.
Harvey, Job.
Lapold, Joseph.
Lawre, Joseph.
Murphey, Edward.
Grub, John.
Hoffacker, Philip.
Clemmons, Joseph.
Remby, Christian.
Thomas, David.

Jones, John.
Murry, Daniel.
Price, Patrick.
Carr, William.
Salyards. Armstrong.
Walter, James.
Goodin, William.
Chaffin, Philip.
Oliver, John.
Hemiger, Joseph.
Jenkins, Enoch.
Evans, Daniel.
Akins, James.
Clare, Philip.
Jaquett, Nathaniel.
Davis, Isaac M.
Huzzard, Anthony.
Snyder, George.

CAMP MARCUS HOOK, *October 18, 1814.*

I certify, on honor, this muster-roll exhibits a true state of the Third company, Sixty-fifth regiment, Pennsylvania militia, now in the service of the United States, and that the remarks set opposite the names of the men are accurate and just.

JACOB CAMPBELL,
Captain.

I believe the above to be a correct muster or pay-roll.

J. L. PEARSON,
Colonel.

I certify that the company commanded by Capt. Campbell is in the service of the United States, under orders of Gen. ———, commanding military district.

By order of the general,

WM. C. ROGERS.
B. Major.

CAMP MARCUS HOOK, *October 18, 1814.*

ROLL OF CAPT. JOHN CAROTHERS' COMPANY.

Muster-roll of Capt. John Carothers' company, in the First regiment, First brigade, Pennsylvania militia, under the command of Col. Maxwell Kennedy, at York, September 5, 1814. (In service from September 2, 1814, to March 5, 1815, from Dauphin county.)

Captain.

Carothers, John.

WAR OF 1812-14.

First Lieutenant.

Henning, John.

Second Lieutenant.

Crangle, Henry.

Ensign.

Orr, Thomas.

Sergeants.

Lyne, John.
Cons, John.
Tomlinson, Isaac.
Emmerson, James.

Corporals.

Hooper, Erastus.
Wilson, McEnier.
Winger, John.
Burton, William.

Privates.

Barr, Robert.
Bevins, Benjamin.
Boyer, William W.
Brown, John.
Bugle, William.
Calendar, Norman.
Capp, Michael.
Elwell, Jacob.
Floyd, James.
Geistweit, Henry.
Harrison, Williamson.
Hartz, Henry.
Hasselbauch, John.
Henry, Joseph.
Housman, Daniel.
Keller, Joseph.
Keller, Samuel.
Kirk, Patrick.
Kline, John.
Krebb, John.
Kurtzel, Jacob.
Macken, Michael.
Magloghlin, William.
Martin, John.
McBride, Jonathan.
McCawen, James.
McChristal, Daniel.
McVanner, Joseph.

WAR OF 1812-14.

Mercer, Caleb.
Miller, Jacob.
Moor, Arthur.
Morningstar, Henry.
Morningstar, John.
Mulhollin, Rudolph.
Nagle, George.
Nickle, John.
Peacock, John.
Peck, Frederick.
Phleger, Jacob.
Pool, Adam.
Robinson, John.
Sellars, George.
Shott, John.
Singer, Benedict.
Steinmill, Philip.
Still, Nicholas.
Walravin, Joseph.

ROLL OF CAPT. JACOB CASH, Jr.'s, COMPANY.

Muster and pay-roll of the company of Junior artillerists, Jacob Cash, Jr., captain, late in the service of the United States, attached to the Light Brigade, under the command of Brig. Gen. T. Cadwalader Date of service, August 26, 1814; discharged, January 3, 1815.

Sergeants.

Randall, Josiah.
Kensill, John.
Clayton, John.
Myers, John P.
Labrouse, Felix.

Corporals.

Mills, Robert.
George, Joseph.
Stephenson, John.
Huff, George.
Wile, Andrew.

Privates.

Abrams, William.
Apple, Adam.
Bamford, Jeremiah.

Baker, Chalkey.
Baft, Luke.
Bender, Jacob A.
Bender, William.
Blair, John W.
Britton, Thomas.
Brooks, John.
Buck, John.
Caner, John.
Cargill, Austin.
Cassey, Martin L.
Clark, Lyman.
Coleman, Daniel.
Collings, Joseph E.
Cook, Samuel.
Cluley, John, Jr.
Cranmer, Thomas.
Dell, William.
Dennison, William.
Dowling, John.
Eckfeldt, John.
Eicleburner, George.
Teil, Jacob.
Erwin, James C.
Erdman, Frederick.
Flaghler, Henry.
Folkrode, Joseph.
Foster, Isaac.
Freymuth, William.
Gardner, Samuel A.
Gardner, Solomon.
William, Goldey.
Graff, Joseph.
Green, Isaac.
Groves, William.
Hansell, Morris.
Hansell, Peter H.
Harberger, Joseph.
Hart, George.
Hay, John.
Hemphill, Thomas.
Herman, John C.
Hoffner, Charles B.
Honeker, Charles L.
Johnston, John.
Jones, George W.

Johnston, Benjamin.
Kauck, George.
Keller, William.
Kurtz, Charles.
Laidley, Robert B.
Larer, Henry.
Laskey, Edward.
Linker, John.
Lyman, Edward.
Lycett, William.
McDonald, Samuel.
McFall, John.
McKibbon, John.
Maul, James.
Mentz, Charles.
Mesker, William.
Miller, Henry.
Morehain, Joseph F.
Purdy, Stephen C.
Reeves, John.
Reynolds, Charles.
Ridgeway, Aquilla.
Riter, Michael.
Ritter, William.
Rockinburgh, George.
Rodgers, William.
Ruddick, John.
Sailor, Henry.
Stratton, William.
Sample, Jared.
Evans, Joseph.
Saunders, Gilford D.
Seybert, John.
Simpson, Michael.
Smith, Peter.
Sost, James.
Snyder, John.
Taylor, George R.
Teil, William.
Thomas, Benjamin.
Thomas, Enoch.
Tigner, William H.
Thomson, Ed. R.
Tress, Thomas.
Tyler, Elnathan.
Vandever, William.

Wallace, William.
Wile, George.
Wile, William C.
Wiley, Eli.
Williams, Alexander.
Williamson, Charles.
Wimley, George.
Wood, Stacy.
White, John.
Eckfeldt, ——.
McKay, John.
Harman, George.
Wright, Joseph, musician.
Brode, Michael, musician.

We certify, on honor, that the above muster and pay-roll is correct, and the remarks set opposite to the men's names is accurate and just.

JACOB CASH, Jr.,
Captain Junior Artillerists.
ANDREWS M. PREVOST,
Lieut. Col. Volunteer Artillery.

ROLL OF CAPT. JOHN CHRISTIAN'S COMPANY.

Muster-roll of Capt. John Christian's company, in the Second regiment, Second brigade Pennsylvania militia, under command of Lieut. Col. John Lotz, at York, Penn'a. (In service from September 1, 1814 to December 4, 1815, from Berks county.)

Captain.

Christian, John.

First Lieutenant.

Alspauch, Matthias.

Second Lieutenant.

Swartz, John.

Ensign.

Zimmerman, Abraham.

Sergeants.

McIntosh, John.
Shoemaker, Henry.
Buck, Peter.
Dornbaugh, William.

Corporals.

Stillwaggey, George.
Kuntz, Abram.
Heisler, Jacob.
Wolfgong, Jacob.

Drummer.

Hoemon, Samuel.

Fifer.

Johnson, John.

Privates.

Albright, John.
Albright, William.
Bar, John.
Bierley, Daniel.
Borger, John.
Boyer, Philip.
Bressler, Jonathan.
Bressler, Peter.
Briner, Leonard.
Christian, Daniel, (waiter.)
Clark, Jacob.
Clay, Abraham.
Cluck, Henry.
Corl, John.
Davolt, John.
Dinger, George.
Dinger, George, Jr.
Dowenspeck, George.
Elliot, Carson.
Fields, George.
Foose, John.
Geist, George.
Grimm, Benjamin.
Grim, John.
Hagmon, Bernard.
Harner, George.
Heim, Andrew.
Heim, John.
Hellinger, Daniel.
Heroff, John.
Hoeman, John.
Houzer, Jacob.
Howzer, John.
Howzer, Michael.

Hummel, Henry.
Jones, Edward.
Kach, George.
Kaup, Jacob.
Koch, Henry.
Lauenberg, Lewis.
Lindon, Isaac.
Long, Michael D.
Miller, Abraham.
Miller, Daniel.
Miller, Jacob.
Moser, Isaac.
Mowrer, David.
Mowrer, Henry.
Moyer, Conrad.
Myers, William.
Noyer, Peter.
Sholhammer, Daniel.
Shrape, John.
Shuee, Peter.
Sloppeck, Adam.
Speek, Daniel.
Stauffer. Jonathan.
Wetzel, Jonathan.
Williamson, Thomas.
Wolfgong, Jonathan.
Wolfgong, Michael.
Wolf, Jacob.
Yost, Daniel.
Zimmerman, Sebastian.
Zimmerman, Solomon.

ROLL OF CAPT. GEORGE F. COLDOVEY'S COMPANY.

Roll of the Second company in regiment, Pennsylvania militia, now in the service of the United States, 23d October, 1814.

Captain.

Coldovey, George F.

First Lieutenant.

Arnt, John.

Second Lieutenant.

Miller, George.

Ensign.

Knidler, John.

Sergeants.

Miller, Jacob.
Lowsh, Lavis.
Koull, John.
Krammis, Jacob.
Dudt, Daniel.

Corporals.

Esterline, Jacob.
Shaff, David.
Wertz, John.
Laudenshleger, William.

Drummer.

Myer, Phillip.

Fifer.

Martz, George.

Privates.

Kammry, Fritrig.
Prich, Henry.
Weaver, Michael.
Robenold, John.
Rickert, Adam.
Quarey, George.
Hitter, Henry.
Gilbert, Jacob.
Kamery, Jonathan.
Buchman, Daniel.
Brunck, John.
Norman, David.
Came, Frietrich.
Mensh, Allick.
Hine, Peter.
Wagner, John.
Wertz, John.
Rednouer, Christophel.
Flowoure, George.
Deal, Peter.
Brish, Jacob.
Steler, Lavis.
Daubert, Henry.
Dups, John.

5—VOL. XII.

Funck, Henry.
Dem, George.
Rudulf, Micheal.
Smith, George.
Bachman, John.
Meitzler, Conrad.
Meitzler, Henry.
Shmyer, George.
Kline, Peter.
Kammery, John.
Defenderfer, Godfried.
Kayser, Peter.
Homan, Joseph.
Finck, Peter.
Karl, George.
Mohn, John.
Shmyer, George.
Shnyter, John.
Richenbach, Phillip.
Richenbach, John.
Hesky, John.
Krinamyer, George.
Klotz, Andras.
Lachleyder, Andony.
Mohr, Henry.
Rinert, George.
Schlicher, George.
Draxel, Daniel.
Shalhamer, Jonathan.
Fegle, Nicholas.
Shubert, David.
Kriling, George.
Finck, Salmon.
Christman, Daniel.
Bachman, Joseph.
Rice, Henry.
Mitzler, Jacob.
Dull, Christian.
Werly, Michael.
Werly, Dabeld.
Greim, Peter.
Smith, Mecheil.
Karsh, Conrath.
Boyer, Christian.
Shnyter, Christian.
Peter, Henry.

Ware, Phillip.
Smith, Conrath.
Finstermayer, Phillip.
Holoig, John.
Kuntz, Christian.
Miller, John.
Hunselman, Andrea.
Leiser, Daniel.
Shnyter, Henry.
Lutz, Christian.
Ohl, Abraham.
Fritz, David.
Jeixtimer, Abraham.
Bar, Phaul.
Rose, Charlis.
Shnyter, Peter.
Lefever, Isaick.
Wagner, Jacob.
Nitz, George.
Dutt, George.
Harpster, John.
Willouer, Christian.
Rinkert, Samuel.

CAMP MARCUS HOOK, *October 23, 1814.*

I certify, upon honor, that this muster-roll exhibits a true statement of the company, —— regiment, Pennsylvania militia, now in the service of the United States, and that the remarks set opposite the names are accurate and just to the best of my knowledge.

GEORGE F. COLDOVEY,
Captain.

I believe the above to be a correct muster of pay-roll.

CHRIST'R J. HUTTER,
Lieutenant Colonel Commanding.

I certify that the company commanded by Capt. George F. Coldovey is now in the service of the United States, under orders of the general commanding military district No. 4, or Fourth military district.

W. SPIRING,
Brigadier General.

October 25, 1814.

ROLL OF CAPT. THOMAS COLLINS' COMPANY.

Pay-roll of Capt. Thomas Collins' company, of United States volunteers, lately under the command of Major John Herkimer, in the service of the United States, discharged at Oswego. Commencement of service, 27th August, 1812; expiration of service, August 26th August, 1813.

Captain.

Collins, Thomas.

Lieutenant.

Marshall, J. H.

Ensign.

Fell, Mahlon, dead.

Sergeants.

Price, Benjamin, promoted to the rank of ensign, April 1, 1813.
McFarland, William.
Beeson, Henry, Jr.
Craig, James.

Corporals.

Colhoun, James.
Trusedale, Allen.
Tibbs, John.
Gard, Moses.

Musicians.

Updegraff, William.
Cuntzman, John.

Privates.

Wood, Seth, appointed second sergeant.
Woods, Clement.
Hibben, Thomas, appointed quarter-master sergeant.
Springer, Job.
Taylor, John.
Price, Simon, employed by Quarter-master Thomas, Buffalo, extra duty.
Lynch, Daniel.
Turner, Hanson.
Pryor, Joseph.
Gilman, Samuel.
Knapp, Jacob.
Farr, William.

Reyner, John.
Stewart, James.
Bleeks, William.
Bson, Henry H.
Henthorn, Noah.
McGuire, Michal.
Butler, Orrick.
Salter, Samuel, discharged for inability.
Springer, David.
Yates, Samuel, furloughed and unable to return.
Bayles, Henry.
Ebbert, William.
Butler, Comfort, furloughed and never returned.
Hoover, Phillip.
Goslin, Richard, employed by Quarter-master Thomas, Buffalo, extra duty.
Gaddis, Rice.
Shiles, Isaac.
Stoops, George.
Askerns, Thomas.
Dixon, William.
Hart, William.
Hunsaker, Henry.
Barnes. Daniel, employed by Quarter-master Thomas, Buffalo, extra duty.
Meason. George, died at Sackett's Harbor.
Gaddis, Abner.
Matt, James.
McCoy, William, employed by Quarter-master Thomas, Buffalo, extra duty.
McClean, Moses, discharged for inability.
Flick, Gersham.
Miller, Richard.
Moore, Samuel.
Firestone, Daniel, died at Buffalo.
Barnes, Otho.
Hyshoe, Adam.
Morris, William.
Orange, Thomas.
Stilwell, James.
Stilwell, Joseph.
White, James.

I certify, that the within pay-roll exhibits a true statement of Capt. Collins' company of United States volunteers, and that the remarks set are accurate and just.

J. H. MARSHALL,
Lieutenant United States Volunteers.

ROLL OF CAPT. JOHN COLUMN'S COMPANY.

Pay-roll of a company of infantry commanded by Capt. John Column, in the service of the United States, of the Second brigade, Pennsylvania, commanded by Brig. Gen. Crooks, attached to the north western army, under Maj. Gen. William Henry Harrison, commencing October 2, 1812, and ending April 2, 1813.

Captain.

Column, John.

Lieutenant.

Stewart, David, volunteered fifteen days.

Ensign.

McDowell, Alexander.

Sergeants.

Chamberlain, John.
Mushrash, Michael.
Morrell, Hugh, volunteered fifteen days.
Dickson, John, volunteered fifteen days.

Corporals.

Ford, Christ, discharged January 24, 1813.
Moorhead, Thomas, discharged December 2, 1812.
Cook, George G.

Musicians.

McClure, Thomas.
Shoop, Michael.

Privates.

Castard, Jesse.
Grey, James.
Spaferd, Rolph A., volunteered fifteen days.
Williams, Daniel, promoted to sergeant.
Grey, William.
Scott, Moses.
Gibson, John.
Collins, Isaac.
Wilson, Andrew.
Dearmond, John.
Dearmond, John C.
Dempsey, John.
Adams, James.
Bunting, John.
Alexander, Hugh.
Andrews, John.

Henry, John.
Dickey, William, volunteered fifteen days.
Myers, George.
Colvin, James.
Bennett, Robert.
Thompson, David.
Douthet, Solomon.
McNice, David.
Royer, Samuel.
Nelson, John.
Harper, John.
Bonce, Daniel, died December 29, 1812.
Grant, Benjamin, volunteered fifteen days.
Craine, Adonija, volunteered fifteen days.
Christy, Henry.
Robison, Isaiah, volunteered fifteen days.
Sterling, James.
McCay, Moses, volunteered fifteen days.
Nangle, Daniel, volunteered fifteen days.
Henry, James, discharged November 4, 1812.
Carnahan, Thomas, discharged November 7, 1812.
Cone, Levenus.
Foust, Jacob.
Anderson, Joseph, sick, absent, October 28, 1812.
Smiley, James.

I certify, on honor, that the within pay-roll exhibits a true statement of Capt. John Colum's company of infantry, and the remarks set opposite the men's names are correct and true.

JOHN COLLOM,
Captain.

October 8, 1813.

ROLL OF CAPT. DAVID COOK'S COMPANY.

Pay-roll of Capt. David Cook's company, Second brigade, First division, Pennsylvania militia, in the service of the United States, under command of Col. John Thompson.
Ribble, or Rivell, John.
Wallace, Thomas.
Spaid, Batmer.
Yarmer, George.
Vulmer, Joshua.
Niles, William C.
Tarrell, David.

Craycraft, Joseph.
Hunter, Robert.
Yagger, Michael.
Whitt, Hugh.
Mackntire, William.
Shafer, Antoney.
Bennett, John.
Richardson, Ekanh, or Ekonoher.
Snider, John.
Cooper, James.
Lervuis, John.
Rutter, John.
Bozorth, Thomas.
May, Daniel.
Cannan, Charles.
Renels, Peter.
Carrey, Edward.
Powewl, Samuel.
McHenery, Barney.
Lodge, George.
Shanon, James.
Cravin, Jacob.
Cuglar, John.
Pratt, John.
William, John.
Conner, Edward.
Cobb, Amer.
Dickerson, Joseph.
Deney, Dennis.
Gosner, Henry.
Whitcraft, William.
Hawkings, George.
Fogg, Samuel.
Rodgers, Robert.
Cambel, Michel.
Hines, James.
Adams, Peter.
Pollard, John.
Rider, George.
Parks, Richard.
Thomas, Amor.
Bishop, Ahigah, or Abijah.
Taylor, John.
Wolbert, or Wolpart, Jacob.
Tulley, James.
Wright, Isaac.

Kelly, Barthmew.
Fitzgerald, George.
Smith, John.
Handy, James.
Stuard, Andrew.
Smith, Henry.
Harris, Michel.
Skilman, John.
Lithtel, Henry.
Cristy, John.
Frances, John.
Thomas, Richard.
Krigmere, John.
Ellis, James.
Buckes, Peter.
Burel, Stephen.
Harvey, William.
Oenes, Michel.
Grimshaw, William.
Mooss, John A.
Storey, Benjamin.
Dilmore, William.
Sharp, Josiah.
Hendrickson, Joseph.
Stephenson, Perry.
Gilling, Daniel.
Rice, William.
Hargain, or Harigan, James.
Cooper, Robert.

We certify, on honor, that the within roll exhibits a true state of the non-commission officers and privates of the militia company commanded by Capt. David Cook.

DAVID COOK,
Captain.

CAMP MARCUS HOOK, *October 17, 1814.*

JOHN THOMSON,
Colonel.

I certify that the militia company commanded by Capt. D. Cook, is in the service of the United States, under order of general commanding Fourth military district.

THOMAS SNYDER,
Brigadier General Commanding.

CAMP MARCUS HOOK, *October 17, 1814.*

ROLL OF HENRY L. CORYELL'S COMPANY.

Muster roll of a company of riflemen under the command of Henry L. Coryell, in the regiment of volunteers in the service of the United States, commanded by Lieut. Col. Joel B. Southerland, from ——————, when last mustered, to time of discharge, 3d of January, 1815. Commencement of service, September 5, 1814.

Coryell, Henry L.
Seidel, John N.
Nezmos, John H.
Stetson, Siles.

Sergeants.

Jackson, William George.
Kerns, L. Andrew.
Till, John.
Lawton, Daniel.

Corporals.

Durand, Francis.
Vanculin, Isaac.
King, Richard.
Freston, William.

Privates.

Dodd, Joseph.
Adler, Bernard.
Adams, John, Sr.
Adams, John, Jr.
Apple, George.
Austin, L. Lewis.
Allison, John.
Blair, Hartman.
Barns, Philip.
Bell, Robert.
Black, William.
Budd, John.
Bissell, B. Allen.
Broom, Thomas.
Barry, B. Josiah.
Bennet, B. John.
Coulter, William.
Corgee, Arthur.
Cornwell, Emerson.

Carrol, John.
Davis, V. Samuel.
Davis, Lewis.
Deamer, John.
Dunwick, William.
Elsworth, David.
Frazure, Antony.
Griskey, Charles.
Grover, Curtis.
Galbreath, James.
Glading, John.
Gillian, James.
Griffith, David.
Gordon, Richard, discharged 5th October, 1814.
Glasby, Joseph.
Holsten, George.
Hammit, Benjamin.
Hawk, Jacob.
Hendricks, William.
Hall, George, October 1, 1814; transferred from the militia.
Holmes, John.
Harvey, Thomas.
Hand, Ezekiel.
Hanar, John.
Hubble, Samuel.
Jameson, Stephen.
Kirk, Philip.
Kane, George.
Keemer, David.
Kelly, John.
Knox, John.
Kinnard, Jacob.
Kinnard, James.
Lower, William.
Louderback, Peter.
Laferty, James.
Lepo, John.
Long, James.
Mirtitis, Sam.
Martin, Ezra.
Mungar, Orisan.
McKane, William.
McGill, James.
McKee, Gabriel.
McDonough, George.
McDonold, Charles.

McKeever, John.
McMullin, Isaac.
McKay, Barnard.
McCall, John, discharged September 27, at Camp Dupont.
Nolen, George.
Powers, Norris.
Parker, Henry.
Remick, John.
Rowland, William.
Rodes, John, September 23, 1814; transferred from the militia.
Rudy, Jacob, transferred into United States Navy, October 24, 1814.
Sherwood, James.
Sherwood, John.
Sherwood, William.
Starkey, George.
Shrank, George.
Tumlin, Stokes.
Thompson, Thomas.
Winnemore, Jacob.
West, James.
Wagner, William.
White, Francis.
Young, Samuel.
Glen, David, substitute for Joseph McAffee.
Scott, James B.

We certify, on honor, that this muster-roll exhibits a true state of Capt. Henry L. Coryell's company of riflemen, of the Pennsylvania regiment of volunteers, for the period therein mentioned, and that the remarks set opposite the names of the men are accurate and just.

H. L. CORYELLE,
Captain.
SAM. SPARKS,
Major.

ROLL OF CAPT. FLORENCE COTTER'S COMPANY.

Muster-roll of a company of militia, under the command of Capt. Florence Cotter, in the First detachment of the First brigade, drafted militia, in the service of the United States, commanded by Lieut. Col. Peter L. Berry, from 26th August, 1814, when last mustered, to 26th September, 1814, inclusive.

Captain.
Cotter, Florence.

Lieutenant.

Roberts, Robert.

Sergeants.

Nonnater, P. P.
George, Joseph.
Gilbert, David.
Rushe, Joseph.

Corporals.

Nassau, Michael.
Stein, Adam.
Ommensetter, Wennard.
Espy, James.

Fifer.

Hays, John.

Privates.

Anderson, John.
Anderson, James.
Biddle, John.
Boulton, Joseph R.
Bloom, George.
Best, John, transferred 8th September, by general orders.
Buchanan, George, transferred 8th September, by general orders.
Clark, James.
Cassidy, Hugh, transferred September 8, 1814, by general orders.
Caldwell, William, 5th September; transferred September 8, 1814.
Childs, John.
Cressman, Henry.
Clark, John F.
Dodgin, John. discharged September 23, 1814.
Dowdney, William.
Etter, Philip.
Flaherty, Edward.
Farner, Casper.
Fletcher, E., transferred September 8, 1814.
Gibson, Alexander.
Goodman, Conrad.
Gibson, James, appointed quarter-master to the battalion, September 16, 1814.
Good. Frederick.
Grimes, Felix.
Harman, Jacob.
Huenes, Melvine.
Hennaberry, Thomas.

Huffnagle, Edward.
Hodge, Michael.
Himes, Christopher.
Hoglin, Cor.
Hagerty, D.
Johnston, Peter.
Jacobs, Ezekiel.
Kibby, Charles.
Kinley, Philip.
Lewis, John.
Laughlin, Michael.
Leonard, William.
Marker, Jacob, transferred September 26.
Manerief, John.
Moore, James.
Mason, Samuel.
Meeker, Daniel.
Moony, Charles.
Muser, Henry, promoted sergeant major, August 26, 1814.
Nonnater, Stephen.
Paul, William S.
Penry, Walter.
Philips, Samuel, missing.
Reynolds, William.
Reeves, Enos.
Russell, Howard.
Richards, B. James.
Roberts, Daniel, transferred September 8, to volunteers.
Springtin, Samuel.
Smith, Joseph.
Steward, Mathew.
Snyder, Simon.
Stricker, John.
Stock, Daniel.
Spade, Henry.
Savage, John.
Tyson, David.
Treese, Abraham.
Tilton, William, transferred September 23, 1814.
Vivan, John.
Williamson, Michael.
Trimble, William, transferred September 8, 1814.
Walls, Henry.
Wallace, Thomas.
Wright, Samuel.

    We certify, on honor, that this muster-roll exhibits a true state of the Fifth company, of the detachment of militia, for the period therein mentioned, and that the remarks set opposite the names of the men are accurate and just.

FLORENCE COTTER,
Captain Fifth company, drafted militia.
PETER P. NONNATER,
First sergeant.
PETER A. BINNS,
Lieutenant Colonel.

CAMP BRANDYWINE, *September 26, 1814.*

I certify that the Fifth company of militia, commanded by Capt. Florence Cotter, is in the service of the United States, under orders of the general commanding the Fourth military district.

THOS. CADWALADER,
Brigadier General commanding.

CAMP DUPONT, *October 7, 1814.*

ROLL OF CAPT. SAMUEL COULSON'S COMPANY.

Pay-roll of a company of infantry commanded by Capt. Samuel Coulson, in the regiment of Pennsylvania militia commanded by Col. Rees Hill, in the service of the United States, commencing on the 29th day of May, and ending on the 5th day of November, 1813, both days inclusive.

Captain.

Coulson, Samuel, died October 12, 1813.

Lieutenant.

Shaw, Levi.

Sergeants.

Carothers, Thomas, promoted to ensign July 17, 1813.
Thompson, Daniel.
McElhatten, James.
Hughs, Barnabas, discharged June 18, 1813.
Kelley, Abraham, promoted June 24, 1813.
Knight, James, discharged October 1, 1813.

Corporals.

Denney, Henry, promoted August 26, 1813; discharged October 13, 1813.
McClelland, Robert, promoted August 26, 1813.
Weldon, John, promoted July 7, 1813.
Kencaid, Robert.

Privates.

Taylor, Matthew.
Galagher, James, discharged October 19, 1813.
Hamilton, Robert.
Given, James.
Musser, John, discharged October 15, 1813.
Stonekin, John.
Blake, Thomas, discharged October 13, 1813.
Allison, John.
Gates, Henry, discharged October 13, 1813.
McDowel, John.
Meek, John, discharged September 1, 1813.
Robison, Daniel.
Parker, Jeremia, discharged October 19, 1813.
Ross, Aaron.
Patterson, David.
Brook, Simeon.
Snyder, George.
Ray, William.
Peterman, Henry.
McCan, George.
Beens, John A.
Cannen, Joshua.
Rhody, John.
Fulton, Hugh, discharged July 13, 1813.
Knox, Andrew.
Achison, Humphrey.
Steen, James.
Roland, Robert.
Wells, James.
Dixon, James.
McGreger, Gabriel.
Brook, Samuel.
McHaffly, Abraham.
Moore, Samuel.
Fouzer, John.
Clarke, David.
Geno, William, died September 1, 1813.
Clark, Jacob.
Dennis, Nicholas.
McCombs, John.
Dunshee, Thomas.
Dugal, James.
Woods, Nathan.
Miller, Henry.
Brown, Francis.

WAR OF 1812-14.

Johnston, Francis.
Miller, James.
Hixon, Jonathan.
Kenneday, John.
Duff, John, died July 9, 1813.
Rogers, James.
Kirkpatrick, John.
McMiller, William.
Colburn, Marre, discharged October 5, 1813.
Denny, Walter, discharged September 29, 1813.
Hershey, John, discharged September 19, 1813.
Findley, Samuel, discharged October 13, 1813.

I do certify, upon honor, that the above roll exhibits a true statement of Capt. Samuel Coulson's company of infantry of Pennsylvania militia, of Col. Rees Hill's regiment, to the best of my knowledge and belief, this 16th May, 1815.

LEVI SHAW,
Lieutenant.

ROLL OF CAPT. WILLIAM CRAIG'S COMPANY.

Pay-roll of a company of infantry, commanded by Capt. William Craig, in the regiment of Pennsylvania militia, commanded by Col. Rees Hill, in the service of the United States, commencing on the 23d day of April, until November 8, 1813, both days inclusive.

Harvey, Isaac, May 5, 1813; died August 6, 1813.
White, James.
Trimble, Alexander.
Robinson, Hugh, promoted to sergeant, July 8, 1813.
Haggerman, Samuel, discharged July 8, 1813, invalid.
Robinson, James.
Cassaday, William.
Fenil, Thomas.
Keister, Michael.
Mitchel, Jesse.
Gray, Israel.
McLaughlin, Michael.
Irwin, Thomas.
Johnston, Uriah.
McVey, Patrick.
Grove, Jacob.
Carney, George.

6—VOL. XII.

Weaver, Daniel.
Brown, Peter.
McClean, Thomas.
Brown, George, sick, and discharged by doctor, August 13, 1813.
Sherbondy, George.
Mahan, Robert.
Berry, John.
Irwin, William, discharged June 13, 1813, casualty.
Carson, James.
Kirkpatrick, Henry.
Wade, George.
McGuire, Daniel.
Russell, John, discharged August 17, 1813, sickness.
Kanaan, Jonathan, discharged September 20, 1813, to take care of a sick man.
Walker, John.
McCormick, James.
Aron, Conrad.
Clark, James.
Black, James.
Serenna, Joseph.
Murphy, James, discharged August 17, 1813, on account of sickness.
McHenry, William.
McCormick, John.
Speese, George, discharged August 18, 1813, over age.
Dougal, Henry.
McClean, Robert.
Shaffer, George, discharged August 19, 1813, on account of sickness.
Young, John, discharged August 17, 1813; cut in the foot.
Geiger, Benjamin.
McClean, John.
McKeever, Matthew, discharged August 19, 1813.
Cochran, William.
Murphy, Jeremiah.
Wadle, James, discharged August 19, 1813.
McKee, John.
Williard, Frederick.
Gray, John.
Amilong, Daniel.
Berlin, John.
Wilty, Philip.
Fox, Jacob.
Gibson, Gedion.
Dixon, Samuel.
Gaut, William.
Dillinger, George.

Campble, Thomas.
Holder, James.
Taylor, John.
Cimmel, John.
Hunter, Thomas.
McQuade, James.
Cassidy, William, Jr.
Morrow, James.
Cole, David.
Leightly, George.
Boyd, John, discharged August 23, 1813.

ROLL OF CAPT. RICHARD M. CRAIN'S COMPANY.

Muster-roll of Captain Richard M. Crain's company, First regiment, First brigade, of Pennsylvania militia, under the command of Col. Maxwell Kennedy, at York, Pennsylvania, (in service from August 31, 1814, to March 5, 1815, from Dauphin county.)

Captain.

Crain, Richard M.

First Lieutenant.

Bailey, Joseph.

Second Lieutenant.

Caruthers, George.

Sergeants.

Piper, Alexander M.
Jacobs, Richard T.
Boyd, James R.
Laveille, Joseph C.

Corporals.

Benjamin, John.
Taylor, George.
Elder, Jacob.
Walburn, John.

Drummer.

Krause, David.

Fifer.

Pool, Jacob.

Privates.

Adams, George.
Barnett, John M.

Barnett, Thomas.
Barnitt, William.
Beissel, John.
Blake, Henry.
Bostwick, Trueman.
Boyer, Samuel.
Boyer, William.
Brotherton, Elisha.
Brown, Thomas.
Burr, H. Henry.
Capp, Samuel.
Carson, William M.
Cochran, George.
Conner, John.
Curtz, Thomas.
Dougherty, Michael.
Eichholtz, George.
Ewing, Nathaniel.
Findlay, William S.
Fleck, John.
Furguson, Matthew.
George, William.
Gleim, Jacob.
Gongaware, George.
Graydon, Alexander.
Grayham, Robert.
Harris, Samuel.
Heister, Jonathan D.
Hitzeberger, Nicholas.
Hoyer, Jacob.
Keighler, John.
Kellar, John.
Kimble, Charles.
Kneply, Jacob.
Krum, Peter.
Kunkle, Jacob.
Lebkicher, Michael.
Lebs, John.
Leech, Richard T.
Leek, Henry.
Mitchell, Thomas.
Murphy, James.
Myre, George.
Nabb, Perry C.
Newell, William.
Reiley, Luther.

Reiley, William.
Robertson, William.
Rodney, John.
Search, John.
Shanning, John.
Sheriman, Henry C.
Shoch, Samuel.
Shrier, John.
Shunk, F. R.
Smith, Henry.
Smith, John.
Stine, Jacob R.
Swoyer, John.
Thompson, John B.
Vanboskirk, Andrew.
Vanderslice, Marcus.
Wallace, Joseph.
Weinman, Samuel.
Whitehill, John.
White, Thomas.
Willis, John M.
Wilson, John.
Youse, Joseph.

ROLL OF CAPT. SAMUEL D. CULBERTSON'S COMPANY.

Roll of Capt. Samuel D. Culbertson's company, Chambersburg, September, 1814.

Captain.

Culbertson, Samuel D.

First Lieutenant.

McClintock, John.

Second Lieutenant.

Harper, George K.

Ensign.

Stevenson, John.

Sergeants.

Calhoun, Andrew.
Calhoun, John.
Rigler, Stephen.
Allison, Alexander.

WAR OF 1812-14.

Corporals.

Greenfield, Hugh.
Wilson, James.
Beatty, Samuel.
Andrew, John.

Privates.

Arntt, John.
Burchett, Henry.
Besore, John.
Brand, Samuel.
Besore, Matthew.
Beaver, George.
Crawford, James.
Crawford, Holmes.
Capron, Augustus.
Cook, William.
Campbell, James.
Crawford, Edward.
Capron, Edward.
Crayton, Peter.
Devine, John.
Denny, William.
Duffield, Joseph.
Denig, John.
Dougherty, John.
Erven, Joseph.
Fahnestock, Benjamin.
Ferry, William.
Grier, Isaac.
Grove, Jacob.
Greenawalt, Henry.
Grove, William.
Hoeflick, Paul.
Holmes, John.
Heyser, William.
Housem, Joseph.
Hutchinson, John.
Harris, George.
Helfmire, Herman.
Hinkle, John.
Johns, Michael S.
Jamison, William.
Jasonsky, George.
Kindline, John.
Kelker, Jacob.
Lindsay, Andrew.

McDowell, William M.
McBride, John.
Murray, Patrick.
McCormick, John.
McKight, George B.
McCulloh, Thomas G.
Merklein, Henry.
Nunemacher, John.
Nochtwine, William.
Oyster, George.
O'Neal, John.
Porter, Samuel.
Reynolds, William.
Riddle, James D.
Reges, Philip.
Reed, John.
Ruthrauff, Samuel.
Richey, William.
Roemer, Adam.
Simpson, George.
Schoepflin, William.
Snider, John.
Shillito, Samuel.
Shane, William.
Stevenson, Daniel.
Smith, Jacob.
Tritle, David.
Thompson, Robert.
Voress, Abraham.
Wolff, Bernard.
Widefelt, Jacob.
Weaver, John.
Whitmore, John.
Watts, John B.
Warden, James.
Wallace, Joseph.
Willison, George.

ROLL OF CAPT. MATTHEW DAWSON'S COMPANY.

Pay-roll of a company of Pennsylvania militia under the command of Capt. Matthew Dawson, of the Fifth battalion, commanded by Maj. David Nelson, in the service of the United States, from October 2, 1812, until April 2, 1813, inclusive.

Captain.

Dawson, Matthew.

Lieutenant.

Ferguson, John.

Ensign.

Scott, Francis.

Sergeants.

Juell, Thomas.
Beens, John I.
Person, George.
Lookart, Robert.

Corporals.

Duglas, Edward.
Gipson, John, died November 18.
Rolston, Jeremiah, died November 29.
Chinoweth, Joshuah, discharged November 14.

Privates.

Crafford, Thomas, discharged January 23, Fort Ferre.
Sampel, William.
Thompson, John.
Sampel, Samuel.
Morland, Isaac.
Morland, John.
Scott, William, discharged January 19.
Cannon, John, October 25, left sick on our march. and did not join again.
Clingensmith, Daniel, drowned March 19.
Gunvell, Jacob L., discharged December 10.
Mercer, Henry.
Beaty, William.
Reed, Andrew.
Marquis, Andrew.
Marquis, Samuel.
Sampson, Thomas.
Zoover, William.
Moats, Christian.

WAR OF 1812-14.

McClurg, William, discharged December 1.
Cherry, Thomas, discharged November 6.
Mears, William, discharged January 23.
Eakrite, or Arkwright, Samuel.
Carpenter, Frederich, discharged January 9.
Graham, James, discharged November 25.
Patterson, Samuel.
Monteath, John H.
Paton, Elija, discharged October 26.
Caster, Benjamin.
McCord, John.
McCrum, Samuel.
Carns, William.
Clark, William.
Hazen, Jeremiah, died February 22.
Boyl, Alexander.
Warner, David.
Watson, Lott.
Bay, William V.
Spear, Thomas.
Byers, Samuel.
Simervil, John.
Cooper, Jacob.
Pool, Jacob.
Vannoston, John.
Baum, Frederick, October 21, left sick on our march, and did not join us again.
Siverlin, John.
Slayman, Francis.
McFadden, Andrew.
Henry, John, discharged October 29.
McIntier, Robert.
Steel, Robert.
McCord, William.
Irwin, John.

I certify, on honor, that this muster-roll exhibits a true state of Capt. Matthew Dawson's company of the Fifth battalion, second detachment, Pennsylvania militia, for the period therein mentioned, and that the marks set opposite the men's names are accurate and just.

MATTHEW DAWSON,
Captain.
FRANCIS SCOTT,
Ensign.

September 6, 1813.

ROLL OF CAPTAIN NICKOLAUS DERR'S COMPANY.

Muster-roll of Captain Nickolaus Derr's company, of the One Hundred and First regiment of Pennsylvania militia, under marching orders to Marcus Hook, on the Delaware river, September 27, 1814.

Captain.

Derr, Nickolaus.

Lieutenant.

Grinewalt, Jacob.

Ensign.

Kistler, Jacob.

Sergeants.

Krimm, Netten.
Kramlich, Jacob.
Seiberlink, Christian.
Kopp, George.

Corporals.

Herbster, John.
Hartman, Peter.
Smith, Conrad.
Peter, Henry.

Drummer.

Krum, Peter.

Fifer.

Smith, Michael.

Privates.

Aiker, Daniel.
Aiker, Daniel, Jr.
Baker, Jacob.
Boger, Christian.
Breiner, George.
Buckman, Andrew.
Deibert, Daniel.
Fenstermacher, Philip.
Folk, George.
Frans, John.
Frey, Adam.
Hander, George.
Hauselman, Andrew.
Hans, Christian.
Hans, Jacob.
Hans, Leohard.

Hardinger, Michel.
Hausman, John.
Heilman, Jacob.
Heller, Christian.
Hetler, George.
Hetler, John.
Holben, Salamon.
Hunsicker, Peter.
Kistler, Henry.
Klotz, Daniel.
Klutz, Andrew.
Kuns, Christian.
Lancknor, Joseph.
Lechleider, George.
Lefaver, Isaac.
Lefaver, William.
Lizer, Daniel.
Lutz, Christian.
Mest, Samuel.
Miller, Abraham.
Miller, Jacob.
Miller, John.
Miller, Peter.
Moyer, John.
Nothstein, Peter.
Peter, Jonas.
Rauche, Daniel.
Rauche, Salamon.
Rex, John.
Rockel, Adam.
Rouche, John.
Sell, Peter.
Sensinger, Daniel.
Sleicher, Valentine.
Snyder, Christian.
Snyder, Jacob.
Snyder, Peter.
Steierwalt, George.
Stein, John.
Verlein, Michael.
Weaver, Jacob.
Wehr, Philip.
Werly, Andrew.
Werly, Theobalt.
Wert, Martin.
Yuxseimer, Abraham.

ROLL OF CAPT. JACOB DIETRICK'S COMPANY.

Muster-roll of Capt. Jacob Dietrick's company, in the Second regiment, First brigade, of Pennsylvania militia, under the command of Adam Riteherd, at York, Pennsylvania, September 5, 1814. In service from September 1, 1814, to March 5, 1815, from Dauphin county.

Captain.

Dietrick, Jacob.

Lieutenant.

Hoffman, Daniel.

Ensign.

Kintzel, Christian.

Sergeants.

Wilson, William.
Deitrick, Jacob.
Sasimon, Peter.
Paul, John.

Corporals.

Russell, John.
Shofstall, Jones.
Gary, Thomas.
Leidy, Abraham.

Privates.

Balsly, Thomas.
Bell, James.
Bell, John.
Brooks, John.
Brubaker, Joseph.
Bumbaugh, John.
Cambell, James.
Cammel, Armstrong.
Clinger, Peter.
Coplens, John.
Cremer, Daniel.
Ettinger, John.
Ettinger, John.
Ferree, Joel.
Fraunk, Abraham.
Garman, John.
Geeseman, John.

Goodman, Henderey.
Haberstick, John.
Halman, Nicholas.
Halsman, John.
Hendrey, Daniel.
Hetrick, Nicholas.
Holman, John.
Holman, Peter.
Hoyer, Peter.
Kean, Daniel.
Lark, Stophel.
Lobe, Peter.
Long, Henderey.
Lower, Jacob.
Lowes, Joseph.
Manigh, Peter.
Matthias, Elgah.
Meek, Jacob.
Menigh, George.
Messner, Christian.
Moore, Christian.
Motor, Christian.
Motter, John.
Moyer, Frederick.
Otto, Conrad.
Powel, Ludwick.
Priser, Hendery.
Rawen, Casper.
Riggle, Andrew.
Ross, William.
Sestor, John.
Shaop, George.
Shnoke, Christian.
Shofestall, William.
Sidel, Hendery.
Snoke, George.
Snyder, Jacob.
Sponcilor, John.
Swab, Jacob.
Swigert, Adam.
Swigert, Peter.
Swisby, George.
Woodside, James.
Workman, Joseph.

ROLL OF CAPT. ADAM DILLER'S COMPANY.

Muster-roll of Capt. Adam Diller's company of infantry in the Sec- regiment, Second brigade, Pennsylvania militia, under the command of Lieut. Col. John Lotz, at York, Pennsylvania. In service from September 1, 1814, to March 5, 1815, from Lancaster county.

Captain.

Diller, Adam.

Lieutenant.

Musser, William.

Ensign.

Muckey, Christian.

Sergeants.

Jonas, David.
Nowman, Christian.
Wagner, William.
Zell, Adam.

Corporals.

Getz, John.
Leyman, John.
Olds, John.
Wheelen, Adam.

Privates.

Bovig, Daniel.
Brobst, Henry.
Butcher, Thomas.
Cooper, George.
Dannavon, Timothy.
Fay, James.
Fix, George.
Fubs, Peter.
Genseman, George.
Grill, William.
Hagerize, Henry.
Harnish, Samuel.
Herbst, Peter.
Hess, Henry.
Heymiller, Henry.
Hood, John.
Karchner, Henry.

Kauffman, John.
Kile, George.
Knox, William.
Kraft, John.
Leininger, John, Jr.
Leisey, George.
Leisey, John.
Lininger, John, Jr.
Ludwick, Philip.
Lutz, Samuel.
Manning, William.
McVay, James.
Mengle, George.
Metzgar, Joseph.
Miller, Philip.
Mull, John.
Nawton, John.
Nibe, Henry.
Overly, Adam.
Rath, Daniel.
Razer, Michael.
Ream, Peter.
Regart, Henry.
Reifsnyder, Benjamin.
Roth, George.
Ruch, John.
Russel, Joseph.
Sander, John.
Sealor, Philip.
Shank, Jacob.
Shappart, John.
Shide, John.
Slough, Abraham.
Smith, Conrad.
Snyder, Henry.
Todd, John.
Trossil, John.
Walborn, Adam.
White, John.
Zimmerman, Peter.

ROLL OF CAPTAIN GEORGE DINCKEY'S COMPANY.

A true list of Capt. [George] Dinckey's company, of the Eighteenth section of riflemen, commanded by Colonel Thom. Humphrey.

Sergeants.

Saeger, Daniel.
Lentz, John.
Traxel, Christian.
Beiper, John.

Corporals.

Deick, Casper.
Kelsy, John.
George, John.
Meyer, Henry.

Bugleman.

Meyer, Daniel.

Privates.

Anawald, John.
Sheirer, Solomon.
Backer, Frederick.
Rencker, Jacob.
Schlosser, John.
Shnyder, Jacob, Jr.
Sigfrid, William.
Shnyder, Samuel.
Meyer, Conrad.
Zillner, Migel.
Handwarck, Frederick.
Mosser, John.
Schad, John.
Yeal, John.
Sigfrid, Solomon.
Meyer, Godfrid.
Sigfrid, Peter.
Shnyder, John.
Deiberd, Peter.
Shnyder, Jacob.
Sigfrid, Andrew.
Haas, Jacob.

I do certify that the within list is a true statement, on honor, this 13th day of November, 1814.

GEORGE DINCKEY,
Captain.
THO. HUMPHREY,
Colonel, P. P. V. R.

WAR OF 1812-14. 97

I do certify, on honor, that the company commanded by Captain George Dinckey is in the service of the United States, under the command of the general commanding the Fourth military district.

THOS. CADWALADER,
Brigadier General Commanding Advance L. B.
CAMP DUPONT, *November 26, 1814.*

ROLL OF CAPT. HENRY DOEBLER'S COMPANY.

Muster-roll of Capt. Henry Doebler's company, in the First regiment, First brigade, Pennsylvania militia, under the command of Col. Maxwell Kennedy, at York, Pennsylvania, September 5, 1814. In service from August 28, 1814, to March 5, 1815; from Lebanon county.

Captain.

Doebler, Henry.

Lieutenant.

Embich, Jacob.

Ensign.

Fasnacht, Frederick.

Sergeants.

Hubley, Andrew D.
Embich, Samuel.
Karch, George.
Johnson, John.

Corporals.

Shindle, Jacob.
Embich, Philip.
Werth, John.
McCool, Joseph.

Fifer.

Millinger, John.

Drummer.

Hefflefinger, William.

Privates.

Bricker, Jacob.
Buckley, Samuel.
Doebler, Lewis.
Dubs, Henry.
Ellinger, Peter.
Embich, Abraham.
Geissaman, John.

7—VOL. XII.

Gerhart, George.
Gillman, Christian.
Greenawalt, Matthias.
Greenawalt, Philip.
Grove, Peter.
Hamilton, John.
Hefflefinger, John.
Hoffman, David.
Honeficaus, Philip.
Hoves, Isaac.
Marshall, James.
Mason, Frank.
Mayer, Henry.
McCloul, John.
McCullough, Samuel.
Miller, Christian.
Millinger, David.
Millinger, Samuel.
Pouler, William.
Rann, Henry.
Reivale, George.
Reivale, Tobias.
Rewalt, John.
Rinal, John.
Schnee, Joseph.
Seigrist, Christian.
Shindel, George.
Shome, Joseph.
Stoever, William.
Uhler, Michael.
Wain, Michael.
Weiss, Jacob.
Wilson, Hugh.
Yeager, Christian.
Yeager, John.
Yeager, Joseph.
Yensell, Martin.

ROLL OF CAPT. JOHN DONALDSON'S COMPANY.

Capt. John Donaldson's Pennsylvania militia, (First regiment, Col. Snyder,) September 25 to November 24, 1814.

Captain.

Donaldson, John.

Lieutenants.

Chamberlain, Aaron.
Hall, John.

Sergeants.

McFadden, John.
Johnson, Abel.
Eiland, Jacob.
Comfort, Henry.

Corporals.

Attzbanch, Jacob.
Jones, Samuel.

Fifer.

Dennis, Michael.

Drummer.

Parks, Robert.

Privates.

Martin, Peter.
Parks, Robert.
Martin, Peter.
Parks, John.
Frederick, Samuel.
Rerrick, John.
Klingerman, Jacob.
Klingerman, George.
Klingerman, John.
Kutz, George.
Nuse, Jonathan.
Cornelius, William.
Johnson, William.
Struble, Peter.
Struble, Henry.
Bower, Joseph.
Linn, David.
Jones, Benjamin.
Curtis, Thomas.
Kimple, Philip.
Black, Robert.
Weykle, Henry.
Frederick, Peter.
Frederick, Jacob.
Reedy, Henry.
Shaw, Samuel.
Lytle, Samuel.
Forster, John.
Turner, John.

Lytle, William.
Snook, Peter.
McGee, John.
Walker, John.
Jordan, George.
Coset, Jonathan.
Meekart, Daniel.
Clement, Michael.
Seaboldt, Christopher.
Wise, John.
Miller, Thomas.
Nelson, Daniel.
Waight, John.
Barbyn, James.
Frock, Jacob.
Glover, John.
Zimmerman, David.
Forster, William.
Forster, William, Jr.
Vanhorn, William.
Stutleback, Jacob.
Weaver, Benjamin.
Binner, Henry.
Norman, William.
Calbetson, Jacob.
Slear, John.
Stirn, Fred.
Bartlow, Francis.
Hollinshead, Francis.
Huff, James.
Miller, Henry.
Harmon, Benjamin.
Thline, (or Kline,) Daniel.
Kiniger, Henry.
McKinley, James.
McKinley, John.
Chamberlin, Uriah.
Thompson, Samuel.
Pearson, John.
Gray, Robert H.
Kelly, John.
Gile, John.
Gibson, John.
McGinnis, John.
Binner, Michael.
Auple, Stophel.

ROLL OF LIEUT. THOMAS DONALDSON'S COMPANY.

Pay-roll of Lieut. Thomas Donaldson's company of drafted militia attached to the First regiment, commanded by Lieut. Col. Joel Ferree, in the service of the United States, from the State of Pennsylvania, Brig. Gen. Richard Crooks, commanding. Commencing October 2, 1812, and ending April 15, 1813.

Lieutenant.

Donaldson, Thomas.

Ensign.

Roberts, Asa.

Sergeants.

Scott, Joseph.
McCombs, Matthew.
Long, John.
Campbell, David.

Corporals.

Robinson, William.
Robinson, James.
Sutherland, Vachel.
Futhey, Benjamin.

Privates.

Ault, George.
Biggar, James.
Bayles, Daniel.
Beaty, William.
Coffman, John, volunteered for fifteen days.
Conrad, William.
Conrad, Henry.
Carlisle, Robert.
Cole, Samuel, volunteered for fifteen days.
Cunningham, Robert.
Dunlap, William.
Adger, James.
French, Richard.
Hughston, Thomas.
Jones, Nathaniel.
Johnson, Samuel.
Johnson, Joseph.
Johnson, John.
Kerr, Robert.
Mires, Mathias.
Mitchel, John.

Pillars, Daniel.
Peoples, Robert.
Price, William.
Hughston, Allen.
Hailey, John.
McIntire, John, volunteered for fifteen days.
McGurk, William.
McCoy, William.
Peeters, Reuben.
Robinson, John.
Russle, Robert.
Rowland, Jonathan, volunteered for fifteen days.
Speers, Samuel, volunteered for fifteen days.
Schoonover, Nicholas.
Sheck, Thomas, volunteered for fifteen days.
Tynan, Robert.
Venoestrand, Peter.
White, David.
Watson, Benjamin.
Kelly, Simon
McClurg, John.
Vernon, Pierce.
Ruble, William.
Clemans, Daniel.
Deems, John, discharged October 22, 1812.
Hainy, Thomas.
Hix, Thomas, volunteered fifteen days.
Leech, James, discharged February 2, 1813, by Dr. Hersey.
Leech, Samuel, discharged February 2, 1813, by Dr. Hersey.
Linvill, Jeremiah, discharged February 2, 1813, by Dr. Hersey.
Duff, James, volunteered fifteen days.
Sanders, Greenberry.
Tuttle, Samuel, discharged November 1, 1812, by a doctor.
Underwood, Obed, discharged December 4, 1812.
Yohe, Peter, discharged October 24, 1812.
McGee, John, died November 21, 1812.
Wonsetler, Jacob, discharged October 22, 1812.
Nangle, Andrew.
Grimo, William.

We certify, on honor, that this pay-roll exhibits a true statement of Lieut. Thomas Donaldson's company of the First regiment of the second brigade, Pennsylvania militia, for the period therein mentioned, and that the remarks set opposite the men's names are accurate and just.

THOMAS DONALDSON,
Lieutenant.

WAR OF 1812–14.

ROLL OF CAPT. JOHN DORNBLASER'S COMPANY.

Muster-roll of Capt. John Dornblaser's company, belonging to a detachment of Northampton, Lehigh, and Pike county militia, commanded by Lieut. Colonel Ch'r. J. Hutter, now in the service of the United States.

Captain.

Dornblaser, John.

First Lieutenant.

Bush, John V.

Second Lieutenant.

Winters, John.

Third Lieutenant.

Fenner, Frederic, elected 10th October, 1814.

Ensign.

Smith, David.

Sergeants.

Morrison, John W.
Hartzell, John.
Hartzell, Jacob.
Fenner, Frederic, promoted.

Corporals.

Teel, Nicholas.
Barret, Henry.
Stocker, Samuel.
Brady, William.

Drummer.

Saylor, Isaac.

Fifer.

Hockman, Jonas.

Privates.

Dietz, John.
Rape, George.
Snyder, Peter.
Ward, John.
Ostertack, John.
Young, John.
Shafer, Joseph.
Nolf, George.
Hoffert, Samuel.
Bunstein, Jacob.
Walter, Conrad.
Young, Adam.

Stocker, David.
Willower, George.
Miller, Abraham.
Wimmer, Joseph.
Price, Freeman.
Kehler, Leonard.
Hutmacher, J., discharged October 17, 1814.
Kehler, Daniel.
Wineland, Christian.
Stoufer, John.
Stocker, Jacob.
Gangwehr, Jacob.
Holman, Jeremiah R.
Nye, Lawrence.
Nye, Andrew, discharged October 20, 1814.
Steiner, Joseph.
Miller, Daniel.
Hahn, Peter.
Hahn, George.
Myer, George.
Schick, Peter.
Keyser, Jacob.
Geres, Frederick.
Swartwood, Jacob.
Winner, John.
Fisher, Philip.
Crawford, John.
Beard, John.
Shepperd, David.
Lowman, John.
Evans, David.
Stine, John.
Barr, James.
Kester, Philip.
Kester, Leonard.
Miller, Henry.
Morris, Obed.
VanHorn, Cornelius.
Barr, Adam.
Cooper, Joseph.
Davis, William.
Clark, John.
Bureau, William.
Arndt, Jacob.
Smell, Samuel.
Erie, or Ihrie, Conrad.

Gower, John.
Myer, Henry.
Serfas, George.
Serfas, John.
Fisher, Dewald.
Crisman, Jacob.
Klinetrup, John.
Mack, John.
Posty, Thomas.
Miller, George, discharged October 17, 1814.
Swenk, John.
Brewer, James.
Smith, Christopher.
Merwine, Jacob.
Huston, John.
Rinker, George.
Rees, Samuel.
McGammon, Alexander.
Strunk, Peter.
Faulk, John.
Coolbaugh, Garret.
Jayne, Peter.
Bunnel, Barnet.
Place, Jacob.
Adams, John.
Horman, Frederick.
Winans, Samuel.
Kincaid, Sylvester.
Vandemark, Peter.
Vanetter, Anthony.
Howe, John.
Impson, Robert.
Vansickle, William.
Steel, Isaac.
Courtright, Levi.
Watson, George.

CAMP MARCUS HOOK, *October 21, 1814.*

I certify, on honor, that this muster or pay-roll exhibits a true state of the company, ―――― regiment, Pennsylvania militia, now in service of the United States, and the remarks set opposite the names are accurate and just, to the best of my knowledge.

JOHN DORNBLASER,
Captain.

I believe the above to be a correct muster or pay-roll.

CHRIST. J. HUTTER,
Lieutenant Colonel Commanding.

I certify that the company commanded by Capt. John Dornblaser is in the service of the United States, under orders of the general commanding the Fourth military district.

W. SPIRING,
Brigadier General.

October 25, 1814.

ROLL OF LIEUT. JOSEPH DRIBLEBIES' COMPANY.

MARCUS HOOK, *October 31, 1814.*

Pay-roll of the company of infantry, under the command of Lieut. Joseph Driblebies, attached and organized by Adjutant General ———, of the ——— brigade, Pennsylvania militia; in the service of the United States, commanded by Lieut. Col. George Weirick, of the Seventy-seventh regiment, Pennsylvania militia.

Lieutenant.

Driblebies, Joseph.

Ensign.

Farnswort, William.

Sergeants.

Achmutz, Samuel.
Colsher, John.
Warner, Thomas.
Hull, Peter.

Corporals.

Rann, Adam.
Mertz, John.
Snyder, Thomas.
Wyall, George.

Drummer.

Fry, John.

Fifer.

Gilger, Adam.

Privates.

Hull, Charles.
Hinkle, Daniel.
Richer, John.
Herner, George.
Kreig, Solomon.
Casner, John.

Casner, Conrad.
Ayres, Lewis.
Ayres, Ellis.
Syby, Frederick.
Weatzel, or Wentzil, Christopher.
Waggoner, George.
Rogers, Arthur.
Smith, Adam.
Goodman, George.
Achmutz, Arthur.
Fagley, John.
Dork, George.
Leader, John.
Hime, George.
Carns, John.
Drumheller, Martin.
Drumheller, Abraham.
Kimble, John.
Kauble, Frederick.
Daniel, Henry.
Farster, Leonard.
Sitz, George.
Read, Michael.
Kimble, Henry.
Slise, Adam.
Kepler, John.
Rabock, Michael.
Foulk, Jacob.
Druchamiller, Michael.
Boyer, Peter.
Rabock, Conrad.
Kline, John.
Rabock, Henry.
Beisel, or Beise, John.
Ritz, George.
Hime, John.
Martin, John.
Lewis, John.
Martin, Daniel.
Huffman, Henry.
Person, John.
Fox, Joseph.
Hummel, Solomon.
Moyer, Solomon.
Holwig, John.
Geise, Henry.

Griem, or Grim, Martin.
Bower, Samuel.
Cocher, Levy.
Herter, John.
Fisher, Henry.
Giesse, Samuel.
Read, Leonard.
Litzel, George.
Hepner, Henry.
Hanabach, Valentine.
Buckner, John.
Farnsworth, Robert.
Creasinger, Henry.
Slaught, Jere.
Foy, Samuel.
Fisher, John.
Tawney, Adam.
Sawer, Conrad.
Heckert, Peter.
Sawer, or Lawer, Peter.
Almond, Jacob.
Heckert, Joshua.
Deiter, Leonard.
Bower, Michael.
Snyder, Daniel.
High, Daniel.
Litle, Ephraim.
Shipman, Elijah.
Dangleberger, I.
Melig, Peter.
Seasholtz, Samuel.
Hahn, or Rann, Philip.
Randolz, William.
Blottenberger, Daniel.
Klook, John.
Kehlor, Frederick.

I do certify, on honor, that this pay-roll exhibits a true statement of the company under my command, from Northumberland county, attached to the regiment under the command of Lieut. Col. George Weirick, Pennsylvania militia.

JOSEPH DREIBELBIES,
Lieutenant.

I believe the above to be a true pay-roll, except Arthur Auchmuty, who received a furlough improper, in my opinion.

GEORGE WEIRICK.
Lieutenant Colonel Commanding.

I certify that the company commanded by Lieut. Joseph Driblebies is now in the service of the United States, under order of the general commanding, Fourth military district.

THOMAS J. ROGERS,
Brigade Major.

ROLL OF LIEUT. PETER DRUM'S COMPANY.

Pay-roll of a company of twelve months' United States volunteer riflemen, commanded by Lieut. Peter Drum, of the independent battalion of volunteers, commanded by Major John B. Alexander, in the service of the United States, who served their terms of service in the Northwestern army, commencing the 11th September, 1812; ending the 11th September, 1813.

First Lieutenant.

Drum, Peter.

Sergeants.

Hardin, Richard.
Fleeger, Peter.
Jamison, John, died 18th August, 1812.

Corporals.

Singer, Samuel.
Shillito, Edward.

Privates.

Gossert, Jacob.
Barton, Henry.
Jamison, Benjamin.
Keck, Isaac.
Knureamer, Jonas.
Kerns, William.
Miller, Henry.
McLane, Samuel.
Mitchul, John.
Pluck, Jacob.
Sicafoos, George.
Sheflor, George.
Thompson, Robert.
Taylor, James, died 6 May, 1813.
Williams, Adam.
Weaver, Abraham.
Walters, Peter.

I certify, on honor, that this pay-roll exhibits a true statement of Lieut. Peter Drum's company of twelve months' volunteers, for the period therein mentioned, and that the remarks made opposite the names of the men are accurate and just.

PETER DRUM,
Lieutenant U. S. V. Riflemen.

ROLL OF CAPT. DUFFIELD'S COMPANY OF ARTILLERY.

Quarter-Master.
Lee, William A.

Sergeants.
Doak, Washington.
Denney, Samuel.
Thomas, James Z.
Fulton, Gardiner.
Erbin, Adam.

Corporals.
Clark, John A.
Teese, Daniel.
Gilbert, John T.
Shallcross, William.
Tyler, Rufus.

Privates.
Hamilton, Benjamin.
Thomas, Moses.
Rees, James.
Schoch, Joseph.
Ristine, Charles.
Matlock, Benjamin.
Shallcross, John.
McMullen, John.
Scates, Lawrence.
Baldwin, Joseph.
Vanaken, Paul.
Schoch, Jonathan.
Dover, Levi K.
Bodine, Jacob.
Shute, Thomas.
Landenberger, Samuel.
Fisher, George.
Bennet, John.
Bordman, John.

Hamilton, James.
Neff, Robert W.
Coon, Christopher.
Solly, Robert.
Robison, George.
Newcamp, John.
Rorar, George.
Clark, Daniel.
Buckius, Rudolph.
Merkle, George.
Worrell, Rudolph.
Miller, James.
Linton, James.
Borger, William.
Frazer, David.
Jenkins, Benjamin.
Retzer, Michael.
Peters, John.
Sparks, Isaac W.
Pennell, Joseph.
Rorar, Joseph.
Delaney, Jacob.
Schoch, Henry.
Scott, Benjamin.
Doran, Francis.
Courtney, Samuel P.
Botner, Joseph.
Worrell, Isaiah.
Lear, James.
Quicksall, Charles E.
Coucker, George.
Worrell, Hawley.
Haines, George.
Marshall, Joseph.
Burk, John.
Hart, Oliver.
Worrell, Stephen.
Thomas, Martin.
Jones, Isaac.
Palmer, Aaron.
Adams, Roderick.
Sparks, Henry D.
Potts, Thomas.
Gray, John.
Rorar, John.
Coon, Jacob.

Shetzline, Michael.
Sanderson, Joseph M.
Fries, Conrad.
Harper, Jacob.
Philips, Henry.
Landenberger, William.
Thomas, William.
Shepherd, Cumberland.
Newlen, Samuel.

    I do hereby certify the within roll to be correct.

THOMAS W. DUFFIELD,
Captain.

A. M. PREVOST,
Major, Volunteer Artillery, Service United States.

CAMP DUPONT, *October 3, 1814.*

    I certify that the company of volunteer artillery, commanded by Thomas W. Duffield, is in the service of the United States, under orders of the general commanding, the Fourth military district.

THOMAS CADWALADER,
Brigadier General Commanding.

CAMP DUPONT, *October 7, 1814.*

ROLL OF CAPT. SAMUEL DUNN'S COMPANY.

Muster-roll of Capt. Samuel Dunn's company, Col. Fenton's regiment, Pennsylvania militia.

Captain.

Dunn, Samuel.

First Lieutenant.

Connell, James.

Second Lieutenant.

Foot, Robert.

Third Lieutenant.

Favouricte, John.

Ensign.

Geddis, William.

Sergeant.

Snively, John.

Privates.

Baker, Samuel, in Capt. Gordon's company.
McHenry, James.
Shannon, John.

WAR OF 1812-14.

Schools, Thompson.
Nevill, William.
Witherow, John.
Brandt, John.
Beams, Jesse.
Byard, George.
Boreoff, Fred'k.
Barclay, John.
Brewster, John.
Baker, Hugh.
Barclay, Andrew.
Buchannon, William.
Connor, James.
Cremer, Samuel.
Clap, William.
Cunningham, John.
Clark, Barney.
Cumings, Thomas.
Davenport, Samuel, in Capt. Hendel's company.
Doyle, John.
Elliot, James.
Elder, Robert.
Fingerty, Joseph.
Flagle, William.
Frush, Jacob, in Capt. Gordon's company.
Gift, Jerry.
Harvy, N.
Holby, Henry.
Hays, Thomas, in Capt. Gordon's company.
Humbert, John.
Hunter, Robert.
Johnston, Robert.
Krotzer, John.
Keever, James.
Keester, M.
Kirkwood, James.
Lang, Benjamin.
Lilly, Elijah, in Capt. Gordon's company.
Lightner, David.
Lang, Tobias.
Mackey, Noah.
McCourtney, William.
McConnell, John.
McConnell, Robert.
Morehead James.
Myres, Adam.

8—Vol. XII.

Miller, John.
McClure, William, in Capt. Gordon's company.
Mateer, Samuel.
Marshall, John.
McKim, James.
Moore, William.
Macilwee, Abr^m.
Murry, John.
McDowell, John, in Capt. Gordon's company.
Nobel, Joseph.
Noble, John.
Over, John.
Phips, Joseph.
Penwell, Thomas.
Plucher, George, in Capt. Gordon's company.
Panther, M.
Ramsey, William.
Roan, Philip.
Runion, Charles.
Shell, Peter.
Shell, John.
Smith, John, in Capt. Gordon's company.
Swanger, John.
Sheetz, William.
Staley, Jacob.
Shipton, Barney.
Stake, John.
Trindell, David.
Woods, William, in Capt. Gordon's company.
Wright, Richard.
Walker, John.
Wrist, George.
Williams, William.
Young, John.
Boggs, John.
Young, John.
Swope, Samuel.

I certify, upon honor, that this muster-roll exhibits a true state of my company. Given under my hand this 8th day of October, 1814.

SAMUEL DUNN,
Captain.
JAMES FENTON,
Colonel.

ROLL OF CAPT. JOHN ELDER'S COMPANY.

Muster-roll of Capt. John Elder's company, in the First regiment, First brigade, Pennsylvania militia, under the command of Col. Maxwell Kennedy, at York, Pennsylvania. In service from September 2, 1814, to March 5, 1815, from Berks and Schuylkill counties.

Captain.

Elder, John.

Lieutenant.

Reed, William.

Ensign.

Conrad, Henry W.

Sergeants.

Stouch, Jacob.
Hess, Daniel.
Walborn, Jacob.
Shive, George.

Corporals.

Reigel, John.
Christ, George.
Miller, John.
Reinoehl, Henry.

Drummer.

Schressler, Conrad.

Fifer.

Wohlhaver, George.

Privates.

Aman, Daniel.
Aman, John.
Baney, Valentine.
Bare, Henry.
Bartow, Benjamin.
Bates, Abraham.
Batton, John.
Beneler, John.
Bonewitz, John.
Brown, John.
Deater, Henry.
Deible, John.

Denger, Peter.
Drane, Michael.
Gessbart, Henry.
Haag, John.
Hautz, John.
Hill, John.
Keefer, Abraham.
Lininger, Jacob.
Lutz, Peter.
Miller, Michael.
Miller, Michael, Jr.
Myswender, Christian.
Reed, Adam.
Riem, John.
Roug, Jacob.
Rourher, Jacob.
Schock, Daniel.
Schreck, Andrew.
Schw-ln, Philip.
Shade, Jacob.
Shade, Samuel.
Shaffer, Abraham.
Sheaffer, John.
Snyder, John.
Snyder, John.
Stall, Jacob.
Stingel, Jacob.
Stolen, John.
Stubb, John.
Unpenkocker, Daniel.
Walborn, Martin.
Weaver, Peter.
Wenrich, John.
Wert, John.
Wertz, John.
Wilhalm, Philip.
Witman, Philip.
Zebach, John.
Zeeman, Jonathan.
Zerb, Adam.

ROLL OF CAPT. PETER FENTON'S COMPANY.

Muster-roll of the Fourth company of drafted militia, under the command of Capt. Peter Fenton, of the First brigade, First division, Pennsylvania militia, in the service of the United States, commanded by Lieut. Col. Peter L. Berry, from November 23, 1814, when last mustered, to the 2d day of January, 1815, inclusive.

Captain.

Fenton, Peter.

First Lieutenant.

Simons, John.

Second Lieutenant.

Shallus, Francis.

Ensign.

Meeser, Henry.

Sergeants.

Honnater, Peter P.
Hickinbottom, Joseph.
Lonton, Joseph.
Nassau, Michael.
Gilbert, David.

Corporals.

Brown, Henry.
Helmbold, Joseph K.
McKenzie, John.
Lewis, John.

Privates.

Bard, Samuel.
Baker, Lewis.
Blum, Philip.
Bolton, John R.
Bowen, Patrick.
Bowen, John.
Bryant, John.
Bryson, William.
Bradley, James.
Butler, James.
Buck, Hugh.
Burkhard, Samuel.
Burns, John.
Carr, John.

Cook, William.
Conrad, Joseph.
Cope, Philip.
Collins, William H.
Cress, Thomas.
Cressman, Henry.
Crozier, Benjamin.
Cunningham, Darby.
Day, John.
Farner, Casper, enlisted and delivered to United States officers at Wilmington, November 30, 1814.
Fredericks, Abraham.
George, Joseph, joined December 31, 1814, by general orders.
Gibson, Jacob.
Gilbert, Michael.
Hennaberry, Thomas.
Hill, Charles.
Huffnagle, Edward.
Huens, Melvin, joined December 31, 1814, by general orders.
Jacobs, Ezekiel.
Jones, Thomas.
Johnson, Peter.
Kinley, Philip.
Kinkaid, John.
Lewis, John B.
Linnard, William.
Manship, Thomas.
Mason, Samuel.
Meguire, Charles.
McKaraher, John.
McFarrand, Alexander.
Murphy, William.
Mooney, Charles.
Nonnater, Stephen.
Nayl, John R., enlisted December 23, 1814, with Capt. Robinson.
Neide, Benjamin.
Pollock, William.
Penry, Walter.
Price, William.
Phillips, Samuel, joined by general orders, December 24, 1814.
Queen, William.
Reeves, Enos.
Rusha, Joseph.
Rampf, William.
Rock, Thomas.
Slater, Jacob J.

Spade, Henry.
Springston, Alexander.
Stotsenberg, Michael.
Stein, Adam.
Stock, David.
Stock, Daniel.
Shafer, Jacob.
Shireman, David.
Tyson, David.
Vivien, John.
Wallace, Thomas.
Walls, Henry.
Wiley, James.
Wright, Samuel.
Williamson, Michael, joined by general orders, December 31, 1814.

We certify, on honor, that this muster-roll exhibits a true state of the Fourth company, of drafted militia, in the service of the United States, for the period therein mentioned, and that the remarks set opposite the names of the men are accurate and just.

PETER FENTON,
Captain.
FRANCIS SHALLUS,
Second Lieutenant.
HENRY MEESER,
Ensign.

Mustered January 2, 1815, and certified by
RICHARD McCALL,
Brigade Major, Light Brigade.

And certified by Samuel Stewart, surgeon, whose signatures are attached to the muster-roll in the hands of James M. Porter, Esquire, paymaster to the militia detachment.

PHILADELPHIA, *January 30, 1816.*

I certify the foregoing muster-roll to be just and true.

WM. BOZORTH,
Major commanding.

ROLL OF CAPT. JEREMIAH FERREE'S COMPANY.

Pay-roll of a company of infantry, under the command of Capt. Jeremiah Ferree, of the First regiment, of Pennsylvania militia, in the service of the United States, commanded by Lieut. Col. Joel Ferree, under the command of Gen. William H. Harrison, from October 2, 1812, to April 2, 1813.

Ridgdon, Stephen.

Carnahan, Alexander.
Hull, Joseph, volunteered for fifteen days.
McCarrell, Hugh, volunteered for fifteen days.
Snodgrass, John K.
Hamilton, William.
Morrow, Alexander.
Keneday, Thomas.
McClelland, George.
Sweeney, Daniel.
Jammison, Thomas.
Kirkland, John.
McKee, John.
Furgeson, John.
Pettygrew, David.
Calhoon, James.
Dickey, James, volunteered for fifteen days.
Guy, Moses.
Smith, Benjamin, volunteered for fifteen days.
Nichle, John.
Adams, James.
Reid, Thomas.
McCreary. John.
Couch, William.
McCleland, William.
McDawes, Alexander.
Stewart, James.
McGowan, Archibald.
Calhoon, John A.
Pumereen, Henry.
Allison, John, died August 5.
Shelly, Thomas.
Reel, John.
Good, Balsor.
Whitchell, Philip.
Purse, Amos.
Day, N.
Wusner, Henry.
Powel, David.
Satsbury, Loramas.
Marshall, Samuel.
McTerron, David.
McGunigal, Hugh.
Dunfred, David.
Lighthill, George.
Powel, Joseph.
Moore, Garret.

Powers, John.
Grayton, Isaac.
McDonald, John.
Renoman, John.
Fowzer, John, volunteered for fifteen days.
Williamson, John, volunteered for fifteen days.
Little, John, volunteered for fifteen days.
Johnston, John.
Darsey, James.
Critchlow, Samuel.
Nichle, James.
Plow, John, volunteered for fifteen days.

I certify, on honor, that this pay-roll exhibits a true statement of Capt. Jeremiah Ferree's company, of the First regiment of Pennsylvania militia, for the period therein mentioned, and that the remarks set opposite the names of the men are accurate and just.

JEREMIAH FERREE,
Captain.

ROLL OF CAPT. JOHN FESMYER'S COMPANY.

CAMP NEAR MARCUS HOOK, *October 15, 1814.*

Pay-roll of a volunteer company of riflemen called the Independent Frankford Riflemen, under the command of Capt. John Fesmyer, attached to the Second brigade, Pennsylvania militia, in the service of the United States, commanded by Lieut. Col. Joel B. Sutherland.

Captain.
Fesmyer, John.

First Lieutenant.
Fesmyer, Christian.

Second Lieutenant.
Enyard, Andrew.

Sergeants.
Northrop, Jeremiah.
Rodgers, Samuel.
Wurts, Peter.
Smith, Jacob.

Corporals.
Shearer, Joseph P.
Rupert, John.
Fulkrod, Samuel.
Lister, Henry.

Musician.

Clift, Powel.

Privates.

Pekey, Samuel.
Rich, Henry.
Hunter, David.
Evans, Hugh.
Barnet, Jacob.
Duffield, Samuel.
Conrod, Casper.
Enyard, William.
Young, Henry.
Barnet, David.
Foster, Samuel.
List, Jacob.
Dingast, Jacob.
Bavington, William.
Carlon, Jacob E.
Grub, Henry.
Mallane, Bartholomew.
Slyhoof, Godfrey.
Lear, Thomas.
Engle, Joseph.
Grub, John.
Tallman, Mathias.
Price, Lewis.
Aris, James.
Engle, Jacob.
Shearer, John.
Snyder, John.
Davis, Jonathan.
Brill, George.
Miller, James.
Stapleton, Abner.
Leahy, David.
Foster, Jacob.
Collumn, Benjamin.
Roarer, David.
Vanfossen, Jesse.
Strous, Joseph.
Thomas, Francis.
Glen, Thomas.
Vandegrift, Levi.
Glen, Joseph.
Brown, Joseph.
Brient, David.

Starne, Isaac.
Carson, Jacob.
Sourman, Jonathan.
Smith, John.
Starne, William.
Newkirk, George.
Wright, Jacob.
Simons, John.
Wartenbee, John.
Lear, Andrew E.
Watson, John.
Fletcher, William.
Gibeson, John.
Todd, John.
Lear, Joseph.
Barret, Robert.
Leister, John.
Smith, William.
Gurdon, John.
Slaugh, Frederick.
Evans, David.
Gilbert, Joseph.
Thomas, Samuel.
Carter, John.
Shetsline, Samuel.
Eger, Martin.
Rial, George H.
Davis, Henry.
Glen, David.
Wilson, William.
Fesmyer, John, Jr.
Fesmyer, Peter.

We certify, on honor, that this pay-roll exhibits a true state of the rifle company attached to the Second brigade, Pennsylvania militia, and that the remarks set opposite the names of the men are accurate and just.

JOHN FESMYER.
JOEL B. SUTHERLAND,
Lieutenant Colonel Commandant.

I certify that the rifle company commanded by Capt. John Fesmyer, is in the service of the United States, under orders of the general commanding the Fourth military district.

THOMAS SNYDER.
Brigadier General.

ROLL OF CAPT. PHILIP FETTERHOFF'S COMPANY.

Muster-roll of Capt. Philip Fetterhoff's company, in the Second regiment, First brigade, Pennsylvania militia, under the command of Lieut. Col. Adam Ritcher, at York, Pennsylvania. In service from September 2, 1814, to March 5, 1815; from Dauphin county.

Captain.

Fetterhoff, Philip.

Lieutenant.

Woodside, Thomas.

Ensign.

Shire, John.

Sergeants.

Baughman, Jacob.
Werner, Peter.
Wenn, John.
Fetterhoff, George.

Corporals.

Frank, Henry.
Enders, Philip.
Howard, James.
Hoffman, John.

Drummer.

Byod, Jacob.

Fifer.

Werley, Henry.

Privates.

Beadle, John.
Bixler, Abraham.
Boardner, Jacob.
Campbell, Conrad.
Chub, Daniel.
Cooper, George.
Deety, David.
Dunckle, George.
Dunckle, Jacob.
Dunckle, John.
Elliot, William.
Fagely, David.
Flesher, Daniel.
Foeght, Frederick.
Franklin, John.

Frantz, Adam.
Frantz, John.
Gardner, James.
Harding, Dennis.
Harman, Daniel.
Harman, Jacob.
Hibsher, Henry.
Hogue, Jacob.
Imshofstall, Lewis.
Keister, Benjamin.
Koch, Henry.
Lankart, Michael.
Lebs, George.
Loudermilk, Adam.
Lower, Christian.
Metz, Henry.
Miller, William.
Motter, George.
Neece, Henry.
Novinger, Isaac.
Novinger, Jesse.
Novinger, John.
Ossman, Andrew.
Ossman, Daniel.
Ossman, Reuben.
Powl, Jacob.
Powl, Lewis.
Reehart, John.
Reist, Peter.
Ritzman, Jacob.
Ritzman, John.
Rumberger, Peter.
Shoop, Jacob.
Shoop, Joseph.
Shoppel, Jeremiah.
Shortess, Thomas.
Shott, Philip.
Shroy, Henry.
Snyder, William.
Umberger, Philip.
Umbortz, Henry.
Weaver, George.
Weis, John.
Werfel, Jacob.
Wert, John.
Willer, Peter.

Woodside, Jonathan.
Yeager, Jacob.
Yeager, Stophel.
Yeartz, Peter.

ROLL OF CAPT. JOHN FINDLAY'S COMPANY.

Roll of Capt. John Findlay's Chambersburg company, September, 1814.

Captain.

Findlay, John.

First Lieutenant.

Snider, John.

Second Lieutenant.

Murphy, Greenberry.

Ensign.

Hershberger, John.

Sergeants.

Severns, Joseph.
Rea, Andrew.
Smith, Henry.
Senseny, Jeremiah.
Fedder, Jacob.

Corporals.

Robison, John.
Lester, George W.
Heck, Jacob.
Bickley, Jacob.

Privates.

Abrahams, Jacob.
Berlin, John.
Bonebrake, Peter.
Baxter, John.
Buchanan, James.
Brindle, John.
Bratton, William.
Blythe, Benjamin.
Baughman, John.
Bucher, John.
Bittinger, Jacob.
Burkholder, Abraham.
Best, Frederick.

Crouse, Daniel.
Campbell, Joseph.
Carberry, James.
Clouse, Conrad.
Cope, Joseph.
Clugston, John.
Cammel, McFarlin.
Draher, Conrad.
Dechert, Daniel.
Dugan, William.
Dixon, James.
Eaton, John.
Eaker, Simon.
Firnwalt, Benjamin.
Fry, Henry.
Fletcher, Thomas.
Ganter, Henry.
George, Jacob.
Gillespy, John.
Glosser, Jacob.
Gelwicks, John.
Helman, Michael.
Hall, Thomas.
Harman, William.
Huston, James.
Helman, Daniel.
Irvin, Isaac.
Jones, Thomas.
Kinneard, William.
Keller, David.
Kaisey, Thomas.
Laufman, Jacob.
Lucas, John.
Monroe, Reuben.
McAfee, Robert.
McAllister, Daniel.
McKesson, William.
McKean, William.
Mills, William.
McElroy, Samuel.
McFaggen, Soyer.
Milone, John.
Mentzer, David.
McFerren, Jacob.
Montgomery, Cammel.
Mumma, David.

Nitterhouse, Ludwick.
Nogel, Samuel.
Nitterhouse, John.
Neff, Jacob.
Nixon, John.
Porter, John.
Ruth, Edward.
Reichert, Jacob.
Radebaugh, John.
Sargeant, Elijah.
Stuard, Charles.
Shillito, Samuel.
Sharp, Daniel.
Sipes, William.
Spitel, Jacob.
Sharp, Ross.
Suttey, Joseph.
Tritle, John.
Todd, John.
Wilson, Joseph.
Wiser, Benjamin.
Walker, James.
Wolfkill, Jacob.
Wallace, Josiah.
White, David.
Wright, Matthew.
Westbay, James.
Woods, Hugh.
White, William.
Young, George.
Zimmerman, George.

Upon the election of Capt. Findley as colonel of the regiment, Lieut. William Young was elected captain of the company in his stead.

ROLL OF CAPT. PHILIP FISHER'S COMPANY.

Muster-roll of Capt. Philip Fisher's company, in the Fifth battalion, First brigade of Pennsylvania militia, under the command of Maj. James McFarlan, at York, Pennsylvania. In service from September 1, 1814, to March 5, 1815; from Lebanon county.

Captain.

Fisher, Philip.

Lieutenant.

Brough, John.

Ensign.

Shey, Thomas.

Sergeants.

Elliot, James.
Shettener, Jacob.
Rambler, Christian.
Bolman, Frederick.
Breird, Henry.

Corporals.

Faver, Samuel.
Ichholtz, Samuel.
Kissinger, Jacob.
Williams, Solomon.

Fifer.

McCoard, James.

Privates.

Achabach, John.
Armold, George.
Ault, William.
Barnit, Isaac.
Bartilbach, Martin.
Brand, Michael.
Bruker, Henry.
Butcher, Thomas.
Cephard, John.
Cornwell, Henry.
Dunbar, Samuel.
Eberly, Jacob.
Eichholtz, Jacob.
Epley, Frederick.
Fogel, John.
Garman, Henry.
Gasshard, Samuel.

Gass, John.
Gingrich, Michael.
Glass, ———.
Goldman, Michael.
Greuk, Frederick.
Greglow, Henry.
Grisher, Jacob.
Hahn, John.
Hoover, William.
Howard, Frederick.
Karich, William.
Kliver, John.
Kromer, David.
Lewis, Evin.
Long, Michael.
Loser, Henry.
Loser, Valentine.
Miller, George.
Miller, Samuel.
Moore, Peter.
Moyer, Peter.
Muckafee, John.
Neaff, George.
Onreider, Henry.
Parsh, Henry.
Pleeher, Jacob.
Ramsey, Daniel.
Ranels, James.
Redick, Henry.
Roland, Abraham.
Smith, Henry.
Spengler, George.
Spengler, Peter.
Sunday, Adam.
Tompkins, Jonathan.
Walts, Christopher.
Waltz, Philip.
Weise, Jacob.
Wittmoyer, George.
Wolf, John.
Wolf, Philip.

ROLL OF CAPT. WILLIAM FISHER'S COMPANY.

Roll of the Third company, in —— regiment, Pennsylvania militia, now in the service of the United States, October 21, 1814.

Captain.
Fisher, William.

First Lieutenant.
Roth, David.

Second Lieutenant.
Lamb, Jacob, promoted October 10.

Third Lieutenant.
Keller, Adam.

Ensign.
Walp, John.

Sergeants.
Johnson, Isaac.
Heyney, John.
Moris, Moris, promoted October 10.
Knacht, Jacob, Sr.

Corporals.
Snyder, John, discharged October 20, 1814.
Shick, Tobias.
Carney, Frederic.
Zeigler, Jacob.

Drummers.
Hess, George.
Sickfried, Paul.

Fifers.
Krankright, Emanuel.
Bush, Henry.

Privates.
Major, William.
Ross, David.
Emrod, (or Himrod,) George.
Albert, George.
Pysher, Henry.
Lomison, Daniel.
Hess, Christian.
Flemmon, (or Fleming,) Abraham.
Kerkhoff, Elias.
Reimer, Peter.
Renner, George.

Wagner, Christian.
Knacht, Jacob, Jr.
Junker, Charles.
Biggle, John.
Kester, (or Caster,) John.
Teal, Michael.
Itterly, Michael.
Flory, Peter.
McCormick, Hector.
Shover, Daniel.
Hilliard, Adam.
Emrich, Jacob.
Kime, John.
Walker, John.
Ernst, Michael.
Bloof, James.
Weed, Silsby.
Lester, Oran.
Walter, George.
Eylenberger, William.
Shelly, Joshua.
Killam, Peter.
Wanauker, Daniel.
Henry, John.
Westfall, Willhelmus.
Galloway, Robert.
Houck, Jacob.
Jones, John.
Gruber, David.
Miller, Joseph.
Hess, Henry.
Miller, Jacob, Jr.
Strouse, Henry.
Warner, Adam.
Roth, John.
Mapus, Frederic.
Miller, John.
Steinmetz, Peter.
Zeigle, Coonrod.
Flick, Jacob.
Kridler, Christian.
Kratzer, Jacob.
Edmond, William.
Kurtz, Jacob.
Menzer, Coonrod.
Flory, John.

Wygant, Peter.
Gross, George.
Houck, Abraham.
Gearhart, George.
Muffly, Christian.
Albert, Isaac.
Shannon, Lanty.
Pensyl, Joseph.
Hopple, Simon.
Fell, Christian.
Bartholomew, Lewis.
Miller, Jacob, Sr.
Michen, John.
Smith, John.
Lebar, Daniel.
Fruitchey, William.
Yoe, Samuel.
Johnson, Jacob.
Nichum, John.
Claywell, Samuel.
Eylenberg, John.
Russell, John.
Protzman, Adam.
Williams, John.
Goriely, Jacob.
Williams, William.
Long, John.
Toch, Benjamin, discharged October 11, 1814.
Kratzer, George, discharged October 14, 1814.
Strouse, Jacob, discharged October 16, 1814.
Keller, Peter, discharged October 17, 1814.

CAMP MARCUS HOOK, *October 21, 1814.*

I certify, upon honor, that this muster-roll exhibits a true statement of the ―――― company, ―――― regiment, Pennsylvania militia, now in the service of the United States, and that the remarks set opposite the names are accurate and just, to the best of my knowledge.

WILLIAM FISHER,
Captain.

I believe the above to be a correct muster of pay-roll.

CHRISTIAN J. HUTTER,
Lieutenant Colonel Commanding.

I certify that the company commanded by Capt. William Fisher is now in the service of the United States, under orders of the general commanding military district No. 4, or Fourth military district.

H. SPERING,
Brigadier General.

October 25, 1814.

ROLL OF CAPT. SAMUEL FLACK'S COMPANY.

List of non-commissioned officers and privates of Capt. Samuel Flack's company, October 10, 1814.

Sergeants.

Warne, George.
Steckel, Samuel.
Opp, Peter.
Caffey, William.

Assistant Sergeant.

Sellers, John.

Corporals.

Newhart, Abraham.
Rude, Samuel.
Regle, John.
Rathman, Thomas.

Privates.

Ackerman, George.
Amey, Joseph.
Anderson, Thomas.
Appleback, George.
Buck, Jacob.
Berier, John.
Berier, Frederick.
Barnt, John.
Cresman, Jonas.
Charles, Sebastian.
Clymer, John.
Crowner, Frederick.
Clines, Adam.
Clark, Samuel.
Coffle, Peter.
Cross, John, joined October 10.
Dull, Joseph.
Dehl, Samuel.
Ditilo, Abraham.

Darrh, Michael.
Eckhert, Samuel.
Fuls, Elias.
Frankenfield, Philip.
Fluck, George.
Fisher, Henry.
Frederick, Joseph.
Frank, John.
Frient, Jacob.
Gobble, Frederick.
Heft, Michael.
Heft, Peter.
Houlshourer, Valentine.
Horne, Sebastian.
Haffner, Peter.
Harwick, Joseph.
Horne, Jacob.
Horne, Sebastian.
Knechel, Bartholomew.
Knechel, William.
King, John.
Keller, George.
Keller, Peter.
Keller, John.
Kitney, Henry.
Lightcap, Solomon.
Lessey, Philip.
Lewis, Peter.
Leach, John.
Mude, George.
McCarty, Edward.
McCarty, John.
Michley, Peter.
Mason, Barnard.
Mongold, Christopher.
Miller, Jacob.
Miller, John.
McCrum, David.
Nicholas, John.
Nicholas, Jacob.
Neace, Jacob.
Opp, John.
Ohle, John.
Ott, Isaac.
Poff, Henry.
Plank, Henry.

Rude, Peter.
Rinkhart, Joseph.
Smith, Robert.
Smith, Jacob.
Strawan, William.
Shive, Daniel.
Simes, Henry.
Siddle, Thomas.
Swarts, Jacob.
Sheats, George.
Snider, Jacob.
Shoch, Jacob.
Shonce, Joseph.
Slight, Henry.
Strome, Jacob.
Smith, George.
Shive, Martin.
Trout, Jacob.
Tatesman, John.
Wireback, Antony.
Wood, David.
Weamer, Adam.
Widener, Jacob.
Wenhold, Henry.
Yealis, John.
Yoest, Jacob.
Stoneback, Michael.
Fluck, Abraham.
Kitchen, Aaron, joined October 10.
Large, Samuel, joined October 15.

CAMP MARCUS HOOK, *October 18, 1814.*

I do certify, upon honor, this muster-roll exhibits a true statement of a company of militia from Bucks, now in the service of the United States, the remarks set opposite the names of the men are accurate and just.

ANDREW APPLE,
First Lieutenant.

I believe the annexed to be a correct muster and pay-roll.

ANDREW GILKYSON,
Lieutenant Colonel.

I certify that the company commanded by Capt. Samuel Flack of Bucks county militia, now in the service of the United States, under orders of the general commanding the Fourth military district.

By order,

W. C. ROGERS,
Brevet Major.

CAMP MARCUS HOOK, *October 18, 1814.*

ROLL OF CAPTAIN JOHN FLANAGAN'S COMPANY.

Roll of Capt. John Flanagan's company, Waynesburg, September, 1814.

Captain.

Flanagan, John.

Lieutenant.

Bivins, William.

Ensign.

McFarlin, Daniel.

Sergeants.

Gordon, Robert.
Cochran, George.
Downey, William.
Foreman, George.

Privates.

Allison, Samuel.
Bowman, John.
Bormest, John.
Bechtel, Christian.
Beaver, David.
Barnet, William.
Blair, Hugh.
Call, William.
Duncan, James.
Fulton, Joseph.
Fry, Jacob.
Fullerton, Loudon.
Fullerton, James.
Getteys, James.
Gettier, George.
Green, Samuel.
Haulman, Peter.
Haulman, Daniel.
Harshman, James.
Heffner, David.
Hartman, Daniel.
Hayden, James.
Koontz, George.
Logan, Daniel.
Logan, John.
Mooney, William.
Misner, Joseph.

McCray, James.
McDowell, William.
Oellig, John.
Obermeyer, Maxamillian.
Price, George.
Ray, Robert.
Roberson, Abraham.
Stonebraker, Adam.
Sheffler, John.
Stoner, John.
Springer, David.
Stewart, Alexander.
Weagley, George.
Weaver, David.

ROLL OF CAPT. JACOB FRYERS' COMPANY.

Muster-roll of Capt. Jacob Fryers' company of Montgomery county.

Captain.

Fryer, Jacob.

First Lieutenant.

Houck, Henry.

Second Lieutenant.

Yost, Jacob.

Ensign.

Smith, John.

Sergeants.

Markley, Jonah.
Bortman, Jacob.
Wannemaker, Jacob.
Fryer, Jacob.

Corporals.

Burger, Peter.
Yost, Peter.
Yost, John.
Houck, George.

Trumpeter.

Yost, Henry.

Privates.

Kulp, George.
Detwhiler, Samuel.
Jones, Lewis.

Neas, Abraham.
Esterline, Samuel.
Bitting, Anthony.
Fryer, George.
Specht, Henry.
Shafer, Frederick.
Sweesholtz, John.
Zern, Abraham.
Smith, John. tailor.
Burger, William.
Witman, Samuel.
Fetser, Jonas.
Beikel, Henry.
Houck, Daniel.
Yost, Daniel.
Shuler, Leonard.
Brecht, William.
Smith, Jacob.
Bitting, Richard.
Smith, Benjamin.
Royer, Henry.
Mowrer, George.
Seehler, Henry.
Ale, Daniel.
Horlocher, Peter.
Hart, David.
Foust, Peter.
Slowneiker, Jonas, (on receipt roll.)
Fox, Frederick.
Burger, George.
Zarn, Adam.
Fox, Jacob.
Huntzberger, Jacob.
Dutterer, John.
Helbert, Michael.
Fox, Barny.
Small, John.
Dutterer, Conrad.
Arb, Peter.
Sheifly, Daniel.
Weidemier, Jacob.
Hoffman, John.
Trace, Peter.
Reider, George.
Wensel, Jacob.
Zepp, Jacob.

Gouckler, John.
Hoff, Daniel.
Long, Henry.
Royer, John.

A true muster roll of Capt. Jacob Fryers' company of Montgomery county, October 14, 1814.

JONAH MARKLEY,
Sergeant.

We do certify, on honor, that the within roll exhibits a true state of the company commanded by Capt. J. Fryers, and that the remarks set opposite the men's names are accurate and just.

HENRY HOUCK,
First Lieutenant.
THOMAS HUMPHREYS,
Colonel First R. P. V. R.

CAMP DUPONT, *November 24, 1814.*

I do certify, on honor, that the company commanded by Capt. J. Fryers is in the service of the United States, under the command of the general commanding the Fourth military district.

THOMAS CADWALADER,
Brigadier General Commanding Advance, L. B.
CAMP DUPONT, *November 26, 1814.*

ROLL OF CAPT. GEORGE FRYSINGER'S COMPANY.

Receipt-roll of a company of militia, commanded by Capt. George Frysinger, of the Third regiment, First brigade, performing a tour of duty under the command of Col. Lefever, who rendezvoused at Hanover, under the general order of the Governor, dated October 15 and 22, 1814. Commencement of service, November 1; expiration of service, December 5.

Captain.

Frysinger, George.

First Lieutenant.

Kitt, William.

Second Lieutenant.

Kiefer, Jacob.

Ensign.

Whillery, William.

Sergeants.

Hostetter, Daniel.

Little, Daniel.
Marris, Joseph.
Wilnight, John.
Craver, George.

Corporals.

Eiler, Jacob.
Cooper, Matthew.
Harris, William.
Slentz, Jacob.
Morningstar, George.
Crilly, Andrew.

Musician.

Haus, Christian.

Privates.

Adelsperger, Michael.
Althoff, John.
Burkert, Lewis.
Bare, Michael.
Baughman, Henry.
Bare, Henry.
Baugher, John, weaver.
Brown, Jacob.
Bart, Jacob.
Bloser, Peter.
Baugher, John.
Crous, John.
Chambers, John.
Dellinger, Daniel.
Doll, Jacob.
Emick, Peter.
Eilen, John.
Flickinger, Samuel.
File, Jacob.
Flone, Jacob.
Fisher, Henry.
Gray, Isaiah.
Gees, John.
Hays, William.
Haus, George.
Holtz, Abraham.
Herman, Joseph.
Hickman, Henry.
Hensel, George.
Hacknay, Thomas.

Henystophel, George.
Hamilton, John.
Horn, Jesse.
Irwin, William.
Jackson, Abraham.
Kanney, Alexander.
Kraft, Michael.
Lang, John.
Lohn, Jacob.
McWilliams, Charles.
Miller, Joseph.
Moul, Henry.
Moul, Peter.
Miller, Samuel.
Miller, Joseph, joiner.
Michael, John.
Miller, John.
Nonemaker, Henry.
Nonemaker, Jacob.
Noll, George.
Rose, Samuel.
Riter, Anthony.
Reichard, John.
Reineman, John.
Riffle, George.
Reinhart, Jacob.
Rutter, Thomas.
Serf, Abraham.
Sipple, James.
Stoddard, Solomon.
Shild, Adam.
Shild, Jacob.
Swartz, Peter.
Snyder, William.
Smith, Samuel.
Stigers, Joseph.
Stephy, Henry.
Stegner, Valentine.
Tarman, Jacob.
Troesler, Jacob.
Unger, Adam.
Unger, George.
Unger, John.
Weloly, David.
Weitnight, Joseph.
Waggoner, Jacob.

Werking, George.
Weeke, Francis.
Willet, George.
Young, Frederick.

I certify the foregoing to be a correct pay-roll of my company.

GEORGE FRYSINGER,
Captain.

Testes:

JNO. FORSTER,
Brigadier General.

ROLL OF CAPT. JOHN FULMER'S COMPANY.

Muster-roll of a company of militia under the command of John Fulmer, captain, in the regiment militia, in the service of the United States, commanded by Col. John Thompson, from the 9th of November, 1814, when last mustered, to the 5th of January, 1815.

Quarter-Master Sergeant.

Saylor, George.

Sergeants.

Thompson, Henry.
Hart, Samuel.
Houghf, Jonathan.
Bowles, John.

Corporals.

Roop, William.
Greening, Richard.
Goodyear, John.
Brown, Jacob.

Privates.

Penagar, Samuel.
Joyce, Benjamin.
Davidson, William.
Cain, Conrad.
Mills, Henry.
Peckworth, Thomas.
Birmingham, John.
Roberts, William.
Brant, James.
McCullough, Edward.
Pearson, Samuel.

McDurman, Thomas.
Groos, Godlieb.
Pipher, John.
Erven, Casper.
Finchem, Edward.
Turner, Joseph.
Mills, George.
Burns, John.
Canon, Denis.
Wentling, George.
Arms, Jacob.
Burdine, John.
Harris, Timothy.
Fegmyer, Lewis.
Parent, John.
Zebley, William.
Powers, John.
Gideon, Peter.
Holaday, Peter.
Ford, Abraham.
Snyder, George.
German name.
Fisher, John.
Mills, John.
McLochlin, John.
More, John.
Young, Henry.
Hess, George.
Hegmon, Fredrick.
Sheelds, George.
Smith, Abraham.
Sheperd, Philip.
Beck, Lewis.
Davis, Peter A.
Evans, Ezra.
Gesnor, Henry.
Sturk, Jacob.
Lake, Adam.
Deroch, Peter.
Davies, David.
Harvey, Job.
Myers, George.
Higins, John.
Dory, James.
Hornketh, Jera[h].
Goucher, William.

Thompson, Caleb.
Barthel, George.
Root, John.
Turner, Stephen.
Jones, John.
Glover, John.
Settel, Nicholus.
Boch, Frederick A.
Smith, Barny.
Kline, Frederick.
Louderboch, William.
Riffert, Jacob.
Wilson, John.
Lasal, John.

We certify, on honor, that this muster-roll exhibits a true state of the tenth company of drafted militia in the service of the United States, for the period therein mentioned, and that the remarks set opposite the names of the men are accurate and just.

JOHN FULMER,
Captain.
JOHN THOMPSON,
Colonel commanding.

ROLL OF CAPT. ABRAHAM GANGWERE'S COMPANY.

Pay-roll of the First company of riflemen commanded by Capt. Abraham Gangwere, attached to the First brigade, Second division, Pennsylvania militia, in the service of the United States, under the command of Brig. Gen. H. Spering, Maj. Gen. Shitz, commanding.

Captain.
Gangwere, Abraham.

First Lieutenant.
Moyer, Daniel.

Second Lieutenant.
Newhart, Jacob.

Third Lieutenant.
Stein, Jacob.

Ensign.
Keller, Adam.

Sergeants.
Dull, John.
Minor, Pitkin.

Quear, Daniel.
Beidlemen, Abraham.
Quear, Jacob.

Corporals.

Keeper. Abraham.
Long, Joseph.
Bickle, Daniel.
Nogle, Joseph.

Musicians.

Keiper, Jacob.
Quear. Daniel.

Privates.

Poyor, John.
Daniel, Daniel C.
Rose, Joseph.
Swenk, Jacob.
Frain, John.
Keik, Daniel.
Moyer, Nicholas.
Keider, Joseph.
Rhoads, Daniel.
Boardst, Solomon.
Ott, Jacob.
Moyer, Abraham.
Rhoads, John.
Yeunt, James.
Litsenbeoreor, George.
Shoemaker, Benjamin.
Kuntz, Philip.
Hilman, Daniel.
Hany, Charles.
Kinkinger, James.
Hoffmon, Peter.
Brobest, Henry.
Hartman, Henry.
Amhiser, Henry.
Fisher, George.
Floats, George.
Good, Henry.
Kentz, George.
Long, Jacob.
Eline, Mathias.
Kemery, Henry.
Loudenslager, Peter.
Loudenslager, John.

Foght, Gollib.
Henry, George.
Gangwer, Thomas.
Hubenstine, David.
Ocker, Henry.
Besh, George.
Shivry, Jacob.
Deal, John.
Shriver, William.
Besh, John.
Woodring, Gabriel.
Good, Michael.
Flexer, John.
Richabauk, Jacob.
Hamor, Jacob.
Druchamiller, Michael.
Miller, John.
Nerfer, John.
Frack, Jacob.
Nogle, Jacob.
Shantz, John.
Miller, John, Jr.
Guishler, John.
Rinebolt, Cornealius.
Hill, George.
Sloufer, William.
Frymon, Michael.
Rider, Frederick.
Rownolt, Solomon.
Kuntz, Peter.
Highleageor, Adam.
Rish, Henry.
Heller, Frederick.
Snider, Henry.
Minic, Peter.
Herner, George.
Rice, Henry.
Seip, Peter.
Braober, George.
Elenrider, Peter.
Trexler, Israel.
Koch, Jacob.
Cladwell, John.
Erad, Jacob.
Fadsinger, Henry.
Keifer, Elias.

Erhard, John.
Hower, Jacob.
Herwig, Henry.
Ott, Jonathan.
Flower, John.
Snider, John.
Musheetz, Jacob.
Poe, Michael.
Sentle, Michael.
Lehr, George.
Nogle, Philip.
Rou, Conrod.
Wile, Conrod.
Louhenbauk, Abraham.
Hillegas, Jacob.
Shontz, Jacob.
Shontz, Henry.
Heller, Jeremiah.
Wetsel, George.
Good, Solomon.

The above statement commences from the 23d day of September, 1814, to the 31st day of October, 1814, making one month and eight days complete.

I certify, upon honor, that this muster-roll exhibits a true statement of the number of men in my company, attached to One Hundred and Eighteenth regiment, First brigade, Seventh division, Pennsylvania militia, in the service of the United States.

ABRAHAM GANGWERE,
Captain.

I believe the above to be correct.

CHRISTOPHER J. ———,
Lieutenant Colonel Commanding.

I certify that the company commanded by Capt. Abraham Gangwere, is now in the service of the United States, under order of Brig. Gen. H. Spearing, commandant militia district.

THOMAS J. ROGERS,
Brigade Major.

MARCUS HOOK CAMP, *October 23, 1814.*

ROLL OF CAPT. REUBEN GILDER'S COMPANY.

Muster-roll of the Second company of drafted militia, under the command of Reuben Gilder, captain, in the service of the United States, commencing on the 26th of August last, and commanded by Lieut. Col. Peter L. Berry, from the 23d of August last, when last mustered, &c.

Captain.

Gilder, Reuben.

First Lieutenant.

Forgraud, William.

Sergeants.

Thomson, David.
Cox, Anthony.
Brown, John.
Brock, John.

Corporals.

Clark, John.
Rhodes, John, transferred to Rifle Corps on 21st instant.
Ruhman, Jacob.
Griffin, Chester.

Privates.

Askins, John.
Akins, John.
Ackly, John.
Benjamin, Caleb.
Bohem, Joseph.
Burck, James.
Buckman, Benjamin.
Brittingham, John.
Bower, John.
Baker, William.
Blandford, George.
Currin, John.
Cremer, George.
Cline, Henry.
Crout, William.
Carlon, Robert.
Caldwell, John, transferred to volunteers.
Denny, Dennis.
Dougherty, Charles, transferred to volunteers.
Dally, Ed^d, transferred to volunteers.
File, William.

Fowler, Elijah.
Gibson, Joseph.
Gilbert, Thomas.
Hammel, John.
Hall, George.
Hawk, George.
Holland, James, transferred to volunteers.
Jones, Evan.
Johnson, William.
Keel, Elias.
Kinsley, George.
Kerlisle, William.
Lukens, Isaac.
Longrew, Sidney S.
Little, John, transferred to volunteers.
Livingston, James.
Little, William.
Miller, Hugh.
Mulhollan, John.
More, Joseph.
McDavis, John.
McGlathery, Mordecai.
McAlloney, (or McAnthony,) Hugh, transferred to volunteers.
McNelly, John, transferred to volunteers.
Marker, George.
Nail, John.
Nichol, Simon, transferred to volunteers.
Nichols, Ithama C.
Newman, John.
Post, Henry.
Pool, Peter S.
Perkins, Lewis.
Roberts, Joseph.
Riley, Hugh.
Shaffer, Joseph.
Smith, John.
Savage, William, transferred to volunteers.
Stewart, F^s.
Taylor, Jeremiah.
Wilson, Hugh, discharged as unfit for duty.
Wilson, Abraham.
Walmir, Philip.
Warnick, Daniel.
Warnick, William, transferred to volunteers.
Wineburner, David, transferred to volunteers.
Yammer, William H.

We certify, on honor, that this muster-roll exhibits a true state of the Second company of drafted militia, of the detachment under the command of Lieut. Col. P. L. Berry, for the period therein mentioned, and that the remarks set opposite the names of the men are accurate and just.

REUBEN GILDER,
Captain Second Company.

I believe the above to be correct.

PETER L. BERRY,
Lieutenant Colonel.

I certify that the Second company of drafted militia, Capt. Reuben Gilder, is in the service of the United States, under orders of the general commanding Fourth military district.

THOS. CADWALADER,
Brigadier General Commanding.

CAMP DUPONT, *October 7, 1814.*

ROLL OF CAPT. HENRY GOOD'S COMPANY.

Muster-roll of Capt. Henry Good's company, in the Second regiment, Second brigade, Pennsylvania militia, under the command of Col. ———— ————, at York, Pennsylvania. In service from September 1, 1814, to March 1, 1815, from Lancaster county.

Captain.

Good, Henry.

Lieutenant.

McMillin, Robert.

Ensign.

Tuttle, Henry.

Sergeants.

Michall, Joshua.
Michall, Abener.
Diekover, Jacob.

Corporals.

Donaly, James.
Diekover, Samuel.
Kinsel, Jacob.
Tovel, George.

Privates.

Albert, Martin.
Baum, William.
Bird, Martin.

Brady, Jacob.
Brenner, Jacob.
Carpenter, Lewis.
Cochrin, Oliver.
Comes, Thomas.
Cowick, Samuel.
Crist, John.
Culverson, John.
Dabilor, Henry.
Daugherty, James.
Douthet, Jonathan.
Eberly, John.
English, Asa.
Farley, Peter.
Fisher, Henry.
Fisher, John.
Flesh, George.
Frankford, Conrad.
Frederick, Abraham.
Fultz, Henry.
Gotshall, David.
Grady, Henry.
Graft, John.
Groover, Samuel.
Haleman, Conrad.
Hoffman, George.
Hoffman, Henry.
House, John.
Kaley, John.
Kauffman, Joseph.
Kipp, Henry.
Knight, Henry.
Lahr, John.
Lemaneer, Elisha.
Locard, John.
Longenaker, John.
Loots, John.
Lorance, John.
Lorman, John.
Lucob, Adam.
Martin, David.
Maus, Henry.
McAlbry, James.
McDarrah, James.
McGonickal, Alexander.
McGowin, Patrick.

McHarty, David.
McMackin, Benjamin.
Murphy, William.
Myars, Isaac.
Newcomer, Christian.
Nicholas, George.
Page, David.
Pagles, John.
Parker, William.
Peter, Henry.
Phillips, George.
Plain, George.
Rafsnider, Andrew.
Robeson, William.
Shaffer, Frederick.
Shallenbarger, Henry.
Shaum, Jacob.
Shickley, George.
Smith, John.
Starmbaugh, Joseph.
Still, Aaron.
Stoner, Christian.
Straum, Michael.
Sumy, Henry.
Swagard, George.
Taylor, James.
Tetrich, Michael.
Troutman, Joseph.
Withers, Jacob.
Worffle, John.
Ziegler, George.

ROLL OF CAPT. GORDON'S COMPANY.

A list of names in Capt. Gordon's company of the Fifth regiment of Pennsylvania militia, in the service of the United States.

Captain.

Gordon, Samuel.

Lieutenants.

Patton, William.
Burns, James.

Ensign.

Miller, William.

Sergeants.

Davison, Hugh.
Mills, Charles P.
Scott, James W.
Gordon, Joseph.

Corporals.

Rodman, John.
Mason, Philip W.
Alsop, William.
Smith, Jacob, deceased.

Musicians.

Shilling, Joseph.
Burgess, William.

Privates.

Authors, Joseph.
Allen, Thomas.
Board, Martin.
Brump, Benjamin.
Barr, George.
Beaverson, Frederick.
Baugher, Henry.
Boarer, Michael.
Baker, John.
Baker, Peter.
Baker, Jacob.
Craupt, Conrod.
Coon, John.
Craig, John.
Cahel, Richard.
Cline, William.
Carver, John.
Davis, George.
Donaho, Richard.
Devilsbess, William.
Dowman, John.
Detrick, Emanuel.
Duncan, Adam.
Eby, Jacob.
Edwards, William.
Ensminger, George.
Fipps, Nathaniel.
Flora, Joseph.
Fisher, John.
Gyger, Henry.
Glaze, George.

Graham, John.
Greenly, John.
Hull, James.
Huber, John.
Huffman, Joseph.
Harden, William.
Harmony, George.
Hardy, James.
Hawk, John.
Irwin, John, made a prisoner.
Johnston, David.
King, Matthew.
Kesmer, John.
Kerper, Peter.
Keifer, Jacob.
Laiton, Henry.
Logan, James.
Lewis, Benjamin.
Leopard, Jacob.
Miller, George.
Mentzer, Daniel.
McClelland, Robert, deceased.
McCawley, John.
McNeal, John.
McConnel, John.
McMullen, Alexander.
Myers, Peter.
Miller, William.
Neal, Joseph.
Peasaker, Abraham.
Quarter, Erasmus.
Robinson, Andrew.
Reesman, William.
Ritter, John.
Rankin, Adam.
Sites, Christopher.
Stumbaugh, Frederick.
Stoupher, Jacob.
Tice, Joseph.
Wolf, William.
Thompson, James.
Curly, Henry.

A list of men left sick from Capt. Dunn's Company, of the Fifth regiment, Pennsylvania militia:
McDowel, John.
Frush, Jacob.

Lilley, Elija.
McClure, William.
Hays, Thomas.
Woods, William.
Baker, Samuel.
Smith, John.
Plugher, George.

I do certify that the above is a correct muster-roll of the men now doing duty in Capt. Gordon's company, except those above mentioned attached to Capt. Dunn. Given under my hand this 24th day of August, A. D. 1814.

WILLIAM PATTON,
Lieutenant Commanding.
JAMES FENTON,
Colonel.

ROLL OF CAPT. JOHN GRAHAM'S COMPANY.

Muster-roll of Capt. John Graham's company, in the Second regiment, First brigade, Pennsylvania militia, under the command of Lieut. Col. Adam Riches, at York, Pa. In service from September 2, 1814, to March 5, 1815, from Dauphin, Berks, and Schuylkill counties.

Captain.

Graham, John.

Lieutenant.

Porter, James.

Ensign.

Turner, John.

Sergeants.

Corbet, James.
Brestel, John.
Boon, William.
Allen, Samuel.

Corporals.

Boon, James.
Umberger, Michael.
McLane, George.
Carter, John.

Musicians.

Straw, John.
Edwards, James.

Privates.

Aunght, John.
Boon, John.
Cathcart, James.
Caverich, Daniel.
Colvins, John.
Darr, Peter.
Deckart, Michael.
Demude, Jacob.
Duncan, John.
Emrich, Thomas.
Focht, Christian.
Focht, Godfrey.
Focht, John.
Fox, Jacob.
Furguson, John.
Gephart, Philip.
Griffith, Thomas.
Hartman, Abraham.
Hembergerger, Jacob.
Hite, Henry.
Huts, John.
Hutton, John.
Jennings, Solomon.
Kenslow, William.
Ketterman, Adam.
Leman, Henry.
Leman, Jacob.
Long, Jacob.
McFadden, Robert.
McKee, Sample.
Michael, Daniel.
Moor, Richard.
Mulholland, James.
Mulholland, Rudolph.
Myer, George.
Myer, Henry.
Myer, Joseph.
Myer, William.
Nigh, Christian.
Phillips, Joseph.
Ponsus, Frederick.
Reedy, Leonard.
Reeser, William.
Reeves, Samuel.
Rider, George.

Rider, William.
Robinson, John.
Rode, Jacob.
Russel, Daniel.
Scot, John.
Shallohamer, George.
Shaum, John.
Shaum, Stophel.
Shoffner, John.
Shrivever, George.
Shriver, Jacob.
Shruck, Henry.
Smith, Henry.
Smith, Martin.
Spancake, Jacob.
Stevenson, Thomas.
Stitzman, John.
Tennis, William.
Ulrich, George.
Ulrich, John.
Wagner, Philip.
Wards, John.
Weaver, Peter.
Wilhelm, Adam.
Wolf, George.
Yerger, Henry.
Zerber, John.
Zimmerman, Henry.

ROLL OF CAPT. JACOB GROSH'S COMPANY.

Muster-roll of the Ninth company (under the command of Capt. Jacob Grosh) of the Second regiment Pennsylvania Volunteer Light Infantry, commanded by Colonel Louis Bache. Attached to the First brigade Second division, Pennsylvania militia.

Sergeants.

Wolfley, George.
Pierce, William.
Williams, Edward.
Cottinger, John I.

Corporals.

Myers, John.
Parker, William I.

Chamberlain, Nathan.
Jones, John.

Drummer.

Keller, Joel.

Fifer.

Steddum, George.

Privates.

Moore, Zachariah.
Ebell, I. W.
Porter, John.
Nicholas, Jacob.
Nagle, Peter.
Rank, Mathias.
Ehler, John.
Bellows, Abraham.
Fetter, Henry.
Leibhart, Henry.
Bell, Edward.
Robinson, Joseph.
Gregg, Mahlon.
Serfoss, John.
Griffin, James.
McCarry, James.
Diffenderffer, Henry.
Toland, Daniel.
Ingles, Moses.
St. John, Stephen.
Temple, William.
DeMiller, William.
Fetterer, Stephen.
Bucher, Joseph.
Black, James.
Amos, Joshua.
Gorrell, James.
Kunitz, Augustus S.
Foulk, William.
Lehman, Lewis.
Law, John.
Caldwell, Timothy.
Sherer, John.
Foltz, John.
Teatsworth, John.
Gregg, Abraham.
Hager, Francis.

WAR OF 1812-14.

Heckrotte, John.
Cramer, John.
McCormick, William.
Chamberlain, Calvin.
Rinehart, David.
Robinson, Richard.
Curry, John.
Davis, Willis, Jr.
Brandt, William.
Heistand, Peter.
Greider, John.
Shirk, Christian.
Johnston, Thomas.
Hughs, Felix.
Donley, Henry.
Lanius, Henry.
Leonard, William.
Cather, Samuel.
Leader, John.
Henry, Joel.
Shanks, John.
Wyatt, John.
Boner, Andrew.
McFall, Joseph.
McFall, John.
Tochill, Edward.
Olewine, Richard.
Gribbin, James, Jr.
Brooks, Andrew.
Frazer, William.
Goshet, Jacob.
Clarnen, James.
Sweeny, Roger.
Mullen, Daniel.
Campbell, James.
Forringer, Henry.
Cushman, Horatio.
Manwaring, Charles.
Cummins, Jacob.
Heck, John.
Asman, James.
Dinsman, William.
Johnson, Jacob.
Hughs, Francis.
Black, Alexander.
Lonny, Daniel.

Mann, Samuel.
Ringgold, James P.

We do certify, on honor, that the foregoing muster-roll exhibits a just and true statement of the foregoing company.

J. HESS,
Lieutenant Commanding.
LOUIS BACHE,
Colonel Second Regiment.

CAMP MARCUS HOOK, *November 29, 1814.*

ROLL OF CAPT. GROSSCUP'S COMPANY.

CAMP DUPONT, *November 13, 1814.*

A true list of Capt. Grosscup's company of the Eighteenth section of riflemen, commanded by Col. Thomas Humphreys.

Sergeants.

Thompson, Edward.
Campbell, Simon.
Grosscup, William.
Freas, Benjamin.

Corporals.

Kerper, Jacob.
McCally, Joseph.
Bayl, Robert.
White, John.

Bugler.

Gilinger, John.

Privates.

Grafly, George.
Kupp, George.
Wack, Jacob.
Rickler, John.
Bilger, Isaac.
Katz, John.
Mink, Adam.
Francis, William.
Heydrick, George.
Wigley, Joseph.
Serber, Joseph.
Townsman, John.
Shepard, Thomas.
Shepard, Joseph.

11—VOL. XII.

Shull, Anthony.
Shermer, Henry.
Dager, Peter.
Yost, John.
Welch, James H.
Weant, John.
Grafly, William.
Bishing, Henry.
Artman, Isaac.
Shafer, Abram.
Shafer, George, Jr.
Gold, Elijah, from October 1.
Rhodeibagh, Thomas.
Keyser, Nathan, from October 1.
Dager, John.
Shafer, George.
Dull, John.
Van Horn, Raber.
Dager, Jacob.
Nail, Daniel.
Francis, Charles.
Harris, John.
Thomas, Amos.
Hentz, Jacob.
Welch, Peter.
Tarrans, John.
Hoffman, Henry, discharged from camp on the 26th of October last.

I do certify, on honor, that the company commanded by Capt. John Grosscup, is in the service of the United States, under the command of the general commanding the Fourth military district.

THOMAS CADWALADER,
Brigadier General Commanding Advance L. B.

CAMP DUPONT, *November 26, 1814.*

I do certify that the within list is correct to the best of my knowledge.

JOHN GROSSCUP,
Captain.
THOMAS HUMPHREY,
Colonel First R. P. V. R.

November 13, 1814.

ROLL OF CAPT. JOHN GUTHRIE'S COMPANY.

A muster and inspection-roll of the quota of militia, drafted from the One Hundred and Fiftieth regiment, in the Second brigade, of the Fifteenth division, Pennsylvania militia, pursuant to brigade orders of the 22d ultimo.

Captain.

Guthrie, John.

Lieutenant.

Gibson, Levi.

Ensign.

McCormick, John.

Sergeant.

McConnell, Jesse.

Privates.

Allison, Robert.
Austin, Samuel.
Barlet, Peter.
Beck, John.
Bell, William.
Best, Nicholas.
Bruner, Jacob.
Byers, John.
Callon, David.
Clark, Robert.
Clinglesmith, Peter.
Cunningham, William.
Delph, Lewis.
Fidler, Peter.
Fiscus, Jacob.
Fish, Robert.
Forman, Charles.
Galbreath, Joseph.
Girt, David.
Gutherie, Alexander.
Gutherie, Thomas.
Heasly, Henry.
Himes, George.
Hosey, Matthew.
Jack, John.
John, John.

Keer, Andrew.
Kefer, Henry.
Kelly, John.
Laird, Oliver.
Latemore, William.
Latshaw, Peter.
Lewis, James.
Maffit, William.
McClane, Jacob.
McKee, Thomas.
McKee, William.
McKibbin, David.
Meredith, Owen.
Meredith, Thomas.
Moor, William.
Moyers, Philip.
Painter, John.
Painter, John.
Patterson, Andrew.
Phillips, David.
Pollock, Thomas.
Polyard, Nicholas.
Read, Patrick.
Rea, Joshua.
Reed, Hugh.
Sheakly, Henry.
Sheffer, Conrod.
Shields, Samuel.
Smith, Abraham.
Smith, James.
Smith, Lewis Steel.
Spears, James.
Stephenson, James.
Thompson, Samuel.
Titus, Timothy.
Weaver, George.
Week, Elisha.
Willson, John.

I do certify the within to be a correct copy from the return of the adjutant of the One Hundred and Fiftieth regiment, Pennsylvania militia, of the quota of drafted militia required from said regiment, in pursuance of your orders of the 12th May, 1812.

ROBERT BEATTY,
Inspector of the Second brigade, Fifteenth division, P. M.
July 21, 1812.

To WILLIAM REED, ESQ., *Adjutant General, P. M.*

WAR OF 1812-14.

ROLL OF CAPT. VALENTINE HAAS' COMPANY.

CAMP MARCUS HOOK, *October 31, 1814.*
Pay-roll of the company of infantry, under the command of Capt. Valentine Haas, attached and organized by adjutant general of the —— brigade, Pennsylvania militia, in the service of the United States, commanded by Lieut. Col. George Weirwick, of the Seventy-seventh regiment, Pennsylvania militia.

Captain.

Haas, Valentine.

Lieutenant.

Shedle, Samuel.

Sergeants.

Eckhart, Jacob.
Hosterman, George.
Boyer, Henry.

Privates.

Hentricks, Andrew.
Johnston, John.
Kleckner, Jacob.
Richter, Frederick.
Overmoyer, David.
Shedler, Jacob.
Bachman, Lorentz.
Binkley, Jacob.
Spaid, Henry.
Hentricks, Ephraim.
Swartz, Peter.
Foltz, Joseph.
Kreitzer, Frederick.
Weller, Isaac.
Gordin, Willis.
Yerger, Adam.
Richenbach, John.
Smith, Joseph.
Keosteller, George.
Yerger, John.
Bortler, Jacob.
Weaver, John.
Rettig, William.
Stock, Peter.
Shoemaker, Peter.
Dake, Jacob.

Yerger, Philip.
Clendinen, John.
Woodling, Henry.
Neitz, Jacob.
Herrold, Philip.
Stahl, Henry.
Smith, John.
Gougler, Jonas.
Kuns, John.
Young, Ludwig.
Jarrutt, Jacob Jerrot.
Duke, George.
Woolf, Daniel.
Trester, John.
Folk, John.
Everhard, Barnes.
Benfort, George.
Buttenstiner, Philip.
Miller, Daniel.
Witmer, Samuel.
Fettor, Benjamin.
Swartzlender, G.
Kesler, Michael.
Kreisher, Henry.
Berger, Joseph.
Hummel, John H.
Doffe, John.
Stimeling, George.
Yeasley, Henry.
Derk, Jonathan.
Bear, Isaac.
Yorton, John.
Deerler, Ludwig.
Moyer, Philip.
Grimm, Henry.
Wagner, George.
Brown, (or Brouse,) Henry.
Berman, Anthony.
Pontious, Henry.
Bous, Frederick.
Hobb, Frederick.
Haas, Henry.
Haas, Daniel.
Everhart, Philip.
Mourer, Jacob.
Sold, Philip.

Desho, (or Rusher,) John.
Smith, Abraham.
Keely, John, discharged October 22.
Alter, Joseph, discharged October 5.

I do certify, on honor, that this pay-roll exhibits a true statement of the company under my command from Union county, attached to the regiment under the command of Lieut. Col. George Weirick, Pennsylvania militia.

VALENTINE HAAS,
Captain.

I believe the above to be a correct pay-roll.

GEO. WEIRICK,
Lieutenant Colonel Commanding.

I certify that the company commanded by Capt. Valentine Haas is now in the service of the United States, order of the general commander Fourth military district.

THOS. J. ROGERS,
Brigade Major.

ROLL OF CAPT. WILLIAM HAIN'S COMPANY.

Muster-roll of Capt. William Hain's company, in the Second regiment, First brigade, Pennsylvania militia, under the command of Col. Adam Richard, at York, Pa., September 5, 1814. In service from August 30, 1814, to March 5, 1815, from Berks county.

Captain.

Hain, William.

Lieutenant.

Salada, George.

Ensign.

McClure, Abraham.

Sergeants.

Shitz, Jacob.
Vaneido, George.
Womelsdorff, Peter.
Arnold, Jacob.

Corporals

Stout, William.
Mathie, David.
Kellar, William.
Ully, George.

Privates.

Achebuch, Peter.
Adams, Richard.
Andrews, George.
Bousman, Abraham.
Case, Charles.
Conrad, Jacob.
Crimes, Henry.
Dehm, Samuel.
Ditzler, John.
Ebling, Henry.
Evans, Joseph.
Farmwald, Daniel.
Fatterman, Michael.
Feg, Henry.
Fidler, Daniel.
Fisher, Jacob.
Fisher, John.
Fisher, Peter.
Folss, William.
Fox, Henry.
Haein, Isaac.
Hartman, Benjamin.
Hassler, Samuel.
Hauk, George.
Heckman, Henry.
Heller, Adam.
Humel, Jonathan.
Kintzle, John.
Kitzmiller, John.
Lanerd, Andrew.
Lanerd, Henry.
Leininger, Jacob.
Marshall, Deiter.
Masser, Nicholas.
Mell, William.
Metz, Jacob.
Meyer, George.
Mick, Adam.
Miller, Henry.
Miller, John.
Miller, Nicholas.
Mumma, Henry.
Neiss, Peter.
Ney, John.
Read, John.

Reifer, George.
Ruth, Leonard.
Seibert, William.
Seltzer, John.
Seltzer, William.
Shultz, John.
Stickler, William.
Stine, William.
Stout, Daniel.
Stout, Daniel.
Stout, Jacob.
Stout, John.
Welsh, Michael.
Wiley, John.
Witmeyer, William.
Zerber, George.
Zimmerman, George.

ROLL OF LIEUT. JOSHUA HAIRE'S COMPANY.

List of non-commissioned officers and privates of the Eleventh company, in the First rifle regiment of Pennsylvania volunteers, under command of Lieut. Joshua Haire, commanded by Col. Thomas Humphrey, in the service of the United States.

CAMP SNYDER, *October 13, 1814.*

Sergeants.

Robinson, James.
Stelle, Isaac.
Todd, Arcturus.
Mathew, Joseph.

Corporals.

Evans, David.
Robison, Benjamin.
Harrah, William.
Heath, John.

Bugler.

Mehinney, John.

Privates.

Anderson, Joseph.
Bear, John.
Barclay, Robert.
Bruner, Paul.

Cisler, Nicholas.
Dennison, John.
Doyle, John W.
Dennison, William.
Dunlap, Isaac.
Engles, Joseph.
Everitt, John.
Friteinger, Christ.
Friece, Joseph.
Fell, David.
Friece, Jacob.
Hall, Gooden G.
Hare, Benjamin.
Harrah, Septimus.
Hughs, Samuel.
Hubbert, Samuel.
James, Benjamin.
James, Mason.
James, Joseph.
Kirkpatrick, Andrew.
Lacy, Jesse.
Lewis, Ephraim.
Marshal, William.
Macintosh, Daniel.
Moyer, Sem.
Mekinsty, Nathan.
Mann, Benjamin S.
Medeary, Isaac B.
Morris, John.
Markely, Daniel.
Megooken, William.
Patterson, William E.
Picker, James.
Ruth, Christian.
Rich, Anthony.
Rodman, Samuel.
Simpson, Job.
Smith, Samuel.
Stoover, John W.
Swartzlander, John.
Thomas, Morgan N.
Thomas, William.
Toy, John.
Trumbower, Philip.
Tanner, Mark.
Williams, John.

Whitingham, John.
Wood, Jonathan.
Pool, Joseph.
Roberts, Robert.
Horn, Samuel.
Horn, William.
Daniels, John F.
Hunter, Joseph.
Patterson, Robert.

ROLL OF CAPT. JOHN HALL'S COMPANY.

October 17, 1814.

Pay-roll for Capt. John Hall's company, in Sixty-fifth regiment, commanded by John L. Pearson, colonel commandant.

First Lieutenant.

Dunbar, Mathew.

Second Lieutenant.

Scofield, William.

Third Lieutenant.

Otty, Thomas.

Ensign.

Dunn, Robert.

Sergeants.

Wise, Jacob.
Dunwoody, Joseph.
Bowers, John, Jr.
Lewis, Jabez.

Privates.

Bittle, Joseph.
Blundat, James.
McFagen, James.
Davis, Isaac.
Fields, William.
McNeal, William.
Corker, Robert.
Burn, Peter.
Boon, Marcus.
Newlin, Moses.
Evens, William.
Bugle, Charles.
Fulton, Joseph.
Pennel, Lewis.

Lewis, Mifflin.
Lewis, Bennet.
Alexander, John.
Hoops, John.
Miles, J. Thomas.
McLary, Edward.
Jones, Jacob.
Richards, Isaac.
Pearce, Thomas C.
Lodge, Able.
Daver, John.
Roberts, Eli.
Davis, Daniel.
Reyner, John.
Lindsey, Samuel.
Jenet, Samuel.
Lainhoff, Joshua.
Standley, John.
Litzenburg, Philip.
Taylor, Samuel.
Humphreys, John.
Uhren, Benjamin.
Armsby, John.
Wiley, Jacob.
Hoiser, John.
Cerril, Benjamin.
Fergonson, John.
Shradan, Denis.
Mann, John.
Hoofstickler, John.
Brannan, George.
Engle, John.
Worrell, Benjamin.
Hughs, James.
McGahey, John.
Downs, Thomas E.
Gamison, Isaac.
Cray, John.
Everheart, James.
Thomas, Mordecai.
King, Peter.
Miller, Samuel, St^{on}.
Miller, Philip.
Evens, Joseph.
Miller, Samuel, Wh^{t}.
Stoneback, Jacob.

Lynch, Samuel.
Shaffener, John.
Longaker, Henry.
Miller, Abraham.
White, John.
Rossiter, Abiza.
Rap, Philip.
Royer, David.
Williams, Able.
Car, Thomas.
Poley, Adam.
Smith, Jacob.
Rossiter, Armet.
Donahower, Jacob.
Shinkle, John.
Phillips, William.
Walker, Samuel.
King, Jacob.
Kulp, Jacob.
Defrain, Peter.
King, Mishad.
Shur, Ezekiel.
Baker, Conrad.
Geger, George.
Shaner or Shawer, Jesse.
Boyer, Jesse.
Defrain, Jacob.
Root, Jacob.
Shurman, Daniel.
Lundy, James.
Root, Daniel.
Rap, John.
Longaker, Joseph.
Job, John.
Brook, Nathan.
Adrekens, James.
Hough, Frederick.
Hause, Mikle.
Stophelbine, Henry.
Zeabar, Isaac.
Laird, Andrew.
Danafelser, William.
McKealher, John.
Haven, or Jlaven, Jacob.
Jones, Isaac.
Hough, George.

Shealer, Martain.
Sheet, Henry.
Rice, Daniel.
Walker, John.
Possey, John.
Scot, Thomas.
Clemans, Alexander.
Young, Daniel.
Nice, Jabez.
Rossiter, Malen.
Litzenburg, George.
Lindsey, Samuel.
Beaty, Miles.
Saylor, John.
Rudabaugh, William.
Enos, Francis.
Griffith, Amous.
Rudolph, Samuel.
Fox, William.
Rively, Andrew.

CAMP SNYDER, *October 18, 1814.*

I certify, on honor, that the within muster-roll exhibits a true statement of the Sixth company, commanded by Capt. John Hall, in the Sixty-fifth regiment, Pennsylvania militia, now in the service of the United States, and that the remarks set opposite the names of the men are accurate and just.

JOHN HALL,
Captain.

I believe the within to be a correct muster or pay-roll.

J. L. PEARSON,
Colonel of the Sixty-fifth Regiment.

I certify that the Sixth company, commanded by Capt. John Hall, in the Sixty-fifth regiment, Pennsylvania militia, John L. Pearson, Lieutenant Colonel, commandant, is in the service of the United States, under the order of the general commanding the Fourth military district.

SAMUEL SMITH,
B. G.

CAMP ———, *October 18, 1814.*

ROLL OF CAPT. GEORGE HAMBRIGHT'S COMPANY.

Muster-roll of Capt. George Hambright's company, in the First regiment, Second brigade, Pennsylvania militia, under the command of Jeremiah Shappell, at York. In service from September 1, 1814, to December 4, 1814, from Lancaster county.

Captain.

Hambright, George.

First Lieutenant.

Musser, Matthias.

Second Lieutenant.

Jordan, Thomas R.

Ensign.

Hambright, Frederick.

Quarter-master Sergeant.

Haverstick, George.

Sergeants.

Wentz, Christopher.
Upperman, John.
Hambright, William.
Hawman, Peter.

Corporals.

Nelson, David.
Clark, John.
Mason, John.
Boyd, Matthew.

Drummer.

Furry, Joseph.

Fifer.

Hasselman, Gotlieb.

Privates.

Ball, Dayton.
Beamer, Andrew.
Boyle, Philip.
Brown, Thomas.
Chambers, Joseph.
Crossen, William.

Cummings, William.
Davis, Joseph H.
Dieffenbach, Henry.
Diehl, Francis.
Dougherty, Hugh.
Doyle, Sylvester.
Emanuel, Joseph.
Foesig, William.
Frick, Jacob.
Frick, William.
Glatz, William.
Graeff, Jacob.
Greider, Godfried.
Gross, Michael.
Haines, Daniel.
Hale, George.
Hassan, John.
Heitz, Charles.
Hentsel, William.
Hughs, James.
Hyser, James.
Kingry, Benjamin.
Levi, Lewis.
Marsh, John.
McDevitt, William.
Mechlin, Matthew.
Messenkope, Adam.
Miller, James.
Miller, John.
Moyers, Philip.
Overman, Henry.
Pugh, William.
Reed, George.
Reitsel, George.
Roberts, Matthias.
Rudisill, William.
Rysinger, George.
Seiner, Jacob.
Scott, Andrew.
Shaw, John.
Shubert, William.
Smith, Christian.
Smith, Thomas.
Strine, Michael.
Swem, Stacy.
Thomas, James.

Thompson, Thomas.
Turner, John.
Watson, Hugh.
Whiteside, John.
Worrell, Lewis.
Young, James.
Zahm, Daniel.

ROLL OF CAPTAIN JOHN HAMILTON'S COMPANY.

Pay-roll of a company of infantry commanded by Capt. John Hamilton, in the Second brigade, Second regiment, under the command of Brigadier General Richard Crooke, from the 2d of October, 1812, to the 2d of April, 1813.

Captain.

Hamilton, John.

Lieutenant.

McDowell, John.

Ensign.

Borts, Michael.

Sergeants.

Carrell, James.
Montgomery, Benjamin.
Nealy, Henry.

Corporals.

Moore, John.
Watts, David.
Arb, Luis.

Privates.

Smith, Simon.
Kerr, David.
Anthony, Samuel.
Kindley, William.
Carnahan, Robert.
Moore, William.
Moore John.
Hauk, Michael.
Brown, Andrew.
Siluire, Henry.
Shilhamer, Phillips.
Perk, Daniel.
Alexander, Joseph.
Gibson, William, died since discharged.
Gorley, David.
McGeary, David.

WAR OF 1812-14.

Almax, Henry.
Taylor, Frederick.
Roley, Easa.
Brice, Ezekiel.
Herriss, William.
Henderson, John.
Miller Jesse.
Elwood, Thomas, left sick at Lisbon, October 22, 1812.
Stoops, John, Sr., left on permit, at Mansfield, December 23, 1812.
Stoops, John, Jr., left on permit, at Mansfield, December 23, 1812.
Linenger, Conrad, left on permit, at Mansfield, December 23, 1812.
Jamison, James, left on permit, at Mansfield, December 23, 1812.
Cunningham, William, left on permit, at Mansfield, December 23, 1812.
Robison, James, left on permit, at Mansfield, December 22, 1812.
McDaide, George, volunteered at Fort Meigs, fifteen days.
Edwards, Henry, volunteered fifteen days, at Fort Meigs.
Wigle, John.
Bush, Christian.
Knapingbarger, John.
Hartman, Jacob.
Whitlinger, John.
Snider, Daniel.
Richey, George.
Miller Jacob.
Trout, John.
Brown, John, volunteered fifteen days, at Fort Meigs.
Brown, William.
Stewart, John.
Stewart, James.
Borland, John.
Kerns, John.
McGeary, James.
Ridenour, John.
Healy, George.
Wagaman, John.
Siluire, John.
McCollaugh, Robert, discharged November 26, 1812.
Everhart, Christian, discharged November 26, 1812.
Hitz, Jacob, discharged October 28, 1812.
Anderson, William, discharged January 4, 1812.

I certify, on honor, that this exhibits a true state of Capt. Hamilton's company, and that the remarks opposite to each name are accurate and just.

JOHN HAMILTON.

September 22, 1813.

ROLL OF CAPT. WILLIAM HAMILTON'S COMPANY.

Muster-roll of a company of riflemen in the actual service of the United States, commanded by Capt. George Musser, in the rifle regiment of the Second brigade, Pennsylvania militia, under the command of Lieut. Col. William Hamilton, from the 5th of September to the ———.

Captains.

Hamilton, William, appointed lieutenant colonel.
Musser, George.

First Lieutenants.

Musser, George.
Hill, Frederick.

Second Lieutenants.

Hill, Frederick.
Wein, George.

Ensigns.

Wein, George.
Eichholtz, Leonard.

Orderly Sergeants.

Eichholtz, Leonard.
McKinzie, Daniel.

Sergeants.

MacKinzie, Daniel.
Huffnagle, George.
Huffnagle, Peter.
Mayers, Jacob.
Musser, Abraham.
Backenstose, William.

Corporals.

Mayers, Jacob.
Musser, Abraham.
Backenstose, William.
Bomberger, John.
Elliot, Robert.
Barton, Matthias.
       er, Peter.
Brislin, Benjamin.
Frailey, Jacob.

Drummer.

Garver, Jacob.

Fifer.

Bowen, Jacob.

Bugler.

Fordney, Samuel.

Privates.

Albright, Jacob.
Albright, William.
Algiger, or Algier, Michael.
Barton, Matthias.
Bomberger, George.
Bonnet, John.
Buchius, John.
Block, John.
Brislin, Benjamim.
Brubaker, Henry.
Brunner, Casper, Sr.
Brunner, Casper, Jr.
Brenner, Henry.
Brenner, Jacob.
Burg, Christian.
Burg, John.
Carson, Robert.
Colsher, Peter.
Danner, Jacob.
Daub, George.
Davis, Samuel.
Davis, Thomas R., appointed quarter-master.
Dealer, William.
Delander, Jacob.
Dellet, Adam.
Deitrich, George.
Duchman, John.
Epler, Lewis.
Ehrman, Michael.
Evans, Jacob.
Elliot, Robert.
Ferree, John.
Ferree, John, Jr.
Ferree, William.
Fraily, Jacob.
Fitzgerald, Thomas.
Fordney, Samuel.
Greaff, Matthias.
Green, John.
Green, Neal.

Hinny, William.
Holmes, Norman, paymaster assistant.
Hoover, John.
Huppart, John, died November 5, 1814.
Hoover, George.
Huffnagle, Peter.
Huffnagle, Michael.
Jones, Samuel.
Jordan, Michael.
Jordan, Casper.
Keller, John.
Kirk, Isaac.
Kitch, Jacob.
Krider, Paul.
Kline, Michael.
Kuhn, Augustus, transferred.
Lightner, Isaac, appointed adjutant.
Lind, John.
Lyon, James.
Mackey, Benjamin.
Metzgar, Philip.
Miller, William.
Muldoon, Charles.
Mulford, Jonathan.
Musketnuss, Adam.
McCan, Francis.
McClure, Robert.
McClure, Samuel.
McKoy, Stephen.
McGonigal, John.
McLean, Andrew.
McLeanagan, Samuel.
McGreanagan, Alexander.
Nagle, George.
Palmer, Moses.
Patterson, John.
Powell, John.
Pile, Henry.
Reese, John.
Reinhart, Jacob.
Reitz, Jacob.
Rexroth, Peter.
Ritter, John, claimed by the United States as a deserter, September 18, 1814.
Rollison George.
Rotharmle, Adam.

Soesholtz, George.
Shartzer, Philip.
Shoebrooks, Edward.
Shufflebottom, Josiah.
Simpson, William.
Smith, Jacob, transferred.
Smith, Jasper, appointed paymaster.
Snodgrass, George.
Spyker, Peter.
Stake, George.
Stoy, Gustavus.
Tindall, William.
Titus, William.
Tripple, Joseph.
Trissler, John.
Wallace, Thomas.
Weidle, Adam.
White, Christian.
White, Levy.
Wise, John.
Zeller, Ephraim.
Jordan, Joseph, waiter.

We certify, on honor, that the foregoing muster-roll exhibits the true state of the company of riflemen in the actual service of the United States, under the command of Captain George Musser, for the period herein expressed, and that the remarks opposite the men's names are accurate and just.

GEORGE MUSSER,
Captain.
DERRICK FAHNESTOCK,
Surgeon.

I certify, on honor, that the foreging muster-roll exhibits the true state of the company of riflemen in the actual service of the United States, under the command of Captain George Musser, as mustered by me this 2d day of December, 1814, in obedience to an order from Major General Scott.

GAB. HIESTER, Jr.,
Brigade Major, Second Brigade, Pennsylvania Militia.

LIST OF CAPT. PETER HANLEY'S COMPANY.

List of non-commissioned officers and privates in the company commanded by Capt. Peter Hanley, of the Eighty-sixth regiment, First brigade, Second division, Pennsylvania militia, now at Marcus Hook, belonging to Col. Conrad Krickbaum's. Entered service September 20, 1814.

Sergeant.

Bevans, Wilder.
Christman, John, Sr.
Christman, John, Jr.
Longenbach, Peter.
March, Rineard.

Corporals.

Rinehard, Benjamin.
Lesig, William.
Burns, Israle.
Rushong, Samuel.

Fifer.

Sheffee, George.

Drummer.

Rushong, Philip.

Privates.

Phillips, George.
Misimer, Joseph.
Gilbrath, William.
Overshine, Jacob.
Misimer, Henry S.
Hanley, Samuel.
Decker, Martin, Jr.
Radebach, George.
Rushong, Jacob.
Ox, William.
Hartranfft, John.
Bryner, George.
Lynderman, Aaron.
Decker, Martin, Sr.
Koch, Jacob.
Hortinstine, Samuel.
Warley, Joseph.
Bolten, John.
Misimer, Samuel, Sr.
Hawbarger, Daniel.

Misimer, Samuel, Jr.
Black, John.
Keely, Henry.
Mayberry, Jacob.
Keeler, John.
Barlow, John.
Barlow, Abner.
Lochman, Henry.
Nap, John.
Prutzman, Adam.
Lockman, Joseph.
Barnhart, John.
Davis, Thomas.
Evans, Robert.
Roads, Jacob.
Pool, Benjamin.
Craver, Henry.
Moyer, Daniel.
Mattes, Abraham.
Sheffee, Jacob.
Crouse, Jacob.
Mayberry, Samuel.
Panabaker, Jacob.
Brant, Samuel.
Yost, Eli.
Hendricks, Jacob.
Prutzman, Abel.
Fillman, Jacob.
Saylor, Godfrey.
Swinehart, George.
Unegobler, George.
Grubb, Jacob.
Fagely, Abraham.
Kutz, Samuel,
Shrader, Frederick.
Samsel, Peter.
Reese, Jacob.
Wilhaur, John.
Althouse, Henry.
Long, John.
Miller, Conrad.
Philman, Samuel.
Place, Peter.
Gephart, Andrew.
Cale, John.
Zuber, Samuel.

WAR OF 1812-14.

Zuber, Henry.
Reninger, John.
Miller, John.
Henrick, Samuel.
Rafesnider, Amos.
Smith, Samuel.
Mull, Henry.
Ale, William.
Bitting, Joseph, Jr.
Miller, Jacob.
Williams, Thomas.
Kepner, Henry.
Miller, Michael.
Weller, Samuel.
Kortz, Valentine.
Althouse, Jacob.
Bitting, Joseph, Sr.
Zoller, George.
Peterman, Jacob.
Smith, Abraham J.
Getman, George.
Walter, Jacob.
Peterman, Jo^n.
Yost, Benjamin.
Misimer, George, discharged October 9, 1814.
Buzard, Henry, discharged October 9, 1814.

I certify the foregoing to be a correct list of the non-commissioned officers and privates now under my command.

PETER HANLEY,
Captain.

October 10, 1814.

CAMP MARKESHOOK, *October 10, 1814.*

I do certify, upon honor, this muster-roll exhibits a true statement of a company of the Montgomery county militia, of the State of Pennsylvania, now in the service of the United States. The remarks set opposite the names of the men are accurate and just.

PETER HANLEY,
Captain.

CONRAD KRICKBAUM,
Lieutenant Colonel.

I certify that the company commanded by Capt. Peter Hanley is in the service of the United States, under order of the general commanding the Fourth militia district.

SAMUEL SMITH,
Brigadier General.

CAMP MARKESHOOK, *October 17, 1814.*

ROLL OF CAPT. MICHAEL HARPER'S COMPANY.

Capt. Michael Harper's company in Col. Snider's regiment, Path Valley, September 5, 1812.

Captain.

Harper, Michael.

Lieutenant.

McKinzie, William.

Ensign.

Campbell, John.

Sergeants.

Irwin, William.
McKinzie, James.
Widney, John.
Barrack, Hugh.

Corporals.

Baker, Jeremiah.
McCullough, Francis.
Campbell, Samuel.
Ginnevin, James.

Privates.

Cannon, John.
Dever, Joseph.
Donnelly, Barnabas.
Evans, David.
Fegan, Barnabas.
Hockenberry, Jeremiah.
Hockenberry, James.
Hockenberry, Peter.
Irwin, George.
Linn, James.
Philips, Samuel.
Scooly, Isaac.
Smith, William.
Scott, Richard.
Taylor, James.
Timmons, Peter.

ROLL OF CAPT. WILLIAM HARPER'S COMPANY.

Pay-roll of a company of infantry commanded by Capt. William Harper, in Fifteenth regiment, Pennsylvania militia in service of United States, commanded by Lieut. Col. Joel Ferree, under Brig. Gen. Richard Crooks.

Captain.

Harper, William.

Privates.

More, Thomas.
Dawson, Thomas, volunteered 15 days at Fort Meigs.
McClain, David.
Freeland, George, volunteered 15 days at Fort Meigs.
Evans, David, volunteered 15 days at Fort Meigs.
Allten, Jesse.
Tams, or Tioms, Samuel.
Brown, John.
Daken, John.
Young, William.
Randle, Enos.
Crego, Samuel.
Hibbs, Jonah.
Pichinpaw, Jacob.
Anderson, Charles.
Humes, Samuel.
Morgan, Robert.
Little, Josiah.
Hall, Jacob.
Wright, John.
Taylor, Barnet, volunteered at Fort Meigs.
Hawkens, Gabriel.
Gerrerd, Cosbly.
Knight, John.
Funk, John.
Evans, Ebreham.
Estle, Joseph.
Crabb, James.
James, Thomas.
Tanner, William, volunteered for fifteen days, at Fort Meigs.
Moreland, James, volunteered for fifteen days.
Slack, George.
Miller, George.
Hickman, Samuel.
Hartly, Edward.

Ankler, David.
Kencade, Robert, volunteered for fifteen days.
McMasters, Robert.
Hupp, Philip.
McGuire, Thomas, volunteered for fifteen days.
Wisman, Jacob.
Hupp, Michael.
Coffman, Joseph, discharged at Mansfield 10th November.
Kelso, Daniel, discharged at Mansfield 10th November.
Gordon, Samuel.
Davis, William.
Stanton, John, volunteered for fifteen days.
Dunn, Moses.
McGinnes, John.
Mason, John.
Scott, Thomas.
Hineman, William.
Coffing, Elijah, volunteered for fifteen days.
Marker, Sampson, volunteered for fifteen days.
Penn, Richard.
Coe, Benjamin.
Marshall, William.
Meadows, Aaron.
Knight, James.
Bell, John, volunteered for fifteen days.
Seaton, George, discharged January 12, 1813.
Sergeant, Abraham.
Stull, John.

I certify, on honor, that this muster-roll exhibits a true statement of Capt. William Harper's company of the First regiment, Pennsylvania militia, for the period therein mentioned, and that the remarks set opposite the men's names are accurate and just.

WILLIAM HARPER.

ROLL OF ENSIGN WILLIAM HARTFORD'S COMPANY.

Pay-roll of a company of infantry commanded by Ensign William Hartford, in the Fifth or odd battalion, commanded by Major David Nelson, of the Second detachment, Pennsylvania militia, commanded by Brigadier General Richard Crooks, in the service of the United States, for the extra pay of said company allowed by the State of Pennsylvania.

Lieutenant.

Walker, Robert, killed by the Indians, 9th March, 1813.

Ensign.
Hartford, William, discharged 2d April, 1813.

Sergeants.
Poe, Adam, discharged 2d April, 1813.
Craige, James, discharged 2d April, 1813.

Corporals.
Joroden, David, discharged 2d April, 1813.
Dillow, Thomas, discharged 17th April, 1813.

Privates.
Brinton, Thomas, discharged 2d April, 1813.
Bruce, William, discharged 2d April, 1813.
Beer, Robert, discharged by sergeant, 20th December, 1812.
Carothers, John, discharged April 2, 1813.
Craige, John, discharged April 17; 1813, fifteen days' volunteer.
Cain, James, discharged 2d of April, 1813.
Huston, John, discharged 2d of April, 1813.
Hall, William, discharged 2d of April, 1813.
Laughlin, Samuel, discharged 2d of April, 1813.
Leitch, Daniel, discharged 2d of April, 1813.
Littell, John, discharged 2d of April, 1813.
Lowman, Philip, discharged 2d of April, 1813.
Miller, James, discharged 2d of April, 1813.
Nelson, John, discharged 2d of April, 1813.
Stewart, John, discharged 2d of April, 1813.
Scott, William, discharged 2d of April, 1813.
Scott, Robert M., discharged 2d of April, 1813.
Smith, John, discharged by sergeant, March 9, 1813.
Shehen, William, discharged April 2, 1813.
Twiford, Manlif.
Wallice, James, discharged April 2, 1813.
Wilson, Henry, discharged April 2, 1813.
Winkler, Rhendey, discharged April 2, 1813.

The case of John Smith is hard. He served within a few days of the passing of the law; yet, as the law says "now in the service," he is cut short. He is a brave fellow.

I certify, on honor, that this pay-roll exhibits a true state of Ensign William Hartford's company, of the Fifth or odd battalion of Pennsylvania militia, for the period therein mentioned, and that the remarks set opposite the names of the men are accurate and just.

WILLIAM HARTFORD,
Ensign.

October 4, 1813.

ROLL OF CAPT. GEORGE HARTMAN, Jr.'s COMPANY.

Pay-roll of a company of drafted ———— regiment, commanded by Capt. George Hartman, Jr., and attached to the ———— regiment, Pennsylvania militia.

Sergeants.

Rentgen, Peter.
Harris, Thomas.
Davis, Sampson.
Neel, Thomas.
Miller, John.

Corporals.

Huston, James.
Hipple, John.
Orner, Lewis.
Roads, Jacob.

Privates.

Smith, Henry.
Roads, William.
Strough, Samuel.
Moses, John.
March, Nicholas.
Miller, George.
Snyder, Peter.
Roberts, Lewis.
Hipple, George.
Powel, Ezekiel.
Moses, Henry.
Watson, Gabrial.
Heck, Jacob.
Scott, John.
Himes, James.
Priser, George.
Griffith, Ebenezer.
Townsand, Caleb.
Wynn, John.
Wynn, Jonathan.
Leiton, Thomas.
Beekley, John.
Clower, Daniel.
Gunn, David.
Lineinger, Jacob.
Martin, Samuel.

Defrain, John.
Lear, Jacob.
Kiser, Nicholas.
Shelich, Valentine.
Snyder, Henry.
Baughdekerch. Henry.
Davidsizer, Jacob.
Hoffman, George.
Snyder, Thomas.
Campbell, George C.
Meezer, John.
Williams, David.
Slighter, Abraham.
Deemer, Michael.
Walter, John.
Snyder, Peter.
Link, Daniel.
Walter, Leonard.
Evens, Owen.
Bignal, George.
Hipple, Henry.
Yeager, Peter.
Custer, William.
Hipple, Peter.
Hipple, Caspar.
Hammer, Jacob.
Kepler, Israel.
Creps, John.
Creps, Thomas.
Harple, John.
Sheeter, Frederick.
Deery, George.
Schristman, Henry.
Essick, George.
Root, Jacob.
Root, Joseph.
Walkingwood, David.
Smith, Henry.
Leacy, William.
Fitzsummons, Caleb.
Ligget, Samuel.
Starrett, William, lame.
Helbert, Jacob.
Watkin, Jesse.
M ller, Isaac.
Stoufer, Jacob.

Roberts, Benjamin.
Griffith, Samuel.
Matson, James.
Hersh, Samuel.
Bush, John.
Root, David.
Emery, William.
Deeds, Frederick.
Widener, Samuel.
Mock, Jacob.
Everhart, Samuel.
Keely, George.
Thomas, Jesse.
Turner, Henry.
Belts, Philip.
March, Henry, lame.
Viant, John.
Kiter, Henry.
Howel, Thomas.
Gregory, John.
Houp, Henry.
Beaven, William.
Snyder, George, lame.
Loyd, Samuel.
Jery, Peter.
Guest, James.
Monroe, David.
Leigtoix, Samuel.

CAMP NEAR MARCUS HOOK, *October 17, 1814.*

I certify, on honor, this muster-roll exhibits a true state of the Second company annexed to the Sixty-fifth regiment, Pennsylvania militia, now in the service of the United States, and that the remarks set opposite the names are accurate and just.

GEO. HARTMAN, Jr.,
Captain.

I believe the above to be a correct muster pay-roll.

J. L. PEARSON,
Colonel of Sixty-fifth Regiment.

I certify that the Second company, in the Sixty-fifth regiment, Pennsylvania militia, commanded by George Hartman, Jr., is in the service of the United States, under order of the ———.

SAMUEL SMITH,
B. G.

WAR OF 1812–14.

ROLL OF CAPT. PETER HARTZOG'S COMPANY.

Pay-roll of Capt. Peter Hartzog's company of drafted militia, attached to the Second regiment, commanded by Col. Patterson, in the service of the United States, from Pennsylvania, Brigadier General Richard Crooks commanding. Commencing of service, October 2, 1812; end of service, April 2, 1815. (3.)

Captain.

Hartzog, Peter.

Lieutenant.

Bowers, Joseph.

Ensign.

Overturf, J.

Sergeants.

Coombs, Edward.
Songster, William.
Hamilton, James.
Yander, Daniel.

Corporals.

Houpt, Jacob.
Freeman, Alexander R.
Hanna, Robert.
Rogers, Stacy.

Privates.

Black, Henry.
Harshberger, Daniel, volunteered fifteen days.
Gono, John.
Brin, William.
Debolt, Rezon, volunteered fifteen days.
Debolt, Tegarden S., volunteered fifteen days.
Danold, Jonah M., volunteered fifteen days.
Blaney, William.
Rifle, Jacob.
Cronton, Abram.
Hafhill, Abram.
Antle, James.
Reed, Jacob.
Robertson, Robert.
Care, John.
Koupt, Tobias.
Smith, Samuel, died March 22, 1813.

White, John, volunteered fifteen days; died April 7.
Rees, James, volunteered fifteen days; died April 9.
Wilson, Thomas.
Numbers, James.
Getzendaner, John, volunteered fifteen days.
Criss, Miceal.
Stuart, James.
Gettry, Solomon, volunteered fifteen days.
Gettry, Joseph, volunteered fifteen days.
Holmes, John.
Defenbough, Daniel.
Proctor, William.
Willey, Richard.
Rumble, Henry.
Wynn, Jonathan.
Hartman, Melchi.
Parson, John.
Willson, Hugh, volunteered.
Price, William.
Coombs, John.
Logan, James.
Mdugal, Levi.
Thompson, Thomas.
Willark, David.
Watson, Joseph.
McCarty, Joel.
McCarty, Hiram.
Tipit, William.
McCann, Hugh.
Hardman, Philip.
Rickets, Philoman.
Owl, Jacob.
Feirst, George.
Crowsore, Christian.
Hall, Ephraim.
Lawriner, Philip.
Vance, Hugh.
Patterson, Jesey.

I certify on honor that this pay-roll exhibits a true statement of my company of the Second regiment of Pennsylvania militia, of the period therein mentioned, and that the remarks set to the men's names are accurate and just.

JOSEPH BOWERS,
Lieutenant.

ROLL OF CAPT. ADAM HAWK'S COMPANY.

Pay-roll of the first company of militia, under the command of Adam Hawk, captain, of the First detachment, Second brigade, of drafted militia, in the service of the United States, commanded by Christian J. Hutter, colonel.

Captain.

Hawk, Adam.

First Lieutenant.

Sailor, Abram.

Second Lieutenant.

Coolbach, Cornelius, promoted October 10, 1814.

Third Lieutenant.

Gorden, William, promoted October 10, 1814.

Ensign.

Pugh, John.

Sergeants.

Sepoch, Jacob C., promoted October 10, 1814.
Troxel, John.
Knouss, John L.
Belles, Peter.

Corporals.

Fitz Randolph, William.
Walter, Samuel.
Wilhelm, Frederick
Lowrey, John.

Privates.

Rohn, John.
Roth, John.
Pigg, Thomas.
Burberger, Henry.
Gruber, Nicholas.
Price, Frederick.
Kreidler, John.
Sirick, Daniel.
Neiterhous, Abram.
Jones, James.
Buss, Henry.
Hess, Peter.

Walter, Jacob.
Snell, Isaac.
Emeck, Henry.
Hackman, Abram.
Herlew, George.
Kern, John.
Kuhn, John.
Wilhour, Andrew.
Walter, Peter.
Hilliard, Joseph.
Ketter, Jacob.
Miksh, Frederick.
Duwalt, Nicholas.
Plotts, Thomas.
Arnold, Robert.
Swarts, Michael.
Roup, John.
Stuher, John.
Jumper, Adam.
Winner, Jacob.
Daniels, John.
Foy, George.
Kouhlein, Michael.
Hulfiesh, William.
Jentry, John.
Coffin, Horatio.
Bauder, John.
Odenwelder, Peter.
Walter, William.
Cuplin, Jacob.
Walter, John.
Medsker, Christian.
Roap, William.
Staher, Christian.
Nauman, Michael.
Siglin, Jacob.
Nagel, John.
Shoop, George.
Siglir, Jesse.
Hawk, John.
Felker, George.
Daniel, Peter.
Detrich, Henry.
Kellor, John.
Shoop, Peter.
Felker, Joseph.

Fushamer, Jacob.
Putz, John.
Remel, Andrew.
Strang, Silvanus.
Wismer, James.
Mantanis, Burris.
Gorden, Abram.
Drake, Joseph W.
Sayre, William.
Lee, Jesse.
Hawk, Peter.
Storm, John.
Wiess, Henry.
Ketts, George.
Andrew, Peter.
Arnold, Adam.
Smith, Melcher.
Burrier, Daniel.
Prony, John.
Depew, Abram.
Strole, John.
Housser, George.
Prim, Joshua.
Kemry, John.
Bush, John.
Utt, Adam.
Prichard, John.
Dinnist, Adam.
Rouse, John.
Smith, Jacob.
Transue, Jacob.
Lee, David.
Pugh, Samuel.
Kleinlup, Peter.
Putz, Peter.
Kailor, Adam.
Carl, John P. M., sergeant; reduced, October 10, 1814, to a private.
Ransberry, Jesse.
Price, Benjamin.
Broadhead, Garret.
Beach, Stephen.

I do certify, on honor, that this muster-roll exhibits a true state of the first company in the First detachment, Second brigade of Pennsylvania militia, that the remarks set opposite the names are accurate and just.

ADAM HAWK,
Captain.

I believe the above to be a correct muster of pay-roll.

CHRIST'R J. HUTTER,
Lieutenant Colonel Commanding Fourth.

I certify that the company commanded by A. Hawk, captain, is in the service of the United States, under orders of the general commanding ——— military district.

H. SPERING,
Brigadier General.

October 25, 1814.

ROLL OF CAPT. PATRICK HAYS' COMPANY.

Capt. Patrick Hays' Mercersburg company, in Col. Jared Irwin's regiment, September 5, 1812.

Captain.

Hays, Patrick.

Lieutenant.

Small, John.

Ensign.

Elder, Samuel.

Sergeants.

McQuown, James.
Small, Jacob.
Williams, Jacob.
Spangler, George.

Corporals.

Herington, Joseph.
Donothen, John.
Leer, Daniel.
Cain, Jacob.

Fifer.

Mull, John.

Drummer.

Wise, Jacob.

Privates.

Bennet, James.
Brubaker, Isaac.
Craig, Samuel.
Cunningham, Joseph.
Crouch, John.
Clapsaddle, John.
Cline, Henry.

Cooper, William.
Campbell, Samuel.
Dunlap, Alexander.
Divilbiss, Frederick.
Deitrick, David.
Dunlap, John.
Elder, James.
Gaster, Peter.
Groscope, Jacob.
Harris, John.
Hodskins, Jacob.
Hissong, Jonas.
Hart, William.
Hallin, John.
Hastler, John.
Heart, John.
Halland, James.
Hodskins, Abraham.
Kyler, Peter.
King, John.
McQuown, Robert.
McFarland, Robert.
McQuown, William.
Mowry, John.
McDowell, James.
McPike, Charles.
Montgomery, Campbell.
McCurdy, William.
Martin, Samuel.
Pettet, Charles.
Suffecool, Henry.
Suffecool, William.
Stewart, William.
Teach, Peter.
Weaver, Henry.
Welker, Daniel.
Walker, James.

ROLL OF CAPT. GEORGE HENDEL'S COMPANY.

Muster-roll of Capt. Hendel's company of volunteers belonging to the Fifth detachment, Pennsylvania militia, now in the service of the United States, at Buffalo, N. Y.

Captain.

Hendel, George.

Lieutenants.

Everly, David.
Philips, Peter.
Sharets, Frederick.

Ensign.

Sanno, Michael.

Sergeants.

Davis, John.
Wormly, Henry.
Winecoop, Isaac.
Ritner, Peter.

Corporals.

Bab, John.
Werehime, Peter.
Devarter, Adam.
Uhler, Philip.

Privates.

Zering, Lewis.
Eslinger, Joseph.
McMickle, Hugh.
Walker, Charles.
Crocket, George.
Hievener, John.
Newport, William.
Smith, Benjamin.
Smith, Samuel.
Rickert, John.
Hinckle, John.
Devenport, Samuel.
Shisler, John.
Beatty, John.
McGregor, Alexander.
Newman, Alexander.
Arny, John.
Galbreath, William.
Husselton, George.

Beaker, Frederick.
Kirtland, William.
Kirtland, Isaac.
McNaughton, Peter.
Hanes, Sollemon.
Kennedy, William.
Phillips, Andrew.
Keigly, Jacob.
Crouse, Andrew.
Ketring, Lorence.
Fisher, Samuel.
Mullen, Alexander.
Dunbar, James.
Bruce, Thomas.
Ford, Samuel.
Manly, Robert.
McGary, John.
Poorman, Christian.
Krider, Jacob.
Barnheiter, John.
Stuard, Henry.
Fireobend, Solomon.
Leehler, John.
Miller, Robert.
Koucher, Charles.
Sidel, Henry.
Andrews, John.
Armstrong, Hiram.
Benizer, Samuel.
Bruce, William, missing July 25.
Boar, Nicholas.
Brumbough, Andrew.
Byers, Jacob.
Bob, Henry.
Bunker, John, missing July 5.
Edeburn, John.
Feyerobend, John.
Fertenbough, Philip.
Guest, John.
Gerhart, Andrew.
Ginkens, John, killed July 25.
Geer, David.
John, Herman.
Herter, George.
Hide, Michael.
Gasperson, George.

Longsdorf, Michael.
Longsdorf, Martin.
Livinger, Henry.
Libe, Christian.
Stookey, Martin.
Messinger, John.
Mullen, James, killed July 5.
Smith, John M.
Smith, Abraham M.
Murry, John.
Munks, James.
Orr, William.
Rensenberger, David.
Rodenbough, Daniel.
Stubbs, Henry, missing July 25.
Stucky, John.
Sholly, Valentine.
Snyder, John.
Warner, John.
Yoe, Conrad.
Speas, Jacob.
Wolf, David.
Krider, John.
Askins, William.
Walker, Jacob.
Dougherty, Robert
Kelsy, George.

I do certify that the foregoing is a correct muster-roll of my company. Given under my hand this 26th day of August, 1814.

GEORGE HENDEL,
Captain.
JAMES FENTON,
Colonel.

ROLL OF CAPT. GAWIN HENRY'S COMPANY.

Muster-roll of Capt. Gawin Henry's company of riflemen, in the Second brigade, Pennsylvania militia, under the command of Col. William Hamilton, at ———. In service from September 1, 1814, to December 4, 1814; from Dauphin and Lancaster counties.

Captain.

Henry, Gawin.

Lieutenant.

Thomas, William.

Ensign.

Ross, Adam.

Sergeants.

Carson, Samuel.
Haws, Dennis.
Glasgow, Alexander.
Miller, Peter.

Corporals.

Hughs, Edward.
Lukins, Jesse.
Price, John.
Schaeffer, George.

Drummer.

Isett, Henry.

Fifer.

Byram, Thomas.

Privates.

Baker, Daniel.
Baumgartner, Windle.
Baxter, William.
Berryman, John.
Best, Thomas.
Blake, Thomas.
Boone, Mordecai.
Brickley, James.
Bryan, John.
Burns, Peter.
Campbell, James.
Casebolt, Isaac.
Cowhick, John.
Crooks, John.
Crossly, Abraham.
Cunkle, Philip.
Earls, Henry.
Fair, George.
Ferguson, John.
Finnerty, Joseph.
Flasher, George.
Fulton, Thomas.
Gastwhite, Joseph.
Gastwhite, Samuel.
Gibson, William.
Green, Griffiths.
Heiney, George.
Heiser, Jacob.
James, Edward.

Johnston, Andrew.
Jones, Jonathan.
Keesel, John.
Lefevre, George.
Linton, John.
Lukins, Aaron.
Lukins, Joseph.
Lytle, Alexander.
Madlam, James.
Madlam, John.
Mayer, Henry.
Mayer, Henry C.
McCurdy, William.
McNamee, James.
McNiel, Archibald.
Milam, William.
Murphy, Benjamin.
Murry, James.
Newman, Jacob.
Nichols, Conrad.
Obert, Peter.
Over, David.
Over, John.
Pheeling, James.
Phoeble, Lewis.
Porter, John.
Ramsey, James.
Reed, King.
Rheim, Samuel.
Ridge, Thomas.
Rupley, George.
Scott, Robert.
Scott, William.
Shirts, Jacob.
Swager, William.
Thomas, Daniel.
Wade, William.
Waggoner, John.
Weaver, William.
Weingarten, Albert.
Weingartner, John.
White, James.
Wilhelm, Adam.
Winemaker, Henry.
Woods, Thomas.
Wyant, George.

ROLL OF CAPT. JOSEPH HERGESHEIMER'S COMPANY.

Pay-roll of Capt. Hergesheimer's company, Second brigade, First division, Pennsylvania militia, in service of the United States, under the command of Col. John Thompson.

Captain.

Hergesheimer, Joseph.

First Lieutenant.

Morrison, William.

Second Lieutenant.

Renshaw, James.

Ensign.

Kline, George.

Sergeants.

Sorber, Jacob C.
Fisher, Charles.
Armstrong, Robert.
Beakley, Edward.

Corporal.

Sugart, George.

Drum-Major.

Green, George.

Privates.

Somerset, George.
Vanhon, William.
Warner, Peter.
Zimerman, Abraham.
Cowher, Daniel.
Zimerman, Jacob.
Link, Frederick.
Good, John.
Henry, William.
Shingle, George.
Selcer, John.
Meroney, David.
Clouse, William.
Hellerman, Jacob.
Homiller, Henry.
Landenberger, Jacob.
Steover, Frederick, Jr.
Berkleboch, Yost.
Pinyard, Bright.
Waxler, Jonathan.

Duy, Christian.
Philips, William.
Kerboch, Michael.
Reed, James.
Strouse, John.
Man, John.
Moul, John.
Young, Martin.
Snovel, John.
Ketler, Adam.
Duy, John L.
Tuston, Edward.
Warner, Philip.
Knor, George.
Stroup, Henry.
Selcer, Henry.
Omensetter, Alhanan.
Widdiss, Jesse.
Bentz Jacob.
Gisel, Jacob.
Zener, John.
Gross, Henry.
Sink, Jacob.
Simon, George.
Gorges, Benjamin.
Gorges, John.
Silvers, Mark.
Fichorn, Samuel.
Sharpnach, Daniel.
Nell, Samuel.
Lehman, George.
Light, John.
Fulmer, Philip.
Somerlot, William.
Schafer, Jacob.
Recher, Jacob.
Wentz, John.
Hoffman, Jacob.
Snider, Edward.
Benner, Jacob.
Peters, Christian.
Hess, John.
Luckens, Elijah.
Didier, John.
Keiser, Enoch.
Marts, Leonard.

Rever, William.
Done, Abraham.
Lawson, Matthias.
Fox, Frederick.
Young, Michael.
Camel, Walter.
Shawaker, Charles.
Dull, James.
Stroup, Peter.
Nicholas, Christian.
Peekey, Joseph.
Felty, Henry.
Waley, John.
Man, Peter.
Gerges, John H., Jr.
Hart, Solomon.
Stace, John.
Kue, John.
Taylor, William.
Shalcross, Benjamin.
Bush, George W.
Smith, Joseph.
Derr, Jacob.

We do certify, on honor, that the within roll exhibits a true state of the company commanded by Capt. Joseph Hargesheimer, of the Second brigade, First division, Pennsylvania militia, under command of Col. John Thompson.

WILLIAM MORISON,
Lieutenant Commanding.

CAMP MARCUS HOOK, *October 17, 1814.*

JOHN THOMPSON,
Colonel.

I do certify that the company commanded by Capt. Joseph Hargesheimer is in the service of the United States, under orders of the general commanding the Fourth military district.

THOMAS SNYDER,
Brigadier General Commanding.

CAMP MARCUS HOOK, *October 17, 1814.*

ROLL OF CAPT. GEORGE HESS' COMPANY.

Muster-roll of Capt. George Hess' Rifle company from Northampton county, September 20, 1814.

Captain.

Hess, George, Jr.

First Lieutenant.

McHose, Isaac.

Second Lieutenant.

Steaver, Joseph.

Ensign.

Meyer, Samuel.

Sergeants.

Boehm, Philip.
Beaver, Daniel.
Bachman, Christian.
Lynn, William.

Corporals.

Lerch, William.
Eikert, Isaac.
Rush, George.
Henn, John.

Musicians.

Weaver, Joseph.
Hinkel, William.

Privates.

Braun, Adam.
Moser, Michael.
Feeman, John.
Sherer, John.
Emery, Samuel.
Laubach, Christian.
Bachman, Jacob.
Seiphert, John.
Mann, John.
Lee, Henry.
Shleyer, Michael.
Knechel, John.
Seigle, Frederick.
Ohl, John.
Beyl, Philip.
Leidich, John.

Long, William.
Shleyer, Daniel.
Reich, Abraham, Jr.
Ohl, Philip.
Leidich, Joseph.
Dany, George.
Rasmy, Henry.
Mill, John.
Henn, Jacob.
Beyl, John.
Beaver, Peter.
Miller, Thomas.
Emery, Andrew.
Weaver, George.
Klace, John.
Bieseiker, Michael.
Fogel, Frederick.
Klace, Jacob.
Bast, John.
Derr, Leonard.
Graham, William.
Lynn, John, Jr.

Witness my hand:

GEORGE HESS, Jr.,
Captain.

We do certify, on honor, that the within roll exhibits a true state of the company commanded by Capt. Geo. Hess, Jr., and that the remarks set opposite the men's names are accurate and just.

GEO. HESS, Jr.,
Captain.

THO. HUMPHREY,
Colonel First R. P. V. R.

CAMP DUPONT, *October 24.*

I do certify, on honor, that the company commanded by Captain George Hess is in the service of the United States, under the command of the general commanding the Fourth military district.

THOS. CADWALADER,
Brigadier General, commanding advance L. B.

CAMP DUPONT, *November 26, 1814.*

ROLL OF CAPT. GEO. HETZELBERGER'S COMPANY.

Receipt-roll of a company of militia commanded by Capt. George Hetzelberger, of the ―――― regiment, performing a tour of duty under the command of Col. Lutz, who rendezvoused at York, under the general order of the Governor dated 26th of August, 1814. Commencement of service, 2d of September, 1814.

Captain.

Hetzelberger, George.

Lieutenant.

Singer, Abraham.

Ensign.

Kruther, Samuel.

Sergeants.

Renshaus, Robinson T.
Sheffner, Henry J.
Good, John.
Diffenderfer, Samuel.

Corporals.

Wright, Samuel.
Gardner, George.
Meyers, John.
Lomax, James.

Privates.

Hutson, John.
Stringfeller, Thomas.
Johnson, David.
Entrichen, Samuel.
Huntwork, Henry.
Jones, Jehu.
Burges, William.
Robinson, James.
Maux, Jacob.
Geshelman, Christian.
Eley, Ab^m.
Gable. Conrod.
Miller, Jacob.
Richwine, Samuel.
Lightner, William.
Kline, Ab^m.
Bodenstaus, Henry.
Fendall, Alexander L.
Lawrence, Thomas.
Zimmerman, John.
Wortz, Henry.

Powel, Mathias.
Long, Isaac.
Garmen, John.
Mushetmess, John.
Denison, Mathew.
Travise, Peter.
Davis, William.
Sylbert, Andrew.
Neff, Henry.
Seisholtz, George.
Underman, Henry.
Detrich, John.
Henwood, Vachel.
Bodenstaid, or Backenstose, George.
Detrich, Michael.
Holsworth, William.
Read, Robert.
Yeatholtz, John.
Garrison, Joseph.
Disert, Andrew.
Ricsickur, Frederich.
Glans, Jacob.
Blickensderfer, Benjamin.
Moir, Jacob.
Howistine, Peter.
Jedy, Jacob.
Moist, Stephen.
Wolf, George.
Seisholtz, George.
Arndt, John.
Syder, William.
Kuitz, Joseph.

ROLL OF CAPT. FREDERICK HOFF'S COMPANY.

A pay-roll of Capt. Frederick Hoff's company of Pennsylvania volunteers, attached to the Fifth battalion, Second detachment, Pennsylvania militia, under the command of Brigadier General Richard Crooks, in the service of the United States. Commencement of service, 2d October, 1812; expiration of service, 16th April, 1813, fifteen day volunteering inclusive.

Captain.

Hoff, Frederick, volunteered fifteen days.

Lieutenant.
Huston, Peter, volunteered fifteen days.

Ensign.
Saylor, Jacob, volunteered fifteen days.

Sergeants.
Cooper, William, volunteered fifteen days.
McGinnis, William, volunteered fifteen days.
Tantlinger, Henry, discharged at the expiration of six months.
Anawalt, Jacob, volunteered fifteen days.

Corporals.
Swinhart, Mathias, volunteered fifteen days.
Larkins, William, volunteered fifteen days.
Fields, Jacob, volunteered fifteen days.
Fox, John, volunteered fifteen days.

Drum-Major.
Lint, John, volunteered fifteen days.

Privates.
Gruber, William, volunteered fifteen days.
Kritzer, John, volunteered fifteen days.
Gribble, Levi, volunteered fifteen days.
Houpt, Valentine, volunteered fifteen days.
Graft, John, volunteered fifteen days.
Cover, Jacob, volunteered fifteen days.
Nelson, Arthur, volunteered fifteen days.
Saylor, Jacob, volunteered fifteen days.
Faith, Thomas, volunteered fifteen days.
Kennedy, George, volunteered fifteen days.
Jones, Samuel, volunteered fifteen days.
Serley, Jacob, discharged at expiration of six months.
Gray, Henry, volunteered fifteen days.
Gray, Samuel, discharged at expiration of six months.
Ganet, Rush, volunteered fifteen days.
Snyder, Adam, volunteered fifteen days.
Nedrow, Philip, volunteered fifteen days.
Nedrow, Peter, volunteered fifteen days.
Hipsher, Andrew, volunteered fifteen days.
Cramer, John, discharged at expiration of six months.
Sterner, John, volunteered fifteen days.
Lingafelter, Michael, volunteered fifteen days.
Houpt, John, volunteered fifteen days.
Pennel, James, volunteered fifteen days.
Stall, David, volunteered fifteen days.
Hartzel, Jacob, discharged at expiration of six months.

Johnston, Tobias, volunteered fifteen days.
Woods, George, volunteered fifteen days.
Whysong, John, volunteered fifteen days.
McNight, John, dec'd January 22, 1813, at Upper Sandusky.
Drury, John, volunteered fifteen days.
Bosh, Joseph, volunteered fifteen days.
Commins, John, volunteered fifteen days.
Howard, David, volunteered fifteen days.
Linn, Alexander, volunteered fifteen days.
Wright, Elija, volunteered fifteen days.
Henry, Peter, volunteered fifteen days.
Davis, John, volunteered fifteen days.

I do certify, on honor, that the within pay-roll is correct, and the remarks set opposite the men's names are accurate and just.

FREDERICK HOFF,
Captain.

ROLL OF CAPT. JACOB HOFFMAN'S COMPANY.

A list of non-commissioned officers and privates belonging to Capt. Hoffman's company of Rifle Rangers, who entered the service on the 14th of September, 1814, and were discharged on the 3d day of January, 1815.

Sergeants.

Supplee, Jesse.
Smith, Samuel.
Miller, Thomas.
Blanckly, George.
Ritter, John.

Corporals.

Furlong, John.
Ramage, Amer.
Saltsburg, Andrew.

Bugler.

Heston, Edward.

Privates.

Hall, John.
Der, John.
Gaul, Frederick.
Brown, James.
Lob, Benjamin.
Saunders, William.
Pearson, Josua.

Degorgen, Francis.
Fenton, Herbent.
Fisher, John.
Penegar, Benjamin.
Bickley, Henery.
Wright, David.
Rambo, David.
Carseley, Charles C.
Lewis, James.
Hughs, George.
Rose, William.
Lewis, Hugh.
Smith, Benjamin.
Rhudolph, Joseph.
McConeghy, John.
Gaskill, Jacob.
Bamfield, Thomas.
Kid, Alexander.
Butler, William.
Crawford, William.
Ray, James.
Hillyards, William.
Donohover, Phillip.
Williamson, Garret.
Sturges, John.
Sloan, Jacob.
Conner, James.
Roberts, Isaac.
Jones, Owen.
Logan, James.
Hanfell, William.
Turner, George.
Campbell, Joseph.
Rodgers, Rheuben.
Wiles, George.
Brame, Henery.
Delany, William.
McDermond, Joseph.
Shronk, Peter.
Kline, Henery.
Campbell, Jacob.
Donely, Charles.
Eaton, John W.
Richardson, Abraham.
Hansell, Joseph.
Hoffman, Jacob.

Davis, John.
Kuhn, Lewis.
Fitzpatrick, George.
Baker, Samuel.

We certify, on honor, that this muster-roll exhibits a true state of the First company of Riflemen, in the service of the United States, for the period therein mentioned, and that the remarks set opposite the names are accurate and just.

JACOB HOFFMAN,
Captain.
J. B. SUTHERLAND,
Lieutenant Colonel.

February 7, 1816.

ROLL OF CAPT. WILLIAM HOLDGATE'S COMPANY.

Muster-roll of Capt. Holdgate's company, in the Second regiment, Pennsylvania volunteers, —— infantry, in the service of the State of Pennsylvania for three months, from the 12th day August last, attached to the First brigade, Second division, Pennsylvania militia, at camp Marcus Hook, commanded by Brig. Gen. Samuel Smith, November 29, 1814.

Captain.

Holdgate, William.

Lieutenant.

Evans, Levi.

Ensign.

Suplee, John.

Sergeants.

Willson, David.
Davis, Thomas.
Ulrich, Jacob.
Gilinger, Henry.

Corporals.

Holdgate, Enos.
Louden, Andrew.
Tippen, George.
Sloan, William.

Musicians.

Haus, Matthias.
Miller, William.

Privates.

Reed, Andrew.
Cain, John.
Roberts, Roberts.
Willson, George.
Kirk, William.
Matson, Robert.
Megee, Henry.
Elliott, Robert.
Carver, Jesse.
Harrison, William.
Thompson, William.
Yates, Benjamin.
Forder, Samuel.
Mealy, John.
Smith, Benjamin.
Linenbough, Jacob.
Earnest, Henry.
McCool, Samuel.
Ramey, Jacob.
Ramey, Benjamin.
Hallman, Henry.
Jones, Job'b.
Brooke, Charles.
Evans, John.
Levering, Wickard.
Enoshs, Alexander.
Levering, Benjamin.
Matson, Jonathan.
McAnall, William.
Peterman, Jacob.
Childs, Jesse.
McMin, Joshua.
Fryer, William.
Carr, John.
Davis, Peter.
Davy, William.
Harrison, John.
Clemmans, Jonathan.
Cleaver, Jesse.
Graham, Thomas.
Whitby, James.
Lentz, Jacob.
Lewellyn, William.
Streper, George.
Martin, Joseph.

Engler, Jonathan.
Shade, Jacob.
Woolf, John.
Roberts, John.
Barr, Lloyd.

CAMP MARCUS HOOK, *November 29, 1814.*

I do hereby certify, upon honor, that the above is a just and true muster-roll of Capt. Holdgate's.

LOUIS BACHE,
Colonel Second Regiment, Pennsylvania Volunteers.

ROLL OF CAPT. JOHN HOLMES' COMPANY.

Pay-roll of a company of volunteers commanded by Capt. John Holmes, of the ——— regiment, performing a tour of duty under the command of Col. ———, who rendezvoused at York, under the general order of the Governor, dated August 26, 1814.

Captain.

Holmes, John.

First Lieutenant.

Downing, John.

Second Lieutenant.

Andrews, James.

Ensign.

Wilson, James.

Sergeants.

Andrews, Nathan.
Ramsey, Joseph.
Robb, John.
Mashbank, Robert.

Corporals.

Ross, James.
Robeson, William.
Wallace, Francis.
Simpson, Robert.

Privates.

Andrews, James.
Ankrim, Archibald.
Alison, Olover.
Alexander, Thomas.
Boon, John.
Brogan, Benjamin.

Cooper, John.
Carlisle, John.
Crosby, Nathaniel.
Corry, John.
Davis, James.
Fox, William.
Ford, Charles.
Laughlen, John.
Lemmon, William.
McNeal, William.
McGee, Patrick.
McLeny, William.
Murdaugh, Robert.
Nilson, John.
Pinkerton, Joseph.
Robison, John.
Riece, Jacob.
Ross, Isaac.
Rogers, William.
Robison, Robert.
Smith, Stewart.
Slack, John.
Turnor, Joseph.
Muse, Thomas.
Farren, James.
Steel, Samuel.
Quigg, James M.
Lemmon, Hector.
Abbitt, Dennis.
Poisel, Henry.
Chinece, John.
Phillips, John.
Ross, William.
Gye, Samuel.
Moore, John.
Dickey, Joseph.
Cowen, David.
Ewing, Alexander.
Lefeber, Samuel.
Wilson, William.
Fleshhalher, Martain.
Watt, David.
Byers, Henry.
Simpson, William.
David, William.
Russell, John.

Worthington, John.
Slegar, Nicholas.
Temanis, George.
Rogers, Ebenezer.
Caruth, Henry.

I certify the foregoing to be a correct roll of my company.

JOHN HOLMES,
Captain.

Test :

B. J. SHIPPEN,
Aid-de-camp to Major Gen. N. Watson.

ROLL OF CAPT. ABR'M HORN'S COMPANY.

CAMP DUPONT, *November 13, 1814.*

A true list of Capt. Abr^m Horn's company, of the Eighteenth section of Riflemen, commanded by Col. Thomas Humphrey.

Captain.

Horn, Abraham, Jr.

First Lieutenant.

Horn, John.

Second Lieutenant.

Dingler, John.

Ensign.

Biglow, Josiah.

Sergeants.

Horn, Melchior.
Moore, Samuel.
Shipe, Jacob.
Luckenbach, John.

Corporals.

Boas, Conrad.
Mixell, William.
Evans, William.
Lattig, George.

Music.

Thomson, William.
Horn, Samuel.
Horn, Joseph.

Privates.

Miller, Peter.
Deatz, Nicholas.
Miller, Hiram.
Doan, John.
Shank, Thomas.
Warmkesel, Frederick.
Hay, Charles.

Jackson, Francis.
Hartly, John.
Mesene, John.
Fortner, Ebenezer.
Shewell, George.
Bossler, John.
Roth, David.
Seiple, John.
Berlin, William.
Dill, Joseph.
Wilhelm, Henry.
Smith, Jacob.
Keisselbach, Aaron.
Cary, Charles.
Breidenbach, John P.
Mattes, Frederick C.
Stucker, Peter.
Grube, John.
Barthold, Alexander H.
Keider, Isaac.
Kelso, James.
Grube, Andrew.
Falkner, John.
Price, Hiram.
Shick, William.
Mettler, Eli.
Barnes, James.
Jackson, John L.
Kilpatrick, Jacob.
Hay, Andrew.
Genther, Charles.
Ward, Adam.
Dingler, George.
Shipe, John.

I do certify that the within list is a true statement, on honor, this 13th day of November, 1814.

J. HORN,
First Lieutenant.
THOMAS HUMPHREYS,
Colonel First R. P. V. R.

I do certify, on honor, that the company commanded by Capt. Ab'm Horn, Jr., is in the service of the United States, under the command of general commanding the Fourth military district.

THOMAS CADWALLADER,
Brig. Gen. Commanding Advance, L. B.

CAMP DUPONT, *November 26, 1814.*

ROLL OF CAPT. THEOPHILUS HUGHES' COMPANY.

Muster-roll of Captain Theophilus Hughes' Company, in the First regiment of Pennsylvania militia, under the command of Lieut. Col. Jeremiah Shappel, at York, Pennsylvania. In service from September 1, 1814, to March 1, 1815; from Schuylkill, Berks, Lancaster, and Bucks counties.

Captain.

Hughes, Theophilus.

First Lieutenant.

Lefever, John.

Second Lieutenant.

Dubelbis, Jacob.

Ensign.

Looser, Christopher.

Sergeants.

Patterson, James.
McClellan, James.
Fortes, Jacob K.

Corporals.

Dunlap, Isaac.
Buffington, William.

Privates.

Ahn, Jacob.
Apple, Jacob.
Blue, John.
Botuff, John.
Boyrele, Samuel.
Britain, Nathan.
Depper, Benjamin.
Dewald, Adam.
Doutt, John.
Dreher, John.
Dribbles, Danis.
Filler, Henry.
Frees, George Adam.
Genger, John.
Heffer, John.
Hendricks, Benjamin.
Hoch, Jonathan.
Hollenbach, Michael.
Honiseiger, George.
Hubner, George.

WAR OF 1812-14.

Kauffman, Benjamin.
Kimmel, John.
Kittner, David.
Kunfer, Peter.
Miller, Adam.
Morberger, John.
Nier, John.
Ream, Peter.
Rebsomer, Anthony.
Rishel, Denneb.
Rishel, Jones.
Rishel, Leonard.
Robonold, Adam.
Sherry, John.
Shew, David.
Shole, Jacob.
Star, Peter.
Stears, Jacob.
Sterner, Daniel.
Sterner, John.
Swenk, John.
Swesh, Peter.
Umbehacker, Ab^m.
Weaver, John.
Weaver, Peter.
Wooding, John.
Yeager, Samuel.
Zerbe, Adam.

ROLL OF CAPT. JACOB HUMMEL'S COMPANY.

CAMP MARCUS HOOK, *October 31, 1814.*

Pay-roll of the company of infantry under the command of Capt. Jacob Hummel, attached and organized by Adj. Gen. ———, of the ——— brigade Pennsylvania militia, in the service of the United States, commanded by Lieut. Col. George Weirick.

Captain.

Hummel, Jacob.

Lieutenant.

Brady, Walter.

Ensigns.

Swartz, Francis B.

Sergeants.

Balty, Stephen.
Eisly, John.
Hammer, John.
James, John S.

Corporals.

Jordan, John B.
Petre, John.
Lisering, Jacob.
Martin, James.

Privates.

Burn, Henry.
Burn, John.
App, John.
Hull, Isaac.
Houzal, John.
Redlien, John.
Newcommer, Abr^m.
Weaver, Frederick.
Morgan, Joseph.
Morgan, James.
Masteller, John.
Haupt, Henry.
Mettler, William.
Overdurf, Peter.
Straw, Jonathan.
London, Zacaria.
Sterner, Henry.
Zeliff, David.
Hoyd, Logwood G.
Ringler, Daniel.
Hoff, Benjamin.
Espy, George.
Buyers, John.
Renn, John.
Mirely, Balser.
Hedrick, Jacob.
Woollican, William.
Corner, Daniel.
Farely, George.
Buchner, John.
McCluchen, Joseph.
Barnhart, John.
Willet, William.
Willet, Samuel.
Woodruff, Elias.

Barr, William.
Roadarmel, John.
Applegate, John.
Bertler, Henry.
Caruthers, Andrew.
Armstrong, John.
Furman, Jonathan.
Rinehard, Frederick.
Garchard, Daniel.
Crutchly, John.
Mahany, William.
Delong, Daniel.
Wagoner, Christian.
Warren, James.
More, David.
Mash, Griggs.
Campbell, John.

I do certify, on honor, that this pay-roll exhibits a true statement of the company under my command, from Northumberland county, atrached to the regiment under the command of Lieut. Col. George Weirick, Pennsylvania militia.

JACOB HUMMEL,
Captain.

I believe the above to be a correct pay-roll.

GEO. WEIRICK,
Lieutenant Colonel Commanding.

I certify that the company commanded by Capt. Jacob Hummel is now in the service of the United States, orders of the general commandant Fourth military district.

THOS. P. ROGERS,
Brigade Major.

ROLL OF CAPT. JOHN HURST'S COMPANY.

A correct muster-roll of Capt. John Hurst's company of Montgomery Rifle Greens, stationed at Camp Boileau.

Captain.

Hurst, John.

First Lieutenant.

Zilling, M.

Second Lieutenant.

Hoover, P.

Ensign.

Beam, Peter.

Quarter-Master.

Weber, Jacob.

Sergeants.

Brown, H. R.
Smith, H.
Wanner, William.
Beam, Enos.

Corporals.

Deweese, Thomas.
Deweese, Jacob.
Spare, John.
Homsher, Jacob.

Bugler.

Thomas, David.

Privates.

Glen, James.
Heller, Daniel.
Deets, Samuel.
Wanner, John.
Deerzy, Jacob.
Thompson, James.
Triple, John.
Seybolt, John.
Owen, John.
Miller, Enoch.
Stilwell, James.
Arney, Michael.
Boure, Mark.
Snyder, John.
Hurst, William.
Wentz, Benjamin.
Ingham, Robert.
Davis, John.
Weber, Jesse.
McKiney, James.
Weber, Jacob, Warcester.
Johnson, Benjamin.
Stong, Ab^m.

We do certify, on honor, that the within roll exhibits a true state of company commanded by Capt. John Hurst, and that the remarks set opposite the men's names are accurate and just.

JOHN HURST,
Captain.
THOMAS HUMPHREY.
Colonel First R. P. V. R.

CAMP DUPONT, *November 24, 1814.*

I do certify, on honor, that the company commanded by Captain John Hurst is in the service of the United States, under the command of the general commanding the Fourth military district.

THOMAS CADWALADER,
Brig. Gen. Commanding Advance, L. B.

CAMP DUPONT, *November 26, 1814.*

ROLL OF CAPT. JOHN HUSTON, Jr.'s, COMPANY.

Muster-roll of the corps of Volunteer Riflemen, commanded by Capt. John Huston, Jr., in the regiment of riflemen under the command of Lieut. Col. Sutherland, attached to the Second brigade, First division, Pennsylvania militia, in the service of the United States, from September 13, 1814, to January 3, 1815.

Captain.

Huston, John, Jr.

Lieutenants.

Jacobs, Henry.
Campbell, Samuel.

Ensign.

Dickinson, Joseph.

Sergeants.

Huston, William.
Fisher, Jacob, died the 10th December, 1814.
Holgate, Reuben.
Nell, Conrad.

Quarter-Master Sergeant.

Dutweiler, Frederick.

Corporals.

Fustin, Abraham.
Hinkle, Samuel.
Roop, John.
Nice, Charles, Jr.

Privates.

Amaigh, Peter.
Anderson, Francis.
Bechtel, Jacob.
Bechtel, George.
Bicking, John.
Bicking, Joseph.
Burnhelter, Jacob
Book, Henry.
Dutz, Henry.

Dehaven, John.
Donoho, James.
Deatz, Henry.
Drace, Michael.
Freas, George.
Freed, Jacob.
Guyer, Benjamin.
Goodman, John.
Holgate, Abraham.
Henry, Jacob.
Holgate, Griffith.
Hein, Abraham.
Jacoby, Martin.
Kirper, John.
Kibler, Samuel.
Knouse, Charles.
Kupp, Frederick.
Lightcap, John.
Lightcap, Michael.
Livezey, Charles.
Mould, Francis.
Nace, John.
Nicholas, Henry.
Ryland, Samuel.
Rynick, John.
Smith, Jacob.
Sign, Simon.
Sausimer, or Sassaman, Peter.
Sign, John.
Sign, George.
Streper, William.
Streper, William, Jr.
Sausimer, or Sassaman, John.
Stallman, John.
Shaffer, Charles.
Saunders, Adam.
Shingle, George.
Smith, John.
Saunders, Isaac.
Sausimer, or Sassaman, Jacob.
Shaffer, Andrew.
Tyson, Philip.
Tarter, Samuel.
Toland, William.
Unruh, John.
Wampole, George.

Wyndolph, Jacob.
Fleming, Frederick.

We certify, on honor, that this muster-roll exhibits a true state of the corps of Volunteer Riflemen, of the Second brigade, First division, Pennsylvania militia, for the period therein mentioned, and that the remarks set opposite the names of the men are accurate and just, the 13th being first altered to the 12th of September.

JOHN HUSTON, Jr.,
Captain.
J. B. SUTHERLAND,
Lieutenant Colonel.

ROLL OF CAPT. THOMAS HUSTON'S COMPANY.

Muster-roll of Capt. Thomas Huston's company, in the Second regiment, Second brigade, Pennsylvania militia, under the command of Lieut. Col. John Lutz, at York. In service from September 1, 1814, to March 1, 1815, from Lancaster county.

Captain.

Huston, Thomas.

Lieutenant.

Karr, David.

Ensign.

Shimp, John.

Sergeants.

Crawley, William.
Hawey, John.
Knopsker, Henry.
Maxvill, Robert.

Corporals.

Applegate, Annanias.
Oneal, Daniel.
Trimble, John.
Todd, Joshua.

Privates.

Adams, William.
Alford, Frederick.
Atwood, Cornelius.
Baker, John.
Barns, Kilion.

Beiler, Philip.
Bell, John.
Berryhill, Stephen.
Bird, John.
Blowers, Henry.
Camble, Moses.
Clark, Andrew.
Clipper, Nicholas.
Cross, William.
Dixon, Patrick.
Dunwoody, John.
Eshelman, Benjamin.
Feltiberger, Jacob.
Fritzlin, Andrew.
Garman, John.
Gohen, John.
Golloher, James.
Hacket, James.
Hamler, Alexander.
Hays, William.
Hide, Nicholas.
Hollinger, Christopher.
Hubley, Henry.
Huston, John.
Jameson, Elias.
Johnson, Robert.
Killgore, William.
Kock, John.
Kopp, John.
Kurtz, Israel.
Leighty, Jacob.
Mantell, Jacob.
McClellan, John.
McGloughlin, Francis.
McGrady, Samuel.
Meldrem, James.
Miller, Abraham.
Miller, Lawrence.
Miller, Martin.
Morgan, Jesse.
Morgan, John.
Mosey, John.
Nagley, Leonard.
O'Donal, Charles.
Otto, John.
Oxer, George.

Peterson, Mark.
Roadvron, Jacob.
Robeson, Anthony.
Robeson, Theadoris.
Sanders, Daniel.
Shank, Robert.
Shiaffer, Jacob.
Shitz, Matthias.
Smith, Adam.
Thatcher, Amos.
Vaughan, John.
Welshhons, Reuben.
White, John.
Wilen, Samuel.
Williams, John.
Wilson, James.
Yeider, John.
Young, John.

ROLL OF CAPT. THOMAS S. JACK'S COMPANY.

Pay-roll of a company of infantry commanded by Capt. Thomas S. Jack, in service of the United States, from the 2d October, 1812, until the 2d April, 1813, ———— brigade, Pennsylvania militia, commanded by Brig. Gen. Crooks.

Captain.

Jack, Thomas S., volunteered for fifteen days.

Lieutenant.

Burgan, James, volunteered for fifteen days.

Ensign.

Hutchison, Daniel.

Sergeants.

Sample, John.
David, Willson.
Lammand, Michael.
Doily, John.

Corporals.

Howard, Samuel.
McClellan, James, volunteered fifteen days.
Weandt, Daniel.
Hemphill, Samuel.

Privates.

Bleeks, John.
Beamont, Jessey.
Beaty, James.
Carnes, Peter.
Cawan, George.
Hill, Joseph.
Hill, Stephen.
Howard, John.
Johnston, John.
McClelan, William.
Neely, David.
Robertson, Thomas.
Sheppard, Paoli.
Shettler, George.
Warner, Jacob.
Varner, John.
Hunter, William.
Grass, Jacob.
Lockwood, Abraham.
Stone, William.
Ray, John.
Harker, Daniel.
Cole, Isaac.
Porter, Daniel.
Shafer, Henry.
Tailour, Henry.
Greer, Alexander.
Malener, John, discharged.
Alexander, Joseph.
McCleur, William.
Comgleton, John.
Hall, John.
Browan, Robert.
Workman, John.
Brantover, David.
Horklin, John.
Hile, James.
Haske, Thomas.
Horner, John.

ROLL OF CAPT. NATHAN JAMES' COMPANY.

List of non-commissioned officers and privates, militia company, Capt. Nathan James, ——— regiment, as a part of the First brigade, Second division, Pennsylvania militia, in the service of the United States, under the command of Andrew Gilkyson, lieutenant colonel, October 30, 1814.

Sergeants.

James, Isaac.
Jones, Griffith.
James, Obia, or Abia.
Riale, Davis.
Miller, William.

Corporals.

Evens, Joel.
Scott, William.
James, John.

Privates.

Vanemaker, Nicholas.
Armstrong, Andrew.
Ashton, John.
Artman, Samuel.
Black, Jacob.
Barton, Silas.
Bartle, Christopher.
Black, Henry.
Callender, Benjamin.
Carman, William.
Cathers, William.
Cautton, Aaron.
Craimer, Jacob.
Craimer, Abraham.
Crager, Samuel.
Carr, Simeon.
Dennison, Samuel.
Elliot, John.
Elliot, Thomas.
Eschout, Michael.
Fulton, Benjamin.
Flack, Henry.
Good, Simon.
Good, Thomas.
Gadis, Alexander.

Gadis, Henry.
Gadis, William.
Gerris, John.
Gordon, Joseph.
Grant, John.
Henry, Frezer.
Hubbs, Jesse.
Harrar, Jesse.
Horn, John.
Hunsman, Jonathan.
Haynin, Samuel.
Harris, Thomas.
Hartzel, John.
James, William.
James, James.
James, I. W.
James, Thomas.
James, John.
James, John C.
James, Abner.
Jobson, Jonas.
Joyce, Thomas.
Kellso, Henry.
Louder, Moses.
Leer, Courtland.
Leaver, George.
Matthew, Benjamin.
Mitchener, Joseph.
McKaffer, Charles.
Mitchell, William.
McConnel, W.
Nash, Joseph.
Nailer, David.
Osbach, John.
Pettit, Henry.
Pennington, James.
Poke, John.
Perringer, Henry.
Price, Charles.
Rockafelser, Sohn.
Roberts, Edward.
Riale, Richard.
Roberts, Thomas.
Rider, Garrit.
Reppard, Jacob.
Swagger, James.

Swagger, Philip.
Smith, John.
Scheffer, William.
Stockton, John.
Starkey, James.
Solomon, John.
Scot, John.
Stout, John.
Syple, David.
Simmerman, John.
Solid, or Solady, John.
Tunis, or Tennis, William.
Thomas, Elias.
Thomas, Mathew.
Vanemaker, P.
Vanhorn, Robert.
Wirmer, Dennis.
Wile, Obadiah.
Young, Isaac.
Aaron, Moses.
Johnston, David.
Shafer, Simon.

ROLL OF CAPT. MATHEW JOHNSON'S COMPANY.

Pay-roll of a company of Pennsylvania militia commanded by Capt. Mathew Johnson, in the Fifth battalion, Second detachment, Pennsylvania militia, commanded by Brig. Gen. Richard Crooks.

Captain.
Johnson, Mathew.

Lieutenant.
Rowan, Charles.

Ensign.
Harvey, John.

Sergeants.
Caughey, James.
Witbrow, James.
Wolf, Abraham.

Corporals.
McElheney, James.
Knight, Daniel.
Heykenall, John.
Rysinger, Daniel.

Privates.

Small, Henry.
Bridgeman, John.
Lezien, Isaac.
McQuistin, David.
Mane, Soloman.
Steel, James.
Latta, John.
Conkle, Henry.
Showalter, John.
Scott, David.
Weatherspoon, John.
Thermburgh, Thomas.
McKain, Robert L.
McKain, Daniel.
Hanna, William.
McNuly, Robert.
Moon, James.
Clark, John.
Henry, David.
Hammon, William.
McCurdy, Alexander.
Wiley, James.
McConnehey, Edward.
Lamis, Isaac.
Campble, Henry.
Grim, Conrod.
Bridgman, Frederic.
McCurdy, Samuel
Thomson, James.
Cooley, Joseph.
Park, David.
Jamison, Daniel.
Smith, William, volunteered for fifteen days.
Clark, Charles.
Diver, John.
Thomson, Samuel.
Hall, James.
Wolf, Isaac.
Yoho, Jacob.
Polinger, Simon.
Kelly, Samuel.
Blain, Thomas.
Ford, George, discharged December 31, 1813.
Smally, Daniel, discharged December 31, 1813.
Shields, William, enlisted March 24, 1813.

Doherty, Edward, discharged December 16, 1812.
Thomson, John.

I do certify, on honor, that this pay-roll exhibits a true state of Capt. Mathew Johnson's company, of the Fifth battalion, of Pennsylvania militia, and the remarks as they stand stated are accurate and just.

MATHEW JOHNSON,
Captain.

ROLL OF CAPT. WILLIAM JOHNSON'S COMPANY.

Receipt-roll of a company of infantry commanded by Capt. William Johnson, of the First regiment of Gen'l Crooks' brigade, Pennsylvania militia.

Captain.

Johnson, William.

Sergeants.

Huey, William M.
Pogue, Samuel.
Dunlavy, Patrick.
Wagstaff, James.

Corporals.

Bell, George.
Burns, Samuel.
Cook, John.
Daughty, Thomas.

Privates.

Bell, George.
Cauch, Philip.
Coulter, Jesse.
Carlisle, Samuel.
Criswell, Robert.
Cline, Jacob.
Chism, or Chisolm, Alexander.
Cooper, Hugh.
Cavit, John.
Casey, William F.
Davis, James.
Dickerson, Zadock.
Eastep, Jacob.
Fletcher, Joseph.
Ferguson, William.
Grinder, or Greiner, Henry.

Gamble, John.
Howel, or Howe, Stephen.
Henry, William.
Hermon, Nathan.
Kip, John.
Logan, John.
Leech, Frederick.
Lockhart, William M.
McMillin, Mathew.
Morrison, William.
Mitchell, Benjamin.
Mitchell, Robert.
Mulvin, Jacob.
Mash, or Marsh, Gravenor.
McNatten, Daniel.
Nickle, James.
Phillips, John.
Ralley, George.
Richey, John.
Smith, Samuel.
South, Joseph.
Springer, Daniel.
Simpson, John.
Wheeler, Charles.
Walker, Andrew.

ROLL OF CAPT. JONATHAN JONES' COMPANY.

Muster-roll of Capt. Jonathan Jones' company, in the First regiment, Pennsylvania militia, under the command of Col. Jeremiah Shappell, at York, Pennsylvania. In service from September 1, 1814, to December 4, 1814, from Berks county.

Captain.

Jones, Jonathan.

Lieutenant.

Morrow, Samuel.

Ensign.

Grove, Simon.

Sergeants.

Jones, Nicholas.
Church, Thomas M.
Baish, Lewis.
Jones, Ezekiel.

Corporals.

Bunn, John.
Bush, Peter.
Hesser, Abram.
Shuridon, William.

Privates.

Aikins, William.
Arp, John.
Babb, David.
Barkley, Alexander.
Barrick, John.
Bayd, John.
Bell, Charles.
Bell, Isaiah.
Borts, David.
Bost, Peter.
Boyer, David.
Briton, Emanuel.
Bunn, Henry.
Carson, John.
Carver, Nicholas.
Cunningham, Jeremiah.
Deturk, Daniel.
Deturk, Samuel.
Eppehamer, Samuel.
Fair, Daniel.
Fees, Abram.
Filman, Philip.
Fox, David.
Fryberger, George.
George, Matthew.
Goodman, Daniel.
Goodman, George.
Gwin, George.
Hamilton, William.
Harpster, Henry.
Heater, Jacob.
Heckman, John.
Hill, Jacob.
Hollebauch, Henry.
Hosler, John.
Jackson, Jacob.
Jackson, William.
Jacobs, James.
Krider, John.
Kutz, Benjamin.

Lapsley, Samuel.
Lawer, John.
Lees, Jacob.
Long, John.
McBride, David.
McCrackin, John.
Miller, Adam.
Miller, Christian.
Mills, Jacob.
Morgan, John.
Null, George.
Null, John.
Ox, Frederick.
Putz, Jeremiah.
Rhoads, Samuel.
Rice, William.
Robison, George.
Row, Jacob.
Russell, Joseph.
Salter, John.
Sloppick, Philip.
Smuck, Samuel.
Spiecie, John.
Stubblebine, Daniel.
Strunk, John.
Surgison, Michael.
Tomlinson, Nathan.
Wall, John.
Weicle, George.
Willhower, Peter.
Worts, George.
Zimmerman, George.

ROLL OF CAPT. JOHN JUNKIN'S COMPANY.

Pay-roll of a company of volunteer Riflemen, commanded by Capt. John Junkin, from the One Hundred and Thirty-fourth regiment, Pennsylvania militia, now in the Fifth battalion of the Second detachment, commanded by Major David Nelson, and in the service of the United States from 2d day of October, 1812, to the 17th day of April, 1813, inclusive.

Captain.

Junkin, John.

WAR OF 1812–14.

Lieutenant.
Oliver, Walter, discharged April 2.

Ensign.
McCune, Samuel B., discharged April 2.

Sergeants.
Clark, Andrew.
Rambo, James.
Rambo, Thomas.
Forkes, Jacob.

Corporals.
Fettiberger, John.
Moore, John.
Kurtz, Frederick.
Branden, Thomas.

Fifer.
Caldwell, James K.

Drummer.
Phinery, Samuel, left the troops a few days after he arrived at Pittsburgh.

Privates.
Rambo, Peter, discharged April 2.
Camble, Josias, discharged January, 1813.
Alexander, John, discharged April 2.
McCord, James.
Simpson, Matthew, discharged April 2.
McCune, Thomas, discharged April 2.
Black, Henry, discharged April 2.
McDonald, John, discharged April 2.
Junkin, Joseph, discharged April 2.
Scott, Francis.
Bowman, Samuel, discharged April 2.
Johnston, John, discharged April 2.
Jordon, Henry, discharged April 2.
Black, Joseph, discharged April 2.
Glenn, James, discharged April 2.
Zahnizor, William, discharged April 2.
Clark, John, discharged January, 1813.
Helverny, Frederick, discharged April 2.
Righel, John.
Moore, Joseph S., discharged April 2.
Pevine, John, discharged April 2.
Clark, Abraham, discharged April 2.

Cannon, Thomas, discharged April 2.
Tait, Washington, discharged January 9, 1813.
Barnhill, David, discharged January 9, 1813.
Troxel, Abraham.
McClusky, James, discharged April 2.
Osburn, Jacob, discharged April 2.
Taylor, Aaron, discharged April 2.
Coyl, Alexander, discharged April 2.
Moore, Samuel.
Gordon, William, discharged April 2.
Gordon. Thomas, discharged April 2.
Thorn, Joseph, discharged April 2.
Gibson, Robert, discharged April 2.
Cook, Solomon, discharged April 2.
Hawthorn, John.
McDonald, John, discharged April 2.
Lowry, John.
Coyle, John, discharged April 2.
Lucus, Charles.
Rose, Chapman.
Williams, Charles.
Rose, Andrew, discharged April 2.
Hill, William, discharged April 2.
Carmical, John, discharged April 2.
McCoy, John.
McCracken, James, discharged January 9, 1813.
Deneston, Alexander.
Simpson, Thomas, discharged April 2.
McDowel, Alen, discharged April 2.
Sheriff, William, discharged April 2.
Mourer, Daniel, discharged April 2.
Senkey, Ezekiel, discharged April 2.
McCurdy, David, discharged early.
Harper, Joseph, discharged April 2.
Hawthorn, Samuel, discharged early.

I certify, on honor, that this pay-roll is correct and just.

WALTER OLIVER,
Lieutenant Commanding.

ROLL OF CAPT. DANIEL D. B. KEIM'S COMPANY.

Muster-roll of the Washington Blues, Berks county, under the command of Capt. Daniel D. B. Keim, and attached to the First regiment of Pennsylvania volunteers, and now in the actual service of the United States.

Captain.

Keim, Daniel D. B.

First Lieutenant.

Betz, Henry.

Second Lieutenant.

Good, Jon. I.

Ensign.

Baird, Samuel, Jr.

Sergeants.

Biddle, James D.
Connor, Samuel.
Maidera, David.
Hobbert, N. P.

Corporals.

Pearce, Henry W.
Roseberry, John W.
Bruckeman, Charles.
Thomas, John R.

Drummer.

Shöner, Henry.

Fifer.

Drenkle, George.

Privates.

Geise, Gerehart.
Hobbert, Robert E.
Laverty, Robert.
Schoenbers, John.
Brooke, William.
Rahn, Jacob.
Potts, David.
Ross, Robert M.
Potts, Thomas.
Klineginna, William.
Bird, William.
Potts, Samuel.
Snyder, George.

Leitz, James.
Metzger, John.
Skeen, William.
Nice, William.
Stichler, Lewis.
Kerchner, Daniel.
Brobst, Christian.
Eckert, James B.
Hahn, George.
Bowen, William.
Brooke, Matthew M.
Boone, Richard.
Koll, John.
Shaffer, Samuel.
Showers, William.
Baird, Thomas.
May, Robert.
Barde, Samuel.
Lindsly, Timothy.
Bannon, John.
Pott, Benjamin.
Seitzinger, Jacob.
Jones, David.
Thompson, William.
Keyser, Henry.
Baide, John.
Wilson, Thomas.
Burhar, Charles.
Stroud, Jonathan.
Yeager, Peter.
Bright, John.
Kepple, Thomas.
Wile, George.
Groul, Samuel.
Green, Joseph.
Seybert, Abraham.
Ely, Elisha.
Neidley, John C.
Smith, Thomas B.
Hubley, James B.
Hanley, John.
Reafsnyder, Thomas.
Mourer, Jacob.
Bell, Adam.
Kendall, Joseph.
Ruth, John.

I do certify the above muster-roll to be a true and complete list of the officers and privates composing the Washington Blues of Berks county, under my command, and in actual service since the 12th of September, 1814.

DANIEL D. B. KEIM,
Captain Washington Blues.

I do hereby certify that the company of Washington Blues, commanded by Captain Keim, is now in the service of the United States, attached to my brigade.

THOS. CADWALADER,
Brigadier General Commanding Advance Light Brigade.
CAMP DUPONT, *October 20, 1814.*

ROLL OF CAPT. PHINEAS KELLEYS' COMPANY.

Pay-roll of Capt. Kelley's company, Bucks county militia, First brigade, Second division.

Sergeants.

Opdicke, Elijah.
Smith, Jonathan.
Rice, Lewis.
Overholt, Jacob.

Corporals.

Addis, William.
Price, John.
Kamp, Adam.
Williams, Joseph.

Privates.

Atkinson, Archibald.
Blakesly, Joel.
Brinton, Thomas.
Bennett, Isaac.
Beatz, Joseph.
Bishop, George.
Cobble, John.
Collins, Robert.
Cooper, William.
Chester, Joel.
Crow, William.
Christman, John.
Coulter, Isaac.
Crow, Israel.
Derr, Michael.
Donehower, Abraham.

Deemer, Michael.
Ettinger, Benjamin.
Eagle, John.
Elwill, William.
Fryling, Jacob.
Flemings, Charles.
Force, Jonathan.
Fonk, Jacob.
Fluck, Peter.
Foolmer, Yost.
Guile, Philip.
Greeow, Henry.
Hogeland, Samuel.
Hill, George.
Hoffman, Philip.
Hibbs, Ely.
Huffman, John.
Hough, John.
Johnston, James.
Jackson, David.
Kinsey, Joseph.
Kelly, Abel.
Kennedy, James.
Kesler, John.
Lovitt, Joseph.
Lazaleer, Britton.
Loyd, William.
Lewis, Henry.
Leer, George.
Long, Peter.
Landis, Joseph.
Lewis, John.
Moon, John.
McCarty, Thomas.
McKinster, James.
Moyers, George.
Overpeck, Conrad.
Overpeck, Henry.
Ott, John.
Peck, Philip.
Peck, Henry.
Phylor, Jacob.
Powers, William.
Raub, Peter.
Rasoner, John.
Raub, Jacob.

Shawger, Adam.
Shawger, William.
Shives, J. W.
Shoemaker, John.
Smith, Joseph.
Shevir, Henry.
Snare, Stephen.
Snorell, Jacob.
Satinger, Joseph.
Shettz, Conrad.
Shettz, Michael.
Shauk, Jacob.
Sharp, Elijah.
Tranger, George.
Tranger, Jacob.
Trumbower, J.
Townsen, Job.
Tranger, Christian.
Titemer, George.
Vandegrift, Jacob.
Wilcocks, Ambrose.
Walter, Nicholas.
Wright, Daniel.
Williams, David.
Allen, Joseph.
Heddich, Henry.
Jacoby, Benjamin.
Carty, John.
Johnston, Robert.
Marshall, Martin.
Beans, John.
Barns, John.
Ogany, John.
Mahan, Cornelius.
Roberts, Stacy.
Reason, Samuel.
Hilliput, Frederick.

We do certify, on honor, that the within muster-roll exhibits a true state of the company, and that the remarks set opposite the men's names are correct and just.

EMANUEL SOLLADAY.
Lieutenant.
ISAAC GRIFFITH,
Major.

CAMP MARCUS HOOK, *October 28, 1812.*

I certify, on honor, that the company commanded by Capt. Kelly, is in the service of the United States, under command of the general commanding the Fourth Military district.

SAM'L SMITH,
Brigadier General.

CAMP MARCUS HOOK, *October 28, 1814.*

ROLL OF CAPT. RICHARD KNIGHT'S COMPANY.

Muster-roll of Capt. Richard Knight's company, in the First regiment, First brigade, Pennsylvania militia, under command of Col. Maxwell Kennedy, at York, Pennsylvania, September 5, 1814. In service from September 1, 1814, to March 5, 1815, from Dauphin county.

Captain.

Knight, Richard.

Lieutenant.

Kline, Philip.

Ensign.

Roberts, George.

Sergeants.

McConnel, Joshua.
Carson, John.
Balsby, Jonathan.
Duncan, William.

Corporals.

Wrightmoyer, Henry.
Swartz, Peter.
Books, John.
Joseu, John.

Privates.

Baker, Jacob.
Blasser, John.
Blasser, Peter.
Bowman, Daniel.
Britz, Ludwick.
Calhoon, William.
Cassel, Jacob.
Colhoon, James.
Cralh, Matthias.

Duncan, James.
Ely, John.
Fisher, Jacob.
Fry, George.
Garverick, John.
Gaul, Philip.
Hains, Sampson.
Harruff, Andrew.
Henning, Samuel.
Hommon, Andrew.
Hommon, George.
Isenhelder, Michael.
Knop, Christian.
Leas, Martin.
Lyter, Joseph.
McIntire, Samuel.
Miller, George.
Miller, Henry,
Miller, Henry.
Miller, William.
Millison, William.
Mooney, Peter.
Moyers, George.
Moyers, Henry.
Orks, William.
Ort, William.
Patrick, William.
Reel, Peter.
Road, John.
Shell, Daniel.
Shroy, Jacob.
Smith, William.
Soul, Abraham.
Soul, Samuel.
Stair, Michael.
Swartz, Abraham.
Updegrove, Richard.
Uriah, George.
Waid, Hugh.
Weaver, David.
Wetzel, Samuel.
Wilson, John.
Wise, George.
Wolf, Jacob.
Yungst, John.
Zimmerman, John.

ROLL OF CAPT. MICHAEL KNORR'S COMPANY.

Pay-roll of Capt. Michael Knorr's company of infantry, of Second brigade, First division, Pennsylvania militia, in the service of the United States, under command of Col. John Thompson, October 17, 1814.

Captain.

Knorr, Michael.

Lieutenants.

Bamford, Enoch.
Brous, Nicholas.

Ensign.

Rimel, John, Jr.

Sergeants.

Gaudin, Charles.
Murcilliott, Peter V.
Bramin, John.
Hilt, Moses.

Corporals.

Faunce, Jacob.
Wilson, Rudolph P.
Hendricks, William.
Rogers, Cormick.

Privates.

Dyer, Charles.
Dungan, John.
Krewson, Joshua.
Folkrod, Philip.
Hill, Benjamin L.
Phillips, William.
Krewson, Isaac.
Markly, Charles.
Roads, Jonathan.
Davis, Jacob.
Snyder, Benjamin.
Scattergood, William.
Heartly, Thomas.
Brown, Clark.
Achuff, Joseph.
McVaugh, Charles.
McDonald, William.
Smith, Benjamin.

Mathias, Joseph F.
White, Joseph.
Strickland, John.
Krewson, Jacob.
Hulings, Thomas.
Richards, John.
Boileau, Jeremiah.
Moore, Henry.
Smith, Frederick.
Judge, Patrick.
Reece, Ezekiel.
Crispen. Moses.
Booth, William.
Simons, Henry.
Bryan, Francis.
Showers, Peter.
Strickland, Abraham.
Hearse, Peter.
Matchner, Joseph.
Foy, John.
Vanhorn, George.
Woodrough, Chancy.
Philpot, Thomas, Jr.
Vanhorn, Derrick.
Stilwell, Isaac.
Cowher, Jacob.
Hilt, Jr., John.
Jentry, Thomas.
Whitesall, Jacob.
Moore, James.
Lowry, William.
Dungan, William.
Keyler, John.
Dougherty, Daniel.
Hoover, Thomas.
Butcher, Joseph.
Ellis, James.
Roberts, Jesse.
Strouse, Jacob.
Christian, Casper.
Rogers, William.
Prentice, Caleb.
Lingerman, Conrad.
Rikle, John.
Billings, John.
Welser, Godfrey.

Pugh, Henry.
Ellis, George.
Boileau, Nathan.
Achuff, John.
Stroup, John.
Roads, John.

I do certify, on honor, that the within roll exhibits a true state of the company under command of Capt. Michael Knorr, First division, Second brigade, Pennsylvania militia, under command of Col. John Thompson.

MICHAEL KNORR,
Captain.

CAMP MARCUS HOOK, *October 17, 1814.*

JOHN THOMPSON,
Colonel.

I do certify that the company commanded by Capt. Michael Knorr is in the service of the United States, under orders of the general commanding Fourth military district.

THOMAS SNYDER,
Brigadier General Commanding.

CAMP MARCUS HOOK, *October 17, 1814.*

ROLL OF CAPT. HARTMAN KUHN'S COMPANY.

Muster-roll of the company of Infantry, called the State Fencibles, under the command of Capt. Hartman Kuhn, in the regiment of Pennsylvania volunteers, in the service of the United States, commanded by Col. Clement C. Biddle, from November 21, 1814, when last mustered, to January 4, 1815.

Captain.

Kuhn, Hartman, August 26, 1814.

First Lieutenant.

Williams, Henry J., August 26, 1814; draws no rations since December 1, 1814.

Second Lieutenant.

Norris, Isaac W., August 26, 1814.

Third Lieutenant.

Canonge, Peter A., August 26, 1814.

Ensign.

McCall, John C., August 26, 1814; draws no rations since December 1, 1814.

Sergeants.

Ker, William, August 26, 1814.
Sonntag, William L., Jr., August 26, 1814; absent with leave since December 17, 1814.
McKean, Joseph K., August 26, 1814.
Young, William, August 26, 1814.
Phillips, William, August 26, 1814; absent with leave since October 18, 1814.

Corporals.

Rockhill, Thomas C., August 26, 1814.
Coxe, Edward D., August 26, 1814.
Fontanges, Peter F., August 26, 1814.
Willing, Thomas, Jr., August 26, 1814.
Patton, John C., August 26, 1814.
Clement, Joseph T., August 26, 1814.

Musician.

Brode, Joseph D., August 28, 1814.

Privates.

Adams, Jacob, August 26, 1814.
Allward, Samuel H., August 26, 1814.
Alman, Joseph, August 26, 1814.
Altemus, Thomas, August 26, 1814.
Baker, Nathan, August 26, 1814.
Barclay, James J., August 26, 1814.
Barclay, Samuel, August 26, 1814; absent with leave since October 27, 1814.
Barnhill, Robert C., August 26, 1814; re-joined on the 12th December, 1814.
Bertrand, Peter, September 18, 1814.
Bickley, Jacob, August 26, 1814.
Billington, William, September 1, 1814.
Boggs, James, September 1, 1814.
Bond, Thomas, August 26, 1814.
Boyd, William, August 26, 1814.
Breban, John, August 26, 1814.
Brittin, Charles, August 26, 1814.
Brown, James, August 26, 1814.
Budd, John B., September 18, 1814; absent with leave since December 26, 1814.
Carey, Henry C., August 26, 1814; absent with leave since December 12, 1814.
Charles, Henry, August 26, 1814.
Choupeau, Peter, August 26, 1814.
Christine, John, August 26, 1814.

Clark, Henry, August 27, 1814.
Cole, James H., August 26, 1814.
Collin, George, September 2, 1814.
Connelly, John M., September 18, 1814.
Coxe, Charles S., August 26, 1814.
Curry, John, August 26, 1814.
Davis, George, August 26, 1814.
Droz, Philibert, August 26, 1814; sick.
Ducker, John, August 26, 1814.
Dunlap, Thomas, August 26, 1814.
Fox, Edward, Jr., August 29, 1814.
Frick, Jacob, August 26, 1814.
Friend, Philip II., August 26, 1814.
Friend, William, August 26, 1814.
Gardiner, Baldwin, August 26, 1814; sick.
Goodwin, Edward, August 26, 1814.
Goodwin, Thomas F., August 26, 1814.
Gravinstine, John K., August 26, 1814.
Green, Edmund, August 26, 1814.
Green, John S., August 31, 1814.
Grice, Charles, August 26, 1814.
Grice, Samuel, August 26, 1814.
Hagner, Charles V., August 26, 1814.
Hagner, George, September 18, 1814.
Henry, John S., August 26, 1814.
Hildebrant, Augustus, August 26, 1814.
Hodge, William L., August 26, 1814.
Hopkins, Thomas, August 26, 1814.
Humes, William, August 26, 1814.
Israel Samuel, August 26, 1814; absent with leave.
Kay, Charles, August 26, 1814; sick.
Kay, Joseph L., August 26, 1814.
Keen, John B., September 22, 1814.
Keen, Joseph, Jr., September 18, 1814.
Kennedy, Isaac P., August 26, 1814.
Kennedy, Samuel, August 26, 1814.
Kerns, Gabriel, Jr., August 26, 1814.
Kline, Jacob C., August 26, 1814.
Kline, Henry S., August 26, 1814; absent with leave since October 17, 1814.
Legget, John, August 26, 1814.
Loughery, John, August 26, 1814; absent with leave since October 17, 1814.
McAlpin, Alexander, September 18, 1814.
McClenachan, John, August 26, 1814.
Molineux, Benjamin, August 26, 1814.

Nevins, Samuel, August 26, 1814; absent without leave since December 31, 1814.
Nidilet, Stephen F., August 26, 1814.
Nones, Abraham B., September 11, 1814; absent with leave since November 10, 1814.
North, William, August 26, 1814; re-joined December 7, 1814.
Ogle, James B., August 26, 1814.
Okie, William, August 26, 1814.
Olds, James D., August 26, 1814; absent without leave since December 24, 1814.
Page, James, August 26, 1814.
Parham, Joseph, August 26, 1814; re-joined December 6, 1814.
Parmantier, Nicholas, September 18, 1814.
Pemberton, John, August 26, 1814.
Pemberton, Nathaniel, August 26, 1814.
Perit, John W., August 26, 1814.
Phillips, Joseph, August 26, 1814.
Pinchin, William, August 26, 1814.
Pollin, Peter, August 26, 1814.
Ray, Joseph, August 26, 1814.
Reynolds, Joel L., August 26, 1814.
Richardson, William, August 26, 1814.
Rink, John, August 26, 1814.
Rittenhouse, William, August 26, 1814; absent with leave since December 20, 1814; appointed midshipman United States Navy.
Robard, Joseph, August 26, 1814.
Roberts, Charles F., September 10, 1814.
Rogers, Joseph, Jr., August 26, 1814.
Roset, John, August 26, 1814.
Rush, Samuel, September 20, 1814.
Schively, George, August 26, 1814.
Selby, James, August 26, 1814.
Selby, Kendal, August 26, 1814; absent with leave since December 11, 1814.
Small, Robert H., August 26, 1814.
Soulié, Lucien, August 26, 1814.
Stiles, James B., August 26, 1814.
Sullivan, John T., August 26, 1814.
Tallman, George L., August 26, 1814.
Topham, John, August 26, 1814.
Watt, Alexander, August 26, 1814.
West, Joseph H., August 26, 1814.
Wetherill, Samuel P., September 5, 1814.
Withington, Samuel, August 26, 1814.
Worl, George, August 26, 1814.
Worrell, William, August 26, 1814.

Wray, Andrew, August 26, 1814.
Young, Thomas, August 26, 1814.

On honor, I certify that the above is a correct muster-roll of the company of State Fencibles, as mustered on the 4th of January, 1815.

H. KUHN,
Late Captain.
CLEMENT C. BIDDLE,
Colonel First Regiment P. V.

ROLL OF CAPT. JAMES LACKEY'S COMPANY.

October 5, 1814.

Pay-roll for the Fifth company, Sixty-fifth regiment, Pennsylvania militia, under the command of Capt. James Lackey.

Privates.

Taylor, Reuben.
White, William.
Robeson, Edward W.
Roberts, George.
Bowers, William.
Dempsey, William.
Goodwin, Jacob.
Lawrence, Joseph H.
Pennell, Samuel.
Degraut, James.
Wells, George.
Patterson, John.
McKinzy, Kenith.
Channel, Powell.
Pierce, Timothy.
Smith, John.
Griffith, Charles.
Hodge, William.
Hersh, George.
Burk, John.
Hunter, Joseph.
Thompson, Benjamin.
Jackson, Hezekiah.
Clare, Benjamin.
McCray, William.
Wilson, Lawrence.
Griffith, Evan.
Peck, Abram.
Salyards, Edward.

Walker, John.
Gilmore, John.
Garman, Henry.
Ford, Richard.
Kelly, Thomas.
Forwood, Jacob.
Bucknell, William.
Bryan, Martin.
Hoskins, William.
Love, Hugh.
Chaffin, Thomas.
Conway, Joseph.
Williamson, David.
Nickles, John.
Hunter, Thompson.
Trimble, Thomas.
Sharp, William.
Sinquet, Samuel.
Sinquet, Daniel.
Cummins, James.
Young, Peter.
Howell, Jacob.
Farrow, John.
Carter, Aaron.
McDonald, John.
Griffith, Samuel.
Murry, Jeremiah.
Waldravin, Levi.
Gallino, John.
Sharpless, Jesse.
Morgan, Davis.
Himes, Francis.
Sill, Oswald.
Rider, David.
Funterwise, John.
Bane, John.
Egee, David.
Hutcheson, Thomas.
Eaches, Isaac.
Youm, William.
Pearson, Henry.
Heck, John.
Frame, John.
Peterson, Peter.
Shimer, Bartholomew.
Rogers, Joseph.

Lewellyn, Thomas.
Sullivan, Samuel.
Cross, John.
Davis, George L.
Haycock, John.
Archer, John.
Farrow, Joseph.
Stanley, Jacob.
Torton, Benjamin.
Everson, Thomas.
Cochran, Thomas.
Epright, Samuel.
Crozier, Jonathan.
Carr, Henry.
Thompson, William.
Brothers, James.
Potter, Atlee.
Sill, William.
White, Isaac.
Cozens, Samuel.
Scott, Mathew.
Kitts, John.
Davis, Emmor.
McKeown, Thomas.
Martin, William.
Rowland, Charles.
Esex, Jacob.
Farrow, George.
King, John.
Hannums, George.
Wizer, John.
Day, James.
Work, Benjamin.
Waidner, Lazarus.
May, Edward.

    I do certify, on honor, that the above pay-roll of the Fifth company, attached to the Sixty-fifth regiment, Pennsylvania militia, is correct.

                            JAMES LACKEY,
                                       Captain.

    I believe the foregoing pay-roll is correct, as witness my hand this 29th day of October, Anno Domini 1814.

                                J. L. PEARSON,
        Colonel Sixty-fifth Regiment, Pennsylvania Militia.

    I do certify, on honor, that the company commanded by Capt.

Lackey, is in the service of the United States, under the command of the general commanding the Fourth military district.

SAMUEL SMITH.
Brigadier General.

CAMP MARCUS HOOK, *October 29, 1814.*

ROLL OF CAPT. SAMUEL C. LANDIS' COMPANY.

Muster-roll of a company of volunteer artillery, under the command of Capt. Samuel C. Landis, in the regiment of volunteer artillery in the service of the United States, commanded by Col. A. M. Prevost, from —— when last mustered, to January 3, 1815.

Captain.

Landis, Samuel C.

Second Lieutenant.

Burden, Henry.

Third Lieutenant.

Lynch, Thomas.

Sergeants.

Pidgeon, William W.
Loper, James.
Pidgeon, James A.
Crocket, Samuel.
Cowen, Jacob.

Quarter-Master Sergeant.

Hufty, John.

Corporals.

Burdec, Lewis.
Larkum, Thomas.
Clowges, Daniel, Jr.
Kidd, Thomas.
Cleary, William.

Drummer.

Lippincott, Samuel.

Fifer.

Burt, Clement W.

Privates.

Ayres, Hiram.
Bruster, Peter.

Buckius, Daniel.
Ball, Richard.
Burkheimer, Henry.
Curtis, John H.
Clawges, Charles S.
Cress, George.
Cannon, Daniel B.
Clawges, William R.
Chapin, Samuel.
Chatten, James N.
Clawges, Thomas.
Cock, Richard T.
Carver, Samuel.
Cornell, John.
Donnick, Samuel.
Defoe, John.
Dartnell, Edmond.
Eckford, Walter.
Emmerson, Erasmus.
Fonde, John P.
Ford, David.
Field, Lawrence.
Grebble, James.
Hoffman, John.
Hall, Joseph.
Hitchcock, Henry.
Hughs, Joshua.
Harkins, John.
Holmes, George.
Hitchner, Mathias.
Jones, Charles F.
Kerley, Jeremiah.
Larkum, John.
Lewis, Benjamin.
Mayhew, David.
Maddock, George.
Makins, William.
McClain, John.
McSweny, George.
Mellish, John G.
McCain, James.
McIlvain, Thomas.
Norwood, Richard.
Phile, Charles.
Philips, Miles C.
Pidgeon, James.

Price, Solomon.
Russel, Thomas.
Robb, Charles.
Shermer, Joseph.
Springer, Francis.
Solomon, Steven A.
Stokes, Abraham.
Shoemaker, Charles M.
Smith, William E.
Seyfert, Anthony.
Stevenson, Robert.
Stow, William.
Toland, James A.
Twis, Abiel.
Tolbert, John.
Tulley, Thomas.
Thacara, James.
Vandegrift, John.
Walter, Charles.
Work, Frazer.
Whiteman, Joseph.
Winkler, Edward.
Lang, John.

We certify, on honor, that this muster-roll exhibits the true state of the company of Washington Artillery, of the First regiment, Pennsylvania artillery, in the service of the United States at the period of its last muster.

SAMUEL C. LANDIS,
Captain Washington Artillery.
S. M. PREVOST.
Lieutenant Colonel Volunteer Artillery, service United States.

ROLL OF CAPT. BENJAMIN LESHER'S COMPANY.

Muster-roll of Capt. Benjamin Lesher's company, in the First regiment, First brigade, Pennsylvania militia, commanded by Col. Maxwell Kennedy, at York, Pennsylvania, September 5, 1814. In service from September 5, 1814, to March 5, 1815, from Lebanon county.

Captain.

Lesher, Benjamin.

Lieutenant.

Leidner, Daniel.

Ensign.

Freylinghouser, Peter.

Sergeants.

Beashor, Benjamin.
Fortney, Jonas.
Achenbach, Jacob.
Wommer, Adam.

Corporals.

Felty, John.
Beany, Martin.
Wetzel, Frederick.
Spengle, George.

Privates.

Beashore, George.
Bush, George.
Capp, David.
Clemens, George.
Derkes, George.
Ehler, Christian.
Ehler, Thomas.
Eysenhower, Henry.
Eysenhower, Martin.
Fearer, Joseph.
Fege, Leonard.
Fege, Peter.
Fisher, George.
Herring, Henry.
Hoffa, Jacob.
Holsaple, John.
Hoover, John.
Keen, Samuel.
Klick, John.
Kunkleman, Daniel.
Lantz, Henry.
Larch, George.
Myres, Henry.
Rice, Samuel.
Ritter, George.
Shuey, George.
Silvus, Nicholas.
Shebely, Henry.
Snobely, John.
Steby, John.
Suter, Christophel.

Updegroff, George.
Wagoner, Jacob.
Weitle, William.
Wenter, John.
Wetzel, Jacob.
Wolf, Daniel.
Wolf, Frederick.
Wolf, Peter.

ROLL OF CAPT. ISAAC LINN'S COMPANY.

Pay-roll of Capt. Isaac Linn's company, belonging to a regiment of Pennsylvania militia commanded by Col. Rees Hill, commencing 18th May, 1813, and ending the 5th November.

Captain.

Linn, Isaac.

Lieutenants.

Oldshen, John.
Meriman, John.
Kendall, Jeremiah.

Ensign.

Lowns, John.

Sergeants.

Shryock, Daniel, appointed wagon-master 19th August, 1813.
Andrews, Thomas, discharged 24th October.
Allen, Jonathan, discharged 24th October.
Lewis, John, discharged 24th October.
Reed, John, discharged November 5.

Corporals.

Davis, Joseph, discharged October 26.
Greenlee, Jacob, discharged October 24.

Drummer.

Shoultz, George, discharged October 24.

Privates.

Anderson, William, discharged November 5.
Crooks, William, discharged October 24.
Fagan, John, discharged November 5.
Martin, George, discharged October 24.
Helmick, Joseph, discharged October 24.
Laylander, James, discharged October 24.
Caufman, Abraham, discharged November 5.

Greenland, John, discharged October 24.
Hilands, John, discharged July 9.
Latta, Ephraim, discharged November 5.
Robbison, Robert, discharged October 26.
Currant, Joel, discharged October 24.
Updegraff, Jacob, discharged August 1
Davis, William, discharged August 22.
Law, Thomas, discharged October 24.
Laughlin, Andrew, died October 18.
Mendingall, John, discharged October 24.
Bell, Samuel, discharged October 24.
Price, James, discharged October 24.
Hartman, Frederick, discharged July 26.
Briant, James, discharged November 5.
Lynch, William, died July 9.
Beeler, John, discharged November 5.
Cumberland, Thomas, discharged October 24.
Alloways, Joseph, enlisted June 23.
Ebbert, Levi, discharged November 5.
Stewart, Robert, enlisted June 27.
Thompson, Thomas, discharged October 24.
Tegret, Hugh, discharged October 26.
Gage, John R., discharged November 5.
Brown, Samuel, discharged November 5.
Brooks, James, discharged November 5.
Ruvendale, Isaac, discharged November 5.
Beehly, Martin, discharged October 26.
Chain, James, discharged November 5.
River, John, died October 18.
Reed, Charles, discharged November 5.
Reed, Thomas, discharged July 1.
Malaby, James, discharged October 24.
McGwiggen, Alexander, discharged October 24.
Johnston, Nicholas, discharged October 24.
Drinen, David, discharged November 5.
Badger, Giles, discharged November 5.
Baner, Daniel, enlisted June 27.
Foredice, William, enlisted June 13.
Vicars, Abel, enlisted June 13.
Rupely, John, on board fleet, August 9.
Craig, William, discharged November 5.
McGinnis, Daniel, discharged November 5.
Clark, John, discharged November 5.
Drenen, John, discharged November 5.
Davis, John, discharged October 24.
Miller, Benjamin, enlisted June 18.

Loey, Stephen, discharged November 5.
Croxton, Abra^m, discharged October 24.
King, Robert, enlisted June 29.
Litman, John, discharged October 24.
Cole, Daniel, discharged August 28.
McFarland, Joseph, discharged October 24.
Dunnom, William, discharged October 24.
Dickason, James, discharged October 24.
Beel, Amos.
Beeson, John, discharged November 5.
Badger, Weyman, discharged November 5.
Evy, Benjamin, discharged August 22.
McClelland, William, enlisted June 1.
Taylor, Jesse, discharged November 5.

I certify, on honor, the above pay-roll to be a true statement of the company under my command, up to the time of discharge.

ISAAC LINN,
Captain.
REES HILL,
Colonel commanding.

ROLL OF LIEUT. JAMES LINNARD'S COMPANY.

Muster-roll of the company of volunteer artillery, under the command of Lieut. James Linnard, in the service of the United States, in the First battalion, commanded by Maj. Andrew M. Prevost.

First Lieutenant.
Linnard, J. M., August 20, 1814.

Second Lieutenants.
Snyder, G. C., August 20, 1814.
Boyd, John, Jr., September 19, 1814.

Third Lieutenant.
Shoemaker, Abraham, Jr., September 19, 1814.

Quarter-Master.
Bigelow, Thomas.

Sergeants.
Donaldson, W. C.
Morgan, Thomas A.
McMullen, Robert.
Prevost, L. M.

Turner, John.
O'Neill, Robert.

Corporals.

Brown, Jesse, August 24, 1814.
Eddowes, John.
Hatfield, N.
McLeod, George.
Stokes, Charles.

Musician.

Hughes, Owen.

Privates.

Andaull, John B., August 24, 1814.
Ayers, Daniel, August 24, 1814.
Ayers, Stephen, August 24, 1814.
Birkey, Samuel.
Bernard, Parker.
Blair, Robert.
Brenno, Felix.
Carson, James, Jr.
Clark, Timothy.
Challoner, Ambrose.
Cherry, James.
Coates, Warwick.
Coxe, James.
Culver, Ephraim.
Culnan, D.
Davis, J. F.
Davis, D.
Dilworth, William.
Elder, William F.
English, Levi.
Fitzgibbons, John.
Flick, George.
Gaw, William.
George, I., or J. D.
Gilfry, John.
Guyot, Felix.
Hall, James.
Hall, Peter.
Hamill, H. H.
Hamilton, William.
Hardy, John C.
Hazlet, H.
Hennessy, Thomas.

Hunter, John C.
Israel, James.
Kearny, Francis.
Lake, William.
Leathem, James.
Leiper, James G. S.
Linehan, James G.
Linehan, M. J.
Marsh, James J.
Martenier, T.
McClernon, William.
McClure, David.
Moody, Samuel.
Norman, John I.
Oswald, Eleazer.
Pearson, Daniel.
Paxson, Phineas.
Plumb, Joseph.
Pickle, George.
Porter, John.
Rosseter, John.
Rayburn, John.
Rudolph, George, discharged on account of bodily infirmity on the —— day of September.
Sausman, Henry.
Selfridge, William.
Sharp, Henry.
Shoemaker, F.
Skerret, William.
Snyder, George K.
Snyder, H^y.
Sparks, Richard.
Stewart, William.
Tittermary, I. C.
Tittermary, R^d.
Webb, William.
Welch, H.
White, George.
Whitehead, W.
Winemore, Thomas.
Workman, Samuel.
Wright, Jarvis.
Young, John.

We certify, on honor, that this muster-roll exhibits a true state of the company of volunteer artillery, of the First battalion of artillery, for the period therein mentioned, and that the remarks set opposite the names of the men are accurate and just.

J. M. LINNARD,
Lieutenant Commanding.
JOHN BOYD,
Lieutenant.

I certify that the volunteer company of artillery, under command of Lieut. Linnard, is in the service of the United States, under orders of the general commanding the Fourth military district.

THOS. CADWALADER,
Brigadier General Commanding.

CAMP DUPONT, *October 7, 1814.*

ROLL OF CAPT. JOHN LOUGHERY'S COMPANY.

Roll and muster of Capt. John Loughery's company of Riflemen, attached to the Second regiment of light infantry, commanded by Lieut. Col. John Purviance, in the service of the United States, from the State of Pennsylvania, Brigadier General Adamson Tannehill commanding. Commencing the September 25, and ending November 24, 1812, both days inclusive.

Captain.

Loughrey, John.

Lieutenant.

Henderson, Robert.

Ensign.

Miller, Samuel.

Sergeants.

Thompson, Alexander.
Mathews, James.
Getty, John.
Oliver, James.

Corporals.

Coleman, John.
Black, James.
Jamison, William Thompson.
Willson, James.

Fifer.

Grimes, William.

Drummer.

Miller, James.

Privates.

Templeton, Samuel.
Templeton, Alexander.
Ewen, Alexander.
McComb, George.
Herrold, William.
Coleman, Archibald.
McCartney, Samuel.
Loughery, James, Jr.
Culberson, Thomas.
Patterson, Samuel.
Wiley, Hugh.
McLean, Alexander.
Jamison, John.
Elder, Robert.
Ewen, James.
Loughery, Joseph.
Marshall, Scott.
Lancy, Daniel.
McClelland, Samuel.
McKisson, Robert.
Dunlap, Robert.
Marshall, Joseph.
Marshall, James.
Bell, John.
Russell, James.
Coleman, Robert.
McKisson, James.
Wooden, John.
Loughery, James.
Young, Michael.
McLure, Thomas.
Deveny, Aaron.
Moorhead, William.
Black, Alexander.
Hunter, Robert.
Miller, Matthias.
Bulman, Nathan.
Lawrence, Randle.
Sleight, Jacob.
Stewart, Watson.
Rankin, George.
McFarland, William.

Adams, David.
Cunning, John.
Spiers, Joseph.
Dickson, James.
Wilson, James.
Cummings, Stephen.
Barr, John.

We certify, on honor, that this muster-roll exhibits a true statement of Capt. John Loughery's company of Rifle volunteers, attached to the Second regiment of infantry, commanded by Lieut. Col. John Purviance, for the period therein mentioned, and that the remarks set opposite the names of the men are accurate and just.

(Signed,)   JOHN LOUGHERY,
Captain.
JOHN PURVIANCE,
Lieutenant Colonel.

ROLL OF CAPT. WILLIAM MAGILL'S COMPANY.

CAMP DU PONT, *November 13, 1814.*

A true list of Capt. Magill's company of the Sixteenth section of riflemen, commanded by Colonel Thomas Humphrey.

Sergeants.

Robinson, James.
Stelle, Isaac.
Todd, Arcturus.
Matthew, Joseph.

Corporals.

Evans, David.
Robison, Benjamin.
Harrah, William.
Heath, John.

Privates.

Wood, Jonathan.
Hall, Gooden, G.
Marshel, William.
Lacy, Jesse.
Thomas, Morgan N.
Thomas, William.
Simpson, Job.
Anderson, Joseph.
Fritsinger, Christian.
Hare, Benjamin.

Ruth, Christian.
Tanner, Mark.
Friece, Jacob.
James, Benjamin.
Friece, Joseph.
McIntosh, Daniel.
Cisler, Nicholas.
McGooken, William.
Dennison, John.
Doyle, John.
Higgens, Joseph.
Rich, Anthony.
Everitt, John.
Williams, John.
Hubbert, Samuel.
Barclay, Robert.
Ditterline, William.
Evans, David, Jr.
Kirkpatrick, Andrew.
Moyres, Sem.
Bruner, Paul.
Dunlap, Isaac.
Shearer, Conrad.
Mekinstry, Nathan.
Harrah, Septimus.
Watt, Alexander.
Engles, Joseph.
Trupsbour, Philip.
Hughs, Samuel.
Whitingham, John.
Lewis, Ephraim.
Mann, Benjamin S.
Medara, Isaac B.
Patterson, William E.
Morris, John.
Smith, Samuel.
McKinney, John.
Stover, John W.
Dennison, William.
Markley, Daniel.
Fell, David.
Picker, James.
Lowdislager, John.
Toy, John.
Roberts, Robert.
Horn, Samuel.

Horn, William.
Daniels, John P.
Hunter, Joseph.
Patterson, Robert.

I do certify that the within list is a true statement, on honor, this 13th day of November, 1814.

WILLIAM MAGILL,
Captain.

THOMAS HUMPHREY,
Colonel First Regiment, Pennsylvania Volunteers.

I do certify, on honor, that the command of Capt. William Magill is in the service of the United States, under the command of the general commanding the Fourth military district.

THOMAS CADWALADER,
Brigadier General, commanding advance L. B.

CAMP DUPONT, *November 26, 1814.*

ROLL OF CAPT. RICHARD MAGUIRE'S COMPANY.

Muster-roll of the rifle company attached to the First battalion, One Hundred and Forty-second regiment, Pennsylvania militia, who have volunteered their services in substitution of the draft required from said regiment.

Captain.
Maguire, Richard.

Lieutenant.
Feltz, John.

Ensign.
Scantlin, John.

Drummer.
Keyler, Peter.

Privates.
Adams, Ignacies.
Adams, Thomas.
Burgoon, John.
Burgoon, Joseph.
Coyler, David.
Curren, Hugh.
Daugherty, John.
Delosier, Daniel.
Elder, James, Esquire.
Elder, Patrick H.
Galagher, Joseph.

Glass, George.
Keene, Christopher.
Lilly, Richard.
Magehan, Joseph.
McCoy, Alexander.
McGaugh, Arthur.
McGehan, James.
McGuire, James L.
Nagle, Jacob.
Noigle, John.
Nowel, John.
O'Conner, James.
Plot, Joseph.
Troxel, Jacob.
Warthin, Stannes Lewis.
Weakland, John.
Will, Jacob.
Will, John.

I do certify that the foregoing is a true copy of a return made to me by Col. Proctor, in substitution of the draft from the One Hundred and Forty-second regiment.

GEORGE GRAHAM,
Brigade Inspector.

ROLL OF CAPT. JOSEPH MARKLE'S COMPANY.

Pay-roll of a troop of twelve-month volunteer Light Dragoons, in the service of the United States, under command of Capt. Joseph Markle, in the squadron under command of Lieut. Col. James N. Ball, attached to the north-western army, under command of Maj. Gen. William Henry Harrison, for the bounty of twenty dollars allowed to each non-commissioned officer, private, &c., by law of Pennsylvania, of March 29, 1813. Expiration of service, September 4, 1813.

Captain.

Markle, Joseph, July 10, 1812.

First Lieutenant.

Fullerton, Humphrey, July 10, 1812; appointed adjutant, October 29, 1812.

Second Lieutenant.

Watts, Daniel, July 10, 1812; killed in the action of Missisinaway, December 18, 1812.

WAR OF 1812-14.

Cornet.

Markle, Jacob, July 10, 1812; promoted to second lieutenant, December 18, 1812.

Sergeants.

Plumer, John C., September 12, 1812.
Daily, Samuel H., September 12, 1812.
Davies, Samuel, September 12, 1812.
Miller, Samuel, September 12, 1812; sick and on furlough for a short time, November 25, 1812; never returned to his duty.

Corporals.

Ryan, James, February 10, 1813; substitute for William Robeson, who deserted January 20.
Skelly, Robert, September 12, 1812.
McGaffin, Robert, September 12, 1812.
Breneman, Henry, September 12, 1812.

Sadler.

Smith, James, September 12, 1812.

Farrier.

Frigs, George, September 12, 1812.

Trumpeters.

Alexander, James, September 12, 1812.
Craig, William, September 12, 1812.

Privates.

Becket, John, September 12, 1812.
Bennet, John, September 12, 1812; wounded at Missisinaway.
Breckenridge, James, February 23, 1813.
Cooper, Robert, September 12, 1813.
Chambers, Joseph, September 12, 1813.
Conner, James, September 12, 1813.
Carpenter, John C., March 29, 1813; not paid.
Cook, Edward, February 10, 1813.
Fleming, Daniel, September 12, 1812.
Francis, Henry, February 10, 1813; died at Delaware, Ohio, June 1.
Hamilton, Samuel, September 12, 1812.
Hissum, Joab, February 10, 1813; substitute for Peter Broadsword, who deserted January 20.
Lowry, Stephen, September 12, 1812.
Logue, William, September 12, 1812.
McClurg, William, September 12, 1812.
McClintock, Jonathan, September 12, 1812.
McClain, John, September 12, 1812.
McGrew, Nathan, September 12, 1812.

McGrew, Findley, September 12, 1812; died at Fort Meigs, about July 13, 1813.
Miller, William, September 12, 1812.
McCammon, John, September 12, 1812.
McCammon, Isaac, February 10, 1813; substitute for Samuel Montgomery, who deserted about September 20, 1812.
Rowan, Stephen, September 12, 1812.
Robison, Jonathan, September 12, 1812.
Redick, John, January 12, 1813; transferred from Capt. Seely's troop; paid at Washington.
Selby, James, September 12, 1812.
Selby, Samuel, March 1, 1813.
Stoflet, Samuel, September 12, 1812.
Byrely, Joseph, February 10, 1813; substitute for William Skelly, who is sick, absent.
McBride, James, February 10, 1813; substitute for Jacob Weaver, who deserted about January 20.
Hall, David, February 10, 1813; substitute for James McGuffin, who deserted January 20.
Rodgers, Samuel, March 1, 1813; substitute for John Robeson.
Gilbert, John, March 12, 1813; substitute for John Millegan, who absented himself without leave.
Neuesum, William, March 17, 1813; substitute for Corporal James Sloan, who deserted February 6.
Brant, Thomas, March 20, 1813; substitute for Sergeant John Marshall, who deserted in February.
Mitchell, William, May 1, 1813; substitute for James Guffy, who deserted February 6.
Thompson, Robert, February 10, 1813; substitute for Mathew Thompson, who deserted January 20.
Thompson, William, September 12, 1812; appointed cornet, March 24, 1813.
Carnahan, Thompson, September 12, 1812; died of his wounds, (received at Missisinaway,) December 20, 1812.
Carnahan, Findley, September 12, 1812; died of his wounds, (received at Missisinaway,) December 30, 1812, at Dayton.
Camble, Robert, September 12, 1812; died of his wounds, (received at Missisinaway,) January 22, 1813, at Dayton.
Burgan, Isaiah, September 12, 1812; died at Delaware, Ohio, May 24, 1813.
Price, Ichabod, February 10, 1813; killed at the siege of Fort Meigs, about May 3, 1813.
Morrison, John, September 12, 1812.
Stone, John, September 12, 1812.
Shepler, Samuel, September 12, 1812.

McGrew, Thomas, September 12, 1812; took sick at Pittsburgh, September 20, and never returned to his duty.

Shull, Charles, September 12, 1812; absent, without leave, from about March 4, until the troop was discharged.

I certify, on honor, that the within pay-roll exhibits a correct list of the troop of Light Dragoons under my command, in the squadron commanded by Lieut. Col. James V. Ball, and that the remarks set opposite the names of the men are accurate and just.

JOSEPH MARKLE,
Captain United States Volunteer Light Dragoons.

ROLL OF CAPT. GEORGE MARK'S COMPANY.

Muster-roll of Capt. George Mark's company, in the First regiment, Second brigade, of Pennsylvania militia, under command of Lieut. Col. Jeremiah Shappell, at York, Pa. In service from August 28, 1814, to March 5, 1815, from Berks county.

Captain.
Marks, George.

Lieutenant.
Boyer, George.

Ensign.
Michael, Christian.

Sergeants.
Conklin, John B.
Reifsnyder, Michael.
Kessler, Charles.
Fritz, Jacob.

Corporals.
Frunk, Jacob.
Briner, Peter.
Bright, Joseph.
Krauser, Samuel.

Musicians.
Rosh, Philip.
Sertzenger, John.

Privates.
Albright, George.
Aston, James.
Aulenbach, Andrew.
Aulenbach, Jacob.
Berger, Daniel.
Bingerman, Henry.

Bingerman, John.
Bingerman, Peter,
Bright, Michael.
Briner, Samuel.
Brotzman, Andrew.
Brown, George, C.
Coleman, George.
Dippery, Jacob.
Ebbert, Joseph.
Egie, Michael.
Ely, Daniel.
Ely, David.
Emmerick, George.
Fisher, Christian.
Forster, John.
Fox, John.
Trill, John.
Trill, William.
Goodman, Jacob.
Graul, Samuel.
Greese, Jacob.
Harff, George.
Heabold, Adam.
Hoffman, Daniel.
Homan, Peter.
Keating, John.
Keller, John H.
Knaur, Nicholas.
Lebo, John.
Manger, Daniel.
McNeal, William.
Moore, John.
Moser, Daniel.
Nagle, George.
Nagle, Peter.
Reeser, Samuel.
Reightmeyer, Jacob.
Sailor, Jacob.
Seifried, Charles.
Seifried, Joseph.
Seifried, Thomas.
Sertzinger, Daniel.
Shenfelder, John.
Sinclair, Samuel.
Snell, John, Jr.
Spang, Christian.

Tobias, John.
Witman, Samuel.
Witman, William.
Wonder, John.
Yeager, Daniel.
Young, Jacob.
Young, Michael.

ROLL OF CAPT. JACOB MARSHALL'S COMPANY.

Muster-roll of Capt. Jacob Marshall's company, in the First regiment, Second brigade, Pennsylvania militia, under the command of Col. Jeremiah Shapplet, at York, Pennsylvania. In service from August 28, 1814, to March 5, 1815, from Berks county.

Captain.

Marshall, Jacob.

First Lieutenant.

Burckher, Henry.

Second Lieutenant.

Hiester, William.

Ensign.

Alston, Lemuel.

Sergeant Major.

Bright, Jacob.

Sergeants.

Engman, John I.
Fraily, John.
Freanor, William.
Lincoln, Jessee.

Corporals.

Jackson, Isaac.
Ely, Jacob.
Shiny, Joseph.
Beyerly, Samuel.

Music.

Philipy, George.
Philipy, Jacob.

Privates.

Allgier, Joseph.
Bennick, George.

Benton, John.
Boon, William.
Bressler, Benjamin.
Buzart, John.
Camp, Jacob.
Clemmence, Ab^m.
Dautrick, John.
Deihl, Henry.
Deihm, Jacob.
Dewees, William.
Drinkhouse, George.
Eberhard, Frederick.
Felise, Jacob.
Felise, Solomon.
Fesis, Samuel.
Fick, Peter.
Fise, John.
Fise, Michael.
Fleicher, Peter.
Foley, Jeremiah.
From, John.
Furman, William.
Gantz, George.
Gerhard, John.
Gilbert, George.
Gross, Ab^m.
Haberacker, Daniel.
Hartman, George.
Hettrick, Henry.
Hill, John.
Hill, Samuel.
Hollenback, David.
Jones, Joseph.
Kelly, John.
Kendel, John.
Klinger, John.
Kremer, Peter.
Leinback, Christian.
Leinback, Daniel.
Loughlin, John, (wagoner.)
Markemer, William.
McKinney, Samuel.
Meek, Dewalt.
Mengel, Peter.
Miller, James.
Miller, William.

Moore, John.
Moyer, William.
Noll, John.
Norton, James.
Ossman, Leon.
Philipi, Peter.
Phyfer, John.
Rehr, Joseph.
Reifsnyder, J. C.
Reitzel, Philip.
Rittner, Jacob.
Rittner, John.
Rorick, Thomas.
Schembers, John.
Smale, Jacob.
Smith, Landle.
Spengler, Henry.
Spiker, George.
Stuart, John.
Thomas, John.
Warner, John.
Wheatly, Alfred.
Wilson, Thomas.
Yauman, John.
Zeibend, Samuel.

LIST OF CAPT. S. MATHER'S COMPANY.

A true list of Capt. Mather's company, of the Eighteenth section of Riflemen, commanded by Col. Thomas Humphrey.

Sergeants.

Rogers, John.
Edgars, William.
Jones, Isaac.
Boyd, Robert.

Corporals.

Warner, Paul.
Straten, Samuel.
Clark, Thomas.

Privates.

Ranson, David.
Wenzel, Lewis.

WAR OF 1812-14.

Oblinger, Christian.
Tolan, Henry.
Hamilton, James.
Rutherford, William.
Roney, Hamilton.
Webster, Benjamin.
Barrel, Samuel.
Stemple, Thomas.
Bisbing, John.
Dean, Joshua.
Shain, Casper.
Stetsenburg, Charles.
Tomilson, Isachar.
Melroy, Ezra.
Cadwalader, Cyrus.
Dull, Gabriel.
Edleman, George.
Brook, Peter.
Davis, David.
Vanderveer, Peter.
Cline, Jesse.
Crotz, John.
Kaskey, John.
Mely, or Melroy, Charles.
Elkens, George.
Newman, Henry.
Hall, Isaac.
Pownall, George.
King, Daniel.
Kelty, Anthony.
Collom, William.
Miller, John.
Sumers, Henry.
McColly, William.
McVey, Jacob.
Wenzel, Anthony.
Hemelright, William.
Webster, David.
Madagan, James.
Vandergrist, John.
German, David.
Madagan, James.
Miller, John.

Entered—September 30, 1814, Lewis Wenzel; Joshua Doan, October 1; Anthony Wenzel, October 1.

James Madagan quit the company October 18, 1814.

I do certify that the within list is a true statement, on honor, the 13th day of November, 1814.

S. MATHERS,
Captain.
THO. HUMPHREY,
Colonel First R. P. V. R.

I do certify, on honor, that the company commanded by S. Mather is in the service of the United States, under the command of the general commanding the Fourth military district.

THOS. CADWALADER,
Brigadier General Commanding Advance L. B.
CAMP DUPONT, *November 26, 1814.*

ROLL OF CAPT. ROBERT MARTIN'S COMPANY.

Pay-roll of a compay of militia, commanded by Capt. Robert Martin, of the One Hundred and Thirty-eighth regiment of Pennsylvania militia, commanded by Lieut. Col. Robert Miller, under the order of Major General Mead, dated January 1, 1814. Commencement of service January 12; expiration of service February 22.

Captain.

Martin, Robert.

Lieutenant.

Logan, William.

Ensign.

Mechlin, Jacob, Jr.

Sergeants.

Stephenson, Hugh.
Lutton, David.
Anderson, Elijah.
McCullouch, Matthew.

Corporals.

Johnston, Thomas.
Riddle, James.
Wilson, Samuel.
Moor, William.

Privates.

Medin, John.
Greham, Mordacai.

Robinson, Samuel.
Love, John.
Mickey, Robert.
Custard, George.
Sullivan, Moses.
Sullivan, John.
Cratty, James.
Gallagher, John.
Forister, William.
O'Harra, William.
Hindman, Robert.
White, Joseph.
Coovert, James.
Davis, Benjamin.
Little, Samuel.
Mecker, Abner.
Mecker, Moses.
Compton, John.
McCandless, James.
Brown, John.
Crutchlow, James.
Crutchlow, Archibald.
Shorts, Richard.
Fleck, Joseph.
Hovis, William.
Bales, William.
Montooth, Alexander.
Roof, Daniel.
McDonald, Daniel.
Painter, Henry.
Brandon, James.
McKinny, Robert.
Crutchlow, Samuel.
Gray, William.
Bryson, Joseph.
Gillaspy, John.
Graham, John.

WAR OF 1812–14.

ROLL OF CAPT. JOHN MAUGER'S COMPANY.

Muster-roll of Capt. John Mauger's company, in the First regiment, Second brigade, Pennsylvania militia, under the command of Col. Jeremiah Shappelle, at York, Pennsylvania. In service from August 28, 1814, to March 5, 1815, from Berks county.

Captain.

Mauger, John.

Lieutenant.

Fisher, Jacob.

Ensign.

Griner, Jacob.

Sergeants.

Breyman, Christian.
Mauger, Henry.
Nagle, Jacob.

Corporals.

Camwell, John.
Mauger, Jacob.
Mauger, Frederick.

Privates.

Auman, Henry.
Bachman, Daniel.
Baker, John.
Barrall, Dewalth.
Boone, Edward.
Boone, Hugh.
Brushall, Jacob.
Christian, Joseph.
Clark, Robert.
Dehart, Jacob.
Folk, Peter.
Fryer, Daniel.
George, Jacob.
Gerber, John.
Gerber, Samuel.
Hains, John.
Heffner, Daniel.
Henricks, John.
Herner, Henry.
Herner, Jacob.

Hopple, Jacob.
Kaup, Michael.
Keely, Jacob.
Kern, Jacob.
Knouse, Samuel.
Knouse, William.
Kochler, George.
Kochler, Henry.
Lafferty, James.
Leffel, William.
Ludwig, Abraham.
Lukins, Daniel.
Meek, Daniel.
Mullen, John.
Mullen, William.
Nagle, John.
Poh, John.
Ringler, Reuben.
Rush, John.
Schoener, John.
Seider, John.
Sidler, Peter.
Smith, Abraham.
Spare, Samuel.
Spatz, Jacob.
Teater, Abraham.
Teater, John.
Yocum, George.

ROLL OF CAPT. JOHN MAY'S COMPANY.

Pay-roll of a company of militia commanded by Capt. John May, of the Second regiment, performing a tour of duty under the command of Colonel Jeremiah Schappell, who rendezvoused at York, under the general order of the Governor, dated 26th August, 1814.

Captain.

May, John.

Lieutenant.

Cohen, Edward.

Ensign.

Regle, George.

Sergeants.

Stell, Andrew.
Ahmond, Paul.

WAR OF 1812-14.   285

Wheeler, George.
Sieger, Jacob.

Corporals.

Oneal, Nicholas.
Shoemaker, Christian.
Glass, Henry.
Hertz, John.

Privates.

Sillyman, Alexander.
Smith, Samuel.
Arnold, George.
Hoyer, John.
Smith, Benjamin.
Goodman, John.
Wendle, Benjamin.
Hann, David.
Hughes, Edward.
Hoffman, Peter.
Beam, Jacob.
Reppert, Daniel.
Beam, John.
Wesly, Daniel.
Kauehel, David.
Odear, Solomon.
Kumrer, Abraham.
Wesner, John.
Smith, Jacob.
Freese, Christian.
Eatzel, George.
Snider, John.
Moyer, George.
Glass, Jacob.
Ham, Daniel.
Homan, John.
Heine, Samuel.
Braucher, Frederick.
Sously, John.
Savage, Jacob.
Merkel, David.
Will, John.
Loehman, Christian.
Davis, John.
Hummel, Andrew.
Coulter, William.
Shoma, Joseph.
Smith, Thomas.

Eisenhower, Daniel.
Finkbone, Jacob.
Heterick, William.
Bradshaw, Robert.
Roush, Peter.
Nease, John.
Stirls, Charles.
Schveier, Nicholas.
Boucher, Peter.
Myer, Jacob.
Rigel, John.
Welsh, John.
Watson, William.
Unger, Samuel.
Miller, Andrew.
Bear, John.
Frounfelter, John.
Mowrer, John.
Fureman, Henry.
Sously, Philip.
Gearhard, John.
Lindenmuth, John.
Hollenbach, Philip.
Wensel, Daniel.
Slear, John.
Cauchel, Andrew.
Stiger, William.
Ahmon, Peter.
Kreitz, George.
Holland, John.
Shoemaker, Charles.

I certify the forgoing to be a correct roll of my company.

JOHN MAY,
Captain.

Test: JEREMIAH SCHAPPELL,
Colonel.

ROLL OF CAPT. McCLEAN'S COMPANY.

CAMP DUPONT, *November 13, 1814.*

A true list of Capt. McClean's company of the Eighteen section of riflemen, commanded by Col. Thomas Humphrey.

Sergeants.

Marple, David.
Stackhouse, John C.
Schreeder, John F.

Corporals.

Cadwalader, Joseph.
Lukens, Cyrus.
Barnes, Benjamin.
Search, William.

Privates.

Laird, John.
Haselet, Abraham.
Barnes, Jesse.
Leech, John.
Barnes, Jacob.
Fitzwater, Abel.
Rice, James.
Grub, John.
Warner, John.
Barnes, Clement.
Sutch, William.
Shelmire, Daniel.
Dunlap, Haselet.
Barnes, Robert.
Roberts, Thomas.
Virtue, James.
Grace, William.
Sandman, Henry.
Banes, or Beans, John.
Hughs, Thomas.
Hobensack, George.
Terry, David.
Yerkes, Philip.
Milnor, Aner, or Abner.
Columns, Judah.
Banes, or Beans, Jesse.
Yerkes, David.

Fisher, Thomas.
Snyder, Simon.
Willard, David.
Yerkis, David.
Sandman, William.
Guy, Jonathan.
Lloyd, David.
Leech, Joseph.
Butcher, Benner.
Beale, William.
Dungan, Amos.
Marple, Elias Y.
Cadwallader, Isaac.
Roberts, John P.

Isaac Cadwallader, second sergeant, promoted to a quarter-master sergeant on the 4th inst.

I do certify that the within list is a true statement, on honor, the 13th day of November, 1814.

J. T. DAVIS,
Lieutenant.

THOMAS HUMPHREY,
Colonel First Regiment P. V. R.

I do certify, on honor, that the company commanded by Capt. McClean is in the service of the United States, under the command of the general commanding the Fourth military district.

THOMAS CADWALADER,
Brigadier General, Commanding Advance Light Brigade.

CAMP DUPONT *November 26, 1814.*

ROLL OF CAPT. JOHN McCLEAN'S COMPANY.

Pay-roll of Capt. John McClean's company, belonging to a regiment of Pennsylvania militia in the service of the United States, commanded by Col. Rees Hill, from the date of entering into service, to November 5, 1813, inclusive.

Captain.

McClean, John.

Lieutenants.

Taylor, Beriah, resigned August 17, 1813.
Gance, Jacob.
Tillard, Robert.

Ensign.

Smith, Samuel, appointed adjutant August 10, 1813.

Sergeants.

Boyd, William.
Taylor, Joseph.
Barton, Joseph.
Death, John.
Routzenger, Adam, appointed sergeant July 14, 1813.

Corporals.

Foly, David, discharged July 27, 1813.
McFall, William, discharged July 14, 1813.
Cox, Levi, appointed corporal July 1, 1813.
Lewis, Thomas, appointed corporal July 1, 1813.
Gue, Joseph, appointed corporal July 15, 1813.
Ryers, Andew, appointed corporal July 1, 1813.

Fifer.

Roberts, William.

Privates.

Donald, William.
Sample, Samuel.
Shaw, William.
Murphey, Barrich, discharged August 14, 1813.
Edwards, John.
McLaughlin, William, discharged August 15, 1813.
Rankin, Robert.
Downer, Jacob, appointed surgeon's mate May 12, 1813.
Sharp, Levi.
Show, Eli.
Patrick, James.
Matthias, Joseph.
Hamilton, Hance.
Campble, Hugh.
Fuller, Thomas, enlisted July 13, 1813.
Hopkins, Josiah.
Phillips, Evan.
Mulvine, Edward.
Williams, William.
Golden, James.
Martin, William.
Allison, Major.
Lewis, Robert.
Law, John.
Simpkins, Amos.

Homan, Michael.
Hunt, Daniel.
Shepperd, Fermand.
King, Joseph.
Cummins, James.
Summions, or Timmons, Peter.
Fulton, Thomas.
Smith, Nicholas.
Riddle, Michael.
Stewart, Daniel.
Bear, John.
Kempson, John, discharged August 3, 1813.
Thomas, Benjamin, discharged August 14, 1813.
Dann, John.
Campble, Stephen, discharged August 19, 1813.
McLaughlin, James.
Coffman, Jacob.
McConnel, William, discharged July 7, 1813.
Helmick, John.
Bice, Thomas.
Booher, Henry.
Woodruff, Cornelius.
McCormack, Moses.
Morgan, James.
Black, John.
Shields, Roger.
Wilkins, Thomas.
Gibney, David.
Roach, Thomas.
Badger, Jeremiah.
Johnston, Elijah, discharged June 22, 1813.
Farquer, Chads.
Wood, Joseph.
Singleton, Jacob.
White, David, discharged July 18, 1813.
Swink, Jacob, discharged July 18, 1813.
Goodwin, Joseph.
Davis, James.
Seals, Isaac.
Morce, Alven.
Bunton, Edmund.
Robinson, James.
Thompson, William.
McClean, William, appointed forage-master May 12, 1813.
Gray, John.
Price, Jacob.

Patton, James, May 16, 1813.
Victor, Laurence.
Colly, David.
Miller, John.
Dougherty, Samuel, April 25, 1813.
Hannahs, James, April 25, 1813.
Maxfield, James, April 24, 1813.
Patrick, William, died April 30, 1813.
Wilson, Joseph, April 22, 1813.
Woods, John.
Cowan, Thomas, dischaged May 14, 1813.

 I do certify, on honor, that the above pay-roll exhibits a true statement of Capt. John McClean's company, belonging to a regiment of Pennsylvania militia in the service of the United States, commanded by Col. Rees Hill, for the period therein mentioned, and the remarks opposite each man's name is correct, to the best of my knowledge. Given at Erie, November 6, 1813.

ROBERT TILLARD,
Lieutenant.
REES HILL,
Colonel commanding.

ROLL OF CAPT. JAMES A. McCLELLAND'S COMPANY.

Pay-roll of a company of twelve month volunteers light dragoons, commanded by Capt. James A. McClelland, in a squadron commanded by Lieut. Col. James V. Ball, late in the service of the United States.

Captain.

McClelland, James A.

First Lieutenant.

Gilmore, Hugh, October 5, 1812; discharged April 2, 1813.

Second Lieutenant.

Ramsay, Thomas, died March 25, 1813.

Sergeants.

Porter, Thomas W., October 5, 1812; discharged October 21, 1813; made first sergeant after death of F. Hertzog.
Hertzog, Frederick, October 5, 1812; died July 11, 1813.
Messmore, George.
Balsinger, Christopher.

Corporals.

Pollock, Stephen.
Lawrence, George.
Keckler, Jacob.

Drummer.

Axton, Jeremiah.

Blacksmith.

Morgan, Morris.

Privates.

Messmore, Solomon.
Parshall, Nathaniel.
Hare, James, killed June 30, 1813.
Ackle, Jacob, killed May 1, 1813.
Tucker, Jacob.
Thompson, John.
Abraham, James.
Bowels, Bazel.
Balsinger, John.
Hannah, Ephraim.
Province, Benjamin.
Gilmore, David.
Christopher, Gideon.
Wheaton, Benjamin, died May 30, 1813.
Breading, James.
Graham, John.
Smith, John, died October 15, 1813.
Williams, William.
McClean, Thomas.
Bowde, Thomas.
Vaughan, Thomas.
Martin, Scott.
Brown, Caleb.
Harrison, Isaac, died August 13, 1813.
Harrison, Jacob.
Daugherty, Samuel, discharged from service—time not known.
Herrod, George.
Griffin, James M., killed December 18, 1812.
Smith, Jeremiah, August, 1813.
Brown, Samuel R., August, 1813; promoted April 2, 1814.

I do certify, on, honor, that the within exhibits a true roll of the men's names belonging to my troop of twelve month volunteer light dragoons, late in the service of the United States.

JAMES A. McCLELLAND,
Captain United States V. L. D.

ROLL OF CAPT. JEREMIAH SNIDER'S COMPANY.

Roll of Capt. Jeremiah Snider's company, from Chambersburg, afterwards commanded by Capt. John McClintock, in Col. Jeremiah Snider's regiment. September 5, 1812.

Captain.

Snider, Jeremiah.

Lieutenant.

McClintock, John.

Ensign.

Aston, Owen.

Sergeants.

Stevenson, John.
Allison, Alexander.
Colhoun, John.
Colhoun, Andrew.

Corporals.

Haslett, Robert.
Tillard, William.
Ruthrauff, H.
Reed, John.

Musicians.

Donaldson, William.
Bickney, Henry.

Privates.

Allen, Timothy.
Andrews, John.
Barnett, Joseph.
Beatty, Samuel.
Blythe, David.
Crain, A. L.
Clunk, Andrew.
Clouser, Daniel.
Cummings, John.
Foot, Robert.
Faber, George.
Grier, Isaac.
Glossbrenner, Peter.
Greenfield, Hugh.
Heist, George.
Hill, Horace.

Hunter, John.
Harvey, Thomas.
Hood, Daniel.
Hutchinson, John.
Lindsay, Andrew.
McKinney, Spencer.
Murray, James.
McConnell, Alexander.
Nabb, Elisha.
Phillipy, Jacob.
Plummer, John.
Rigler, Stephen.
Shannon, William.
Simpson, George.
Swan, Moses H.
Taylor, William.
Wilson, Joshua.
Wilson, James.
Wilson, David.
Wolff, Bernard.

ROLL OF LIEUT. JOSEPH McCOY'S COMPANY.

Pay-roll of a volunteer company of Riflemen, called the Southern Rangers, under the command of Lieut. Joseph McCoy, attached to the Second brigade Pennsylvania militia in the service of the United States, commanded by Lieut. Col. Joel B. Sutherland.

CAMP NEAR MARCUS HOOK, *October 15, 1814.*

First Lieutenant.

McCoy, Joseph.

Third Lieutenant.

Decker, Peter T.

Ensign.

Wiggins, Thomas.

Quarter-master Sergeant.

Cooper, William.

Sergeants.

Youchley, John.
Cook, Philip.
Finch, William.
Grover, Thomas D.

Corporals.

Crowell, Nathanial.
Wood, Charles.
Lector, William.
Shaffer, George.
Ails, Joseph.

Bugler.

Hill, John, Jr.

Privates.

Abraham, William.
Allen, Thomas P.
Auld, David.
Black, Thomas.
Bell, James.
Boyd, John.
Bailey, Robert.
Cambel, Alexander.
McClemens, John.
McComb, William.
Cook, William.
McCalla, Alexander.
Cope, William.
Christersin, Charles.
McCarty, Daniel.
Conely, Joseph.
O'Donel, Henry.
Donely, Alexander.
Devanport, Alfred.
Dumphy, James.
Elwell, Robert.
McFerron, John.
McFelly, John.
Fury, John.
Fury, Patrick.
German, Daniel.
Green, Job.
Geary, or Gerry, Edward.
Hill, John.
Hopkins, John.
Hale, Moses.
Hale, Warwick.
Hood, James.
Hunterson, John.
Hassel, Joseph.

Hurley, George.
Hawkins, John.
Hughes. Patrick.
Hasser, John.
Hoffnar, Richard.
Johnson, William.
Jones, David.
Johnson, Henry.
Johns, Thomas.
Truat, Thomas.
Kelter, David.
Keho, Thomas.
King, William.
Lyons, Joseph.
Lomax, Caleb.
Lockwood, Oliver.
Marker, John.
Marcelus, Cornelius E.
Lawrence, Charles.
North, David.
McNelly, Barney.
Nailer, William.
Painter, Lemuel.
McPile, Joseph.
Pistar, John.
Rhoads, John.
Ross, Walter.
Rivel, George.
Richards, Thomas.
Singleton, James.
Sweeney, Hugh.
Stagg, Tunis.
Shear, George.
Shaffer, Joseph L.
Tool, Arthur.
Thomas, Joseph.
Tittermary, David.
Veasey, Hesekiah.
Wiler, John.
Wiggins, Petit.
Whitehead, Caleb.
Young, George.
Wheldon, James.
White, Samuel.
Witman, Charles.
Irvine, Samuel.

Linnard, Thomas.
Grady, Thomas.

We certify, on honor, that this pay-roll exhibits a true state of the rifle company attached to the Second brigade, Pennsylvania militia, and that the remarks set opposite the names of the men are accurate and just.

PETER J. DECKER,
Lieutenant Commandant.
JOEL B. SUTHERLAND,
Lieutenant Colonel Commandant.

I certify that the rifle company commanded by Lieut. Joseph McCoy is in the service of the United States, under orders of the general commanding the Fourth military district.

THOMAS SNYDER,
Brigadier General.

ROLL OF CAPT. JAMES McCULLOUGH'S COMPANY.

Muster-roll of Capt. James McCullough's company, in the Fifth battalion, First brigade, Pennsylvania militia, under command of Maj. McFarland, at York, Pennsylvania. In service from September 3, 1814, to March 5, 1815, from Lancaster county.

Captain.

McCullough, James.

Lieutenant.

King, Robert.

Ensign.

Dayton, John.

Sergeants.

Ramsay, John.
Steward, John.
Hanna, John.
Crawford, Theophilus.

Corporals.

Carbison, James.
McCue, John.
Johnson, John.
White, Joseph.

Privates.

Ailes, Amos.
Armstrong, Andrew.
Awcrum, Samuel.

Baker, Frederick.
Brow, John.
Brubaker, Jacob.
Carpenter, Daniel.
Carpenter, Richard.
Curtis, John.
Devet, Conrad.
Donnelly, Patrick.
Doubts, Samuel.
Evans, John.
Gamble, John,
Green, Edward.
Hamilton, James.
Hannum, Davis.
Hervey, Moses.
Howell, John.
Jackson, William.
Kunkle, George.
Lemon, William.
Long, Hugh.
Long, Moses.
Long, William.
Maxwell, Martin.
McCartney, George.
McConkey, Andrew.
McCrabb, David B.
McCullough, Hugh.
Modenville, John.
Moore, Christian.
Moore, Isaac.
Murdock, John.
Peter, Samuel.
Ramsey, Nathaniel.
Reed, James.
Robinson, John.
Ruse, Henry.
Sletter, John.
Trimble, George.
Walton, Isaac.
Warden, George.

ROLL OF CAPT. THOMAS McELHENNY'S COMPANY.

Muster-roll of Capt. Thomas McElhenny's company, in the Second regiment, First brigade, of Pennsylvania militia, under command of Lieut. Col. Richer, at York. In service from September 3, 1814, to March 5, 1815, from Dauphin and Lebanon counties.

Captain.

McElhenny, Thomas.

Lieutenant.

Finny, Thomas.

Ensign.

Borry, John.

Sergeants.

Jemeson, John.
Strop, John.
Fisburn, David.
Rees, Jacob.

Corporals.

Hamilton, William.
Spuk, Michael.
Bentor, Jacob.
Denius, Jacob.

Fifer.

Woolhaver, Henry.

Privates.

Bailer, John.
Baird, James.
Balm, George.
Bashore, Adam.
Bashore, Henry.
Basler, John.
Bassford, John.
Bluher, Henry.
Breight, John.
Brownewell, John.
Bush, Frederick.
Cape, Henry.
Cinty, Patrick M.
Dasher, Henry.

Deihl, Jacob.
Earley, Christian.
Feegan, Daniel.
Feesick, John.
Fortney, John.
Fronkford, Henry.
Funk, Martin.
Gebeny, Hugh.
Gels, Jacob.
Haneson, John.
Harvy, Henry.
Heims, John.
Hexenhiser, Henry.
Horner, George.
Johnson, James.
Kaffeman, Philip.
Kelay, John.
Keller, Jacob.
Kenny, Patrick M.
Kramer, John.
Kurtzman, Daniel.
Lance, John.
Laughlin, James M.
Leob, Christopher.
Luton, John.
Miller, John.
Mingle, Benjamin.
Moyer, Henry.
Moyer, Jacob.
Moyer, Michael.
Nagle, Frederick.
Nelenour, Philip.
Nigh, Adam.
Noaker, Benjamin.
Olwine, Warner.
Plessly, Frederick.
Rawland, John.
Rees, David.
Reeson, Samuel.
Ritter, Enoch.
Robison, George.
Rudy, Samuel.
Smith, Henry.
Sponprot, Christian.
Stukey, Frederick.
Swier, John.

Swigart, Martin.
Switzer, John.
Tui, John.
Ulrich, Jacob.
White, George.
Yingst, Jacob.
Yingst, John.
Young, John.

ROLL OF CAPT. McGLATHERIE'S COMPANY.

A complete muster-roll for the second (Capt. McGlatherie's) company of the Second regiment, volunteer light infantry, under the command of Col. Louis Bache, under the order of the Commander-in-chief of the Commonwealth of Pennsylvania, of August 27, 1814, and attached to the First brigade, Second division, Pennsylvania militia.

Captain.

McGlatherie, William.

First Lieutenant.

Bisson, John.

Second Lieutenant.

Wanner, John.

Ensign.

Bisbing, George.

Sergeants.

Jamison, John.
Hauss, John.
Osborne, Richard.
Lewis, Nathan.

Corporals.

Bachman, John.
Lowry, Job.
Colson, Jesse.
Lutz, Abraham.

Drummer.

Kline, John.

Fifer.

Weaver, Jacob.

Privates.

McGlatherie, Samuel.
Custard, Paul.
Buck, William.
Deem, Adam.
Dyer, John.
Spear, Philip.
Roberts, John.
Deem, Henry.
Roberts, David.
Pluck, John.
Bacher, or Baker, John.
Baker, Jacob.
Garney, or Carney, Henry.
Bisson, William R.
Barton, William.
Morris, Samuel.
Boyer, Benjamin.
Levering, Jacob.
Zerfass, Jacob.
Thomas, Owen.
Painter, Isaac.
Pluck, George.
Dyer, Henry.
Shearer, Jacob.
Gerhard, Nicholas.
Berritt, or Barret, John.
Hendricks, Joseph.
Martin, John.

I do hereby certify, upon honor, that the above is a correct muster-roll of Capt. McGlatherie's company, this 29th day of November, 1814.

JOHN WANNER,
Second Lieutenant.
LOUIS BACHE,
Col. Second regiment Penn'a Vol. Light Infantry.

ROLL OF CAPT. DANIEL McKOWN'S COMPANY.

Pay-roll of a company of infantry commanded by Capt. Daniel McKown, in the —— regiment of Pennsylvania militia, in the service of the United States, commanded by Col. Rees Hill. Commencement of service, May 25, 1813; expiration of service. November 8, 1813.

Captain.
McKown, Daniel.

First Lieutenant.
Cuningham, Robert.

Second Lieutenant.
Simpson, Joseph.

Third Lieutenant.
Gordon, Samuel.

Ensign.
Stepheson, William.

Sergeants.
Hill, William.
Moerehead, James, promoted to sergeant, June 25, 1813.
McLoud, David, promoted to sergeant, November —, 1813.
Kirkpatrick, David M.
McKillip, Mathew.

Corporals.
Sampson, George.
Rutan, Nicholas.
Martin, James, promoted September 14.
Loyel, John, promoted September 14.
Anderson, William.

Privates.
Housman, John, discharged June 20, 1813.
McGuire, Joseph, substitute for John Guinn
McKee, Hugh.
Mansfield, Christopher.
Gibson, William.
Alaxander, Samuel, discharged August 21, 1813.
Cowan, Joseph, discharged September 1, 1813.
Stilwell, Elias, appointed drum major May 22, 1813.
Horrell, Christ.
Horrell, Johnston.
Archard, David.
Bowars, Jacob.
Black, Abraham.

Blair, Thomas.
Blair, Alaxander.
Collins, Isaac.
Crice, Andrew.
Collins, Joseph, discharged August 15, 1813.
Coon, Henry.
Carson, Brien.
Cline, George.
Carrans, John.
Carney, William.
Dunlap, William.
Davis, William.
Deeds, John.
Dickey, Henry.
Dobins, James, discharged August 17, 1813.
George, Henry.
Gartley, George.
Hiles, Fredrick.
Sloan, John, substitute for John Guire.
Huffman, Adam.
Hart, William.
Hair, Christ, discharged June 5, 1813.
Hylands, William.
Jay, John.
Johnston, Henry.
Jones, Joseph.
Kiser, John.
Kister, Philip.
Kelly, Robert, discharged July 5, 1813.
Kenaday, John.
Loghrey, Thomas, discharged June 26, 1813; enlisted June 27, 1813.
McCartney, Alaxander.
Mathias, David.
McLaughlin, Charles.
McKean, Samuel, discharged August 19, 1813.
McHenry, Neal.
McClintock, Samuel.
Moak, John.
McVain, John.
Millar, Peter.
McLain, David.
Milliron, John.
McMillan, Thomas.
Patterson, Robert, absent; confined.
Novenmire, Daniel.
Piper, Isaac.

Quail, John.
Robison, James.
Rosberry, Robert.
Russel, Joseph, discharged June 26, 1813; enlisted June 27, 1813.
Reek, Henry.
Riddel, John.
Roads, Abraham.
Smitley, Mickal.
Spoon, John.
Swanger, Jacob, discharged September 1, 1813.
Starnbarger, John.
Swanger, Peter.
Snyder, Jacob.
Snyder, David.
Shrum, George.
Gibson, Charles, substitute for John Shirey.
Sadler, William.
Teell, Jebes, discharged August 10, 1813.
Thompson, Thomas.
Walker, George.
Weever, Nicholas.
Millar, William, substitute for Abraham Wever.
Wiley, Robert.
Williams, Richard, discharged May 23, 1813; enlisted, May 24, 1813, in the marine service.
McGuire, Samuel.

I certify, on honor, that the within pay-roll exhibits a true statement of my company, and that the remarks set opposite the men's names are accurate and just, to the best of my knowledge.

DANIEL McKOWN,
Captain.

ROLL OF CAPT. JOHN McMILLIN'S COMPANY.

Muster-roll of Capt. McMillin's company of militia, belonging to the Fifth detatchment from Pennsylvania, in the service of the United States, at Buffalo, New York.

Captain.

McMillin, John.

Lieutenants.

Chamberlain, Joseph.
Lynn, William.
Blythe, Samuel.

Sergeants.

Cooper, David.
Reed, Peter.
Cunningham, Andrew.

Corporals.

Reed, Henry.
Scott, Samuel.
Douglass, Thomas.
Cunningham, James.

Privates.

Adair, William.
Armstrong, John.
Agnew, Samuel, missing at Bridgewater battle.
Arvin, William.
Bradley, George.
Burk, Michael.
Baltsley, Jacob.
Buchanan, William.
Bear, John.
Bower, Lewis.
Bower, Philip.
Beard, William.
Beighler, John.
Burns, Henry.
Boreland, Thomas, deceased.
Blake, Samuel.
Blythe, Calvin.
Cunningham, John.
Curbaugh, John.
Comfort, Jacob.
Creamer, Peter.
Chapman, William.
Cook, John.
Chamberlain, David.
Degrott, Cornelius.
Derbon, Thomas.
Edwards, Charles.
Greg, James.
Galaher, Patrick.
Geipe, John.
Gates, Frederick.
Himer, William.
Hagan, Robert.
Harman, Henry, missing.
Humes, Abraham.

Hensel, Andrew.
Hinier, William.
Heron, John.
Iser, Philip.
Isier, Mathias.
Jones, Jacob.
Kimes, Henry.
Kepner, John, missing.
Long, Aquilla.
Long, Martin.
McSherry, Frederick.
Lease, George, deceased.
Moore, Christopher.
McLief, James.
Majors, Jacob.
McDermot, James.
McCaleb, Hugh.
McMaster, James.
Mills, Joseph.
Morgan, Jacob.
McWilliams, James.
McAfee, Joseph.
Noel, David.
Newcomer, Christopher.
Norbeck, Jacob.
Orbison, James.
Pope, William.
Pepple, Abraham.
Rogers, John.
Rumel, John.
Riffle, Leonard.
Ray, Samuel.
Smeltser, Joseph.
Seabrooks, James.
Spencer, George W., killed at the battle of Bridgewater.
Threoder, Jacob.
Sweutzel, Frederick.
Thomas, Peter.
Thomas, William.
Troxel, Anthony.
Thatcher, Charles.
Vance, David.
Valentine, Charles.
White, Thomas.
Wolfkill, Henry, died July 10.
Woods, Joseph.

Woods, William.
Woods, John.
Williams, Andrew.
Wiggins, James.
Melker, Jacob.

I do certify that the above and foregoing is a correct muster-roll of Capt. McMillan's company. Given under my hand this 27th day of August, A. D. 1814.

JOSEPH CHAMBERLAIN,
Lieutenant Commandant.
JAMES FENTON,
Colonel.

ROLL OF CAPT. THOMAS McQUAIDE'S COMPANY.

Pay-roll of a company of riflemen commanded by Capt. Thomas McQuaide, in the service of the United States, from August 2, 1812, until April 2, 1813, Second regiment, Second brigade, Pennsylvania militia, commanded by Brig. Gen. Richard Crooks.

Captain.

McQuaide, Thomas.

Lieutenant.

Mickey, Isaac.

Ensign.

Crofard, Hugh.

Sergeants.

McClelland, John.
Christey, John.
McQurton, James.
Matther, James.

Corporals.

Irvan, Hugh.
Dotey, Nathaniel.
Kelley, Alexander.
Wiley, Albert.

Privates.

Robston, David.
Galaher, Philip.
Frame, William, volunteered fifteen days.
McIlwain, David.
Lesley, James.

WAR OF 1812-14.

Shearer, Robert.
Shedrick, Robert.
Mickey, Daniel.
Pirkey, Christopher.
Wiman, Jacob.
Hartman, Michael.
Jinkeson, George, volunteered fifteen days.
Boyd, Robert.
Pollans, William.
Hunter, Samuel.
Borland, John.
Camble, Henry, volunteered fifteen days.
Brow, John.
Dickey, William.
McCalley, John.
Jonnston, John, Sr.
Smith, James.
Weaver, David.
Haleday, James.
Brown, William.
Pepels. Samuel.
Moor, William, Jr.
Cochran, William.
Andrew, John.
Means, Charles.
Marrs, John.
Kelley, John.
Cochran, Jesse.
Rickard, Andrew.
Sands, James.
Breeker, George, volunteered fifteen days.
Mime, John, volunteered fifteen days.
Row, Michael.
Moor, William, Sr., discharged December 22.
Wiley, Robert, on furlough.
McQuaid, Andrew, on furlough.
Brice, Henry, discharged December 22.
Dickey, David, on furlough.
Christey, Joseph, on furlough.
Woods, William.
Johnston, John, discharged December 21.
Horn, Solomon, on furlough.
Buchanon, William.
   I do certify that the within rolls are accurate and just.
THOS. McQUAID,
Captain.

ROLL OF CAPT. HENRY MEYERS' COMPANY.

Muster-roll of a company of infantry called the State Guards, commanded by Capt. Henry Meyers, and belonging to the First regiment of Pennsylvania volunteers, commanded by Col. Clement C. Biddle. Commencement of service, September 17, 1814.

Captain.
Meyers, Henry.

First Lieutenant.
Fisler, Jacob H.

Second Lieutenant.
Billington, George.

Third Lieutenant.
McCaraher, Alexander.

Ensign.
Miller, Daniel H.

Sergeants.
Geyer, Andrew.
Benner, George.
Richard, George.
Harman, George.
Heyberger, Jacob, absent on furlough.

Corporals.
Dungan, William.
Colloday, Joseph S.
Meyer, Peter C.
Warn, Thomas.
Rush, Thomas M.
Burkard, Jacob.

Fifer.
Benner, J. L.

Drummer.
Vaenlan, Jeremiah.

Privates.
Andrew, Nicholas.
Buzby, Hezekiah.
Burrow, Jacob, absent on furlough.
Benner, Henry.
Bealer, Tobias.
Bruce, William.
Bartlesan, Peter.
Buck, John.

Brook, John, Jr.
Barcroft, Stacy B.
Barnes, Isaac.
Bartholomew, Joseph.
Bicknell, Charles.
Barry, John.
Colladay, William.
Cooper, James, Jr.
Corry, Walter A.
Comly, Joshua.
Christian, Thomas.
Clark, David W.
Dunlap, Sallows.
Gravenstine, William.
Gillins, Theodore.
Garrison, John.
Gardiner, Robert.
Gardiner, Jacob H.
Goodwin, Courter.
Gobright, Christian.
Hansell, James.
Hollenbush, Henry.
Hamilton, John.
Hartzog, Peter.
Hauze, John.
Hill, Joseph.
Harman, Jacob, Jr.
Houpt, Henry.
Hollahan, John.
Jackaway, Nathan.
Kookagey, John.
King, Joseph.
Keyser, Joseph.
Knight, Isaiah.
Keehnell, Samuel.
Kennedy, William D.
Lauderback, Peter.
Link, Peter.
Link, John.
Larkey, John.
Lyons, Mordecai.
Meyers, George G.
Mills, Smith.
Murphy, John.
Morris, John.
Mingle, John, Jr., absent on furlough.

Magee, Hugh S.
Mitchell, Elijah.
McDowell, Daniel.
McClintock, Joseph A.
Noxson, Joseph G.
Newman, Daniel.
Owens, Owen.
Peterson, Samuel.
Pollock, John.
Price, Isacher.
Parham, Robert.
Pennell, Henry H.
Porter, McKinney.
Reilly, Joseph S.
Reed, Alexander W.
Rush, John.
Reabsam, Philip.
Roberts, Israel.
Snyder, Peter.
Sagers, Samuel H.
Stout, George.
Skinner, William.
Shinn, Caleb.
Shunk, Isaac.
Shuster, Lawrence.
Smith, Joseph.
Smith, Jacob.
Seckel, Joshua C.
Shinkel, Jacob.
Strock, Joseph.
Saunders, Peter.
Stinger, Thomas H.
Slanter, Jacob.
Thompson, Thomas.
Wilstack, John A.
Weiss, William.
West, Richard L.
Warnock, John.
Van Staveren, William.
Yeager, Joseph.
Boyer, I.
Brackenridge, George W.
Clymer, Jacob.
Pool, William.
Everitt, Jonathan.

HENRY MEYERS,
Captain.

WAR OF 1812–14. 313

I believe the above muster-roll to be correct.

CONDY RAGUET,
Lieut. Col. First Regiment Pennsylvania Volunteers.

I certify that the State Guards, commanded by Capt. Henry Meyers, is in the service of the United States, under orders of the general commanding the Fourth military district.

THOMAS CADWALADER,
Brigadier General Commanding.

CAMP DUPONT, *October 7, 1814.*

ROLL OF CAPT. HENRY MEYERS' COMPANY.

Muster-roll of a company of infantry under the command of Capt. Henry Meyers, in the Fourth detachment, Pennsylvania militia, now in the service of the United States, commanded by Col. Lewis Rush, from May 13, 1813, when last mustered, to June 18, 1813.

Captain.

Meyers, Henry.

First Lieutenant.

Coles, William.

Second Lieutenant.

Geyer, George.

Third Lieutenant.

Sagar, Michael.

Ensign.

Suter, John, May 27; now in service of United States.

Sergeants.

Speel, George.
Witt, Abraham, Jr.
Bayard, George.
Haas, Charles.
Whitecar, Joseph.

Corporals.

Travellier, John.
Stetson, Silas.
Perpignan, Peter.
Landis, Samuel C.

Drum-Major.

Tripner, George.

Fifer.

Lechler, George E.

Privates.

Allman, Joseph.
Anthony, Thomas.
Apple, John.
Bignal, William.
Black, John A.
Baymont, Jacob, furloughed May 18, six days, and never returned to camp.
Baker, Peter.
Brown, Joseph.
Blume, George.
Boggs, David.
Baker, Bart.
Brown, John.
Brittenham, Joshua.
Crouse, Michael.
Cooper, George.
Cooper, George A.
Cole, Francis.
Cornell, Nathan.
Clark, John.
Dubois, Henry.
Dahoff, Jacob.
Dunfee, Samuel, left camp without leave, and never returned.
Decoster, Charles.
Deforest, John.
Evens, John.
Fulmer, John, Jr.
Fries, John.
Gross, John.
Good, Frederick.
Gossler, George.
Hampton, Benjamin.
Hagerthy, Daniel.
Hammel, Samuel.
Holliday, Richard.
Hartranoff, Michael.
Harington, Jonathan.
Jones, Thomas.
Kiel, John.
Kreamer, Philip.
Kirkpatrick, John.
Kemp, John.
Lewis, Francis.

Ludwick, John.
Lane, William.
Lancaster, William, Jr.
Lehman, Charles.
Love, Thomas.
Lauck, David.
Lafourge, George.
Leatherberry, Peregrin.
Lower, Christian.
Lambsbach, John.
McKee, Andrew.
Mavis, Peter.
Miller, John.
Moor, Thomas.
Millen, John.
Mawig, William.
Mulhunn, John.
Mulherring, John.
Nagel, William.
Newman, Daniel.
Norberry, Joseph.
Ogden, Abraham.
Patton, William.
Powell, William.
Pfaff, Conrad.
Phile, Daniel.
Pugh, Henry W.
Phillips, Henry R.
Raphonn, John.
Raser, Matthias.
Reed, Peter.
Reedy, John.
Rock, Thomas.
Reed, Thomas.
Sheppard, Jacob.
Sagerthy, William.
Shannon, John.
Shronk, Joseph.
Sweitzer, Frederick.
Sweeny, William.
Steinberg, Peter.
Stull, John.
Strèmback, Jacob.
Snowden, Thomas.
Simpson, David.
Sybert, Joseph.

Steimberg, Jacob.
Sheppard, James.
Shermer, John.
Stewart, John I.
Snyder, John Christian.
Trueman, John.
Walker, John.
Wiley, James H.
Warwick, Charles.
Wells, Thomas.
Walter, George.
Landis, Samuel C., promoted to Fourth corporal.

We certify, on honor, that this muster-roll exhibits a true state of Capt. Henry Meyers' company, of the Fourth detachment ——— regiment, of Pennsylvania militia, for the period therein mentioned, and that the remarks set opposite the names of the men are accurate and just.

HENRY MEYERS,
Captain.

Upon the return of the detachment to the city, the muster-roll had undergone no alteration since the above period.

HENRY MEYERS,
Captain.

I do certify, upon honor, that I believe the above return and remarks to be accurate and just.

LEWIS RUSH,
Colonel Fourth Detachment, Pennsylvania Militia.

August 6, 1813.

ROLL OF CAPT. NER MIDDLESWARTH'S COMPANY.

Muster-roll of the Union Rifle volunteers, of Union county, commanded by Capt. Ner Middleswarth, and attached to the battalion of riflemen commanded by Capt. John Uhle, in the Light Brigade, commanded by Brig. Gen. Thomas Cadwalader, now in the actual service of the United States, at Camp Dupont, October 27, 1814.

Captain.

Middleswarth, Ner.

First Lieutenant.

Mertz, Isaac.

Second Lieutenant.

Aurandt, John.

Ensign.

Devore, Daniel.

Sergeants.

Fryer, Jacob.
Weiser, Daniel.
Steese, Frederick.
Wikle, George.

Corporals.

Frederick, Abraham.
Layer, Daniel.
Swineford, Albright.
Long, Jacob.

Privates.

Moyer, George.
Gilbert, Jacob.
Wales, John.
Miller, Jacob.
Loehr, Peter.
Butler, Jacob.
Smith, James.
Freadley, Ludwick.
Royer, Samuel.
Melchor, Stock.
Kratzere, Henry.
Grub, Jacob.
Gill, Jacob.
Loehr, Jacob.
Dracksel, Jacob.
Dreese, Henry.
Sness, Henry.
Wirick, Henry.
Koones, John.
Bowerson, Daniel.
Moyer, Jacob.
Wiant, George.
Mertz, Samuel.
Klemence, George.
Abraham, Kaley.
Ely, Esher.
Bird, John.
Miller, Daniel.
Thirston, Israel.
Gilmore, Robert.
Carrol, Henry W.

Campbell, Elias.
Michel, John.
Wakey, John.
Keterman, John.

I do certify that the above muster-roll is correct as stated. Witness my hand this 29th October, 1814.

NER MIDDLESWARTH,
Captain Union Volunteers.

The above is correct.

JOHN UHLE,
Captain commanding the First battalion Rifle in the service of the United States, at Camp Dupont.

I do certify, on honor, that the company commanded by Capt. N. Middleswarth, is in the service of the United States, under the command of the general cammanding the Fourth military district.

THOMAS CADWALADER,
Brigadier General commanding advance Light Brigade.

CAMP DUPONT, *November 26, 1814.*

ROLL OF CAPT. JOHN R. MIFFLIN'S COMPANY.

Muster-roll of the First Company Washington Guards, under command of John R. Mifflin, in the First regiment of Pennsylvania volunteers, commanded by Col. Clement C. Biddle, from August 27, 1814, to October —, 1814.

Captain.

Mifflin, John R., promoted to captain September 15; first lieutenant from August 27.

First Lieutenant.

Wharton, Thomas J., promoted to first lieutenant September 16; second lieutenant from August 27.

Second Lieutenant.

Traquair, Thomas, promoted to second lieutenant September 19; ensign from August 27.

Third Lieutenant.

Baker, John S.

Ensign.

Brown, John M., promoted to ensign September 20; first sergeant from August 27.

WAR OF 1812-14.

Sergeants.

Milnor, John, Jr.
Davis, Thomas.
Carpenter, Charles.
Moore, John P.
Nice, George.

Corporals.

Kintzing, Tench C., on furlough, granted October 1, for four days.
Emerich, William B.
Reese, Charles B.
Bedwell, George.
Robbins, James, on furlough, granted September 28, for five days.

Fifer.

Christie, John.

Drummer.

Christie, Robert, absent on furlough.

Privates.

Able, George.
Allen, Richard.
Anderson, Edwin.
Austin, Alexander.
Ashmead, Isaac.
Barger, William.
Burkart, Valentine, on furlough, granted September 30, for four days.
Burkart, Peter.
Burkart, Adam L.
Benson, David, on furlough. granted October 2, for four days.
Bringhurst, B.
Breintnall, Thomas.
Child, Cephas G.
Christie, William.
Cox, John R.
Cox, Charles James, on furlough, granted September 28, for six days.
Carson, Thomas W., on furlough, granted September 29, for four days.
Clinton, George C.
Campbell, Ephraim.
Clause, John H.
Condon, William.
Catz, Jacob.
Chevalier, C. C., sick, absent.
Campbell, Robert.
Clayton, Edward, sick, absent.

Christien, Thomas.
Donaldson, George, on furlough, granted September 28, for four days.
Donaldson, Andrew.
Delicker, George.
Duncan, John H.
Durborrow, John.
Dehaven, H.
Eldridge, Anthony.
Elliott, J. S.
Ewing, Thomas W.
Ernest, David.
Freed, Anthony.
Folwell, Thomas, on furlough, granted October 2, for four days.
Fries, John, September 1.
Gray, Samuel N.
Graham, William.
Grim, Henry.
Goodman, George.
German, Thomas D.
Hartley, Nicholas.
Hicks, John.
Hill, Thomas.
Hockley, George W., absent on command of Gen. Cadwalader.
Harper, John.
Hay, William.
Hailer, Frederick.
Hirckle, Robert.
Hall, Edward E., died September 28, at Philadelphia.
Hutton, James.
Humphreys, Andrew.
Jobson, Samuel.
Kean, James C.
Kempton, Joseph B.
Keyser, Joseph.
Kintzing, H.
Lees, William L.
Lesh, Henry.
Lauk, David.
Major, William.
Metzker, John.
Mahany, J. J.
Mifflin, Lemuele.
Morrell, James.
McMullen, William.
Miles, Ephraim.
Newell, William.

Nice, Washington.
Owen, John.
Porter, Henry.
Pinkerton, J. O.
Pratt, James D.
Phillips, Benjamin, on furlough, granted October 1, for four days.
Rodgers, Robert.
Revoudt, William.
Robbins, Benjamin.
Smith, W. S.
Shreeve, John.
Servess. Charles.
Seybert, Adam.
Scott, Robert.
Stager, Cornelius.
Turner, Joseph M.
Thompson, James.
Thompson, James C.
Thornton, Joseph.
Thomas, James C., absent on furlough, granted September 30, for four days.
Tustian, Thomas.
Turner, Edward.
Wager, William S.
Wright, William.
Whitaker, Joseph.
Wilson, Thomas.
Webb, John, absent on furlough, granted October 1, for four days.
Whiteman, Benjamin.
Wucherer, John.
Wetherstein, Joseph.
Wiltberger, Joseph W.
Watson, James.
Wiltberger, Isaac, September 1.
Capp, John, October 2.
Bryan, John Y., October 2.

I certify that the above muster-roll exhibits a true statement of the first company of Washington Guards, and the remarks set opposite the names are just and true.

JOHN R. MIFFLIN,
Captain First Company Washington Guards.

CAMP DUPONT, *October 1, 1814.*

I believe the above muster-roll to be correct.

CONDY RAGUET,
Lieutenant Colonel First Regiment P. V.

I certify that the first company of Washington Guards, commanded by Capt. John R. Mifflin, is in the service of the United States, under orders of the general commanding the Fourth military district.

THOS. CADWALADER,
Brigadier General Commanding.

CAMP DUPONT, *October 7, 1814.*

ROLL OF CAPT. HENRY MILLER'S COMPANY.

Pay-roll of the company of infantry under the command of Capt. Henry Miller, attached and organized by adjutant general ———, of the ——— brigade, Pennsylvania militia, in the service of the United States, commanded by Lieut. Col. George Weirick.

Captain.

Miller, Henry.

Lieutenant.

McMullen, John.

Sergeants.

Williams, Benjamin.
Rarick, John.
Rhule, Philip.
Francis, William.

Corporals.

Spaht, Adam.
Wilson, Forster.
Spangler, George.
Robinson, Richard.

Privates.

Solomon, Abraham.
Mayer, John.
Shaffer, Jacob.
Faught, George.
Fry, John.
Norman, John.
Spangler, Christ.
Rarick, John.
Dunsife, Daniel.
Smith, John.
Panier, Peter.
Gearhart, Samuel.
Shaffer, William.

Crosgram, Samuel.
Forster, William.
Hosenfluke, Henry.
Thompson, James.
Driesbaugh, John.
Egbird, Cyrus.
Mayer, William.
Gerick, Jacob.
Herger, Henry.
Snyder, Michael.
Kleckner, Anthony.
Driesbaugh, Thomas.
Mangle, David.
Gill, William, discharged October 24, 1814.
Slear, George.
Gill, John.
Hasenpluke, Samuel.
Dar, Elias.
Faris, Garret.
Oilert, William.
Fox, Conrad.
Roate, John.
Rayer, Henry.
Phelps, Ira.
Zimmerman, Jacob.
Wright, John.
Spear, Robert.
Spegelmair, Daniel.
Shaw, Samuel.
Kleckner, Isaac.
Cooke, Andrew.
Stitzer, David.
Black, Robert.
Kleckner, Abraham.
Richley, William.
Bitting, Charles.
Mayer, John.
Babb, John.
Ritter, Henry.
Baker, George.
Babb, Conrad.
Bosler, George.
Saugh, or Slough, Benjamin.
Faught, Jacob.
Sander, Michael.
Barber, John.

McClay, John, appointed assistant deputy quarter-master general, October 9, 1814.
Mayer, William.
Baker, Peter.
Corall, George, appointed sergeant major, September 26, 1814.

ROLL OF CAPT. ANDREW MITCHEL'S COMPANY.

Return of the names of the men composing Capt. Andrew Mitchel's company.

Captain.

Mitchel, Andrew.

First Lieutenant.

McKeehan, Samuel.

Second Lieutenant.

Mitchel, James.

Sergeants.

McBride, Robert.
Derr, Andrew.

Privates.

Kingsborough, John.
Thompson, Peter.
Cooper Thomas.
Cope, Philip.
Bilew, John.
Montgomery, John.
Ripton, Peter.
Shulds, James.
Mathers, Robert.
Campbell, Daniel.
Long, Michael.
Thompson, Joseph.
McClelland, Elias.
Lytle, George.
Styner, Joshua.
McEntire, Thomas.
Long, Joseph.
Browneller, John.
Ripton, John.
Mathers, Thomas.
Wilt, John.

House, John.
Cooper, William P.
Cooper, Jesse.
Redick, Jacob.
Moor, John.
Barber, John.
McKibben, Samuel.
Cooper, Joseph.
Weekline, George.
Ritchie, William.
Bilew, Joseph.
McMenomy, Patrick.
Callen, James.
Derr, Joseph.
Fulton, John.
Herron, Thomas.
Epright, Philip.
Wood, Samuel.
Clark, William.
Corothers, William.
Campbell, John.
Tanneyhill, James.
Thrush, Solomon.
Dixon, John.
Ross, Samuel.
Ross, John.
Carson, Andrew.
Watsbougher, George.
Myer, John.
Sever, Abraham.
Devalt, John.
Dougherty, George.
McClelland, Robert.
Booth, Jonathan.
Roudebaugh, Henry.
Kelly, Morgan.
Dimpsey, Timothy.
Doud, Robert.
Davis, James.
Spangler, Samuel.
Logan, William.
Spidle, Mark.
Bisline, John.
Anders, Frederick.
Saudy, George.
Dennison, Samuel.

Branyan, William.
Jenning, Israel.
Garner, John.
Keel, Henry.
Willing, Michael.
McMullen, John A.
Holmes, David.
Hughes, William.
Jones, William.
Irvine, Presley.

The above and within roll is a just and true return of the men and their names, now in service and under my command, as part of the detachment to march to Erie, from the Fifth brigade, Seventh division, Pennsylvania militia, agreeable to a requisition of the President of the United States, and the order of the Governor of the State of Pennsylvania. Certified under my hand at Carlisle, March 5, 1814.

        ANDREW MITCHELL,
           Captain.
       JAMES FENTON,
        Colonel Commandant.

ROLL OF CAPT. WILLIAM MITCHELL'S COMPANY.

Muster-roll of a volunteer company of Infantry, under the command of Capt. William Mitchell, in the service of the United States, in the First regiment, Pennsylvania militia, commanded by Col. Clement C. Biddle, from September 6, 1814, when last mustered, to October 3, 1814, inclusive.

Captain.

Mitchell, William.

First Lieutenant.

Mitchell, Jacob, on command.

Second Lieutenant.

Cain, Dennis.

Third Lieutenant.

McCollin, William.

Ensign.

Hoffman, Frederick.

Sergeants.

Burden, Benjamin.
Fritez, Peter F.
Butcher, William.

Gross, Michael.
McGlue, Luke.

Corporals.

Schreiber, Theodore.
Allen, William.
Smith, John.
McGinly, William, on furlough.
Thibault, William.
Branson, John.

Acting Sergeant.

Leacock, William S.

Acting Corporal.

Clayton, Solomon.

Drummer.

Mitchell, George, sick in Philadelphia.

Privates.

Anderson, Jacob.
Aston, John.
Brown, Gowan A., on furlough.
Brady, James.
Brown, Joseph.
Borie, Simon.
Boulou, Augustus.
Barbazet, James.
Barbazet, Jacob.
Brown, Thomas.
Bruner, Henry.
Brown, James.
Bavis, Aaron.
Bomb, Conrad.
Barth, John.
Bright, Michael.
Brady, Alexander.
Bruce, Thomas.
Caruth, William.
Couden, Joseph.
Carpenter, Joshua.
Couden, Samuel.
Comegys, Benjamin.
Coombes, Joseph.
Carpenter, George.
Crumbly, Jacob.
Curby, Michael.
Crussel, Thomas A., absent without leave.
Cathrall, Edward.

Deforest, George.
Davis, Benjamin.
Downie, David.
Dutheyou, John.
Devon, Samuel.
English, Benajah.
Eckfeldt, George.
Foote, Lewis H.
Fries, Adam.
Gold, Paul.
Gravell, George.
Gray, Patrick.
Gross, Jacob.
Hesselpoth, Henry.
Haywood, Robert.
Houck, William.
Ivins, Isaiah.
Jones, Joseph.
Kreider, Anthony.
Linton, John, on furlough.
Lutz, John.
Lutz, Jacob.
Lower, John.
Latourna, Joseph.
Mills, David R.
Meyers, John H.
Miles, John, sick in Philadelphia.
McCormick, Henry.
McIlhenny, John.
McDonald, Richard, absent without leave.
McAllister, William, on furlough.
Newnam, Eli.
Polain, Philip.
Pickering, William.
Porter, James.
Payne, George.
Pringle, John, on furlough.
Pool, Joseph.
Rawlings, George.
Rhinehart, Joseph.
Robinson, William.
Rumpf, Peter.
Reess, Samuel.
Ryan, David.
Stackhouse, Samuel.
Schreiner, Nicholas.

Schreiner, William.
Shaw, Joseph.
Smith, Samuel.
Strickland, John, Jr.
Steever, James G.
Stephens, William, on furlough.
Shubert, Isaac.
Tacy, Joseph.
Tanier, John.
Thomas, Thomas.
Thatcher, Charles.
Wallis, Edward.
Williamson, Samuel.
Wallace, John.
Yard, Jacob.

I certify, on honor, that this muster-roll exhibits a true state of Capt. William Mitchell's company, of the First regiment of Pennsylvania militia, for the period therein mentioned, and that the remarks set opposite the names of the men are accurate and just.

WILLIAM MITCHELL,
Captain First Company, Union Guards.

I believe the foregoing muster-roll to be correct.

CONDY RAGUET,
Lieutenant Colonel First Regiment P. V.

I certify that the First company of Union Guards is in the service of the United States, under orders of the general commanding the Fourth military district.

THOS. CADWALADER,
Brigadier General Commanding.

CAMP DUPONT, *October 7, 1814.*

ROLL OF CAPT. ANDREW MOORE'S COMPANY.

Pay-roll of a company of infantry commanded by Capt. Andrew Moore, in the service of the United States, from October 2, 1812, until April 2, 1813, Second regiment, Second brigade, Pennsylvania militia, commanded by Brig. Gen. Richard Crooks.

Captain.

Moore, Andrew.

Lieutenant.

Flanigin, Andrew.

Ensign.

Allen, Elisha.

Sergeants.

Bailey, Andrew.
Gallagher, John.
Marrow, John, left sick at Canton, October 30, and returned home
Swain, Hiram.

Corporals.

Hughs, Reef.
Brewin, Elias.
McClelland, William.
Dunn, John, discharged December 20.

Privates.

Allen, David, discharged October 20.
Brown, Solomon.
Brown, Christopher.
Burt, Daniel, left sick at Canton, October 30.
Bright, David, died since the time expired.
Bardlow, Daniel, discharged December 19.
McDole, Alexander.
Uptecraft, Jacob.
Jewell, William.
Conquers, Samuel.
Mitchel, John.
Mitchel, Lewis.
Tissue, Sebastian.
Sills, John.
Steel, Isaac.
Lappin, Robert.
Gilliland, William.
Gilliland, Adam.
Fuller, James.
Shanks, Mathew.
Neighbours, William.
Miller, John.
Russell, James.
Low, Daniel, died since the time expired.
Evins, John.
Tissue, Edward, volunteered for fifteen days.
Vanhauten, Cornelius, volunteered for fifteen days.
Emberson, John, volunteered for fifteen days
Campbell, Jonathan, volunteered for fifteen days.
Wood, Lewis.
Wood, William.
Lewis, John.
Freeman, Edward.
Kemp, Solomon.

Kemp, William.
Heaney, Isaac.
Reynolds, William.
Swick, Martin.
Thompson, Aaron.
Maekelfresh, Eli.
Harris, Joseph.
Robbins, John.
Whetzell, Andrew.
Fisher, Michael.
McKee, John.
McCauce, James.
Daugherty, Patrick.
Yauger, Henry.
Miller, Pressley, discharged December 14.
Tharp, Job, left sick at Mansfield, December 23.
Wilson, William, discharged December 14.
Inks, John, discharged December 14.
Tharp, David, discharged October 19.
Weer, James, discharged October 19.
Coflier, James, discharged October 19.
McKearns, Charles, left sick at Canton, October 30.
Flick, Jacob, left sick at Canton, October 30.
Mareland, Robert.
Marble, Daniel.
Canon, Daniel.
McClean, Alexander.
Jackson, Robert.
Elliot, Benjamin, discharged October 19.
Leynard, Stephen.

We certify, on honor, that the above, according to the best of our knowledge, is accurate and just.

ANDREW MOORE,
Captain.
JOHN GALLAGHER,
Sergeant.
HIRAM SWAIN,
Sergeant.

ROLL OF CAPT. THOMAS MOORE'S COMPANY.

Muster-roll of Capt. Thomas Moore's company, of the Second regiment, Second brigade, Pennsylvania militia, under command of Lieut. Col. John Lotz, at York, Pennsylvania. In service from September 1, 1814, to March 5, 1815; from Berks county.

Captain.

Moore, Thomas.

First Lieutenant.

Tilton, William.

Ensign.

Baum, George.

Sergeants.

Moore, Samuel.
Stighter, Jacob.
Stout, Jacob.

Corporals.

Meffet. Peter.
Christ, Thomas.
Aurand, Peter.
Chadwick, Thomas.

Drummer.

Homan, Jacob.

Fifer.

Rightmire, David.

Privates.

Alguire, Jacob.
Baum, Jonas.
Bingamon, John.
Cyder, Jacob, waiter.
Dager, John.
Goodman, George.
Greaff, Frederick.
Habacker, Christian.
Habacker, Samuel.
Heller, John.
Homan, Jacob.
Hyneman, Frederick.
Isabue, Matthew.
Keen, John.

Kepner, John.
Kricher, George.
Kroh, John.
Lewis, Joseph.
Lotz, Daniel.
Lotz, Nicholas.
Lotz, William.
Lumberger, Michael.
McKay, Joseph.
Meffet, Peter.
Moore, Thomas.
Mulenberger, Francis.
Nagle, George.
Philippy, Jacob.
Porter, Richard.
Prutegonan, Abraham.
Reinhart, Ab^m.
Roland, George.
Row, Jacob.
Row, William.
Stout, Benjamin.
Stout, John.
Stout, Samuel.
Weisman, John.
Witman, Charles.
Witman, John.
Witman, William.
Wood, Joseph.
Wunder, George.
Wunder, Peter.
Young, Daniel.
Zimmerman, George.

ROLL OF CAPT. JOHN B. MOORHEAD'S COMPANY.

Muster-roll of Capt. John B. Moorhead's company, in the First regiment, First brigade, Pennsylvania militia, commanded by Col. Maxwell Kennedy, at York, September 5, 1814. In service from September 1, 1814, to March 5, 1815; from Dauphin county.

Captain.

Moorhead, John B.

Lieutenant.

Manley, John.

Ensign.

Habel, David.

Sergeants.

McCord, John.
Fishburn, Deitrich.
Hammil, William.
Louer, Simon.

Corporals.

McCord, William.
Drummond, Francis.
McNair, Thomas.
Ramsey, Thomas.

Privates.

Anghts, George.
Bear, Jacob.
Brown, John F.
Burnett, Archibald E.
Collins, Reuben.
Cowden, James.
Cowden, Matthew B.
Cromwell, John.
Cross, John.
Enk, Jacob.
Espey, David.
Foster, George W.
Fraizer, Andrew.
Gilchrist, John.
Haverstick, John.
Hollsman, Henry.
McKissick, Thomas.
Moore, Thomas H.
Moorhead, Robert.
Myer, Benjamin.
Pearson, Samuel.
Pollock, John.
Quig, William.
Shannan, Edward.
Simmons, Joseph.
Simonton, John W.
Stephen, Andrew.
Sterrett, Joseph.
Sturgeon, Allen.
Sturgeon, Robert.
Unger, David.
Wallace, John.

Welsh, Andrew.
Welsh, John.
Wheeler, Joseph.
Willson, William.
Zhent, Jacob.

ROLL OF CAPT. DAVID MORELAND'S COMPANY.

Muster-roll of Captain Moreland's company of volunteers belonging to the Fifth detachment, Pennsylvania militia, under the command of Col. James Fenton.

Captain.

Moreland, David.

First Lieutenant.

Thompson, Robert.

Second Lieutenant.

Neeper, John.

Ensign.

Cadwallader, Amos.

Sergeants.

Steigleman, John.
Kibler, John.
Rodgers, Richard.
Strock, George.

Corporals.

Adams, James.
Abercrombie, John.
Waggoner, Sebastian, missing July 20.
Rodgers, James.

Musicians.

Beems, David, deceased.
Myers, John.

Privates.

Askins, William, in Captain Hendel's company.
Barrickstresser, or Bergstreser, George.
Bower, Jacob.
Bergstresser, Solomon.
Bice, Samuel.
Barclay, William.
Bower, Peter.
Buck, George.
Buck, Robert.

Burd, Frederick.
Byers, Joshua.
Baughman, John.
Camp, Daniel.
Keiner, Jacob.
Clark, Thomas.
Dougherty, Robert, in Capt. Hendel's company.
Dysinger, David.
Dysinger, George.
Deckard, Philip.
Dunbar, Robert.
Dansville, Thomas.
Ewens, Moses.
Evinger, Peter.
Fry, Daniel.
Fry, Joseph, killed July 5.
Fry, Abraham.
Gillim, Jacob.
Goodlander, John.
Garland, John.
Gushard, Isaac.
Gallagher, John.
Gutshall, George.
Hollebaugh, Henry.
Hoobler, John.
Hollebaugh, Mathias.
Hays, Robert.
Hamaker, Jacob.
Hamilton, John.
Hochenberry, Joseph.
Irwin, George.
Jacobs, John.
Jordan, David.
Kesler, Adam.
Kesler, Peter.
Kennedy, Archibald.
Kelsey, George, in Capt. Hendel's company.
Kenny, Jacob.
Ledick, Jacob.
Moses, John.
McMurray, Ezekiel.
McCoy, Thomas.
Martin, James.
Miller, William.
Neeper, James.
Otto, Peter.

WAR OF 1812-14.

Potter, Jacob.
Presser, Henry.
Gray, George.
Rodgers, Robert, deceased.
Robison, George.
Ross, Henry.
Stumbaugh, Philip.
Shreffler, George.
Scott, James.
Strock, Joseph.
Sheaffer, Jacob.
Sheaffer, William.
Spanaberger, Michael.
Stuart, Richard.
Shaw, George.
Sleighter, John.
Shumbaugh, George.
Sheets, Samuel.
Stambaugh, Jacob.
Tate, Wiliam.
Taylor, Joseph.
Wilson, Joseph.
Wolf, Adam.
Welsh, Robert.
Wendt, George, taken prisoner July 5.
Wilson, Samuel.
Weaver, Michael.
Wallace, William.
Young, Abraham.
Rouse, Godfrey.
Shreffler, John.

I do hereby certify that the above and foregoing is a correct muster-roll of my company. Given under my hand this 22d day of September, A. D. 1814.

DAVID MORLAND,
Captain.
JAMES FENTON,
Colonel.

22—VOL. XII.

ROLL OF CAPT. WILLIAM MORGAN'S COMPANY.

Pay-roll of non-commissioned officers and privates, under the command of Capt. William Morgan, of the First company of First brigade, Third division, of Pennsylvania militia, now in the service of the United States, encamped at Marcus Hook, for the 10th day of October, 1814.

Sergeants.

Morgan, James.
Smith, Caleb.
Mather, John.
Brook, Lewis.
Crozer, Charles.

Corporals.

Trainer, Daniel.
Urain, William.
Davis, George.
Smith, Isaac.

Quarter-Master Sergeant.

Atmore, Isaac.

Privates.

Delainey, George.
Davis, Joseph.
Dickason, Enoch.
Lee, James.
Low, Robert.
Palmer, William.
Gill, William.
Smith, John.
Taylor, Thomas.
Brown, Samuel.
Burns, Isaac.
Morgan, Jonathan.
Lewis, Vernon.
Davis, Jonathan.
Dunn, George.
Maul, Jeremiah.
Mace, William.
Smith, Davis.
McClelin, William.
Vallentine, Robert.
Rhudolph, Joseph.

Hibberd, Aaron.
Jones, John.
Gore, John.
Handley, Henry.
Eppright, William.
Wright, Samuel.
Litzenburg, Adam.
Rhudolph, Joseph, 2d.
Rhudolph, Thomas.
Schrimger, John.
Lindsey, James, Jr.
Grim, Jacob.
Arment, Benjamin.
Latch, John.
Smith, David.
Fraim, William.
Ramsey, Enoch.
Fraim, James.
Kamp, Hezekiah.
Pennell, Evan.
Fraim, John.
Jones, Isaac.
Hoven, John.
Lindsey, Samuel.
Wright, James.
Kerns, John.
Williamson, Lewis.
Jones, Israel.
Gare, John, Jr.
Crozer, John.
Fines, Philip.
Trites, John.
Humphrey, Samuel.
Trites, William.
Wright, William.
Orr, William.
Ewing, John.
Forsyth, John.
Price, James.
Flahady, Michel.
Cox, Isaac.
McDade, Hugh.
Morton, John.
Armstrong, William.
Little, John.
McDonnal, John.

Stewart, John.
Wells, George.
Holdt, James.
Yoecome, George.
Hoff, John.
Ely, George.
Garey, Alexander.
Worrell, Elias.
Cozens, John.
Byers, Jacob.
Vernor, Jonathan.
Waters, Edward.
Stewart, William.
Hardey, Joshua.
Flounders, Septamus.
Free, John.
Hail, William.
Green, Joseph.
Green, John.
Heppelfinger, John.
Lithgaw, Robert.
Sharpless, Isaac.
O'Harrah, John.
McDougal, James.
Warrell, John H.

CAMP MARCUS HOOK, *October 18, 1814.*

I do hereby certify, on honor, that this muster-roll exhibits a true statement of the first company in the Sixty-fifth regiment, Pennsylvania militia, now in the service of the United States, and that the remarks set opposite the names are accurate and just, to the best of my knowledge and belief.

WM. MORGAN,
Captain.

I believe the within to be a correct muster pay-roll.

J. L. PEARSON,
Colonel Sixty-fifth regiment.

I certify that the first company in Sixty-fifth regiment, Pennsylvania militia, commanded by Capt. William Morgan, is in the service of the United States, under the order of the general commanding the Fourth military district.

SAM'L SMITH,
Brigadier General.

CAMP ——, *October —, 1814.*

ROLL OF CAPT. WILLIAM MORRIS' COMPANY.

Pay-roll of Capt. William Morris' company of Pennsylvania militia, belonging to the regiment of Pennsylvania militia commanded by Col. Rees Hill from the date of organization to the 5th day of November, 1813, inclusive. Commencement of service, May 5, 1813.

Captain.

Morris, William.

Lieutenants.

Weaver, Daniel.
Isgrig, William.
Crum, Cornelius, resigned June 5.
McIlroy, John, promoted from ensign June 5.

Ensign.

Love, William, promoted from sergeant June 5.

Sergeants.

Creswell, Alexander, promoted orderly sergeant June 5; discharged November 5.
Newingham, Henry.
Stratton, John, discharged November 5.
Metzebaugh, Joseph.
Wilson, William, promoted from corporal June 5.
Brotherland, John, promoted from corporal June 30.
Eckley, Joseph, promoted from corporal September 5.

Corporals.

Hollinshead, Samuel, discharged November 5.
McNamara, John, discharged November 5.
Riddle, John B., discharged October 13.
Mack, John, promoted from private June 5.
Scott, Benjamin, promoted from private June 5.
Galbraith, John, promoted from private September 5.

Privates.

Elsworth, Samuel.
Kelly, William.
Gutrie, William.
McCammon, John.
Dean, George.
Ewing, David.
Dearment, William.
Thomson, Matthew.
Shoup, George.

Fagin, Asaph, discharged October 13.
Weston, Joseph.
Wilson, George.
Wharton, Samuel.
Shaw, James.
McGiffin, Samuel.
Flener, Jonathan.
Strong, Daniel.
McKeehan, Samuel.
Burns, Isaac.
Kimberlin, Henry.
Duncan, Daniel, discharged October 13.
Nelson, William.
Walls, Jacob.
Cornelius, Jacob.
Bingham, John.
Williamson, Hugh.
David, William.
Clark, Samuel.
Bolinger, Jacob.
Long, John, discharged October 13.
Black, Robert.
Dun, John, discharged September 15.
Stewart, William, discharged November 5.
Thomson, Rees.
Getties, Robert.
McKeehan, David, died 15th.
Switchal, Jacob.
Taylor, William Wilson.
Larrimore, Thomas.
Boweroock, Jacob.
Camberlin, John.
Ilyte, James, discharged October 13.
Fitzimons, Henry.
Long, Henry.
Glen, James, discharged October 13.
Bingham, Hugh.
Lightner, Matthias.
Scott, John.
Hewet, Henry.
Shade, George.
Logan, Robert.
Johnson, Hugh, discharged October 13.
King, Patrick.
Swartz, Michael.
Shortbill, Thomas.

Grady, George, volunteered on board August 11.
Griffin, John.
Irwin, Samuel.
Forsley, Thomas.
Kint, Nicholas.
Fleming, John, July 16.
Ralston, Thomas.
Rickets, Hezekiah.
Booth, Thomas, discharged August 18.
Clabaugh, Henry.
Johnston, Thomas, died May 29.
Hanen, William, discharged.
Smice, John.
Campbell, Hugh.
Rudy, Daniel, discharged October 13.
Morehead, Samuel.
Stewart, James, discharged.
Hollis, William, discharged November 5.
Dougherty, Edward.
Clemans, Robert.
Stewart, John, discharged October 13.
Hawkenbery, Adam, July 16.
Johnson, Anthony, on furlough till the end of term.
Baugher, Henry.
Lennox, John.
Gooshorn, Samuel.

  I certify, on honor, that the within pay-roll is just and true, and the remarks set opposite the men's names are correct, to the best of my knowledge.

W. MORRIS,
Captain.
REES HILL.
Colonel commanding.

November 5, 1813.

ROLL OF CAPT. WILLIAM MORRIS' COMPANY.

  The following men, returned as members of my company, on a tour of duty to Erie, in the service of the United States, are returned by me as having neglected or refused to march, April 14, 1813, viz:

Armstrong, Andrew.
Campble, Isaac.
Carman, James.

Carolus, John.
Carven, John.
Corbin, Esel.
Couch, William.
Covenhoven, Hezekiah.
Cowen, Samuel.
Cryder, Daniel.
Deckert, Peter.
Dickey, John.
Dorsey, Edward B.
Dry, George.
Duff, John.
Eberly, Jacob.
Evans, Roland.
Ewing, Thomas.
Feagen, Asaph.
Foster, William.
Ginter, William.
Glazier, Charles.
Glenner, Jonathan.
Graffius, Martin.
Green, Charles.
Hemphill, Samuel.
Henderson, John.
Hollinger, Jacob.
Humphreys, Richard.
Johnston, William.
Lemon, Samuel.
Longenecker, Jacob.
Luitton, John.
Maguire, James.
Martin, Isaac.
Massey, Daniel.
McGeehan, David.
Miller, Frederick.
Miller, John, Esq.
Montgomery, Thomas.
Neff, Andrew.
Nelson, William.
Plummer, John.
Porter, James.
Porter, Samuel.
Reed, Robert.
Shint, Nicholas.
Shough, William.
Shrock, Andrew.

Sinkey, James.
Steel, John.
Thomas, John.
Warfield, Emanuel.
Westbrook, Levi.
Whiteman, Michael.
Williams, Samuel.
Wilson, George.
Woods, William.
Yocum, John.

WILLIAM MORRIS, 33,
Captain.

ROLL OF CAPT. JOSEPH MURRAY'S COMPANY.

Muster-roll of a volunteer company of Infantry, under the command of Capt. Joseph Murray, in the First regiment of Pennsylvania volunteers, in the service of the United States, commanded by Col. C. C. Biddle, from November 24, 1814, when last mustered, to January 4, 1815. Commencement of service, September 6, 1814.

Captain.

Murray, Joseph.

First Lieutenant.

Corcelius, William.

Second Lieutenant.

Stratton, John.

Third Lieutenant.

Ogle, Peter L.

Ensign.

Rogers, Andrew.

Sergeants.

Decoster, Charles.
Irvin, Frederick.
Carson, William.
Thomas, Jehu.
Howell, Amos.

Corporals.

Horn, John.
Headman, Andrew.
Morrison, And.
Keen, Moses.

Maley, John.
Roberts, Joseph.

Drummer.

Tryer, John.

Privates.

Avis, Joseph.
Armstrong, Thomas.
Baen, William.
Benner, George.
Burn, Michael.
Bell, John, deceased October 26.
Bell, Thomas.
Budd, John.
Baker, John.
Clark, John.
Crothers, Samuel.
Cunitz, Lewis.
Chrystler, John.
Childs, Robert.
Campbell, William.
Cramer, Charles.
Durr, John.
Demick, Caleb.
Davis, Joseph.
Fox, George W.
Fizone, Anth.
Fizone, Jacob.
Field, John.
Girvin, John.
Huff, George William.
Hays, Archer.
Harvey, Robert.
Headman, Jacob.
Hellem, Jacob.
Holahan, Jacob.
Horn, Peter.
Hobson, William L.
Heppard, William.
Johnson, Jesse.
Johnson, Jacob.
Jones, Holvell.
James, Samuel.
Keith, Robert.
Leyer, Henry.
Lyndall, Samuel.

Leinan, Daniel.
Lauck, Joseph.
McMullin, Daniel.
McCafferty, Hugh.
Moore, William.
Merkel, Conrad.
Maxfield, Thomas.
Mifflin, Thomas.
Miller, Richard.
Nice, John.
Porter, John.
Simpson, John.
Sommerl, William.
Sourman, Yerkes.
Snyder, Henry.
Shute, William.
Smith, Charles, discharged November 15.
Shinn, Ezra.
Tash, Thomas.
Whitman, Samuel.
Whitman, Henry.
Wood, Edward.
West, William.
Collins, Joseph, servant.
Johnston, Peter, servant.

We do certify, on honor, that this muster-roll exhibits a true state of Capt. Murray's company, of the First regiment, Pennsylvania volunteers, for the period therein mentioned.

JOSEPH MURRAY,
Captain.
CLEMENT C. BIDDLE,
Colonel First regiment, Pennsylvania Volunteers.

ROLL OF CAPT. GEORGE MUSSER'S COMPANY.

Muster-roll of Capt. George Musser's company, in the Rifle regiment, of the Second brigade, Pennsylvania militia, under the command of Lieut. Col. William Hamilton, at York, Pa. In service from ——— to ———; from Lancaster county.

Captains.

Hamilton, William.
Musser, George.

WAR OF 1812–14.

First Lieutenants.

Musser, George.
Hill, Frederick.

Second Lieutenants.

Hill, Frederick.
Weir, George.

Orderly Sergeants.

Eichholtz, Leonard.
McKinzell, Daniel.

Sergeants.

McKinzell, Daniel.
Huffnagle, George.
Huffnagle, Peter.
Mayers, Jacob.
Musser, Abraham.
Backenstos, William.

Corporals.

Mayers, Jacob.
Musser, Abram.
Backenstos, William.
Bomburger, John.
Elliot, Robert.
Barton, Matthias.
Colspher, Peter.

Corporals.

Brissler, Benjamin.
Fraily, Jacob.

Drummer.

Garron, Jacob.

Fifer.

Bower, Jacob.

Bugler.

Fordney, Samuel.

Privates.

Albright, Jacob.
Albright, William.
Algier, Michael.
Balsmer, Moses.
Barton, Matthias.
Block, John.
Bomberger, George.
Bonnet, John.

Brenner, Jacob.
Breslin, Benjamin.
Brubaker, Henry.
Bruner, Casper, Sr.
Bruner, Casper, Jr.
Bruner, Henry.
Buchers, John.
Burg, Christian.
Burg, John.
Carson, Robert.
Colsher, Peter.
Danner, Jacob.
Daub, George.
Davis, Samuel.
Davis, Thomas R.
Dealer, William.
Delander, Jacob.
Deleet, Adam.
Dietrich, George.
Duchman, John.
Elliot, Robert.
Eplar, Lewis.
Eshman, Michael.
Evans, Jacob.
Ferree, John.
Ferree, John, Jr.
Ferree, William.
Fitzgerrald, Thomas.
Fordney, Samuel.
Frailey, Jacob.
Greaff, Matthias.
Green, John.
Green, Neal.
Hinny, William.
Holmes, Norman.
Hoover, George.
Hoover, John.
Huffnagle Michael.
Huffnagle, Peter.
Huppert, John.
Jones, Samuel.
Jourdon, Casper.
Jourdon, Joseph, waiter.
Jourdon, Michael.
Keller, John.
Kirk, Isaac.

Kitch, Jacob.
Kline, Michael.
Krider, Paul.
Kuhn, Augustus.
Lightner, Isaac.
Lind, John.
Loesholtz, George.
Lyon, James.
Mackey, Benjamin.
McCan, Francis.
McClure, Robert.
McClure, Samuel.
McCoy, Stephen.
McGonigal, John.
McGrenagan, Alexander.
McLean, Andrew.
McLeanagan, Samuel.
Metzgar, Philip.
Miller, William.
Muldoon, Charles.
Mulford, Jonathan.
Musketnuss, Adam.
Nagle, George.
Patterson, John.
Pole, Henry.
Powel, John.
Reinhart, Jacob.
Reitz, Jacob.
Rexroth, Peter.
Ritter, John.
Rollison, George.
Rotharml, Adam.
Ruse, John.
Shartzer, Philip.
Shoebrooks, Edward.
Shufflebottom, Josiah.
Simpson, William.
Smith, Jacob.
Smith, Jasper.
Snodgrass, George.
Stake, George.
Stoy, Gustavus.
Syker, Peter.
Tindal, William.
Titus, William.
Tripple, Joseph.

Trissler, John.
Wallace, Thomas.
Weidel, Adam.
White, Christian.
White, Levy.
Winters, Stacy.
Wise, John.
Zeller, Ephraim.

ROLL OF CAPT. JOHN NAGLEE'S COMPANY.

Pay-roll of a company of Northern Liberty Artillerists, under the command of Capt. John Naglee, in the regiment of artillery in the service of the United States, commanded by Lieut. Col. A. M. Prevost. In service from September 8, 1814, to January 3, 1815.

Captain.

Naglee, John.

First Lieutenant.

Baker, Michael.

Second Lieutenant.

Baker, George N.

Third Lieutenant.

Swab, Joseph.

Sergeants.

Naglee, Joseph.
Foering, Samuel.
Hay, Peter.
Lesher, Charles.
Preston, William, on furlough since December 6, to work at fortification.

Quarter-master Sergeant.

Landle, George.

Corporals.

Limeburner, John.
Rush, Thomas.
Craft, William.
Millard, Charles.

Privates.

Andrews, Abraham.
Bowers, Joshua, on furlough since December 6, 1814, to work at fortification.

Brewster, James.
Brautigam, John.
Bedeman, Jacob.
Boshart, John.
Benner, Whiteman.
Boylin, James.
Bisbing, George.
Biedelman, Jacob R.
Carter, John, on furlough from November 23, 1814.
Clothier, Samuel, on furlough from November 28, 1814, to work at fortification.
Cramp, John, on furlough from November 28, 1814, to work at fortification.
Collar, Michael.
Deal, John, on furlough November 28, 1814, to work at fortification.
Dillman, Christian.
Eager, William, on furlough November 28, 1814, to work at fortification.
Emmons, Samuel.
Emerrick, Frederick, on furlough November 28, 1814, to work at fortification.
Fisher, Henry.
Frederickson, John.
Fagundus, George.
Gable, Daniel.
Graul, Daniel.
German, Vincent.
Hoffman, Samuel, on furlough November 28, 1814, to work at fortification.
Hewston, Robert.
Hammit, Isaac, on furlough December 20, 1814, to work at fortification.
Hodge, Richard, on furlough November 28, 1814, to work at fortification.
Hymbach, Adam.
Heiss, William.
Hunneker, John.
Hoeckley, Christian.
Ireland, Edward, on furlough December 6, 1814, to work at fortification.
Justice, Joseph P.
Jones, George.
Keiter, William.
Jefferries, William.
Kivlin, James.
Keiter, James.

Luffberry, John, on furlough November 28, 1814, to work at fortification.
Luffberry, Samuel, on furlough November 28, 1814, to work at fortification.
Luffberry, Andrew, on furlough November 28, 1814, to work at fortification.
Murphy, Charles, on furlough November 28, 1814, to work at fortification.
Marks, Samuel.
Nell, John.
Oneil, John, on furlough December 26, 1814, to work at fortification.
Pennington, William, on furlough November 28, 1814, to work at fortification.
Pitcher, Henry, on furlough November 28, 1814, to work at fortification.
Poat, Henry.
Pickering, Joseph.
Poat, Christian.
Painter, George, on furlough December 8, 1814, to work at fortification.
Rice, Peter, on furlough November 28, 1814, to work at fortification.
Rice, John J., on furlough November 28, 1814, to work at fortification.
Reaver, Henry.
Rhile, Henry.
Sutten, William.
Sutton, John.
Streeten, William, on furlough November 28, 1814, to work at fortification.
Shibe, Casper, on furlough November 28, 1814, to work at fortification.
Sickfret, Joseph, on furlough November 28, 1814, to work at fortification.
Streeby, Joseph.
Scheetz, Jacob.
Shermer, Jacob.
Smith, George F.
Sheerer, Isaac.
Seddenger, John.
Stackhouse, Stephen, on furlough.
Tossleson, Nelson, on furlough.
Vandusen, Nicholas.
Vice, David, on furlough November 28, 1814, to work at fortification.
Walter, Phillip.
Wagner, William.

23--Vol. XII.

Williamson, Henry.
Willcox, Stephen.
Zigler, George.
Jackson, Jacob L., servant to captain.
Bowen, David, servant to lieutenant.

Those persons named on furlough have been employed, and have received full wages for their labor, and have been settled with by the United States pay-master for only the time actually in service.

See United States pay-roll, in hand of Col. Prevost.

JOHN NAGLEE,
Late Captain of the Northern Liberty Artillery.

I certify the above return to be correct to the best of my knowledge, and Capt. Naglee's signature to be genuine.

ANDREW M. PREVOST,
Late Lieut. Col. First Reg. Vol. Artillery, Service of United States.

ROLL OF LIEUT. ALEXANDER NAPIER'S COMPANY.

Muster-roll of the Third company of drafted militia, under the command of Lieut. Com. Alexander Napier, in service of the United States. Commencing on the 25th day of August last, commanded by Lieut. Col. Peter Berry, and from the 23d of August, when last mustered.

Lieutenant Commandant.
Napier, Alexander, August 26.

Lieutenant.
Fisher, John P.

Acting Ensign.
Howell, Lemuel.

Sergeants.
Boddy, John.
Hergesheimer, John.
Alexander, Joseph.
Brelsford, Francis.

Corporals.
McManame, Tole.
Day, John.
Triall, Peter A.
Lippencott, William C.

Privates.

Arther, James.
Bones, John.
Bradly, James.
Barret, Persel.
Butler, James.
Broom, Elias.
Buck, Hugh.
Coleman, Jonathan.
Collins, William H.
Cope, Philip.
Cade, Jonathan.
Conagan, Darby.
Croser, Benjamin.
Denney, Jacob.
Davis, David.
Danely, John.
Dugen, Daniel.
Force, Samuel.
Frances, John.
Gebart, Joseph.
Hannah, Samuel.
Hill, Charles.
Herder, Peter.
Hofman, Christopher.
Hammel, James.
Jeffres, Richard.
Kennard, George M.
Loyd, Henry.
Loper, Uriah.
Macentee, Bernard.
Mills, James.
Manship, Thomas.
McKarraker, John.
Mackneme, or McNamee, John.
McMean, or McMinn, Samuel.
Ogden, Robert.
Ogden, John.
Pancost, Thomas.
Petit, Amos C.
Roch, Thomas.
Rhamp, William.
Smith, John.
Sherkey, James.
Stotsenburg, Michel.

Shaffer, Philip.
Willey, James W.
Wells, Jesse.
Yeager, Benjamin.
McNulty, John, transferred to volunteer.
Freeland, Joseph, transferred to volunteer.
Bowden, Zachariah, transferred to volunteer.
Wolf, Jacob, discharged by the colonel, being over age.
Gilmore, Patrick, transferred to volunteer.
Germon, Francis, transferred to volunteer.
Vivans, John.
Dicks, Henry, transferred to volunteers.
Burk, Thomas.
Siscoe, James, transferred to volunteers.
Cooper, George.

We certify, on honor, that this muster-roll exhibits a true state of the third company of the drafted militia for the period therein mentioned, and that the remarks set opposite the names of the men are accurate and just.

(Signed)
ALEX'R NAPIER,
Lieutenant commandant.
JOHN P. FISHER,
Lieutenant.

I believe the above to be correct.

PETER L. BERRY,
Lieutenant Colonel.

I certify that the third company of drafted militia commanded by Lieut. A. Napier, is in the service of the United States, under orders of the general commanding Fourth military district.

THOS. CADWALADER,
Brigadier General commanding.

CAMP DUPONT, *October 7, 1814.*

ROLL OF CAPT. THOMAS NEEL'S COMPANY.

Muster-roll of Capt. Thomas Neel's company, of the Second regiment, First brigade, Pennsylvania militia, under the command of Lieut. Col. Adam Risher, at York. In service from September 9, 1814, to March 5, 1815; from Lancaster county.

Captain.

Neel, Thomas.

Lieutenant.

Milligan, Robert.

Ensign.

Noble, Andrew.

Sergeants.

McClure, James.
Milliner, Isaac.
Jones, John.
Doughty, Henry.

Corporals

Horner, Matthew.
Patterson, James.
Caughy, John.
Rippy, Henry.

Privates.

Badger, George.
Barkley, James.
Boyd, John.
Bunting, William.
Clark, Jonathan.
Clark, Samuel.
Collins, Thomas.
Connelly, Patrick.
Creamer, Christian.
Davis, Jesse.
Dolly, Abraham.
Donnelly, James.
Dunkle, George.
Dunkle, John.
Dunn, William.
Earhart, Adam.
Eckley, James.
Evans, Abraham.
Fentermacker, Adam.
Fitz, Jacob.
Fraslier, James.
Gavel, John.
George, William.
Gregg, Nathaniel.
Hamilton, Samuel.
Hastins, John.
Hays, John.
Hemphill, John.
Herron, John.
Hetherington, James.
Hopper, Samuel.

Kerns, Christian.
Kidd, John.
Labaser, James.
Lemmon, Isaac.
Loomas, Francis.
McCanna, Taurance.
McClelland, William.
McClung, Samuel.
McCmin, Hugh.
McConnel, William.
McCord, James.
McCrea, William.
McGlaughlin, James.
McKerrigan, William.
Milligan, James.
Montgomery, William.
Murray, James.
Nicholas, Richard.
Norton, John.
Patman, George.
Patton, Robert.
Pickle, John.
Pierce, Richard.
Pocock, Thomas.
Reed, Joseph.
Rodgers, Hugh.
Sampson, John.
Sampson, William.
Skean, Joseph.
Sott, William.
Stiles, William Francis.
Suiter, James.
Swisher, Henry.
Taylors, James.
Wallace, William.
Whitesides, Thomas.
Wilson, Thomas.
Wilson, William Josiah.
Wivle, Samuel.

ROLL OF CAPT. PETER NUNGESSER'S COMPANY.

A complete muster-roll for the Fourth (Capt. Nungesser's) company of the Second regiment volunteer Light Infantry, under the command of Col. Louis Bache, under the order of the commander-in-chief of the Commonwealth of Pennsylvania, of August 27, 1814, and attached to the First brigade, Second division, P. A. M.

Captain.

Nungesser, Peter, Jr.

First Lieutenant.

Lombeart, Charles.

Second Lieutenant.

Segreaves, Henry.

Ensign.

Barnett, William, Jr.

Sergeants.

Peirsol, Andrew.
Mush, John.
Hickman, Conrad.
Nagle, John.

Corporals.

Geno, Lewis.
Arndt, Benjamin F.
Osterstock, Jacob.
Reichart, George.

Drum-Major.

Horne, Charles.

Fife-Major.

Stroup, George.

Privates.

Arnold, Thomas.
Schooley, William.
Bishop, Peter.
Barnes, Stephen.
Bachman, Samuel.
Bachman, Jacob.
Cary, Isaac.
Diley, Valentine.
Dehart, John.
Reichart, Philip.
Reichart, John.

Yohe, Jacob.
Hawk, Thomas.
Skelley, John.
Wallace, Robert.
Otto, John.
Morgan, Joseph.
Garron, William.
Simons, John.
Troxell, Michael.
Hutter, Christian.
White, Samuel.
Levers, William.
Jarman, John.
Stucker, Jacob.
Frants, Simon.
Everhart, Peter.
Ludwick, John.
Levan, Samuel.
Newhart, John.
Easterwood, Laurence.
Young, John.
Bellows, Joseph.
Snyder, William.
Ferren, John.
Gemming, or Jennings, Edward.
Drumheller, Philip.
Ervine, or Erwin, Scott, appointed sergeant major.

   I certify the above to be just and true, on my honor.

C. LOMBAERT,
Lieutenant.

CAMP MARCUS HOOK, *November 29, 1814.*

LOUIS BACHE,
Lieut. Col. Second Regiment Penn'a Vol. L. I.

ROLL OF CAPT. ANDREW OAKS' COMPANY.

Greencastle company, Capt. Andrew Oaks, September 5, 1812, in Col. Jared Irwin's regiment.

Captain.

Oaks, Andrew.

Lieutenant.

Wilson, Thomas.

Ensign.

Zeigler, George.

Sergeants.

Cramer, Peter.
Gudtner, Jacob.
Fletter, Jacob.
Pennel, James.

Corporals.

Dugan, William.
Sharer, George.
Garresene, Jacob.
Brady, Thomas.

Fifer.

Sites, Henry.

Drummer.

Poper, Jacob.

Privates.

Brendlinger, Henry.
Byerly, Joseph.
Bettes, George.
Bolton, William.
Bender, Samuel.
Carroll, William.
Dugan, Patrick.
Evans, Evan.
Foster, William.
Fletcher, Thomas.
Gaff, John.
Gordon, William.
Garner, John.
Keller, Richard.
Martin, Samuel.
McCurdy, James.
McLaughlin, Samuel.
Ovelman, William.
Plummer, Thomas.
Snyder, John.
Scully, William.
Sreader, John.
Stuff, George.
Smith, Samuel.
Shaffer, George.
Uller, George.
Wilhelm, Christian.
Weidner, Samuel.
Weidner, Daniel.

ROLL OF CAPT. GABRIEL OLD'S COMPANY.

Muster-roll of Capt. Gabriel Old's company, in the Second regiment, Second brigade, Pennsylvania militia, under the command of Lieut. Col. John Lootz, at York, Pennsylvania. In service from September 1, 1814, to March 5, 1815, from Berks county.

Captain.

Old, Gabriel.

Lieutenant.

Fistee, John.

Ensign.

Shook, William.

Sergeants.

Muislan, Rudolph.
Lexan, Isaac.
Graff, William.
Arens, George.

Corporals.

Graff, Daniel.
Wiltman, John.
Lehman, Jacob.
Langbien, Jacob.

Drummer.

Marro, William.

Fifer.

Treler, Jonas.

Privates.

Adams, William.
Aker, Jonathan.
Bichel, Abraham.
Bowman, John.
Boyer, Abraham.
Boyer, Daniel.
Breash, George.
Brown, Andrew.
Danner, Jacob.
Delong, Michael.
Dor, William.
Eisenhart, Jacob.

Esse, George.
Fegeley, George.
Fisher, Jacob.
Fisher, John.
Flauer, Adam.
Flauer, Samuel.
Folk, Peter.
Frasher, William.
Friniot, John.
Gaest, Valentine.
Gilgert, Jonas.
Glausee, Jacob.
Hausknechs, Jacob.
Hill, Peter.
Hoffman, Gideon.
Hoffman, Joseph.
Hughes, Jeremiah.
Kamp, Jacob.
Kamp, Samuel.
Kaup, Andrew.
Kayser, John.
Keefer, Jacob.
Kercher, Benjamin.
Kimerling, John.
Kreisher, Nicholas.
Leib, Reuben.
Letwyler, Abram.
Long, Daniel.
Menker, Henry.
Menker, John.
Miller, Philip.
Noll, John.
Old, George.
Polzgrove, Jacob.
Reeder, John.
Reifsnyder, Moses.
Reininger, John.
Roof, Henry.
Roof, John.
Rowzahn, Christian.
Rowzahn, David.
Shaffer, Jacob.
Shaffer, Nathan.
Sherer, Michael.
Simmons, William.
Smith, Andrew.

Snyder, John.
Snyder, John K.
Stout, Samuel.
Strome, John.
Stroup, George.
Weaver, Henry.
Weaver, Peter.
Winder, Jacob.
Wiser, Jacob.
Woalison, George.
Young, Daniel.
Ziegler, Benjamin.

ROLL OF CAPT. DANIEL OLDENBERGH'S COMPANY.

Muster-roll of a company of Infantry under the command of Capt. Daniel Oldenbergh, in the service of the United States, commanded by Col. C. C. Biddle, of the First regiment, Pennsylvania volunteers. Commencement of service, August 27, 1814; when last mustered, inspected, and discharged, January 4, 1815.

Captain.

Oldenbergh, Daniel.

First Lieutenant.

Wright, George C.

Second Lieutenant.

Snyder, John.

Ensign.

Fawkes, Richard.

Sergeants.

Allison, Walter.
McClure, Robert.
McCoy, Kenneth.
Wile, John.
Colladay, Charles.

Corporals.

Emerick, Benjamin.
Buckingham, Edward.
Savoy, Francis.
Snyder, David.

Privates.

Bastian, Charles.
Butcher, John.

Bates, William.
Bolen, Henry.
Bucker, Joseph.
Broadnix, James.
Brown, Maurice.
Blair, William.
Clark, George E.
Clark, George.
Cable, Charles.
Critz, Peter.
Countryman, Christopher.
Course, William.
Davis, Robert.
Evens, Ellis.
Finn, Henry.
Frazier, John.
Hall, Benjamin.
Hute, Henry.
Hassel, Daniel.
Harman, Andrew.
Hulan, Henry.
Hamilton, William.
Hollick, John.
Mullock, Edward.
Kirkland, George.
Kellam, Benjamin.
Linch, Daniel.
Lincoln, John.
Marker, Jacob.
Marker, Philip.
Morris, John.
Makeson, George.
Makeson, Henry.
Mark, Conrad.
Morgan, John.
Mires, Henry.
Mackarahar, Daniel.
Olwine, Samuel.
Paskel, Edward.
Rambow, David.
Kettring, Jacob.
Sinclair, Samuel.
Shuster, John.
Smith, Thomas.
Spregle, John.
Scrivinger, or Schriminger, John.

Stevens, Joseph.
Sifert, John.
Thompson, Peter.
Tichner, Richard.
Turner, John.
Wright, John.
Wattles, Alex.
Wray, Thomas.
Stinger, Daniel.
Weaver, William.

We certify, on honor, that this muster-roll exhibits a true state of Capt. Daniel Oldenbergh's company of infantry in the First regiment Pennsylvania volunteers, for the period therein mentioned, and that the remarks set opposite the names are accurate and just.

CLEMENT C. BIDDLE,
Colonel First Regiment Pennsylvania Volunteers.
DANIEL OLDENBERGH,
Captain Infantry Volunteers.

ROLL OF CAPT. JOHN OTT'S COMPANY.

CAMP DUPONT, *November 13, 1814.*

A true list of Capt. John Ott's Volunteer Rifle company of the Second Co^n, First battalion, under the command of Col. Thomas Humphrey.

Captain.

Ott, John.

Lieutenant.

Wild, Joseph.

Ensign.

Jumgerd, Caspar.

Sergeants.

Wittman, Frederick.
Knepply, Jacob.
Ox, Matias.
Wind, Peter.

Corporals.

Jenners, Thomas.
Haller, Elias.
Hearline, Melcher.
Fogel, William.

Bugler.

Weber, Henry.

WAR OF 1812-14.

Drummer.

Jacoby, Philip.

Fifer.

Weber, Earhard.

Privates.

Shapar, Peter.
Nederrour, Daniel.
Heager, Philip.
Jacoby, Philip.
Brown, John.
Gangwer, Jacob.
Stoll, Frederick.
Hofman, John.
Dotra, Matias.
Paul, Samuel.
Trapp, John.
Buchaker, Philip.
Romig, Daniel.
Meuer, Henry.
Henn, John.
Guerd, John.
Gangwear, Daniel.
Loskerge, or Boskerg, John.
Rigenback, Leonard.
Buchaker, Peter.
Shafar, Simon.
Mastaller, Henry.
Bouter, Henry.
Trapp, George.
Hearline, Philip.
Weber, Peter.
Wild, Peter.

This is a true list of all the men in my company, November 13, 1814.

JOHN OTT,
Captain.
THOMAS HUMPHREY,
Colonel First Regiment P. V. R.

I do certify, on honor, that the company commanded by Capt. John Ott is in the service of the United States, under the command of the general commanding the Fourth military district.

THOMAS CADWALADER,
Brigadier General Commanding Advance Light Brigade.
CAMP DUPONT, *November 26, 1814.*

ROLL OF CAPT. WILLIAM PAINTER'S COMPANY.

Pay-roll of Capt. Painter's company, Second brigade, First division, Pennsylvania militia, in the service of the United States, under command of Col. John Thompson.

Alexander, Wolf.
Annadown, Henry.
Bosick, Henry.
Bartle, George.
Barris, Thomas.
Blecker, Jacob.
Bailey, John.
Beverlin, James.
Buck, Frederick G.
Buchanan, Alexander.
Baites, Isaiah.
Burch, David.
Baker, Frederick.
Barnholdt, John.
Britton, Edward.
Bentley, John.
Clymer, George.
Cooper, James.
Cryser, Samuel.
Cox, Menan K.
Cake, Matthias.
Duncan, Nathaniel.
Deboufre, James.
Emery, Henry.
English, Michael.
Eyres, Joseph.
Fox, Samuel.
Fox, Anthony.
Franks, Henry.
Gaun, George.
Goldsmith, Jeremiah.
Gable, John.
Hubbert, Benjamin.
Harman, John.
Hillman, Oliver.
Howard, Richard.
Hughes, William.
Hoover, David.
Hamilton, John.

Haines, Robert.
Hearty, Charles.
Hemphill, Adam.
Hargrove, William.
Higgins, Frederick.
Hollingsworth, John.
Hollowell, John.
Jaggers, Jonathan.
Jackson, Benjamin.
Johnson, Daniel.
Kessler, Martin.
Lowe, Thomas.
Koch, J.
Ludlow, Isaac.
Locke, Nathaniel.
Miller, Jacob.
Moxley, John.
Montgomery, Robert.
Miller, William.
Murphy, Arthur.
Morgan, Nicholas.
Nice, Frederick.
Nace, Jacob.
Pool, John.
Parker, Nathaniel.
Quinlin, William.
Rudy, Jacob.
Riter, John.
Rookstull, Jacob.
Seybert, William.
Rout, Jacob.
Steinauer, Adam.
Stele, Thomas.
Sneck, Jacob.
Smith, Henry.
Stevenson, Dennis.
Smith, Philip.
Stone, John.
Smith, Christian.
Thomas, Jacob.
Trexler, Jonathan.
Thompson, Robert.
Thompson, Constant.
Thomas, William.
Thomas, Israel.
Thompson, William.

24—Vol. XII.

Ulrich, Frederick.
Ulrich, Henry.
Kerum, Thomas.
Vantine, Joseph.
Warton, Isaiah.
Worman, Samuel.
Weever, John.
Watson, Christian.
Yunker, Jacob.
Young, John.

We certify, on honor, that the within roll exhibits a true state of the militia company commanded by Capt. William Painter, and that the remarks are accurate and just, and that the names therein contained are non-commission officers and privates.

WM. PAINTER,
Captain.
JOHN THOMPSON,
Colonel.

CAMP MARCUS HOOK, *October 17, 1814.*

I certify that the militia company commanded by Capt. William Painter, is in the service of the United States, under orders of the general commanding Fourth military district.

THOMAS SNYDER,
Brigadier General commanding.

CAMP MARCUS HOOK, *October 17, 1814.*

ROLL OF CAPT. JAMES PERLE'S COMPANY.

Muster-roll of the First company drafted militia, under the command of Capt. James Perle, of the First brigade, First division, Pennsylvania militia, lately in the service of the United States, commanded by Lieut. Col. Peter L. Berry, from the 23d of November, 1814, to the 2d of January, 1815, when last mustered, and that day discharged by order of Gen. Cadwalader.

Captain.

Perle, James.

First Lieutenant.

Forgrave, William.

Second Lieutenant.

Hanna, William.

Ensign.

Taylor, Charles.

Sergeants.

Breidenbaugh, Valentine.
George, Israel.
Bovard, William.
Hergesheimer, J.

Corporals.

Frederick, Philip.
Houtzell, John.
Ogden, Robert.
Alexander, John.
Pancost, T. F.

Privates.

Arthur, James.
Bowen, Clement R.
Biggard, James.
Brelsford, F.
Broom, Elias.
Bartram, David.
Brotherton, John.
Blume, George.
Cost, George.
Cassady, Humphrey.
Campbell, John.
Comman, William.
Coleman, Jonathan.
Coles, Michael.
Clark, Robert, discharged November 14, 1814.
Douden, T. C.
Dickhart, Jacob.
Dicks, Bartley, or Barclay.
Dallman, John.
Davis, David.
Donald, Manes O.
Evaland, William.
Estwick, Henry.
Edwards, Thomas.
Espey, James.
Etwine, Jacob.
Flowers, George.
Force, Samuel.
Fry, John.
Fletcher, Joshua.
Greer, Joseph.
Good, F.
Hunt, James.

Hight, Charles.
Hoffman, Gabriel.
Hoffman, Christian.
Hurder, Peter.
Hassett, Edward.
Kennard, George.
Little, Elijah.
Link, Frederick.
Lippencott, William.
Leatherberry, Pery.
Lewis, Joseph.
McElroy, William.
Mace Joseph N.
McGlincy, John.
Matthews, John.
McMane, Samuel.
McNamee, John.
Philips, Rowland.
Prichett, Richard.
Rooth, George.
Russell, J. W.
Rivall, Adam.
Russell, Howard.
Regnault, George.
Schaeffer, Peter.
Story, Jeremiah.
Stokely, Prettymor, or Prettyman.
Stewart, James.
Simons, John.
Swartz, Gotleib.
Sourman, I. P.
Schaeffer, Philip.
Stricker, John.
Smith, John.
Trexler, Jacob.
Tryall, P. A.
Wharton, Fishburn, died November 9, 1814.
Williams, Samuel.
Walker, William.
Walnut, J. W.
Wardle, Philip.
Yeager, Benjamin.
Young, Jacob.
Ricketts, George.

We certify, on honor, that this muster-roll exhibits a true statement of the First company of drafted militia, lately in the service

WAR OF 1812-14.

of the United States, for the period therein mentioned, and the remarks set opposite the names of the men are accurate and just.

JAMES PERLE,
Late Captain.

PHILADELPHIA, *January 31, 1816.*

I certify that the foregoing muster-roll is just and true.

WM. BOZORTH,
Major Commanding.

ROLL OF CAPT. MICHAEL PETRE'S COMPANY.

Muster-roll of Capt. Michael Petre's company in the Second regiment, First brigade, Pennsylvania militia, under the command of Col. Adam Richards at York, Pennsylvania. In service from September 1, 1814, to March 5, 1815, from Berks and Lancaster counties.

Captain.

Petre, Michael.

Lieutenant.

Salada, Jacob.

Ensign.

German, Jacob.

Sergeants.

Levy, Daniel.
Moyer, George.
Ozwald, George.
Griersy, Jacob.

Corporals.

Clause, Daniel.
Smith, Joseph.
Eckler, Jacob.

Musicians.

Daniel, John.
Manner, Charles.

Privates.

Allen, David.
Bonewitts, Adam.
Bowman, Solomon.
Dautrich, George.
Dippery, John.
Feitler, Leonard.
Filbert, Peter.
Fisher, Peter.

Fox, John.
Gibson, John.
Greiger, John.
Hammer, Jacob.
Hoffman, George.
Holgate, George.
Klein, Benjmain.
Klinger, John.
Kolb, Nicholas.
Krick, Jacob.
Krill, William.
Kutz, John.
Leininger, Peter.
Lindemuth, Samuel.
Lissfall, Philip.
Manner, Samuel.
McAnally, William.
More, Anthony.
Nagle, John.
North, John.
Pappert, Jacob.
Pierce, David.
Preisg, Christopher.
Preisg, Michael.
Senex, James.
Smith, William.
Williams, George.
Wissner, Jacob.
Wormelsdorff, Daniel.

ROLL OF CAPT. JOHN PHILIPS' COMPANY.

Pay-roll of Capt. John Philips' company of United States volunteers, lately under the command of Maj. John Herkimer, in the service of the United States; discharged at Oswego, August 26, 1813; commencement of service, August 28, 1812.

Captain.

Philips, John.

Lieutenant.

Wood, Joseph.

Sergeants.

Kalor, Frederick.
Kramer, Balthaser.
Kelley, Matthew.

WAR OF 1812–14.

Corporals.

Daugherty, Zadoc.
Shaw, James.
Philips, Peter.

Privates.

Nailor, John.
Daugherty, William.
Tipton, Thomas.
Dorff, Richard.
Cassady, Edward.
Caseman, John.
Black, James.
Ramage, James.
Hannahs, John.
Iliff, Stephen.
Smith, Thomas.
Bear, David.
Morgan, David.
Havel, Philip.
More, Samuel L.
Handin, Cato, discharged December 9.
Parke, John, furlough to April 1; not returned.
Denney, Miller, furlough to March 1; not returned.
Darling, James, discharged December 9.
O'Nail, Charles.
Clovous, Matthias, discharged February 17.
Philips, Theophilous, discharged December 9.
Bothwell, John.
Ogle, Lewis.
Parke, Andrew.

I certify that the within exhibits a true statement of Capt. John Philips' company.

JOSEPH WOOD,
Lieutenant United States Volunteers.

ROLL OF CAPT. JAMES PIPER'S COMPANY.

Muster-roll of Capt. Piper's company of volunteers belonging to Fifth detachment, Pennsylvania militia, now in the service of the United States, at Buffalo, State of New York.

Captain.

Piper, James.

Lieutenant.

Woodburn, James.

Ensign.

Huston, Andrew.

Sergeants.

Weakley, William L.
Weakley, James.
Smith, James.
James, Henry.

Corporals.

Kable, Daniel.
McCulloch, William, Sr.
McCulloch, William, Jr.

Privates.

Morrison, Ezra.
Orr, Samuel.
Stitt, James.
McIntire, James.
Collins, Valentine.
Turner, Joseph.
Casner, Jacob.
Spangler, Peter.
McGaw, Thomas.
McGlaughlin, Samuel.
Jones, William, deceased August 5, 1814.
Bull, John.
Thomas, Enoch.
Williamson, David.
McWilliams, John.
Kelly, John.
Patterson, Hugh.
Walker, John.
Marlin, Thomas.
Thompson, William.
Sowers, Samuel.
Ingram, Samuel.
Wacob, William.
McGlaughlin, Robert.
Donley, Michael.
Harper, Samuel.
Carothers, Andrew.
Brown, Alexander.
Buchanan, Robert.
Trago, Joseph.
McKinney, John.
Brown, William.
Graham, James.

Watts, James.
Ramsay, James.
Kinkaid, William.
Jones, Joshua.
Huston, John.
Miller, Robert.
Woodburn, Robert.
Davidson, Andrew.
Gamble, Benjamin.
Lindsay, William.
Oliver, John.
Boner, John.
Miller, Jacob.
Brown, William, Jr.
Burk, William.
Felker, William.
Garrad, John.

I do certify that the above is a correct muster-roll of my company. Given under my hand this 23d day of August, A. D. 1814.

JAMES PIPER,
Captain.
JAMES FENTON,
Colonel.

ROLL OF CAPT. THOMAS F. PLEASANTS' COMPANY.

Muster-roll of a company of volunteers under the command of Thomas F. Pleasants, in the First regiment of volunteers, commanded by Col. Clement C. Biddle. Commencement of service, August 29.

Captain.

Pleasants, Thomas F.

First Lieutenant.

Montgomery, John C.

Second Lieutenant.

Rawle, Francis W.

Ensign.

Biddle, Richard.

Sergeants.

Dickinson, John B.
Harrison, Samuel B.
Howell, John L.

Shober, Samuel L.
Sparhawk, Thomas.

Quarter-Master.

Hampton, John H.

Corporals.

Burn, Joseph, Jr.
Smith, William.
Willig, George.
Richards, George W.
Williamson, John G.

Privates.

Alter, Jacob.
Armstrong, Andrew, September 1.
Bankson, John P.
Bell, Thomas.
Bicknell, Daniel D.
Biddle, James C., secretary to the general.
Blackwood, William.
Carrell, John, Jr.
Catherwood, Robert.
Caldwell, William.
Carson, James B., September 1.
Cox, William S.
Clement, Jacob.
Claypoole, James T.
Claypoole, David.
Coney, David.
Dale, Richard S.
Darrah, Thomas.
Dillingham, William H.
Durney, Paul.
Erringer, Jacob, September 1.
Fisher, S. Rhoads.
Garrigues, James.
Garrigues, Elmslie, September 1.
Glentworth, James, Jr.
Govett, Charles.
Govett, Robert, September 29.
Griffith, John T.
Gallager, William.
Guest, Jonathan, September 1.
Hawkins, William.
Haverstick, Charles, September 1.
Hildeburn, Samuel.
Hopkins, James H.

WAR OF 1812-14.

Hopkinson, John.
Hopkinson, Francis.
Hopkins, John, September 1.
Houston, John H.
Israel, Joseph.
Jones, Edward P.
Kittera, John M.
Lake, Thomas.
Lapsley, David, Jr.
Marrigault, Charles I., September 1.
Marshall, Thomas A.
McCorkle, Joseph P.
McClintock, Ralph.
Mitchell, Benjamin.
Montgomery, James H., September 29.
Montgomery, Samuel P., September 1.
Mills, William M.
Morris, Thomas W., secretary to the brigade major.
Musser, William, September 1.
Peter, John W.
Philpot, William.
Purdon, Joseph R.
Richard, A. G., stewart of the hospital.
Roberts, Allen.
Rumsay, William.
Rumsay, Andrew.
Rush, Joseph.
Shubert, John R., September 1.
Smith, William.
Snowden, Charles, September 1.
Spring, Marshall B., September 29.
Stewart, Washington.
Taylor, Levi.
Taylor, Robert B., September 1.
Thackara, William W.
Thompson, Benjamin A.
Todd, John N.
Warrance, William, September 1.
Wasson, Joseph.
Wartmough, Edmund C.
Weaver, John, September 1.
Wells, John F.
Condy, Thomas D., September 1; discharged by order of Gen. Bloomfield.
Cox, Henry P., dead.
Malcoln, N. G.

Russell, George.
Wertz, C.
McSparran, William.

We certify, on honor, that this muster-roll exhibits a true state of the company in the First regiment of volunteers, for the period therein mentioned, and that the remarks set opposite the names of the men are accurate and just.

THOMAS F. PLEASANTS,
Captain of the Third Company Washington Guards.

I believe the above muster-roll to be correct.

CONDY RAGUET,
Lieut. Col. First Regiment Pennsylvania Volunteers.

I certify that the Third company of Washington Guards commanded by Capt. Thomas F. Pleasants, is in the service of the United States, under orders of the general commanding the Fourth military district.

THOS. CADWALADER,
Brigadier General Commanding.

CAMP DUPONT, *October, 1814.*

ROLL OF CAPT. PURDY'S COMPANY.

CAMP DUPONT, *13.*

A true list of Capt. Purdy's company of the Eighteenth section of riflemen, commanded by Col. Thomas Humphrey.

Hart, Samuel.
Hart, Louis F.
Hart, William, Jr.
Hart, William.
Jones, Ashforby.
Hart, John.
Carrell, Joseph.
Baird, John.
Carr, Joseph.
Kirkpatrick, John.
Vansant, Wilhelmus.
Coughlin, Thomas.
McDowell, Samuel.
Darrach, Henry.
Polk, James.
Craven, James.
Brown, James.
Hervey, William.
Scout, Lewis.

Tyson, Malichi.
Washman, Jesse.
Gill, John.
Bennet, Aaron.
Brady, Benjamin.
Crawford, John.
Roberts, Daniel.
Silvey, William.
Wells, John.
Craven, John M.
Shelmine, Abraham.
Young, Samuel.
Neal, Thomas.
Bodle, John.
Slack, Bernard.
Wilson, Ezekiel.
Buskirk, Isaac.
Yerkes, Andrew.
Vansant, William.
Vankorn, or Vanhorn, William.
Long, William.
Daniels, William.
Dougherty, David.
Robinson, Watson.
Scott, Andrew.
Leedom, Samuel.
Courson, Benjamin.
Ovem, Joseph.
Jones, David.
Wood, Josiah H.
Bennet, George.
Webster, Charles.
Search, James.
Search, Lot.
Rogers, James.
Banes, Lemen.
Thomas, Benjamin.
Roseman, Robert, discharged at the end of one month's service, and received but two dollars.

CAMP DUPONT, *November 13, 1814.*

This is to certify that the within is a true return of the non-commissioned officers, musicians, and privates belonging to Capt. Wm. Purdy's company of riflemen stationed at this place.

LEMEN BANES,
Orderly Sergeant.
THOS. HUMPHREY,
Colonel First Regiment P. V. R.

CAMP DUPONT, *November 26, 1814.*

I do certify, on honor, that the company commanded by Capt. Wm. Purdy is in the service of the United States, under the command of the general commanding the Fourth military district.

THOS. CADWALADER,
Brigadier General Commanding Advance L. B.

ROLL OF CAPT. CONDY RAGUET'S COMPANY.

Muster-roll of a company of Pennsylvania militia, under the command of Capt. Condy Raguet, in the Fourth detachment, in the service of the United States, commanded by Col. Rush, from 13th May, 1813, when last mustered, to 18th June, 1813.

Captain.

Raguet, Condy.

First Lieutenant.

Mifflin, John R.

Second Lieutenant.

Ash, Michael W.

Third Lieutenant.

Anthony, Thomas.

Ensign.

Traquair, Thomas.

Sergeants.

Pleasants, Thomas F.
Montgomery, John C.
Howell, John F.
Wharton, Thomas I.
Rawle, Francis W.

Corporals.

Wartmough, John G.
Sykes, Samuel M.
Burrows, Thomas.
Brown, John M.

Fifer.

Christie, John.

Drummer.

Green, Anderson.

Privates.

Ashbridge, Joseph H.
Anderson, Edward.
Armor, James.
Burkhart, Valentine.
Baker, John S.
Banks, John.
Biddle, Richard.
Benson, David P.
Burns, Joseph, Jr.
Bredin, B. B.
Burns, William.
Bedwell, George.
Buckley, Clement A.
Clinton, George C.
Cist, Charles.
Child, Cephas G.
Cox, Charles I.
Carrell, John, Jr.
Carpenter, Charles, Jr.
Correy, James.
Cobb, William.
Cobb, Joseph.
Cain, Richard.
Campbell, Ephraim.
Clause, John H.
Cuthbert, Anthony.
Davis, George, Jr.
Davis, Thomas, Jr.
Dickinson, John B.
Delaker, George.
Durborrow, John.
Eldridge, Phineus.
Emerick, William B.
Fricke, George I.
Fling, Daniel.
Freeman, T. W.
Freed, Anthony.
Frithmuth, Jacob.
Grim, Henry.
Gibbs, George.
Gill, Edward.
Goodman, George.
Greenwood, Frederick.
Hall, James.
Huber, Tobias.

Hay, William.
Howell, John L.
Harrison, Samuel B.
Huddle, Bankson.
Huckle, Francis.
Harberger, G.
Harley, Francis.
Jobson, Samuel.
Knight, Joseph.
Kintzing, Tench C.
Keemer, George.
Keen, James C.
Kempton, Joseph.
Moore, John P.
Milnor, John, Jr.
Milnor, Isaac, Jr.
Marshall, Thomas A.
McKeever, Rees W.
Major, William.
Metzker, I.
Mahany, I. I.
McKeever, James.
Martin, John P.
McPherson, I.
Nice, G.
Pinkerton, I. O.
Plocher, I. I.
Peale, C. L.
Porter, H^y.
Rees, C. B.
Robbins, James.
Rovoudt, William.
Richards, G. W.
Richard, A.
Rogers, Rob.
Ranten, James.
Shober, Samuel L.
Schreiner, Charles.
Smith, G. W.
Sparhawk, Thomas.
Smith, W. S.
Simler, G.
Shreeve, I.
Steel, R.
Servoss, Charles.
Seybert, Adam.

Turner, Jos^h. M.
Twibell, G.
Thomson, B. A.
Thompson, J. M.
Wager, W. S.
Worrell, Norris.
Wharton, James S.
Willig, George.
Vanpelt, I. K.

We certify, on honor, that this muster-roll exhibits a true state of Capt. Raguet's company, of the Fourth detachment of Pennsylvania militia, for the period therein mentioned, and that the remarks set opposite the names of the men are accurate and just.

CONDY RAGUET,
Captain.

Upon the return of the detachment to the city the muster-roll had undergone no alteration since the above period.

CONDY RAGUET,
Captain.

I do certify, upon honor, that I believe the above return and remarks to be accurate and just.

LEWIS RUSH,
Colonel Fourth Detachment P. M.

August 6, 1813.

ROLL OF CAPT. WILLIAM RAWLE, Jr.'s, COMPANY.

Muster-roll of the second troop of Philadelphia Cavalry, commanded by Capt. William Rawle, Jr., in the service of the United States, under the command of Brig. Gen. Cadwalader. Mustered on the 2d of October, 1814.

Captain.
Rawle, William, Jr.

First Lieutenant.
Scott, John M.

Second Lieutenant.
Schlatter, William.

Cornet.
Hall, John.

Quarter-master Sergeant.
Nagler, Henry.

25—Vol. XII.

Sergeants.

Fullerton, E. Spencer.
Allen, Miller.
Erwin, Robert.
Say, Benjamin.

Corporals.

Watson, John.
Potter, John.
Sickeld, George L.
Worknot, Conrad.

Musician.

Adler, Christian F.

Privates.

Allen, Samuel.
Alexander, Samuel.
Byerly, John.
Bany, Joseph.
Chrystler, Jacob.
Caldwell, James.
Carlton, George.
Callahan, Thomas.
Corfield, Jesse.
Fitter, William.
Friburg, Joseph.
Gray, Robert E., sent a substitute
Gray, Joseph.
Gilpin, John.
Geisse, Philip.
Humphreys, John.
Hancock, Robert, discharged on account of sickness.
Ingersoll, Edward.
King, William.
Kneass, Christian.
Korkhauss, Henry.
McKensie, Richard.
Milnor, Robert.
Manœver, Louis.
Newlin, Thomas.
Owens, Thomas.
Osburn, Jeremiah.
Primrose, John.
Rogers, Evans.
St. Clair, William.
Sickell, Laurence.
White, Charles.

White, William.
Woolpped, Frederick.

The within muster-roll contains a true exhibit of the state of the troop on this day.

W. RAWLE, Jr.
Captain Second Troop Cavalry.

CAMP DUPONT, *October 2, 1814.*

I certify that the Second troop of Philadelphia cavalry is in the service of the United States, under orders of the general commanding the Fourth military district.

THOMAS CADWALADER,
Brigadier General Commanding.

CAMP DUPONT, *October 7, 1814.*

ROLL OF CAPT. JOHN RAWLIN'S COMPANY.

A list of the volunteer rifle corps, commanded by Capt. John Rawlins, quartered at Camp Boileau, Philadelphia, October 24, 1814.

Captain.
Rawlins, John.

First Lieutenant.
Young, John L.

Second Lieutenant.
Armstrong, Edward.

Ensign.
Haley, John, Jr.

Privates.
Haley, William.
Vaughan, Jonathan.
Guinn, John.
Holland, James.
Rorman, George.
Grant, John.
Robeson, Jonathan.
Wells, John.
Sedenger, George.
Colflesh, David.
Marker, Jonathan.
Haley, Isaac.
Sedenger, John.
Sedenger, William.
Smith, William.

Williamson, Morris.
McGee, John.
Jones, John.
Stillwagon, John.
Smith, William, farmer.
Murphy, James.
Fritz, Henry.
Young, William.
Carpenter, Joel.
Daugherty, Thomas.
Calden, John.
Fryar, Charles.
Ferlenden, Garret.
Hurst, William.
Tunis, William.
Haffman, William.
Litzenberg, Simon.
Jarrett, John.
Elwell, Elijah.
Horn, William.
Hair, William.
Lynce, or Lentz, Christopher.
Priest, William.

I certify, on honor, that the within roll or list exhibits a true state of the company under my command.

JOHN RAWLINS,
Captain.
THOS. HUMPHREY,
Colonel First Regiment P. V. R.

November 7, 1814.

I do certify, on honor, that the company commanded by Capt. John Rawlin is in the service of the United States, under the general commanding the Fourth military district.

THOS. CADWALADER,
Brigadier General Commanding Advance L. B.
CAMP DUPONT, *November 26, 1814.*

ROLL OF CAPT. HENRY READ'S COMPANY.

Muster-roll of the Benevolent Blues, under the command of Major Samuel Shacks, in the service of the United States, commanded by Capt. Henry Read, from the Northern Liberties.

Captain.
Read, Henry.

First Lieutenant.
Emry, Abraham.

Second Lieutenant.
Hess, William.

Ensign.
Ruby, Felix M.

Privates.
Will, Isaac.
Long, Jacob.
Clark, William.
Benner, Henry.
Moore, Charles.
Brindle, John.
Beck, Daniel.
Cahill, Richard.
Reap, Andrew.
Baker, Jacob.
Refile, or Rafael, Joseph.
Reap, Philip.
Wittistine, Richard.
Will, George.
McCauly, James.
Thomas, George.
Shoeman, William.
Ketz, Jacob.
Krouscope, George.
White, John.
Emry, Jacob.
Tappa, John.
Hamerick, John.
Dehart, Abraham.
Butz, Henry.
Boyfull, Philip.
Weckerly, Abraham.
Wistor, William.

Keyser, Henry.
Young, George.
Capehart, James.
Kyser, William.
Shade, John.
Hymer, Stephen.
Henry, Peter.
Clothear, Joseph.
Sim, Jacob.
Lister, George.
Gockler, Godlip.
Einwachte, William.
Bates, Charles.
Shettle, Henry.
Wolbert, Frederick.
Saffron, John.
Croely, Samuel.
Archey, Charles.
Lechler, Joseph.
Eyers, D. Ryers.
Bender, Charles.
Breder, Henry.
Godfry, Fillinger.
Wickerly, Jacob.
Rink, John.
Stull, Adam.
Berkenbine, William.
Cline, Philip.
Shoman, John.
Schank, Robert D.
McGrady, John.
Buck, John.
Stull, John.
Gosline, Joseph.
Montgomery, Joseph.
Shaffer, John.
Sedingsher, Jacob.
Rensell, George.
Miller, John A.
Hummel, John.
Earl, Samuel R.
Walters, Jacob.
Colldavy, William.
Bozard, Peter.
Walling, Lusty.
Miller, Conrad.

Worthington, Thomas.
Rink, Jacob.
Selzer, Henry.
Lentz, Alexander.
Carson, John.
Balt, John.
Senderting, or Senderling, Jacob.
Wyble, Thomas.
Streeker, Charles.
Vanderslice, Isaac.
Trexler, John.

I do certify, on honor, that the within roll exhibits a true state of the volunteer infantry called the " Benevolent Blues," under my command, and the remarks set opposite the names are accurate and just, and the names therein contained are non-commissioned officers and privates.

           HENRY READ,
              Captain.

CAMP MARCUS HOOK, *October 18, 1814.*
I certify the within to be correct.

           SAM. SPARKS,
             Major Battalion.

I certify that the Benovolent Blues, commanded by Capt. H. Read, is in the service of the United States, under orders of the general commanding Fourth military district.

           THOMAS SNYDER,
           Brigadier General Commanding.

CAMP MARCUS HOOK, *October 18, 1814.*

ROLL OF CAPT. GEORGE RECORD'S COMPANY.

Muster-roll of Capt. George Record's company of Pennsylvania militia, belonging to the regiment commanded by Col. Rees Hill, from the 5th day of May, until November 8, 1813.

Captain.

Record, George.

Lieutenants.

Wilson, John.
Shannon, John.
Moore, Archibald.

Ensign.

Long, Joseph.

Sergeants.

Lamborn, Isaac.
Hunter, John.
McEwen, Henry.
Smith, Peter.
Eakens, Robert.

Corporals.

Green, Thomas.
Tate, Robert.
Bathurst, Henry.
Freeby, George.

Fifer

Dunn, Samuel.

Drummer

Rice, John.

Privates.

Hull, John.
Bowers, Joseph.
McClearn, Joseph.
Morrison, Joseph.
Murray, George.
Hearper, George.
Murray, William.
Pierce, Brittain.
Rineheart, Frederick.
McClintock, John.
Smith, Arthur.
Sneveley, John.
Gibbons, John.
Bartwell, Solomon.
Bready, William P.
Righley, George.
Sayers, William.
Waggoner, William.
McKee, William.
McCloskey, Alexander.
Stewart, Hugh.
Cronimiller, Martin.
Underwood, John.
Moyers, Henry.
Hannah, Andrew.
Hearper, Henry.
Kemmerer, John.
Sheaffer, Michael.
Shook, Charles.

Mays, William.
Adamson, William.
Taylor, William.
Sharp, David.
Brosios, Jacob.
Bright, George.
Lyons, William.
Landas, John.
Silhamer, John.
Newel, William.
Williams, Enoch.
McKinney, Samuel.
McNall, James.
Hoover, William.
Askey, Samuel.
McClelland, Hugh.
Emrick, Joseph.
Packer, Johnston.
McCray, Robert.
Shirk, John.
Lucas, John.
Meanes, Edward.
Lucas, Noble.
McKelips, Alexander.
Berger, Jacob.
Moore, William.
Allison, Samuel.
Boyd, Alexander.
Stewart, Archibald.
Moore, John.
Senser, Jacob.
Blair, William.
Ammerman, Joseph.
Huff, William.
Mitchel, David.
Mitchel, James.
McClain, John.
Stephenson, Thomas.
Cook, John.
Gardener, Samuel.
Brien, George.
Fleming, John.
Smith, Joseph.
McNitt, John.
Ross, James.
Hagerty, James.

Cochren, Samuel.
McCoy, John.
Acreman, John.
Glass, James.
Long, David.
Smith, Philip.
Woolf, Jacob.

ROLL OF CAPT. JEREMIAH REES' COMPANY.

Muster-roll of Capt. Jeremiah Rees' company, of the Fifth battalion, First brigade, Pennsylvania infantry, under the command of Lieut. Col. Lefever, at York, Pennsylvania. In service from August 30 and 31, 1814 to March 5, 1815; from Lancaster, Berks, and Lebanon.

Captain.

Rees, Jeremiah.

Lieutenant.

Knepley, Conrad.

Ensign.

Dill, James.

Sergeants.

Eichelberger, Peter.
Deal, Daniel.
Garmin, Philip.
Kendle, Henry.

Corporals.

Missimer, John.
Newman, Peter.
Darr, John.
David, George.

Privates.

Adams, Isaac.
Badorf, Henry.
Bridegum, David.
Coleman, John.
Deckert, Daniel.
Defenbauch, John.
Dingler, Samuel.
Dubert, Henry.
Feag, John.

Fidler, Henry.
Fisher, Frederick.
Fisher, Michael.
Foltz, Henry.
Forry, John.
Foust, John.
Friberger, John.
Gable, Samuel.
Glinger, Daniel.
Griss, Adam.
Hahn, John.
Hain, Adam.
Heepner Daniel.
Hosler, John.
Katterman, John.
Katzaman, Anthony.
Keich, Michael.
Krick, Peter.
Lutz, George.
Matthew, Samuel.
Mell, John.
Metz, Henry.
Miller, Henry.
Noll, George.
Noll, Jacob.
Reed, Jacob.
Reedy, Daniel.
Riggler, Jacob, Jr.
Rutter, Joseph.
Sheetz, Henry.
Shell, Peter.
Shingler, Jacob.
Siler, John.
Sipple, William.
Sollady, Lawrence.
Spotz, Conrad.
Stoner, Rudolph.
Stronk, John.
Troutman, Michael.
Wolf, Jacob.
Zeller, Valentine.
Zimmerman, Henry.

ROLL OF CAPT. HENRY REGES' COMPANY.

Chambersburg company, Capt. Henry Reges, in Col. Jeremiah Snider's regiment, September 5, 1812.

Captain.

Reges, Henry.

First Lieutenant.

Senseny, Jeremiah.

Second Lieutenant.

Musser, John.

First Sergeant.

Fleck, Peter.

Privates.

Boyle, John.
Baughman, John.
Cunningham, Robert.
Cook, John.
Crawford, Edward.
Dobbin, Arthur.
Denig, John.
Essig, John.
Erwin, Isaac.
Favorite, John.
Gelwicks, John.
Grice, William.
Good, Joseph.
Gilmore, John.
Grim, Philip.
John, Christian.
Lester, George W.
Lemon, Josiah.
Lamar, Isaiah.
McMurray, Robert.
Mumma, John.
Mannon, Hugh.
McConnell, Hugh.
McAnulty, Hugh.
Martin, John.
Martin, Benjamin.
McConnell, James.
Pollack, William.
Runnion, Richard.
Radebaugh, John.

WAR OF 1812-14.   897

Robinson, John.
Reilly, John.
Snyder, Jacob.
Stall, Joseph.
Smith, Henry.
Schools, Thompson.
Severns, Joseph.
Sailer, Daniel.
Whitney, John.
Wise, James.
Wilson, George.
Zimmerman, George.

ROLL OF CAPT. JOHN REITZEL'S COMPANY.

Muster-roll of Capt. John Reitzel's company, in the Rifle regiment of the Second brigade, Pennsylvania militia, under command of Lieut. Col. William; Hamilton, at York, Pennsylvania. In service from November 1, 1814, to December 4, 1814, from Lancaster county.

Captain.

Reitzel, John.

First Lieutenant.

Heinitch, Henry C.

Second Lieutenant.

Jeffries, James

Ensign.

Greenwood, Frederick.

Sergeants.

Sherrer, Thomas.
McCurdy, John.
Coleman, Richard.
Rigg, William A.

Corporals.

Spelland, Maurice.
Fultz, John.
Howard, William.
Sanders, Hugh.

Bugler.

Heintinch, Frederick.

Privates.

Andrew, Good.
Arthur, William.

Bailey, Stephen.
Bedel, Benjamin.
Bell, William.
Benner, Harman.
Binkley, Felix.
Bitner, Abraham.
Callihan, Edward.
Cunningham, Samuel.
Dunder, John.
Eckert, Jeremiah.
Fisher, Joseph.
Fitzgerrald, Edward.
Foultz, William.
Graeff, George, Jr.
Harsh, John.
Hornberger, Stephen.
Jackson, John.
Johnson, Daniel.
Keyler, Daniel.
Layman, Henry.
Marrow, John.
McCoy, Charles.
McGrand, Barney.
Messersmith, John.
Michael, John.
Michael, William.
Moore, Anselm.
Prutzman, John.
Rees, Jacob.
Reiley, John.
Schaum, John.
Sloan, Elijah.
Smith, John.
Smith, Michael.
Smith, Nathaniel.
Stall, Samuel.
Stornleach, George.
Taylor, John.
Thorne, John.
Truby, John, captain's waiter.
Wilhelm, John.
Young, Peter.
Zanzinger, Henry.

ROLL OF CAPT. JONATHAN RHOADS' COMPANY.

A muster-roll of Capt. Jonathan Rhoads' rifle company, attached to the First battalion of the One hundred and Twenty-eighth regiment, who have offered their services to the Governor in substitution of the drafted militia from the One Hundred and Twenty-eighth regiment, of the First brigade, Twelfth division, Pennsylvania militia.

Captain.

Rhoads, Jonathan.

Lieutenant.

Bowmon, Peter.

Ensign.

Zimmorman, Philip.

Privates.

Alexander, James.
Alexander, John.
Alexander, William.
Berkey, Christian.
Bisacker, Daniel.
Bisacker, Frederick.
Borron, George.
Bounbrack, Jacob.
Brucker, Henry.
Dinning, David.
Dinning, John.
Emmet, Joseph.
Faith, William.
Fleck, Peter.
Flout, Henry.
Frownhizer, John.
Gardner, Peter.
Gohn, John.
Hess, George.
Horner, Daniel.
Horner, Samuel.
Horner, Solomon.
Howard, David.
Huffmon, Philip.
Keiser, Conrad.
Metzler, Henry.
Mowrer, Adam.
Rhoads, Jacob.

Ritter, Elias.
Seese, John.
Shaver, David.
Shoemaker, Jacob.
Showmon, David.
Smiley, Robert.
Stall, Jacob.
Starn, Mathias.
Storm, William.
Tom, David.
Whright, Frederick.
Youngman, George.
Youtzler, William.

We, the subscribers, officers of the above company, do respectfully offer our service to his Excellency Simon Snyder, Governor of the Commonwealth of Pennsylvania, as above stated. Witness our hands at Stoystown.

JONATHAN BHOADS,
Captain.
PHILIP ZIMMERMAN,
Ensign.

BRIGADE INSPECTOR'S OFFICE, *June 15, 1812.*

ROLL OF CAPT. WILLIAM RICHARDSON'S COMPANY.

We, the subscribers, non-commissioned officers and privates of ——— militia company, commanded by Capt. Wm. Richardson, regiment of ———, as a part of the First brigade, Second division, Pennsylvania militia, of the State of Pennsylvania, in the service of the United States, under the requisition of the President, of the 4th of July, 1814, ———, &c., under command of Lieut. Col. Conrad Kirkbaum, October 29, 1814.

Ensign.

McVey, David.

Sergeants.

Bealer, Thomas.
Carrier, Abraham.
Melligan, Joseph.
Mitchel, John.
Sheive, Jacob.

Corporals.

Riland, William.
Dagen, Lewis.

Whitman, Thomas.
Widner, Samuel.

Drummer.

Atkison, Samuel.

Privates.

Smith, Lee.
Weld, Michael.
Harner, Joseph.
Argue, Robert.
Gregor, George.
Doyle, or Dole, Levi.
Preston, George.
Gouldy, David.
Jenkins, John.
Rodenbock, John.
Hinkner, Jesse.
Kinear, Daniel.
Rambo, Andrew.
Rambo, Jonas.
Carrahan, Timothy.
Doyle, George.
Coats, John.
Griffith, Lewis.
Sullender, Isaac.
Mason, George.
Calahan, John.
Drain, John.
Washer, Joseph.
McDermond, John.
Percy, William.
Armstrong, William.
Matson, William.
Puff, Berkhard.
Tool, William.
McCoy, William.
Whitby, John.
Frantz, John.
VanCoursen, or Han Courson, John.
Cox, John.
Cox, Charles.
Cook, Daniel.
McMichael, John.
Highland, Thomas.
Sheppard, William.

Harvey, John.
Eve, John.
Eve, Abraham.
Bailey, Abraham.
Cressman, Samuel.
Smith, John.
Garner, John.
Frantz, Tobias.
Colar, Caspar.
Kruzal, or Knezel, John.
Beaver, Henry.
Shire, or Share, Samuel.
Waters, Samuel.
Greenwolt, Henry.
Miller, Andrew.
Butler, Joseph.
Hirst, John.
Shart, James.
Beaver, John.
Benner, Henry.
Bruner, Henry.
Rhambo, Isaiah.
McClain, Charles.
Esswick, John.
McClelland, Joseph.
Peters, Samuel.
Rawn, Daniel.
Rymar, Philip.
Stewart, John.
Buckwalter, Joseph.
Hartenstine, John.
Beaver, John.
Kugler, Michael.
Daniels, Samuel.
Graham, John.
Evans, Charles.
Duffield, Richard.
Dagar, George.
Goshaw, John.
Harning, or Horning, Jesse.
Fleck, Adam.
Mattes, or Mathias, John.
King, John.
Arnin, or Arnan, Jesse.
Benner, William.
Newberry, John.

Peters, John.
Hogston, William.
Wills, Michael.
Garner, Henry.
Sheppard, James.
Earnest, Jesse.

ROLL OF CAPT. ABRAHAM RINKER'S COMPANY.

CAMP DUPONT, *November 13, 1814.*

A true list of Capt. Abraham Rinker's company of the Eighteenth section of Riflemen, commanded by Col. Thomas Humphrey.

Sergeants.

Knouse, Peter.
Lehr, Peter.
Marck, Jacob.
Strouse, John.

Corporals

Shiffert, John.
Nunemacker, George.
Stoer, or Starr, Conrad.
Keck, John.

Musician.

Wotring, Fortinant.

Privates.

Bower, Henry.
Sickfrit, Daniel.
Hertzel, Henry.
Mayer, George.
Smith, Adam.
Hartzel, Jacob.
Reinbold, John.
Luckes, Solomon.
Strouse, George.
Yoe, Jacob.
Deily, Christian.
Hartzel, Adam.
Steinberger, Peter.
Kershner, Conrad.
Doll, Charles.
Kloeckner, Solomon.
Whiteman, John.

Shoudt, Michael.
Wotring, Fertinant.
Nunemacker, Henry.
Keck, David.
Lehr, Michael.
Lehr, Adam.
Mansch, Adam.
Hartzel, Andrew.
Diffenderfer, Jonathan.
Deily, Jacob.
Yost, Nathaniel.
Whiteman, Jacob.
Moritz, George.
Hantzel, Solomon.
Gordan, Jacob.
Horlocher, George.
Good, Adam.
Kunckel, Lewis.
Beidelman, Jacob.
Hicker, Adam.
Lower, Michael.
Swander, Henry.
Fetzer, Daniel.
Shaffer, George.
Billig, John.
Eschenbach, Daniel.
Bortz, George.
Newhard, Frederick.
Steinberger, Jacob.
Spangler, Jones.
Sharrer, Adam.
Bachman, Jacob.
Rou, or Rau, John, quit the company September 23, 1814.
Klotz, Peter, quit the company September 23, 1814.
Ealer, John.
Mansch, Peter.
Frantz, Henry.
Moll, Peter.
Coock, Peter, enlisted in the army of the United States October 2, 1814.

We do certify that the within list is a true statement, on honor, this 13th day of November, 1814.

ABRAHAM RINKER,
Captain.
THOS. HUMPHREY,
Colonel First R. P. V. R.

WAR OF 1812–14.

I do certify, on honor, that the company commanded by Capt. A. Rinker is in the service of the United States, under the command of the general commanding the Fourth military district.

THOS. CADWALADER,
Brigadier General Commanding Advance L. B.
CAMP DUPONT *November 26, 1814.*

ROLL OF CAPT. GEORGE RITTER'S COMPANY.

Muster-roll of Capt. George Ritter's company, in the First regiment, Second brigade of Pennsylvania militia, under command of Lieut. Col. Jeremiah Shappel, at York, Pennsylvania, September 5, 1814. In service from August 28, 1814, to March 5, 1815; from Berks county.

Captain.

Ritter, George.

First Lieutenant.

Berdow, John.

Second Lieutenant.

Moyers, Isaac.

Ensign.

Slotman, Daniel.

Sergeants.

Berninger, Philip.
Breidigam, Abra^m.
Clauser, William.
Fox, John.
Heaffer, Henry.

Corporals.

Acker, Daniel.
Berdow, Abr^m.
Berninger, Jacob.
Heaffer, Mathias.
Lorah, Michael.
Moyer, Jacob.

Musicians.

Bingenman, Yost.
Slotman, John.

Privates.

Adams, John.
Andy, Jacob.
Andy, Jacob B.

Andy, John B.
Andy, Matthias.
Barker, John.
Barkop, John.
Beaver, Devald.
Beaver, John.
Behm, John.
Bierman, John.
Borger, Henry.
Bouman, Jacob.
Boyer, John.
Brown, Jacob.
Clark, David.
Daupert, Peter.
Dillinger, Daniel.
Edinger, Christopher.
Ely, Daniel.
Emrich, John.
Feagely, Henry.
Flicker, Jacob.
Folck, Henry.
Fox, Engel.
Gerver, Henry.
Gilbert, Samuel.
Gregory, Peter.
Gregory, Samuel.
Gruber, Michael.
Haas, Adam.
Haas, George.
Haist, George.
Heanih, Henry.
Herbst, Samuel.
Herp, Jacob.
Himelreich, Jacob.
Himelreith, John.
Hoffman, Jacob.
Hoppes, Jacob.
Keller, George.
Kister, Conrad.
Kline, George.
Lees, Peter.
Lehman, Christian
Ludwig, George.
Miller, John.
Moon, Daniel.
Moyer, Abraham.

Ohrantz, John.
Olinger, David.
Paulus, John.
Peterson, Severon.
Preis, George.
Ruppert, Abraham.
Ruppert, Herman.
Rush, John.
Sheiry, John.
Sheiry, Nicholous.
Smith, William.
Specht, Peter.
Sprigelmoyer, Henry.
Steller, Henry,
Weller, George.
Weastler, John.
Windbigler, Philip.
Yost, George.

ROLL OF CAPT. JOHN ROBERTS' COMPANY.

Muster-roll of Capt. Roberts' company of the Fifth detachment, Pennsylvania militia, now in service of the United States at Buffalo, New York.

Captain.

Roberts, John, deceased.

First Lieutenant.

Reddig, Thomas.

Second Lieutenant.

Gibson, John.

Third Lieutenant.

Cox, Jacob.

Sergeants.

Wimer, Jacob.
McGahan, Jesse.
Turbett, Thomas.
Ritter, Daniel.

Corporals.

Allen, Hugh.
Byrns, William.
Duck, Philip.
McGuire, John.

Musician.

Weaver, John.

Privates.

Burker, John.
Kettering, Michael.
Wilson, Andrew.
Dredge, John.
Martin, Paul.
Caotsner, Isaac.
Wilson, James.
Pawders, Joseph.
Houtz, Samuel.
Nigh, Philip.
Lusk, William.
Atkinson, George.
Kennedy, John.
Marrow, Edward, missing.
Shirky, Cannel.
Fishborn, Jacob.
Timmons, Thomas.
Maury, Jacob.
Blair, James.
Patterson, James.
Cole, Henry.
Magee, Morrison.
Abbot, John.
Dennis, William.
Clark, William.
McBride, Joseph.
Morrow, James.
Wolf, George.
Elsroth, Samuel.
Allen, Thomas.
Bougher, George.
Humes, Joseph.
McGrew, James.
Thompson, William.
Robinson, John.
Kinny, David.
Oyler, John.
Mawry, Adam.
Hold, Thomas.
Early, Samuel.
McCaleb, Alexander.
Davis, James.
McCandless, Robert.

Melhorn, Henry, deceased.
Krull, John C.
Swartz, John.
Freeman, Seth.
Bougher, John.
Murphy, Francis.
Bovard, John.
Bowers, George, missing.
Morgan, Michael.
Carson, Samuel, deceased.
Kelly, Patrick.
Coyle, Peter.
Heyner, Jacob.
Armor, William.
McWilliams, James.
Sancker, John.
Kissel, Frederick.
Fry, John, Sr.
Alexander, Andrew.
Mewhirter, William.
Carlisle, Samuel.
Chambers, Alexander, steward.
Kitring, Jacob.
Kinkle, John.
Whitmer, William.
Miller, Frederick.
Banker, Jacob.

I do certify that the above and foregoing is a correct muster-roll of the company now under my command at Buffalo, the 24th day of August, 1814.

THOMAS REDDIG,
Lieutenant.
JAMES FENTON,
Colonel.

ROLL OF CAPT. ANDREW ROBINSON'S COMPANY.

Roll of Capt. Andrew Robison's company, Greencastle, September, 1814.

Captain.

Robison, Andrew.

First Lieutenant.

Brotherton, John.

Second Lieutenant.

Mitchel, James.

Ensign.

Besore, Jacob.

Sergeants.

Walker, James.
Snively, Andrew.
Wilson, Thomas.
Fleming, Archibald.

Corporals.

Randall, John.
Bellows, George.
Sackett, George.
Aiken, Alexander.

Paymaster.

Carson, William.

Privates.

Armstrong, William, Jr.
Allison, John.
Bratten, William.
Bruce, Robert.
Billings, John.
Beatty, Henry.
Bradley, Samuel.
Brotherton, William H.
Brotherton, James.
Brotherton, Robert.
Baird, Frederick.
Boggs, John.
Core, Benjamin.
Clark, Walter B.
Clark, William.
Clark, George.
Carpenter, Frederick.

Coffroth, William.
Camlon, James.
Deman, Jesse.
Dennis, John.
Davison, James.
Dugan, William T.
Foreman, Samuel.
Flora, George.
Fullerton, David.
Garner, John.
Guinea, Robert.
Guinea, Hugh.
Gordon, Edward.
Gallagher, William.
Graff, John.
Gearhart, Frederick.
Gallagher, Peter.
Harger, William.
Henneberger, John.
Hughes, Joseph.
Irwin, William.
Johnston, James.
Keyser, Jonathan.
Kennedy, Matthew.
Krepps, William.
Kuy, George.
McCune, John.
McCallister, Adam.
McGaw, James.
McCord, James.
McGraw, William.
Miller, William H.
Moreland, William.
McConnell, John.
McCutchen, Samuel.
Miller, John.
McLane, Archibald.
McCutchen, Abraham.
McCoy, John.
McLanahan, John B.
McClellan, John.
Nigh, Samuel.
Owen, Robert.
Poe, James.
Park, John.
Poper, Jacob.

Piper, J.
Reed, John.
Rice, Roger.
Rankin, A. B.
Rowe, John, Sr.
Rogers, John.
Shira, John.
Stewart, Charles.
Sayler, Adam.
Shearer, John.
Statler, Samuel, or Emanuel.
Schreder, John.
Sites, Henry.
Speckman, George.
Snyder, John.
Smith, Robert.
Shaup, John.
Uller, George.
Vanderaw, William.
Welsh, Thomas.
Wilson, James.
Wallack, George.
Wilhelm, Christian.
Wise, Christian.
Weaver, John.
Walker, Thomas.
Young, Alexander.

ROLL OF CAPT. JAMES ROBINSON'S COMPANY.

CAMP DUPONT, *November 13, 1814.*

A true list of Capt. James Robinson's company, of the Eighteenth section of Riflemen, commanded by Col. Thomas Humphrey.

Sergeants.

Ladds, Samuel.
Boggs, John.
Maires, Samuel.
McClelland, George.

Corporals.

Kettler, Andrew.
Koplin, Philip.
Harner, John.
Gregory, Abraham.

Bugler.

Zaine, Jesse.

Privates.

Vandike, Charles.
Mather, Francis.
Carr, Robert.
Brough, John.
Hesson, John.
Deweese, Henry.
Raizor, Peter.
Sturges, Nathan.
Keesey, John.
Keesey, David.
Teaney, William.
Jones, Abraham.
Williams, Levi.
Daniels, David.
Kid, William.
Keyser, Samuel.
Nuss, Frederick.
Tyson, Joseph.
Keesey, William.
Betson, Peter.
Peters, Philip.
Beard, Joseph.
Beard, John.
McClelland, Joseph.
Hiltner, John.
Porter, John.
Crawford, William.
Gilkey, Samuel.
Griffith, William.
Hiltner, William.
McCalla, Nathan.
Byrne, Michael.
Kattz, Henry.
Fogerty, Jeremiah.
Cleaver, Thomas.
Neill, John.
Llewellyn, John.
Reed, John.
Keesey, Jacob.
Streeper, Peter.
Painter, George.
Davis, Zachariah.

Clayer, Frederick.
Stroud, John.
Fisher, John.
Mathers, William.
Gouldey, John.
Schrack, David.
Bean, William.
Saylor, John.
Walker, John.
McNabb, Edward.
Neill, John.
Rees, David.
Walker, Ralph.
Whiteman, Thomas.
Tyson, Isaac.
Jones, Israel.
Kinsey, John.
Newcomb, Hezekiah.
Raizor, Aaron.
Moore, Jonathan.
Tyson, Abraham.
Melnor, Isaac.
Currin, Arthur.
Hughes, Francis.
Keesey, Jesse.
Neiley, Mathew.
Miller, John.
Foster, George.
Roberts, Levi.
Zieber, Jacob.
Lyde, or Leidy, Conrad.
Lyde, or Leidy, Philip.
Conrad, John.
Walker, Jacob.
Royer, John.
Kittler, William.
Hipple, John.
Boggs, John.
Vanforsen, John.
Thompson, Benjamin.
Mitchell, John.
Smith, Zopher.
Zaine, Nathan F.
Boyer, John.
Deweese, Jacob.
Patterson, Robert.

I do certify that the within list is a true statement, on honor, this 13th day of November, 1814.

JAMES ROBINSON,
Captain.
THOS. HUMPHREY,
Colonel, First regiment P. V. R.

I do certify, on honor, that the company commanded by Capt. James Robinson is in the service of the United States, under the command of the general commanding, the Fourth military district.

THOS. CADWALADER,
Brigadier General commanding advance L. B.
CAMP DUPONT, *November 26, 1814.*

ROLL OF CAPT. JOHN ROBINSON'S COMPANY.

Muster-roll of Capt. John Robinson's company of the Fifth battalion, First brigade, Pennsylvania militia, under command of Maj. McFarland, at York. In service from September 5, 1814, to March 5, 1815; from Lancaster county.

Captain.

Robinson, John.

First Lieutenant.

Robinson, William.

Ensign.

Pendel, Benjamin.

Sergeants.

Miller, David.
Persley, Bertholomy.
Carn, William.
Zink, Samuel.

Corporals.

Miller, John.
Orr, James.
Weaver, George.
Zink, John.

Privates.

Adair, John.
Angel, John.
Armstrong, John.
Arnold, Joseph.
Aron, John.
Babb, Samuel.

Bailey, Valentine.
Baker, Abraham.
Barefoot, William.
Barge, Philip.
Bowers, Jacob.
Bowman, Henry.
Browbender, Andrew.
Brown, John.
Chambers, David.
Clark, John.
Clendenin, William.
Close, Charles.
Cole, Rudolph.
Cummins, Jonathan.
Cummins, William.
Douthn, John.
Evans, Caleb.
Evans, Samuel.
Evets, John.
Fickley, Jacob.
Frame, Jesse.
Frazer, James.
Frey, Peter.
Fritz, John.
Gambell, William.
Garmby, John.
Gilkison, William.
Graham, Thomas.
Greenfield, John.
Greer, Samuel.
Henderson, John.
Henry, Jacob.
Horman, Jesse.
Hughs, Robert.
Humpshire, John.
Hunter, Abraham.
Johnston, James.
Kimbell, Thomas.
Kirkwood, Samuel.
Landers, George.
Line, Jesse.
McDonald, John.
McGowan, Philip.
Meekilips, Samuel.
Megroty, Charles.
Moore, John.

Murry, William.
Nelson, James.
Powel, John.
Quin, Thomas.
Reed, John.
Shaw, David.
Snyder, Adam.
Stephon, Peter.
Stoutzenberger, David.
Strome, Erhart.
Sulons, Richard.
Swiner, Alexander.
Tangert, Jacob.
Taylor, Francis.
Weaver, Adam.
Weaver, John.
White, Clempson.
Wolf, Daniel.
Woods, Thomas.
Wright, Samuel.
Yeger, John.

ROLL OF CAPT. MATTHEW RODGERS' COMPANY.

Pay-roll of Capt. Matthew Rodgers' company of Pennsylvania militia, belonging to the regiment of Pennsylvania militia, commanded by C. Rees Hill, from the 5th day of May, 1813, to the 5th day of November following, inclusive.

Captain.

Rodgers, Matthew.

First Lieutenant.

Criswell, James.

Second Lieutenant.

McCoy, John.

Third Lieutenant.

Hallman, Michael.

Ensign.

Elliott, Robert, volunteered on board the fleet August 5.

Sergeants.

Butler, William.
McKillip, Samuel.
Dunn, James.
Edmiston, Samuel.

Robb, William.
Crafford, Samuel.

Corporals.

McAlister, Robert.
Fear, Richard, volunteered on board the fleet August 9.
Rhea, James.
Shields, Joshua.
Miller, Jacob.
Maloy, William.

Fifer.

Lutz, William.

Drummer.

Baker, Henry.

Privates.

Piper, Jacob.
Okeson, Daniel.
Kanady, John, July 9.
Reed, Robert.
Dobbs, Andrew.
McConnel, Francis.
Roberts, William.
Laughlin, Thomas.
Goosehorn, Robert.
Thornburgh, John, June 14.
Kanady, Thomas.
Alexander, William.
McConnel, George.
Hurl, Robert.
Sims, James, volunteered on board the fleet July 26.
Fisher, George.
Gurtin, John.
Metlan, Alexander, volunteerd on board the fleet August 9.
Kanady, Samuel.
Hogg, Robert.
Rice, John, volunteered on board the fleet August 10.¶
Stewart, James.
Hogg, William.
Martin, Nathaniel.
Crain, Robert.
Bell, Robert.
McFaddin, Samuel.
May, David.
Crouce, John.
Seinor, Adam, June 23.
Moss, William.

WAR OF 1812-14.

Alford, Fielding, volunteered on board the fleet July 26.
Swallow, Benjamin.
Myres, Alexander.
Gregory, Elinathan, June 23.
McCrum, Michael, June 14.
Sweesy, David.
Adams, John, volunteered on board the fleet August 2.
Hoyt, Henry, volunteered on board the fleet August 7.
Allison, James.
Pedan, John.
Cooper, John.
McDowel, James.
Allison, Robert.
Hazlet, Jacob.
William, Allen, volunteered on board the fleet August 3.
Work, Robert.
Henry, William, volunteered on board the fleet July 26.
Luvenfass, Henry.
Alexander, James.
McKinny, Charles.
Swisher, Daniel, volunteered on board the fleet July 27.
Mitchel, James, volunteered on board the fleet July 26.
Tool, Jacob, volunteered on board the fleet July 26.
Stoneroad, Valentine.
Irvin, John B.
Worly, Daniel.
Sweesy, Samuel, volunteered on board the fleet August 3.
Brothers, Joseph.
Elliott, William P.
Marshall, Joseph.
Galloway, John.
Shular, William, volunteered on board the fleet July 26.
Korcle, John.
Robison, William.
Grasmire, Daniel.
Jones, Daniel, volunteered on board the fleet July 27.
Lemon, Neal.
Sells, Henry.
McDonald, Alexander.
Stinson, John.
Curtis, Samuel.
Jenkins, William.
Ross, David.
Humphreys, Thomas.
Dysert, John.
Marsh, Jehu, July 11.

Shimp, David.
Reynolds, John.
Mays, James.
Metland, or Maitland, William.

I do, upon honor, certify that the within pay-roll is correct to the best of my knowledge, this 5th of November, 1813.

MATTHEW RODGERS,
Captain.
REES HILL,
Colonel Commanding.

ROLL OF CAPT. CHARLES ROSS' COMPANY.

Muster-roll of the First troop, Philadelphia city cavalry, commanded by Captain Charles Ross, of the light brigade of Pennsylvania volunteers, in the service of the United States, from August 27, to December 20, 1814, commanded by Brigadier General Thomas Cadwalader, (excluding commissioned officers and their servants.)

Sergeants.

Smith, John R. C.
Stocker, Anthony, September 17, 1814.
Leaming, Thomas F.
Bacon, Job.

Corporals.

McConnell, Matthew.
Harrison, Henry, September 6, 1814.
Tunis, Jehu R.
Simmons, John B., October 27, 1814.

Quarter-Master.

Donaldson, John, Jr., September 5, 1814.

Trumpeter.

Lamsback, John, October 20, 1814.

Privates.

Bolton, James M., discharged September 4, 1814.
Bready, Clement L.
Brown, William J., November 1, 1814.
Bryant, John Y.
Craig, William.
Cushing, Augustus.
Davis, Edward.
Donaldson, Edward M., discharged November 2, 1814.
Elfreth, John, September 22, 1814.

Fisher, William W.
Fox, Charles P.
Gratz, Joseph.
Hall, Nathan, September 6, 1814.
Harlan, Joshua, Jr., September 7, 1814.
Hart, William H.
Hugg, George W.
Inskeep, John, Jr., September 12, 1814.
Jackson, Samuel.
Jacobs, Samuel H.
Kintzing, Abraham, Jr.
Krug, Fred. V., September 5, 1814.
Lardner, Lynford.
Lehman, William.
Lewis, Warton, September 22, 1814.
Lloyd, Hugh P., September 23, 1814.
Matthews, Matt., September 1, 1814.
McCallmont, George, September 12, 1814.
McCrea, John.
McMurtrie, Henry, September 1, 1814; discharged September 24 1814.
Morrell, John W., September 9, 1814.
Nixon, Henry, September 12, 1814.
Norris, Charles, September 5, 1814.
Pettit, Charles, September 4, 1814.
Say, Thomas, September 5, 1814.
Simmons, William S.
Sink, Lawrence.
Smith, Francis G.
Smith, John C., September 1, 1814.
Smith, William H.
Stuchert, George T.
Taylor, Thomas H.
Moses, Thomas, September 17, 1814.
Toland, Henry, Jr.
Twells, Conrad.
Vanuxem, Lewis C.
Warder, John R., September 5, 1814.
Warner, John.
Wharton, Robert, discharged October 16, 1814.
Whelan, William, discharged October 18, 1814.
Witmer, Henry, September 22, 1814.
Wikoff, Henry, September 13, 1814.
Willing, George, October 1, 1814.
Willing, William, September 1, 1814.
Worley, Francis, September 1, 1814.

I certify that this pay-roll has been by me examined and compared with the original muster-rolls of the said troop, now in possession of John Donaldson, Jr., paymaster of the squadron, and that the sums stated, amounting to four hundred and twenty-eight dollars and fifteen cents, were due from the State of Pennsylvania to the said First Troop of Philadelphia City Cavalry, acting as videttes, on the 20th day of December, 1814.

CHARLES ROSS,
Captain First Philadelphia City Troop of Cavalry.

The above is correct.

THOS. CADWALADER,
Brigadier General, late Commanding Light Brigade.

ROLL OF CAPT. JOHN F. RUHE'S COMPANY.

A complete muster-roll of the Fifth (Capt. Ruhe's) company of the Second regiment volunteer light infantry, under the command of Col. Louis Bache, under the order of the Commander-in-Chief of the Commonwealth of Pennsylvania, of 27th August, 1814, and attached to the First brigade, Second division, Pennsylvania militia.

Captain.
Ruhe, John F.

First Lieutenant.
Blumer, Jacob.

Ensign.
Fatzinger, Solomon.

Sergeants.
Miller, William.
Dobbins, William.
Kauffman, George.
Gangwere, Isaac.

Corporals.
Mohr, John.
Gangwere, Andrew.
Swander, Daniel.
Miller, John.

Drummer.
Keiper, George.

Fifer.
Klotz, John.

Privates.
Raser, Benjamin.

Statter, John.
Seip, Christian.
Kuchline, Peter.
Nagle, Leonard.
Weaver, William.
Weal, John.
Houk, David.
Statter, Henry.
Ebner, Henry.
Gudekunst, Adam.
Huber, David.
Keiper, William.
Ruhe, Charles.
Martz, George.
Swenk, Mathias.
Haveracher, George.
Keiper, Peter.
Seip, Jacob.
Good, John.
Mickly, Jacob.
Beery, Peter.
Horn, Samuel.
Keiper, Daniel.
Derr, Abraham.
Balliott, Barthold.
Klotz, Andrew.
Mohr, Jacob.
Kuchline, William.
Houk, Jacob.
Spinner, George.
Hutter, Charles L.
Gossler, Jacob.
Wilson, John.
Weaver, Charles.
Gross, Henry.
Wagner, John.
Ginkinger, William.
Reep, John.
Reichard, Henry.

CAMP MARCUS HOOK, *November 29, 1814.*

I do hereby certify, upon honor, that the above is a just and true muster-roll of Capt. Ruhe's company.

JACOB BLUMER,
First Lieutenant.
LOUIS BACHE,
Colonel First Regiment, P. V. I.

ROLL OF CAPT. WILLIAM RUNKLE, Jr.'s, COMPANY.

Muster-roll of the Northern Liberty Guards, under the command of Capt. William Runkle, Jr., in the battalion of volunteers, in the service of the United States, commanded by Maj. Samuel Sparks, from September 16 to December 31, A. D. 1814.

Captain.

Runkle, William, Jr.

First Lieutenant.

Wilt, Abraham, Jr.

Second Lieutenant.

Perpignan, Peter.

Ensign.

Snyder, Henry.

Orderly Sergeant.

Coats, Thomas, Jr.

Sergeants.

Stinemetz, John S.
Kline, Benjamin.
Friend, John H.
Hellings, William.

Quarter-master Sergeant.

Getz, George A.

Corporals.

Souder, Jacob.
Goodman, Charles.
Mintzer, Peter.
Shinn, Josiah.
Ash, Nicholas.

Drummer.

Fenemore, Daniel.

Privates.

Angel, John.
Abraham, David.
Appell, Henry.
Apple, Valentine.
Beck, William.
Brandt, Thomas.
Brooks, Benjamin.
Brooks, James.

Barger, Benjamin.
Balm, Jacob.
Brown, Jacob.
Bissoon, John.
Brunner, John.
Bowman, Zachariah.
Cole, William.
Cromwell, Oliver.
Cummings, John.
Carlin, Mahlon.
Carlin, George.
Cunningham, Samuel.
Cownover, Jacob.
Clurg, McSamuel.
Day, Stephen.
Deal, Christian.
Deal, John.
Darr, Jacob.
Eisens, Daniel.
Englehart, John.
Engard, John.
Fisher, Frederick.
Fisher, John.
Fraley, Enoch.
Fraley, Joseph.
Fagundas, Peter.
Funk, James.
Foulke, Henry.
Gill, McMichael.
Green, Joseph.
Gravenstine, Jacob.
Goods, George.
Hymer, Peter.
Hetzell, Barny.
Hyneman, William.
Hughes, James.
Jones, John.
Jeffries, Daniel.
Kates, H. John.
Keage, McWilliam.
Kingsmore, John.
Lonaback, Christian.
Lonaback, Frederick.
Lentz, John.
Letford, William.
Loller, Thomas.

Levering, Robert.
Meyweg, William.
Montgomery, Alexander.
Meyers, Anthony.
Meridith, Thomas.
Meyers, Henry.
Miller, George.
Nelson, John.
Magee, Andrew.
Painter, John.
Palmer, Amos.
Rorig, Peter.
Royer, George.
Rose, Thomas.
Roseberry, Charles.
Mager, William.
Pritchard, William.
Snyder, Peter.
Streeper, George.
Smith, Jacob.
Sparks, John.
Seybert, John.
Thomson, John.
Teas, John.
Upman, John.
Vietmayer, Daniel.
Walton, Daniel.
Weyant, Peter, degraded from a corporal.
Wirsham, John.
Wolfe, Jacob.
Weaver, George F.
Walters, Charles.
Weaver, Michael.
Woolley, Samuel.
Wheeler, Samuel.
Yeager, John.
Yenricht, John.
Zebley, Benjamin.

We certify, on honor, that this muster-roll exhibits a true state of the Northern Liberty Guards, of a battalion of volunteers, for the period therein mentioned, and that the remarks set opposite the names of the men are accurate and just.

W. RUNKEL, Jr.,
Captain.
SAMUEL SPARKS,
Major Commanding Battalion.

ROLL OF CAPT. JOSEPH SANDS' COMPANY.

Muster-roll of Capt. Joseph Sands' company of the Riflemen, of Montgomery county, Pennsylvania.

Captain.

Sands, Joseph.

First Lieutenant.

Sands, James.

Second Lieutenant.

Rodearmel, Samuel.

Ensign.

Pilger, John.

Quarter-Master.

Rhoads, Jacob.

Sergeants.

Perry, Richard.
Lessig, John.
Rafesneider, William.
Niman, Michael.

Musician.

Sands, William.

Privates.

Zimerman, Abraham.
Wardman, John.
Albright, John.
Stroman, Jacob.
Leavengood, John.
Grove, George.
Rafesnider, Joseph.
Weasner, John.
Grove, John.
Yocom, David.
Beachtel, John.
Kean, Andrew.
Missimer, Solomon.
Geiger, Charles.
Ruth, Samuel.
Yeager, Samuel.
Leavengood, Joseph.

Fritz, Jacob.
Wamback, Bartholomew.
Niman, William.
Mauger, Martin.
Shaner, Joseph.
Conrad, Thomas.
Keyser, Henry.
Weasner, Henry.
Ritemire, George.
Bowman, George.
Geyer, Abraham.
Specht, Jacob.
Smith, Henry.
Davis, Richard.

We do certify, on honor, that this roll exhibits a true state of the company commanded by Capt. Joseph Sands, and that the remarks set opposite their names are accurate and just.

JAMES SANDS,
Lieutenant Commanding.
THOS. HUMPHREY,
Colonel First Regiment P. V. R.

CAMP DUPONT, *November 24, 1814.*

I do certify, on honor, that the company commanded by Capt. J. Sands, is in the service of the United States, under the command of the general commanding the Fourth military district.

THOS. CADWALADER,
Brigadier General, Commanding Advance Light Brigade.

CAMP DUPONT, *November 26, 1814.*

ROLL OF CAPT. GEORGE SCHWENK'S COMPANY.

Muster-roll of Capt. Schwenk's company, in the Second regiment, Pennsylvania volunteer light infantry, in the service of the State of Pennsylvania for three months, from the 12th day of September last. Attached to the First brigade, Second division, Pennsylvania militia, under command of Brig. Gen. Samuel Smith, November 29, 1814.

Captain.

Schwenk, George.

First Lieutenant.

Teany, James.

Second Lieutenant.

Schwenk, Henry.

Ensign.

Setsler, John.

Sergeants.

Smith, James.
Coffman, Archibald.
Gross, John.
Major, John.

Corporals.

Weller, John.
Sheen, Peter.
Groff, Samuel.
Hovis, John.

Privates.

Ruff, Michael.
Rawn, Joseph.
Buzzard, John.
Teany, Henry.
Hartenstine, Eli.
Stewart, James.
McClenand, John.
Saylor, Arnold.
May, Joseph.
Updegraff, Mark.
Schrock, Jacob.
Ringler, Samuel.
Schrader, John.
Schwenck, Jacob.
Bower, Jacob.
May, Frederick.
Cline, Michael.
May, John.
Garber, Joseph.
Jefferis, Joseph.
George, Martin.
Faw, John.
Wireman, John.

We do certify, on honor, that the above muster-roll exhibits a just and true statement of the above mentioned company.

GEORGE SCHWENK,
Captain.
LOUIS BACHE,
Colonel Second Regiment P. V. L. I.

ROLL OF CAPT. JOHN SCHWEPPENHEISER'S COMPANY.

Muster-roll of Pennsylvania militia, First division, Second brigade, Sixth company, under the command of Capt. John Schweppenheiser, in the regiment of Col. John Thomson, in the service of the United States, commanded by Col. John Thomson, from the 11th of September, 1814, when last mustered, to January 5, 1815.

Captain.

Schweppenheiser, John.

First Lieutenant.

Urwiler, George.

Second Lieutenant.

Cooper, Francis.

Ensign.

Painter, Nicholas.

Sergeants.

Weiser, John.
Shafer, John, Jr.
Smith, Henry.
Derick, William.
Slemmer, Mathias.

Corporals.

Miller, George.
Dubois, Benjamin.
Stretch, Nathen.
Shane, George.

Drummer

Schweppenheiser, Philip.

Privates.

Brummel, Samuel.
Brown, Benjamin.
Boyer, Nicholas, sick at home.
Baker, William.
Brumm, John.
Bunting, William.
Brown, James.
Bauchman, Christian.
Bruner, Soloman.

Crossdill, John.
Comley, Benjamin.
Commerlo, John.
Coleman, John.
Danely, John.
Emery, Jacob, October 31, 1814, when he was discharged by order of the doctor.
Frick, Jacob.
Gladding, Joseph.
Genter, Nicholas.
Garrison, Benjamin.
Goldsmith, George.
Genter, Valentine.
Graff, Henry.
Hickey, John.
Hummel, Jacob.
Hines, William.
Haris, Alexander.
Hinkle, Conard.
Hoe, George.
Hanse, Jacob.
Harrison, George.
Hubbert, Samuel.
Irving, Jacob.
Jones, William.
Kennedy, Andrew.
Krull, Michael.
Knapp, John.
Lee, George.
Lindsey, John.
Lisley, Christian.
McMahon, Andrew.
Maine, James.
Miller, John.
Mingle, Christian.
Millich, Simon.
Miers, George.
McCronogal, Nathaniel.
McWaber, John.
Newman, Henry.
O'Coner, John.
Painter, Adam.
Pember, Charles.
Richmond, Isaac.
Robberts, Daniel.
Ross, John.

Robison, Benjamin.
Schockaw, Henry.
Shafer, Adam.
Senterling, Frederick.
Snell, Andrew.
Shafer, John.
Sansom, John, sick at home.
Smith, Abraham.
Shafer, Jacob.
Taylor, Lemuel.
Wood, Stephen T.
White, Hugh.
Wipert, John.
Walters, Adam.
Weaver, Alexander.
Wilt, Henry.
Williams, John.
Wible, Jessee.
Hull, Henry W.
Young, Andrew.
Young, Thomas.
Zigler, Jacob.
Rusk, George.
Etinger, William.
Thorn, John.

We certify, on honor, that this muster-roll exhibits a true state of the Sixth company of Pennsylvania militia, service of the United States, regiment of Col. John Thompson, for the period therein mentioned, and that the remarks set opposite the names of the men are accurate and just.

JOHN SCHWEPPENHEISER,
Captain.
JOHN THOMPSON,
Colonel Commanding.

February 16, 1816.

ROLL OF CAPT. GEORGE SENSENDERFER'S COMPANY.

A correct muster-roll of Capt. George Sensenderfer's company of Montgomery Rifle Greens, stationed at Camp Boileau.

Captain.
Sensenderfer, George.

First Lieutenant.
Schneider, Henry.

Second Lieutenant.
Borkert, George.

Ensign.
Stoflit, Michael.

Sergeants.
Smith, Jacob.
Bucher, Dieter.
Smith, Daniel.
Smith, George.

Corporals.
Stitzer, Daniel.
Sasaman, Jacob.
Gilbert, John.
Gilbert, Mathies.

Privates.
Smith, George.
Yorgy, John.
Gilbert, Jacob.
Herpst, Peter.
Wiehn, John.
Linsenbigler, Henry.
Reifnider, Jacob.
Drease, Conrad.
Dengler, George.
Gilbert, Anthony.
Yerger, John.
Deeker, John.
Drase, John.
Herpst, John.
Yerger, Mareks.
Deeker, Peter.
Yerger, Isaac.
Kepner, John.
Linsenbigler, Lewis.
Swinehard, Daniel.

Swinehard, David.
Yorgy, Mathies.
Reigner, Conrad.
Wise, John.
Hauberger, Peter.
Beydenman, Samuel.
Frederick, John.
Kortz, Michael.
Erb, John.

We do certify, on honor, that the within roll exhibits a true state of the company commanded by Capt. George Sensenderfer, and that the remarks set opposite the men's names are accurate and just.

GEORGE SENSENDERFER,
Captain.

THOS. HUMPHREY,
Colonel First R. P. V. R.

CAMP DUPONT, *November 24, 1814.*

We certify, on honor, that the company commanded by Capt. George Sensenderfer, is in the service of the United States, under the command of the general commanding the Fourth military district.

THOS. CADWALADER,
Brigadier General Commanding Advance L. B.

CAMP DUPONT, *November 26, 1814.*

ROLL OF CAPT. JAMES SERRILL'S COMPANY.

Pay-roll of the Delaware county Fencibles, commanded by Captain James Serrill, attached to the Thirty-second regiment of Pennsylvania militia. Date of entering service, September 21, 1814.

Captain.

Serrill, James.

First Lieutenant.

Leiper, George G.

Second Lieutenant.

Serrill, James, Jr.

Ensign.

Serrill, George.

Sergeant Major.

Adams, Moses.

Sergeants.

Pearson, John B.
Jones, Richard R.

Rose, David, Jr.
Oakford, Joseph.

Corporals.

Wood, Henry.
Shallcross, Joseph.
Urian, Andrew.
Farrell, John C.

Musicians

Warner, James.
Holmes, Robert.

Privates.

Martin, Thomas J.
Wetherall, John.
Trites, Casper.
Rively, John.
Rively, Andrew.
Dobbins, John.
Fines, William.
Stannard, Lewis B.
Bonsall, Charles.
Attmore, Charles.
Helmes, Aaron.
Noblet, Andrew.
Stroop, John.
Bonsall, Enoch.
Ormsby, Edward.
McNulty, Matthew.
Paschall, Jesse Z.
Smith, Daniel.
Williamson, George.
Bonsall, Reuben.
Hanse, Clement.
Gibson, Charles.
McSweeny, Miles.
Helms, Cad. M.
Enberg, Andrew.
Siddons, Marshall.
McCormick, William.
Brown, John.
Bonsall, Evan.
Lutkin, John.
Duey, Jacob.
Bonsall, Jon^a S.
Kinsey, William.
Helms, William.
McLane, John.

Ash, Thomas.
Cox, William.
Shaw, John.
Johnson, George W.
Jones, William.
Ash, Thomas P.
Quicksall, Jonathan.
Fleming, Thomas.
Humphries, William.
Frazier, John.
Meyers, John.
McCleester, John.
Glover, William.
Bonsall, Joshua.
Bonsall, Samuel, Jr.
Bonsall, Thomas.
Bonsall, Samuel.
Palmer, Samuel.
Merion, Thomas.
Hooper, Joseph.
Clark, Robert.
McGilton, John.
Bunting, Samuel.
Painter, Philip.
Meyers, George.
Smith, Davis.
Smith, Clement.
Long, Peter.
Mackey, Cornelius.
Smart, David.
Hayes, Nathan.
Bonsall, David.
Brooks, Isaac.
McGinley, Daniel.
Statton, John.
Hahn, John.
Ross, George.
Williams, Thomas.
Wells, Moses, Jr.
McCullough, Thomas.
Smith, William.

CAMP MARCUS HOOK, *October 14, 1814.*

I do certify, upon honor, this muster-roll exhibits a true statement of the Delaware County Fencibles, a volunteer company of militia of the State of Pennsylvania, now in the service of the United States, the remarks set opposite the names of the men are accurate and just.

JAMES SERRILL,
Captain.

I believe the annexed to be a correct muster and pay-roll.

WILLIAM C. ROGERS,
Brigade Major.

I certify that the Delaware County Fencibles, commanded by James Serrill, is in the service of the United States, under orders of the general commanding the Fourth military district.

SAMUEL SMITH,
Brigadier General.

CAMP MARCUS HOOK, *October 17, 1814.*

ROLL OF CAPT. ABR'AM SHAFER'S COMPANY.

List of non-commissioned officers and privates of the militia company commanded by Capt. Abr^{am} Shafer, as part of the Second brigade, Second division, Pennsylvania militia, in the service of the United States, under the requisition of the President, of the 4th of July, 1814, and subsequent thereto, * * * under the command of Lieut. Col. Christian I. Hutter, November 10, 1814.

Sergeants.

Drumheller, Jacob.
Sellers, Cornelius.
Brunner, Andrew.
Brumfeld, Israel.
Dotterer, Jacob.

Corporals.

Hess, John.
Unangst, John.
Lynn, Peter.
Weaver, George.

Privates.

Sigfried, George.
Unangst, Philip.
Heager, Peter.
Engleman, Ab^m.
Hartman, Solomon.
Jacoby, John.
Zeigler, Jacob.
Kleimer, George.
Klik, Philip.
Miller, Jacob.

Welsh, John.
Laubach, Rudolph.
Reish, David.
Hoffman, Henry.
Cooper, John.
Christman, John.
Weaver, Tobias.
Freeman, Jacob.
Roth, Philip.
Beidleman, John.
Loyd, Martin.
Hess, Jacob.
Best, Henry.
Ruch, Christian.
Blaylor, or Beyler, Lazarus.
Ruth, Michael.
Trauser, Jacob.
Reigle, Henry.
Fehr, Abraham.
Lutz. Michael.
Lantz, Jacob.
Peyfer, Philip.
Hartzel, Samuel.
Waldenslager, Samuel.
Lougbach, George.
Jacoby, George.
Woodring, Jacob.
Grotz, Henry.
Peyfer, John.
Stem, John.
Best, Jacob.
Hartzell, Ab^m.
Garis, Frederick.
Spangleberg, or Spangenberg, F.
Spangenberg, Jacob.
Raub, Jacob.
Stem, Henry.
Miller, Frederick.
Miller, Jacob.
Frankenfield, H.
Raub, William.
Raub, John.
Brotzman, Joseph.
Walter, Leonard.
Mittig, Peter.
Transer, Peter.

WAR OF 1812-14.

Rouch, Daniel.
Sander, George.
Rouch, John.
Fatick, George.
Rouch, Solomon.
Mest, Samuel.
Rex, John.
Hauseman, John.
Peter, Jonas.
Lauchnor, Joseph.
Rauchle, Adam.
Sliger, Valentine.
Deibert, Daniel.
Sensinger, Daniel.
Klotz, Andrew.
Buckman, Andrew.
Miller, Peter.
Sensinger, Peter.
Hause, Christian.
Klotz, Daniel.
Hanse, Leonard.
Harlen, John.
Hanse, Jacob.
Stirwald, George.
Archer, or Acker, Daniel, Sr.
Acker, Daniel, Jr.
Magers, Carl.
Fry, Adam.
Bogers, Samuel.
Miller, Jacob.
Hiller, Christian.
Hedler, John.
Dapbeider, George.
Breiner, George.
Hedler, George.
Miller, Ab^m.
Frantz, John.
Mest, Martin.
Rex, Jacob.
Natstone, Peter.
Sell, Peter.
Favour, William.
Kromlich, Jacob.
Heidenreich, John.
Kob, George.
Hartman, Peter.

ROLL OF CAPT. JOHN SHEFFER'S COMPANY.

A complete muster pay-roll of a company of militia, commanded by Capt. John Sheffer.

Captain.

Sheffer, John.

First Lieutenant.

Bowman, Henry.

Second Lieutenant.

Levers, Joseph, promoted.

Third Lieutenant.

Horner, Hugh, promoted.

Ensign.

Dreisbach, Adam.

Sergeants.

Steckel, Peter.
Mulhollan, Arthur.
Gressler, John.
Hertz, Peter.

Corporals.

Shefer, Peter.
Edelman, John.
Millham, Jacob.
Merch, John.
Chester, John.

Drummer.

Fuldon, John.

Fifer.

Donner, John.

Privates.

Dilcher, Henry.
Mosser, George.
Derhamer, Abraham.
Deal, John.
Mosser, Henry.
Keiner, John.
Roth, Peter.
Houser, Jacob.

Mosser, Peter.
Frey, Michael.
Shlegel, Conrad.
Steinmetz, John.
Walker, Jacob.
March, Henry.
George, Joseph.
Best, George.
Leinberger, Adam.
Kester, Laurence.
Gress, or Kress, Henry.
Derr, Jacob.
Osterdock, William.
Kester, Jacob.
Brown, William.
Kemrer, Frederick.
Musselman, Michael.
Best, Jacob.
Kester, William.
Shefer, John, Sr.
Kester, Conrad.
Bachman, Conrad.
Sneneberger, Christian.
Person, Abraham.
Dieter, John.
Dieter, Henry.
Eberts, Frederick.
Shefer, John, Jr.
Kase, Peter.
Vogal, Jacob.
Breder, George.
Huber, Jacob.
Klepinger, Jacob.
Renner, Philip.
Laubach, Simon.
Balliott, Abraham.
Hamsher, Adam.
Anthony, Peter.
Engler, George.
Patterson, Ludwig.
Sensebach, Godfried.
Patterson, Henry.
Bartelme, Henry.
Snyder, Henry.
Repe, Henry.
Lind, John.

WAR OF 1812-14.

Oblinger, Peter.
Steckel, Peter, Jr.
Sigfried, Isaac.
Wesner, John.
Bush, Jacob.
Heckman, Joseph.
Anthony, George.
Bile, Abraham.
Deshler, Jacob.
Hahn, John.
Wittes, Isaac, discharged October 20.
Hubler, John.
Kruber, Jacob.
Comas, Daniel M.
Swap, Jacob.
Klinetop, Ludwig.
Smith, Joseph.
Box, Nicholas.
Bock, Joseph.
Blare, or Blase, Peter.
Sold, Conrad.
Smith, Abraham.
Barthelme, Ludwig.
Shumaker, Frederick.
Zegenfuse, Andrew.
Muffly, Daniel.
Myer, Conrad.
Beer, George.
Rosbrugh, John.
Wise, Francis.
Kep, John.
Blase, Nicholas.
Miller, John.
Rishel, Michael.
Diemer, George, died October 15, 1814.
Deal, Henry, joined October 19, 1814, being on furlough; discharged October 21.
Rohrer, Daniel.

CAMP MARCUS HOOK, *October 22, 1814.*

I certify, upon honor, that this muster-roll exhibits a true statement of the —— company, —— regiment, Pennsylvania militia, now in the service of the United States, and that the remarks set opposite the names are accurate and just, to the best of my knowledge.

JOHN SHEFFER,
Captain.

I believe the above to be a correct muster of pay-roll.

CHRISTIAN J. HUTTER,
Lieutenant Colonel Commanding.

I certify that the company commanded by Capt. John Sheffer is now in the service of the United States, under order of the general commanding military district.

H. SPERING,
Brigadier General.

October 25, 1814.

ROLL OF CAPT. THOMAS SHRIVER'S COMPANY.

Pay-roll of a company of Riflemen, commanded by Capt. Thomas Shriver, of the One Hundred and Thirteenth regiment, performing a tour of duty under command of Col. Lutz, who rendezvoused at York, Pennsylvania, under the general order of the Governor, dated August 26, 1814. Commencement of service, September 3.

Captain.

Shriver, Thomas.

First Lieutenant.

Gartner, Israel.

Second Lieutenant.

Small, Joseph.

Ensign.

Boyer, Henry.

Sergeants.

Renshaw, James.
Gartner, John M.
Gortman, Jacob.
All, Peter.

Corporals.

Miller, John.
Krone, Jacob.
Schreder, William.
Whiteford, Samuel.

Drummer.

Schlossar, George.

Fifer.

Koontz, Henry.

Privates.

Hald, Jacob, miller.
Eichelberger, Charles.
Peters, William.
McCurtin, John A.

Jacoby, Elisha.
Streibig, Peter.
Frey, Jacob.
Hass, Jeremiah.
Zeigler, John.
Norris, William.
Wolery, George.
Ennis, John.
Miller, Christian.
Miller, Henry.
Kleinfelter, Henry.
Ford, Daniel.
Stotebeck, Frederick.
Kaler, Frederick.
Zeigler, Philip.
McIntire, George.
McKinny, Michael.
Nicuffer, William.
Reisinger, David.
Brown, Jacob.
Irwin, Christopher.
Taylor, Joseph.
Corbin, Thomas.
Kuch, John.
Sheffer, George.
Clingman, Daniel.
Mann, Abraham.
Koch, Jacob.
Owings, John.
Smith, Charles.
Stump, John.
Blue, John.
Frey, Daniel.
Rupp, Christ.
Markle, George.
Conn, George.
Huber, Nicholas.
Deitch, Philip.
McLaughlan, Jeremiah.
Inerst, H.
Ernst, Christian.

I certify the within to be a correct roll of my company.

THOMAS SHRIVER,
Captain.

Test:

JNO. ADDAMS,
Brigadier General.

ROLL OF CAPT. JACOB SHURTZ'S COMPANY.

CAMP DUPONT, *November 13, 1814.*

A true list of Captain Jacob Shurtz's company of the Eighteenth section of Riflemen commanded by Col. Thomas Humphreys.

Sergeants.

Ettwine, John.
Lawall, George.
Wagner, John.
Hummel, Jacob.
King, John.

Corporals.

Wolf, John.
Wolf, Henry.
Buss, John.
Kaemerer, Nich^l.

Musicians.

Stehr, Ab^m.
Lawall, Michael.
Lawall, Peter.

Privates.

Koeher, John.
Beil, John.
Fry, Daniel.
Fry, John.
Fry, Michael.
Blum, John.
Clayder, John.
Gross, Samuel.
Becker, Christ.
Coleman, Joseph.
Colver, Jacob.
Engel, George.
Flick, Jonas.
Handsher, Jacob.
Cutting, Levy.
Dorwart, John.
Dreher, Fred^r.
Huber, John.
Kinkel, John.
Junkin, Peter.
Kinnart, Isaac.
Kirkenthal, John.
Kreidler, Daniel.

Moser, Joseph.
Overly, David.
Roth, Casper.
Roth, Jacob.
Roth, John.
Santee. John.
McSwain, W.
Transer, Mathias.
Unangst, John.
Wagner, George.
Young, George.
Ziegefuss, Jacob.
Heberling, George.
Fry, Conrad, promoted the 1st of November, 1814, to ensign.

We do certify that the within list is a true statement, on honor, this 13th day of November, 1814.

JACOB SHURTZ,
Captain.
THOMAS HUMPHREY,
Colonel First R. P. V. R.

I do certify, on honor, that the company commanded by Capt. Jacob Shurtz is in the service of the United States, under the command of the general commanding the Fourth military district.

THOMAS CADWALADER,
Brigadier General Commanding advance, L. B.
CAMP DUPONT, *November 26, 1814.*

ROLL OF CAPT. ISAAC SILVERTHORN'S COMPANY.

Pay-roll of Capt. Isaac Silverthorn's company, belonging to the Seventeenth regiment, Pennsylvania militia, under the command of Lieut. Col. John C. Wallace, being part of a brigade doing duty at Erie, by order, and under the direction, of Major Gen. David Mead, commencing the 24th day of July, and ending the 5th day of August following, A. D. 1813.

Captain.

Silverthorn, Isaac.

Ensign.

Sterrett, David, attached from Capt. Lee's company.

Sergeants.

Hunter, John, attached from Capt. Cole's company.
Crane, Elihu, attached from Capt. Salsbury's company.
Dimpsey, John, attached from Capt. Cole's company.

Corporals.

Cowgill, Jonah, attached from Capt. Morris' company.
Bunting, Samuel, attached form Capt. Morris' company.
Sterrett, Robert, attached from Capt. Lee's company.

Privates.

Kelley, George, attached from Erie Light Infantry.
Leech, John, attached from Capt. Morris' company.
Brewster, Alexander, attached from Capt. Morris' company.
Culbertson, James, attached from Capt. Coneattee's company.
Spry, Benjamin, attached from Capt. Coneattee's company.
Long, John, attached from Capt. Cole's company.
Swan, John, attached from Capt. Cole's company.
Collumn, Benjamin, attached from Capt, Coneattee's company.
Taggart, Cardiff, attached from Capt. Cole's company.
McCreary, Samuel, attached from Capt. Cole's company.
Kennedy, Robert, attached from Capt. Cole's company.
Lungan, Peter, attached from Capt. Cole's company.
McClelland, William, attached from Capt. Cole's company.
Martin, Nathaniel, attached from Capt. Lee's company.
Dunn, William, attached from Capt. Lee's company.
Hodge, Alford, attached from Capt. Coneattee's company.
Akers, Daniel, attached from Capt. Salsbury's company.
Dunlap, John, attached from Capt. Lee's company.
Gray, John, attached from Capt. Morris' company.
Braddish, Joel.

I certify, upon honor, that the above pay-roll is correct.

ISAAC SILVERTHORN,
Captain.
JOHN C. WALLACE,
Lieutenant Colonel Commanding.

ROLL OF CAPT. ISAAC SMITH'S COMPANY.

Muster-roll of Capt. Isaac Smith's company in the One Hundred and Fifty-second regiment, First brigade, Pennsylvania militia, under the command of Lieut. William Cochran at York, Pennsylvania. In service from September 2, to ———; from Dauphin, Lancaster, &c.

Captain.

Smith, Isaac.

First Lieutenant.

Lentz, Michael.

Second Lieutenant.

Buchanon, Nathan.

Ensign.

Taylor, John.

Sergeants.

Black, Thomas.
Taylor, George.
Freeburn, James.
Shaeffer, Henry.

Corporals.

Fullen, Tilson.
Hummel, Samuel.

Privates.

Bittinger, Peter.
Black, John.
Bower, Adam.
Bower, Jacob.
Bower, Michael.
Braught, Adam.
Chubb, Peter.
Clark, John.
Cline, Philip.
Frank, Frederick.
Fred, Abraham.
Freeburn, Thomas.
Gray, Jacob.
Huston, Samuel.
Hylard, Guy.
Jury, Abraham.
Jury, George.
Lentz, George.
Lingefelter, Jacob.
Lorge, William.
Mash, Peter.
Miller, John.
Nablet, John.
Peters, Christian.
Reed, John.
Rutter, Isaac.
Sewers, Daniel.
Sinn, George.
Sweigart, David.
Urich, Joseph.
Wilson, Daniel.

ROLL OF CAPT. JACOB SNYDER'S COMPANY.

Muster-roll of Capt. Jacob Snyder's company in the Second regiment, Second brigade, Pennsylvania militia, under the command of Lieut. Col. Lutz at York, Pennsylvania. In service from September 2, 1814, to (time not mentioned) from Lancaster county.

Captain.

Snyder, Jacob.

First Lieutenant.

Scott, John.

Second Lieutenant.

Fordney, Casper.

Ensign.

Welsh, George.

Sergeants.

Sansom, Bonom.
McGivern, Patrick.
Scott, Archibald.
Fordney, Philip.
Lehman, Josiah.

Corporals.

Hartley, Nicholas.
Jackson, John G.
Miller, Henry.
Nagle, Rudolph.

Drummer.

Leeher, Anthony.

Privates.

Bennet, Isaac.
Bortle, Jacob.
Brown, John.
Brown, William.
Bruner, George.
Buckley, John.
Campbell, Robert.
Christ, John.
Collens, Andrew.
Donner, Jacob.
Ferree, Henry.
Fetter, Frederick.
Finfrock, George.
Garlack, Henry.

Geider, Christian.
Goldsmith, Charles.
Hainy, James.
Hamilton, Robert.
Hart, Lewis.
Hatz, John.
Hauntch, Nathaniel.
Hauntch, William.
Hoover, Jacob.
Joudon, Joseph.
Kauts, Joseph.
Kee, William.
Keiler, Henry.
Ketch, John.
Kreamer, George.
Kreamer, John.
Lambert, John.
Lawrence, John.
Leinback, Joseph.
Leonhard, Philip.
Lithgow, Alexander.
Lutz, Coleman.
McCurdy, Archibald.
McGinniss, John.
McLaughlin, Barney.
Menida, James.
Miley, John.
Nauman, Jacob.
Ostler, William.
Pickle, Isaac.
Roth, George.
Roth, Jacob.
Russel, Thomas.
Schucker, Peter.
Seider, John.
Slauter, John.
Smith, Matthias.
Spreaker, Andrew.
Stace, Charles.
Wagner, John.
Waters, Richard.
White, Joseph.
Wineland, Emanuel.
Young, Adam.
Young, John.

ROLL OF CAPT. JOHN SNYDER'S COMPANY.

Muster-roll of the Selinsgrove Rifle Volunteers of Union county, commanded by Capt. John Snyder, and attached to the battalion commanded by Capt. John Uhle, in the light brigade commanded by Brig. Gen. Thomas Cadwalader, now in the actual service of the United States, at Camp Dupont, November 14, 1814.

Captain.

Snyder, John.

First Lieutenant.

Rhoads, Jacob.

Second Lieutenant.

Selen, Anthony C.

Ensign.

Barkstreser, George.

Sergeants.

Thornbaugh, Mathias.
Shriner, Jacob.
Harlon, Isaac.
Graever, Philip.

Corporals.

Hausman, John.
Lebo, Daniel.
Dering, William S.
Stock, Conrad.

Privates.

Hilbush, Henry.
Bloom, Henry.
Hoote, Henry.
Keefer, Henry.
Botthof, Henry.
Miller, John.
Filman, John.
Hall, John.
Ulrick, John.
Rhem, John.
Kersteler, John.
Hays, James.
Harlon, James.
Fisher, David.
Hauck, George.

Boddory, George.
Buchley, George.
Weiser, George.
Ulrick, Benjamin.
Gemberling, Samuel.
Haislett, Samuel.
Coldron, Solomon.
Vandike, James.
Maus, John S.
Essick, or Essig, John.
Steel, William.
Gaugler, William.
Sassaman, John.
Arnold, Peter.
Robison, Isaac.
Strayer, Jacob.
Vanandey, Jacob.
Walburn, Jacob.
Schlutterback, Peter.
Shipman, Abraham.
Minier, William.
Silverwood, Thomas.
Lebo, Paul.
Rupp, John.
Wise, Christian.
Lambert, John.
Hoey, Samuel.
Hair, Valentine.
Thursby, Thomas.
Antee, or Andy, Charles.

I do certify that this muster-roll is correct as stated. Witness my hand this 21st November.

JACOB RHOAD,
First Lieutenant.
JOHN UHLE,
Capt. commanding the First batt'n of Riflemen at Camp Dupont.

I do certify, on honor, that the company commanded by Capt. John Snyder is in the service of the United States, under the command of the general commanding the Fourth military district.

THOS. CADWALADER,
Brigadier General Commanding Advance L. B.

CAMP DUPONT *November 26, 1814.*

ROLL OF CAPT. PETER SNYDER'S COMPANY.

Muster-roll of Capt. Peter Snyder's company, in the Second regiment, First brigade, of Pennsylvania militia, under the command of Lieut. Col. Adam Ridsher, at York, Pennsylvania. In service from September 2, 1814, to March 5, 1815, from Dauphin, Schuylkill, Lebanon, and Berks counties.

Captain.

Snyder, Peter.

Lieutenant.

Bonawits, Benjamin.

Ensign.

Moody, Robert.

Sergeants.

Leahy, John.
Spayd, Christian.
Snyder, John.
Hughes, Charles.

Corporals.

Manly, David.
Hauthorn, George.
Heppick, Joshua.
Hargesloger, Michael.

Privates.

Alberty, Lawrance.
Albright, John.
Andrew, Jacob.
Bale, John.
Barket, Peter.
Belleman, John.
Boddorff, John.
Boyer, John.
Brown, Jacob.
Bullinger, Daniel.
Bullinger, Jacob.
Cassel, Frederick.
Cassel, Michael.
Conrad, John.
Critzon, John.
Cunningham, Robert.
Curry, William.
Diel, John.
Duncan, John.
Ebbert, Henry.

Eckler, Henry.
Ettle, David.
Eversole, Abraham.
Felty, Martin.
Fritz, Michael.
Gross, Michael.
Grundon, James.
Harrow, Henry.
Hays, Richard.
Hays, Solomon.
Hedrick, Peter.
Hemperly, Michael.
Hite, Jacob.
Hostler, Jacob.
Hummel, Frederick.
Hummel, Joseph.
Johnson, David.
Jontz, George.
Kramer, Michael.
Lukinbill, John.
McBride, James.
McElrath, John.
Mosey, David.
Moyer, David.
Murray, Francis.
Night, John.
Reigle, Jonathan.
Remly, George.
Sawyer, John.
Seiler, Peter.
Shaffer, George.
Shaffer, John.
Smith, John.
Snyder, Godfrey.
Souser, Michael.
Stine, George.
Stine, John, Jr.
Strouse, William.
Winter, Jacob.
Wolf, John.
Woltz, John.
Woltz, Michael.
Wright, James.
Wyrich, David.
Zarver, Benjamin.
Zarver, Philip.

WAR OF 1812–14. 455

ROLL OF CAPT. MICHAEL SPANGLER'S COMPANY.

Pay-roll of a company of volunteers, commanded by Capt. Michael Spangler, of the First regiment, performing a tour of duty, under the command of Col. Maxwell Kennedy, who rendezvoused at York, under the general order of the Governor, dated 26th August, 1814. Commencement of service, August 28, 1814.

Captain.

Spangler, Michael.

First Lieutenant.

Barnitz, Jacob, Jr.

Second Lieutenant.

McCurdy, John.

Ensign.

Doll, George F.

Sergeants.

Hay, John.
Kuntz, John.
Kurtz, Charles.
Schall, Joseph.

Corporals.

Wilson, David.
King, Adam.
Updegraff, Daniel.
Hahn, Michael.

Privates.

Altemas, Jerman W.
Briegle, John.
Briegle, George.
Burns, William.
Baumgartner, Daniel.
Beard, George.
Burns, Anthony F.
Bull, Walter.
Burns, John.
Connelly, James.
Coil, Daniel.
Coodie, Richard.
Carney, Dennis.
Cooker, Peter.

Duvall, Grafton.
Dunn, George.
Divine, John.
Dougan, James.
Eshbaugh, Christian.
Frey, Jacob.
Fisher, John.
Gibson, James.
Glessner, Jacob.
Grimes, Peter.
Gartnur, Jacob.
Heckert, Daniel.
Hays, Samuel.
Holter, George.
Herbst, Jacob.
Hoffart, David.
Holt, Aaron.
Ingram, Hugh.
Ilgenfritz, George.
Keller, Abraham.
Kergher, Frederick.
Kerr, Joseph.
Kaufman, David.
Kaufman, Andrew.
Giese, John.
Lavan, Jacob.
Lottman, Jacob.
Lehman, Jacob.
Leitner, George M.
Laub, George.
McCoscar, Hugh.
Murphy, Edward W.
Miller, Thomas.
Miller, Michael.
McClean, John.
McAnulty, John.
McAleer, Hugh, Sr.
McAleer, Hugh, Jr.
Mundorff, Henry.
McKoneghen, Joseph.
Noell, Jacob.
Nes, William.
Nes, Samuel.
O'Conner, Peter.
Pierson, Robert.
Reisinger, Jacob.

Raup, Emanuel.
Rupp, Jacob.
Reisinger, George.
Stuck, Charles.
Sheffer, Jacob.
Spangler, George W.
Stewart, Hugh.
Schlieger, Henry.
Sieres, Peter.
Smith, Chester.
Stroman, Charles.
Stoehr, Jacob.
Sinn, John.
Trimble, David.
Thompson, Thomas.
Taylor, John.
Thompson, Enoch.
Wisenall, Jacob.
Witz, Frederick.
Woodyear, Joseph.
Wolff, Henry.
Warson, William.
Miller, John.
Heckman, William.
Joseph, Leitner.

I certify the foregoing to be a correct pay-roll of my company.

M. H. SPANGLER,
Captain.

Test:

J. FORSTER.
Brigadier General.

ROLL OF CAPT. JACOB F. SPARKS' COMPANY.

* Muster-roll of the non-commissioned officers and privates of a company of drafted militia of the late One hundred and Fortieth regiment, Pennsylvania militia, under the command of Jacob F. Sparks, in the service of the United States from September 12, 1814, to January 5, 1815.

Sergeants.

Arbigust, William.
Keanny, John.
Martin, Thomas.
Kettler, John.

Corporals.

Gardner, John.
Shisler, George.
Boake, Israel P.
Getz, George.

Musicians.

Copple, Jacob.
Gassey, Remond.

Privates.

Falbourt, Joseph.
Berk, William.
Bowman, Daniel.
Bowman, Casper.
Boyer, John.
Boyer, Henry.
Butler, Joseph.
Bryant, William.
Brown, Samuel.
Chatham, John.
Copple, George.
Cubler, Jacob.
Creely, John.
Dixey, John.
Ervine, John.
Ellott, Robert.
Fawpell, George. •
Flood, John.
Griner, George.
German, William.
Gosner, Christopher.
Harden, John.
Hempshire, Jacob.
Havenstrite, Jonas.
Harvy, James.
Hartrums, or Hartramps, George.
Ireland, Jacob.
Johnson, Job.
Kettler, David.
Keglar, Thomas.
Lesher, George.
Lutz, John G.
Louderback, John.
Lyon, Samuel.
Lawrence, James.
Mettia, Samuel.

Moore, George.
Morrow, William.
Manderfield, Charles.
McKover, Isaac.
McCowen, John.
McCarty, Bernard.
McCoy, Edward.
Morrison, Alexander.
Mounery, Richard.
Nordike, Benoni.
Ross, William.
Rossnickle, John.
Riaki, William.
Rutter, Henry.
Rue, John.
Reid, William.
Smith, Jonathan.
Smith, Robert.
Stevenson, William.
Sturges, Joseph.
Siddons, John.
Story, William.
Taylor, James.
Thomas, Joshua.
Ulirick, Jacob.
Wright, William.
Westenberger, George.
Wilson, Richard.
Young, Jacob Jr.
Young, Jacob.
Young, Samuel.
Shaffer, Thomas C.

We certify, on honor, that this muster-roll exhibits a true state of Capt. Jacob F. Spark's company of the Sixty-seventh regiment of infantry, of the Second brigade, First division, Pennsylvania militia, late in the service of the United States, commanded by Col. John Thompson for the period therein mentioned, and that the remarks set opposite the names of the men are accurate and just.

JOHN THOMPSON,
Colonel.
JACOB F. SPARKS,
Captain.

PHILADELPHIA, *March 18, 1816.*

ROLL OF CAPT. SOLOMON SPARKS' COMPANY.

Pay-roll of Capt. Solomon Sparks' company of Riflemen, attached to the Second regiment of riflemen commanded by Col. William Piper, in the service of the United States, from the State of Pennsylvania, Brig. Gen. Adamson Tannehill, commanding. Commencing the 25th (?) and ending the 24th of November, 1812, (both days inclusive.)

Captain.

Sparks, Solomon.

Lieutenant.

Piper, James.

Ensign.

Fletcher, David.

Sergeants.

Armstrong, Joseph.
Paxton, John.
Wilson, James.
Steckman, Philip.

Corporals.

Mortimore, John.
Sparks, James.
Steckman, Valentine.
Wilson, William.

Fifer.

Whitestone, Solomon.

Drummer.

Lysinger, Samuel.

Privates.

Stover, Henry.
Piper, David.
Holler, Solomon.
England, James.
Clinger, Henry.
Young, Frederick.
Steckman, John.
Phillips, Jacob.
Corn, or Carn, Philip.
Hammelton, Robert.
Morris, Joseph.
Sparks, Joseph.
Hinish, John.
Swartz, David.

Barndollar, Peter.
Donaldson, Reason.
Wassing, Henry.
Pickering, Joshua.
McCasling, Samuel.
Henry, Ather, or Achar.
Casner, Daniel.
Smith, Samuel.
Means, Edward.
Casner, Jacob.
Runard, Jacob.
Sparks, Abraham.
Means, Joseph.
Richey, Henry.
Sparks, Joseph.
Cook, William.
Griffith, Abel.
Gardner, James.
Griffith, Evan.
Smith, Henry.
Deal, John.
Runard, David.
McCarty, William.

ROLL OF CAPT. JAMES W. SPROAT'S COMPANY.

Muster-roll of a volunteer company of Light Infantry, called the Germantown Blues, commanded by Capt. James W. Sproat, late in service of the United States, attached to the Second brigade, First division, Pennsylvania militia. Commencement of service, September 8, 1814; discharged January 2, 1815.

Captain.

Sproat, James W.

First Lieutenant.

Wilson, John.

Second Lieutenant.

Ent, William.

Ensign.

Barwell, John.

Sergeants.

Coit, Gabriel.
McCully, William.
Junkart, Christopher.

Corporals.

Butler, George H.
Mower, Rudolph B.
Williams, Daniel.

Privates.

Hess, John.
Gilbert, Anthony.
Nell, John.
Buddy, John.
Moyer, Charles.
Snyder, George W.
Salter, John W.
Keysel, Herman.
Ulmer, George.
Hess, William.
Koagi, Andrew.
Hofman, George.
Blair, Samuel.
Brooker, Samuel.
Steel, John.
Reger, Samuel.
Sanno, Frederick D.
Cooke, John.
Nagle, Christian.
Buckius, Albert.
Hess, Christian.
Fraley, Henry.
Stroup, Daniel.
Boehm, William.
Sorber, Elias.
Singlewood, Charles.
Shorwaker, John.
Williams, Luke.
Meridith, Samuel.
Corwell, William.
Benner, Isaac.
Stadelman, John.
Johnes, William.
Felty, Peter.
Warner, John.
Widdis, George.
Vanhorn, Edward.
Duval, John.
Smith, Jacob.
Buddy, Charles.

Keyl, Baltus.
Heileg, John D.
Sinclair, William.
Norton, Thomas.
Crout, William.
Wunder, Jacob.
Moyer, William.
Lower, John H.
Decart, Michael.
Burwell, Isaac.
Zigler, William.
Bowhard, Augustus, appointed a cadet in the United States army September 28, 1814.
Magarge, Jonathan.
Maclain, John.
Gover, William.

I certify the above to be correct.

JAMES W. SPROAT,
Captain Germantown Blues.
SAMUEL SPARKS,
Major.

GERMANTOWN, *March 20, 1816.*

ROLL OF CAPT. JACOB STAKE'S COMPANY.

List of men belonging to a company commanded by Jacob Stake, in the Second brigade, Seventh division, Pennsylvania militia, and belonging to the Fifth detachment, under the command of Col. James Fenton.

Captain.
Stake, Jacob.

First Lieutenant.
Favourite, John.

Second Lieutenant.
Foot, Robert.

Ensign.
Miller, William.

Sergeants.
Snively, John.
Baker, Jacob.
Baker, Samuel.
Wescoat, William.

Corporals.

Over, John.
Keever, Jacob.
Shannon, John M.
Scholes, Thomson.

Drummer.

Boggs, John.

Privates.

Creamer, Samuel.
Hawk, John.
Long, Benjamin.
Crotzer, John.
Rone, Philip.
Reed, William.
Davenport, Samuel.
Stake, John.
Swanger, John.
Trindle, David.
Smith, John.
McDowell, John.
Brant, John.
Beams, Jesse.
Holby, Henry.
Pluher, George.
McComb, George.
Erwin, John.
Myers, Adam.
Nevel, William.
Young, John.
Miller, John.
Clark, Barnabas.
Baker, Hugh.
McLay, or Maclay, John.
Hunter, Robert.
Staily, Jacob.
Rist, George.
Young, John.
Meteer, Samuel.
Bender, Matthias.
Borough, Frederick.
Brackenridge, Alexander.
Johnston, Robert.
Johnston, David.
Leopard, Jacob.
McNeal, John.

McClure, William.
Byard, George.
Keever, James.
Flyle, Abraham.
Runion. Charles.
Beaty, John.
Harmony, George.
Ramsen, William.
Lilly, Elisha.
Stoufer, Jacob.
Kline, William.
Sheets, William.
Fipps, Joseph.
Marshall, John.
Hill, Edward.
Frush, or Crush, Jacob.
Henderson, Hugh.
Ensminger, George.
Clapp, William.
McConnel, John.
Allen, Thomas.
Early, James.
Baker, John.
Carver, John.
Neff, George.
Davis, Benjamin.
Stewart, John.
Frits, Michael.
Campton, James.
Morehead, James.
Cunningham, John.
Baker, Peter.
Hardy, James.
Cummins, Thomas.
McConnel, Robert.

I do hereby certify that this is a true list of the members composing my company. Witness my hand this 18th day of March, 1814.

JACOB STAKE,
Captain.
JAMES WOOD,
Major.

ROLL OF CAPT. JOSEPH STARNE'S COMPANY.

Pay-roll of Capt. Joseph Starne's company of volunteers, attached to the Second brigade, First division, Pennsylvania militia, under command of Col. John Thompson, in the service of the United States.

Captain.

Starne, Joseph, extra duty.

First Lieutenant.

Levering, Aaron.

Second Lieutenant.

Conrad, John.

Ensign.

Kline, Peter.

Sergeants.

Tibbin, Daniel.
Kerper, George.
Righter, Charles.
Strouse, Jacob.

Corporals.

Levering, Charles.
Levering, John.
Righter, Michael.
Smith, Jacob B.

Music.

Moore, Charles.
Ashton, James.

Privates.

Levering, Joseph.
Wilt, Cristopher.
Stretzell, Joseph.
Keely, George.
Ozeas, Joseph.
Hinkle, Peter.
Fight, Casper.
Shuster, Jacob.
Struper, John.
Coulston, James.
Shuster, Charles.
Ingram, Joseph.
Tibbin, John.
Rex, Henry.
Goodman, George.
Shain, William.

WAR OF 1812-14. 467

Spencer, Samuel.
Keely, Charles.
Hart, William.
Hutzell, Peter.
Rex, John.
Shinkle, John.
Snyder, William.
Henry, William.
Moyer, Joseph.
Toole, Samuel.
Adams, Jacob.
Weaver, Samuel.
Halloway, Windel.
Taylor, James.
Kulp, James.
McClellan, Samuel.
Kurtchner, Cristopher.
Bloome, Samuel.
Wilner, John.
Green, John.
Miller, George.
Gorgas, Samuel.
Merwine, Peter.
McGuire, Archibald.
King, John.
McCan, John.
Moyer, Benjamin.
Dehaven, William.
Hamburg, William.
Rittenhouse, Abraham.
Rex, Francis.
Graham, Jacob.
Laurence, John.
Merwine, Charles.
Keely, Jacob.
Ulmer, John.
Himelwright, John.
Flein, Peter.
Struper, Joseph.

We certify, on honor, that the within roll exhibits a true state of the volunteer company commanded by Capt. Starne, and the remarks set opposite the names are accurate and just.

AARON LEVERING,
First Lieutenant Commanding,
JOHN THOMPSON,
Colonel.

CAMP MARCUS HOOK, *October 17, 1814.*

I certify that the volunteer company commanded by Capt. Starne is in the service of the United States, under orders of the genera commanding Fourth military district.

THOMAS SNYDER,
Brigadier General, Commanding.

CAMP MARCUS HOOK, *October 17, 1814.*

ROLL OF CAPT. WILLIAM STEEL'S COMPANY.

Muster-roll of Captain William Steel's company, in the Fifth battalion, First brigade, Pennsylvania militia, commanded by Maj. William McFarland at York, September 5, 1814. In service from September 5, 1814, to March 5, 1815, from Chester county.

Captain.

Steel, William.

Lieutenant.

Wiley, David.

Ensign.

Lefever, Samuel.

Sergeants.

Ramby, Robert.
Gibson, Robert.
Jones, Jesse.
Maxwell, John.

Corporals.

Gibson, John R.
Russell, Isaac.
Ford, John.
Patterson, Samuel.

Privates.

Armstrong, John.
Bear, Henry.
Boyd, James.
Brown, Joseph.
Brown, Joseph.
Bunting, James.
Burkalwice, Ab^m.
Carswell, James.
Chamberlain, Obed.
Cloud, George.
Cloud, Jacob.
Cochran, John E.
Copee, John.

Corry, William K.
Cummins, Jesse.
Curtz, Jacob.
Dance, Isaac.
Darling, John.
Davis, John.
Dean, Matthias.
Drenning, John.
Dugan, Philip.
Dunlap, Enoch.
Fitzgerrald, John.
Flemming, William.
Gibson, John.
Gibson, William.
Gilmore, John.
Harris, Reuben.
Henderson, Archibald.
Hinston, Moses.
Hollis, George.
Hollowell, John.
Irwin, Alexander.
Irwin, Benjamin.
Irwine, William.
Kennedy, John.
Lawrence, Sentman.
Leming, Thomas.
Lewis, Absolom.
Lewis, Collin.
Lowry, James.
Mack, Joseph.
Money, Charles.
Mullin, Charles.
Murdock, John.
McClellan, John.
McCrachan, James.
McGinnis, Joseph.
Nolen, Robert.
Porter, John.
Powel, Thomas.
Quigly, Thomas.
Russell, James.
Sentman, Laurence.
Shute, James.
Simcox, William.
Smith, Joseph.
Smith, William.

Sorence, John.
Stewart, James B.
Stinson, William.
Stone, Gaust.
McWilliams, James.
Wilson, Robert.
Wood, William.
Wright, William.

ROLL OF CAPT. CORNELIUS STEVENSON'S COMPANY.

A complete list or muster-roll of the volunteer company of Washington Artillerist, commanded by Capt. Cornelius Stevenson, in the service of the United States.

Captain.

Stevenson, Cornelius.

First Lieutenant.

Landis, Samuel C.

Second Lieutenant.

Burden, Henry R.

Sergeants.

Pidgeon, William W.
Loper, James.
Pidgeon, Joseph A.
Crockett, Samuel.

Corporals.

Lynch, Thomas.
Cress, George.
Burdick, Lewis.
Cowen, Jacob.

Fifer.

Burt, Clement W.

Drummer.

Lippincott, Samuel.

Privates.

Curtis, John H.
Clawges, Charles S.
Russell, Thomas.
Kerley, Jeremiah.
Clawges, Daniel, Jr.
Shermer, Joseph.

Kelsey, John C.
Mayhew, David.
Long, John G.
Hoffman, John.
Foland, James A.
Philes, Charles.
Clawges, William R.
Maddock, George.
Eckford, Walter.
Milliman, John.
Ayres, Hiram.
Vandegrift, John.
Stothoff, Garret.
Pidgeon, Christopher.
Springer, Francis.
Twiss, Abiel.
Lang, John.
Makins, William S.
Hough, G. W.
Hunter, Samuel.
Weatherby, or Weatherly, David.
Brewster, Peter.
Clark, David W.
Solomon, Stephen N.
Donnick, Samuel.
Stokes, Abraham.
Cannon, Daniel B.
Tolbert, John.
Hall, Joseph.
Shoemaker, Charles M.
Bockius, Daniel.
Kid, Thomas.
Larkum, Thomas.
Greble, James.
Bashford, N.
Clawges, Thomas.
Larkum, John.
Cone, Joseph.
Emerson, Erasmus.
Cock, Richard T.
Loper, James.
Smith, William E.
McSweeny, George.
Pidgeon, James.
Meyers, Peter.
Abbit, Frederick.

Seffert, or Seyfert, Anthony.
Walter, Charles.
Hitchcock, Henry.
Lee, James F.
Robb, Charles.
Jones, Charles F.
Work, Frazer.
Ball, Richard G.
Burkhimer, Henry.
Whiteman, Joseph.
Winkler, Edward.
Carver, Samuel.
Mellish, John G.
Hughes, Joshua.
Cornell, John.
Defoe, John.
Tully, Thomas.
Lewis, Benjamin.
Stow, William.
Chapin, Samuel.
Harkins, John.
Chattin, James N.
Ford, David.
Thackara, James.
Price, Solomon.
Clary, William D.
Norwood, R.
Holmes, George.
Hitchner, Matthias.
Field, Lawrence.
Fonde, John P.
Hufty, John.
McLean, John.
McKean, James.
Philips, Miles C.
Stevenson, Robert.
Dartnell, Edmond.
McIlvain, Thomas.

I certify the above to be a true list or roll of the volunteer company of Washington Artillerists.

CORNELIUS STEVENSON,
Captain.

A. M. PREVOST,
Major Volunteer Artillery, U. S. service.

I certify that the Washington Artillery is in the service of the

United States, under orders of the general commanding the Fourth military district.

THOS. CADWALADER,
Brigadier General Commanding.

CAMP DUPONT, *October, 1814.*

ROLL OF CAPT. ROBERT STORY'S COMPANY.

Roll and muster of Capt. Robert Story's company of infantry, attached to the Second regiment of militia, commanded by Col. John Purviance, in the service of the United States, from the State of Pennsylvania, Brig. Gen. Adamson Tannehill commanding. Commencing the 25th September, and ending the 24th November, 1812, (both days inclusive.)

Captain.

Story, Robert.

Lieutenant.

Means, Robert.

Ensign.

Stewart, Christopher.

Sergeants.

Christy, Andrew.
White, William.
Weakley, William.
Ross, John.

Corporals.

Martin, Thomas.
Anderson, Thomas.
Gipson, John.
Connan, Edwin.

Fifer.

Bell, John.

Drummer.

Bell, William.

Privates.

Bell, Walter.
Hulyard, Isaac.
Walise, Samuel.
Stanorl, John.
Martin, William.
Crofford, Samuel.
Celsor, Andrew.
Taylor, Pickert.
Uddewit, Henry.

Armstrong, George.
Jackson, John.
Stewart David.
Porter, James.
Cross, David.
Moore, William.
Gildersteres, Jeremiah.
Adams, Joseph.
Gaylor, or Taylor, Richard.
Campbell, Robert.
Campbell, Henry.
Straeyrs, Signe.
Brown, John.
Hartley, John.
Waddle, Robert.
Moore, Robert.
Sutton, Samuel.
McDarmart, George.
Weeks, John.
Stanlorf, Joseph.
Studebaker, Joseph.
McCannon, William.
Beeher, Solomon.
Black, Samuel.
Waddle, Thomas.
Bradley, Andrew.
McMunway, Alexander.
Osburn, Samuel.
Martin, John.
Sutton, Robert.
Gilmore, Hugh.
Cruthers, Thomas.
Cruthers, John.
Sanderson, George.
Jordan, John.
Black, Samuel.
Mathews, John.

We certify, on honor, that this muster-roll exhibits a true state of Capt. Robert Storey's company, of the Second regiment of infantry, commanded by Lieut. Col. Purviance, for the period therein mentioned, and that the remarks set opposite the names are correct and just.

ROBERT STOREY,
Captain.
J. PURVIANCE,
Lieutenant Colonel.

ROLL OF CAPT. WILLIAM STUART'S COMPANY.

Pay-roll of a company of light infantry, commanded by Capt. William Stuart, of the ——— regiment, performing a tour of duty, under the command of Col. ———, who rendezvoused at York, under the general order of the Governor, dated 26th August, 1814.

Captain.

Stuart, William.

First Lieutenant.

Potts, James W.

Second Lieutenant.

Perry, John D.

Ensign.

Baily, Israel.

Sergeants.

Rogers, John.
Norton, Jacob G.
Norton, James.
Pawel, David.

Privates.

Stone, William.
Pawel, John G.
Pawel, Abel.
Pawel, Aaron.
Murphy, John.
Reed, William.
Bradley, Richard.
Thomas, Charles M.
McKee, William.
Windle, Moses.
Sweeney, James.
Hamill, John C.
Dunn, James.
Strand, Peter.
Cooper, David.
Rolinson, Thomas.
Scantlin, James.
Watters, Joseph.
Chalfant, William.
Benner, Jacob H.

Harlan, Lewis.
Tinny, Neal.
Miller, Samuel.
Pawel. John.
Davis, George.
Brackenrige, Samuel.

   I certify the foregoing to be a correct roll of my company.

                              WILLIAM STEWART,
                                               Captain.

   Test: W. FORSTER,
                                          Brigadier General.

ROLL OF CAPT. LINDSEY STURGEON'S COMPANY.

   A roll of the First company, in the Ninth regiment and First brigade of Fifth division, Pennsylvania militia, commanded by Capt. Lindsey Sturgeon.

Cox, Jacob.
Lague, Patrick.
Timmens, Thomas.
Hull, George.
Heiner, Jacob.
Burget, John.
McIvain, Robert.
Boreland, Thomas.
McTaggert, William.
Young, Andrew.
Myers, John.
Bawer, George.
McCulip, Alexander.
Filler, Solomon.
Cole, Michael.
Wise, Jacob.
Swartz, Paul.
Marfert, Richard.
Strawsbaugh, George.
Rautseng, John.
Glass, Jacob.
Henderson, William.
Pape, William.
Abbott, John.
Harman, Henry.
Carnes, Samuel.
Duncan, Adam.
Baugher, George.

Marks, Michael.
Swenzel, Frederick.
Kepner, John.
Alexander, Andrew.
Bear, John.
Lemping, Jacob.
Davis, James.
Crall, John C.
Thompson, David.
Baugher, John.
Henystophel, Uriah.
Harman, Jacob.
Grass, John.
McPherson, James.
McWilliams, James.
Wirich, Christopher.
Filler, Jacob.
Sauger, John.
Stiehel, John.
Fitter, Peter.
Deeher, Peter.
Benard, John.
Wear, John.
McIlvain, William.
Lochart, Moses.
Feter, Joseph.
Kitte, George.
Speck, Andrew.
Emlet, Michael.
Eck, Peter.
Wear, Michael.
Swartz, John.
Shecky, Conn.
Britton, John.
Mailhorn, Henry.
Cole, Henry.
Longgart, George.
Hilt, Jacob.
Spitler, Adam.
Clark, William.
Oyler, John.
Little, Peter.
Whitford, John.
Ritter, Daniel.
Kelly, Patrick.
Snyder, George.

McKinney, John.
Gilbert, Jacob.
Thompson, William.
Bankart, Jacob.
Kuhn, John.
Giesler, Jacob.
Parr, Conrad.
Shitt, Henry.
Sell. Jacob.
Shitt, Daniel.
Syphert, John.
Hays, William.
Shitt, Jacob.
Stombaugh, Jacob.
Bawersacks, Jacob.
Swartz, Nicholas.
Miller, Abraham.
Dansville, Thomas.
Sheets, Samuel.
Patterson, James.
Culberson, Samuel.
McClure, John.
Craige, William.
Geisle, Frederick.
King, Jacob.
Queen, Arthur.
Blake, Samuel.
McMaster, James.
Wolf, George.
McGrew, James.
Morgan, Michael.
Coile, Peter.
Swartzman, Anthony.
Hupert, Jacob.
Armstrong, John.
Price, William.
Lightfoot, William.

I do hereby certify that the foregoing are the names of all the persons who are put under my command by a requisition made by the President of the United States, agreeably to an act of Congress.

LINDSEY STURGEON,
Captain.

G. WELSH,
Brigade Inspector.

SAMUEL GALLOWAY,
Major.

March 9th, 1814.

ROLL OF CAPT. JOHN SWIFT'S COMPANY.

Pay-roll of the Second company of Washington Guards, commanded by Capt. John Swift, of the First regiment of Pennsylvania volunteers, in the service of the United States, from the 25th of August, 1814, to the 4th day of January, 1815, four months and ten days.

Captain.

Swift, John.

First Lieutenant.

Ellick, Clemmens S.

Second Lieutenant.

Gratz, Benjamine.

Third Lieutenant.

McElwee, Charles B.

Ensign.

Stockton, Francis B.

Sergeants.

Woodward, William H.
Billington, Henry.
Eyre, George L.
Ashburner, Adam.
Ammerman, A. B.

Corporals.

West, Thomas R.
Seckle, William.
Billington, John.
Helmbold, H. K.
Newkirk, Matthew.
German, Francis.
McKinsey, James.

Privates.

Alcock, John H.
Ashman, Daniel.
Anderson, William.
Abbott, William.
Bastian, Joseph, Jr.
Ball, B. W.
Bedford, Joseph.
Berresford, R. H.
Burr, Joseph.
Burke, William.
Brown, John A.

Brown, John M., substitute for William Hoover.
Carpenter, S. H.
Curry, George.
Curry, Thomas.
Coppuck, Daniel.
Canby, Isiah.
Clark, Joseph A.
Cope, John.
Chamberlain, John.
Cline, William.
Cooke, James T.
Cooke, Joseph.
Corkin, James, J.
Cooper, George.
Denckla, Henry.
Dick, Archibald.
Douglass, George.
Erwin, John.
Elton, Anthony, Jr.
Evans, Samuel.
Elton, Anthony.
Elton, Joseph.
Evans, William M.
Emerick, George.
Ebsworth, George D.
Fullen, James.
Fenton, William.
Fennel, Edward.
Gihon, James.
George, John.
Hamilton, John W.
Hines, William.
Hart, John.
Haas, Adam.
Hoffman, William.
Hart, Mordicai.
Hines, Joseph.
Hopper, James W.
James, Thomas.
Jones, William.
Johnston, Thomas.
Jones, Joseph.
King, Edward.
Keyser, Jacob.
Lawrence, John.
Lehman, Charles.

WAR OF 1812-14. 481

Lasher, Francis.
Lovering, William.
Lindsay, William.
Lane, John.
McKensey, Alexander.
McCoy, William.
Marchment, Steᵛ.
Morrell, Peter.
Myuck, Joseph.
Murlock, Isaia R.
McPherson, John.
McCalpin, Andrew.
North, Francis A.
Oat, Israel.
Perry, John.
Redmand, Thomas.
Russet, Robert.
Rickards, William.
Riley, Peter.
Schrunee, George.
Sellers, Robert B.
Singer, John, Jr.
Shinn, John.
Smith, William.
Smith, John I.
Sarver, Thomas.
Summers, W. I.
Stemble, George S.
Shinn, Samuel Z.
Sinex, Thomas.
Sheaf, John V. W.
Steel, James.
Speal, George.
Thompson, Shubut.
Thomas, John.
Tilton, William.
Vanpelt, Alexander.
Vaughan, Thomas.
Wilson, Napier.
West, Charles S.
Willes, Joel.
Wyant, Jacob.
Wandall, Abraham.
Young, James H.
Bockius, William.

We certify, on honor, that to the best of our knowledge, that this
31—VOL. XII.

exhibits a true state of the Second company of Washington Guards, of the First regiment, Pennsylvania volunteers, in the service of the United States, for the period herein mentioned.

BENJ. GRATZ,
Lieutenant Commanding.
CLEMENT C. BIDDLE,
Colonel First Regiment P. V.

ROLL OF CAPT. TAYLOR'S COMPANY.

Muster-roll of Capt. Taylor's company, in the Second regiment of Pennsylvania volunteers, Light Infantry, under the command of Col. Louis Bache, in the service of the State of Pennsylvania, for a tour of duty, commencing the 5th day of September, and ending the 5th day of December, 1814, attached to the brigade of militia, under the command of Brig. Gen. Samuel Smith, at Camp Marcus Hook.

Sergeants.

Taylor, William H.
Darlington, Ziba.
Painter, John.
Hall, John.

Corporals.

Logan, John.
Vibber, Russell.
Worthington, Eber.
Myers, Henry.

Fifer.

Burkess, Jacob.

Drummer.

Davis, George.

Privates.

Brinton, Joseph H.
Brinton, Ethan.
Brinton, William.
Brinton, James.
Brinton, John.
Brinton, Thomas H.
Brinton, Joseph.
Black, Robert.
Cox, William.

Darlington, Amos.
Daily, William.
DeWolf, Thomas.
Ehrenzeller, Jacob.
Evenson, Eli.
Gamble, Robert.
Greer, James.
Gardiner, Archibald.
Hall, Lewis.
Iddings, Joseph.
Keehmle, Jacob.
Lindsay, John.
Marshall, Stephen.
Matlack, Jonathan.
Matlack, Nathan.
Morrow, Hiram.
Nelson, Joseph.
Nichols, Isaac.
Pierce, Myers.
Parry, Caleb.
Pearson, Harper.
Pearson, George.
Rice, Thomas.
Sweeney, Thomas.
Shields, William.
Townsend, William.
Townsend, Granville S.
Taylor, Vernon.
Frederick, William.
Baily, Hiram.
Yearsley, Nathan.
Evans, Thomas B., appointed sergeant's mate.

CAMP MARCUS HOOK, *November 29, 1814.*

I do hereby certify, upon honor, that the above is a just and true muster-roll of Capt. Taylor's company.

TITUS TAYLOR,
Captain.
LOUIS BACHE,
Colonel Second Regiment, Pennsylvania Volunteer Light Infantry.

ROLL OF CAPT. EDMUND TIPTON'S COMPANY.

We, the subscribers, members of a company of infantry commanded by Capt. Edmund Tipton, belonging to a regiment commanded by Col. Rees Hill, now in the service of the United States, do acknowledge to have received of John Phillips the sums annexed to our names, respectively, this —— day of November, 1813.

Captain.

Tipton, Edmund.

First Lieutenant.

McCabe, John.

Second Lieutenant.

Vantrees, Isaac.

Third Lieutenant.

Cox, John.

Fourth Lieutenant.

Denlinger, Christian.

Ensign.

Madden, Patrick.

Sergeants.

Calderwood, John.
McCune, Benjamin.
Moore, Jesse.
Hewit, Peter.
Shafer, Jacob.

Corporals.

Mathers, James.
Rees, Thomas.
Law, Abraham.
Parks, James.
Westover, Zaduck.

Drummer.

Ross, Elisha.

Privates.

McLin, John W.
Harbst, John.
Welsh, William.
Sackett, Azarah.
McWilliams, James.

Williamson, James.
Cahr, Joseph.
Patton, Samuel.
Wilson, James.
Shank, John.
Metzenbaugh, Daniel.
Moore, Abraham.
Tipry, Abraham.
Moore, Ephraim.
McMillen, John.
Luckart, George.
Burgart, Samuel.
Buell, Joseph.
Laughlin, Hugh.
Parker, Ira.
Walls, Jonathan.
Emy, John.
Baily, George.
Thomson, William.
Bumbarger, Joseph.
Kelly, Davis.
Newel, Joseph.
Gardner, William.
Gearhard, John.
Gallagher, James.
Hopkins, James.
Elliott, John.
Doil, Dennis.
Jones, James.
McClilland, James.
Johnston, David.
•Vanpoll, Henry.
Jamison, John.
McClelland, Joseph.
Willerman, Jacob.
Raub, Henry.
Maury, or Maurer, Jacob.
Burns, Daniel.
Kephard, Henry.
Kemberling, Ludwig.
Baily, William.
Smith, John.
Sharp, Thomas.
Ellis, William.
Dunn, Alexander.
Lanzer, Abraham.

Miller, Henry.
Gibson, Jesse.
Shoener, Solomon.
Daly, Henry.
Hyle, John.
Wilson, Abraham.
Fulton, Henry.
Ganoe, Samuel.
Mung, Henry.
Ganoe, James.
Hunter, John.
Hunter, Samuel.
Smithly, Martin.
Smock, Abraham.
Smithly, Stofel.
Keighly, Jacob.
Brown, Joseph.
Boyd, Alexander.
McCleland, Nathaniel.
Stewart, Isaac.
Gibson, Gideon.
Dixon, Samuel.
Dellinger, George.
Fox, Jacob.
Gaud, William.
Aurand, John.

ROLL OF CAPT. JAMES TODD'S COMPANY.

Muster-roll of Capt. James Todd's company, of the Second regiment, First brigade, Pennsylvania militia, under the command of Col. Adam Richards, at York, Pa. In service from September 1, 1814, to March 5, 1815, from Dauphin and Lebanon counties.

Captain.

Todd, James.

Lieutenant.

Ward, John.

Ensign.

Winter, Henry.

Sergeants.

Ward, Isaac.
Fox, John.

Mchight, William.
Duey, Simon.

Corporals.

Martin, James.
Fisher, George.
Todd, Samuel.
Johnson, Samuel.

Drummer.

Bomberger, William.

Fifer.

Winter, Samuel.

Privates.

Albert, John.
Beasore, Peter.
Beck, Jacob.
Binner, George.
Brown, Jacob.
Click, John.
Culp, Lewis.
Dibbins, John.
Emmeriety, Jacob.
Failer, George.
Feauver, John.
Felty, George.
Fersling, George.
Firnedald, George.
Folmer, John.
Fusick, Dewald.
Goodman, Peter.
Heelderich, John.
Hileman, John.
Hoofnagle, Benjamin.
Hoofnagle, John.
Hoover, Conrad.
Hossinger, Stofle.
Howser, John.
Hunsaker, Philip.
Knoll, George.
Koch, Henry.
Krimner, Peter.
Kyser, Conrad.
Leas, Daniel.
Light, Felix.
Lunning, Casper.

Lutz, George.
Martin, John.
McCright, Alexander.
Morton, James.
Moury, Conrad.
Muse, John.
Obrian, Samuel.
Painter, George.
Pruss, George.
Pruss, John.
Secondevrst, John.
Seemon, John.
Shafer, Adam.
Shink, George.
Snodgrass, Robert.
Speller, Henry.
Stoner, Henry.
Todd, David.
Unglrst, Peter.
Weiser, Benjamin.
Welkmore, Davis.
Wenny, Andrew.
Winter, John.
Wolburn, Henry.
Wolburn, Jacob.
Wolburn, John.
Wolf, John.
Wolmer, George.
Yonker, John.

ROLL OF CAPT. WILLIAM J. TROTTER'S COMPANY.

Muster-roll of the Third company of Rifleman in, the service of the United States, in the First battalion of the Second brigade, First division, Pennsylvania militia, under the command of William J. Trotter, Lieut. Col. Joel B. Sutherland. From September 14, 1814, to January 3, 1815.

Captain.

Trotter, William J.

First Lieutenant.

Deal, Peter.

Second Lieutenant.

McKinney, Thomas R.

WAR OF 1812-14. 489

Third Lieutenant.

Graves, William.

Quarter-master Sergeant.

Gamble, Cyrus.

Sergeants.

Briggs, Russel T.
Gray, Hugh.
Wilson, William H.
Jefferis, Benjamin D.

Corporals.

Cooper William.
Tubbs, Zediac.
Toy, John M.
Matlock, James.

Bugler.

Ayres, John.

Privates.

Avis, John.
Bullenger, John.
Adle, Godfrey.
Baisly, Abraham.
Combs, John.
Cooper, John.
Decamp, David.
Kucer, John.
Caster, Jonathan.
Dayley, Dennis.
Daten, Lewis.
Ebert, Peter.
Emerick, David.
Fetters, James.
Fullingsby, William.
Greer, Henry.
Hilman, Elikum.
Holland, William.
Heller, Joseph.
Hutchinson, Joseph.
House, Peter.
Hill, Jacob.
Homerick, Paul.
Hopkins, Alexander.
Hoover, Anthony.
Hunter, Abraham.

Hamilton, Archibald.
Jordon, Thomas.
Jerman, Reuben.
Kelley, James.
King, Francis.
Kerbough, John.
Mayres, John, sick at last muster.
McCu, Edward.
Milward, John.
Moses, Henry.
Meredith, Jehu.
McKoy, George, died since discharged.
McFate, John, died since discharged.
Painter, Martin.
Pote, Henry.
Parker, John.
Porter, Isaac.
Patton, William.
Rookstool, John.
Ray, William.
Rookstool, Samuel.
Russel, Joseph.
Roman, Francis.
Samson, John.
Surles, Thomas.
Smith, Conrad.
Sharp, John G.
Sutton, Oswin.
Stevens, John.
Suker, Jacob.
Stuttler, Philip.
Stratton, William.
Sweaney, David.
Sutton, Joseph.
Sharp, John, Jr.
Sheets, Peter.
Turner, William.
Town, Joseph.
Vandergrief, George.
Wilson, Job.
Wasey, Samuel.
Wister, George.
Wooner, William.
Winemore, John.
Swift, Crispin.

We certify, on honor, that this muster-roll exhibits a true state of the Third company of the First battalion of Riflemen, Second brigade, First division, Pennsylvania militia, for the period therein mentioned, and that the remarks set opposite the names of the men are accurate and just.

SAMUEL SWIFT,
Major.
WILLIAM GRAVES,
Lieutenant.
J. B. SUTHERLAND,
Lieutenant Colonel.

ROLL OF CAPT. JOSEPH WADSWORTH'S COMPANY.

Pay-roll of a company of Infantry, commanded by Capt. Joseph Wadsworth, of the Second regiment, Second detachment, Pennsylvania militia, commanded by Lieut. Col. Robert Patterson, in the service of the United States. Commencement of service October 2, 1812; expiration of service April 2, 1813.

Captain.

Wadsworth, Joseph, died at fort Meigs after the expiration of the tour.

Lieutenant.

Conrad, Jacob, died on his return home after the expiration of the tour.

Ensign.

Craft, George, resigned on the 22d of January, 1813.

Sergeants.

Gusey, Valentine.
Wherley, Daniel, appointed clerk to the district paymaster.
Gallaher, Thomas, promoted to first sergeant.
Stickle, Henry, promoted to second sergeant.

Corporals.

Shaw, John, promoted to third sergeant and elected ensign; volunteered fifteen days.
Moore, Alexander, promoted to fourth sergeant.
Jackson, John.
Coulter, Samuel.

Privates.

Allison, William, discharged on the 22d December; allowed fourteen days to go home.
Barton, Roberts, promoted fourth sergeant.
Crosier, Kenada, promoted first corporal.

WAR OF 1812-14.

Hill, Joseph, promoted second corporal.
Armstrong, John C., promoted third corporal.
Sayres, Reuben, promoted fourth corporal.
Tobs, Samuel.
Marthers, Robert.
McLain, John.
Frazier, Even, discharged December 16; allowed sixteen days to go home.
Blana, Thomas.
McCrorey, William.
Monteeth, James, discharged December 15; allowed sixteen days to go home.
Kelley, James.
Phillips, John.
Nahlon, Jonathan.
Homan, Ucal, discharged October 26, 1812.
Miller, Ephraim.
Ammons, George.
Chandler, Isaac H.
Ammons, Jacob.
Miller, Eli.
Harford, Charles, discharged October 17, 1812.
Shion, Jones.
Doney, Isaac.
Langley, Jonathan, discharged October 19, 1812.
Luce, Henry.
Hutchinson, James.
Hutchinson, Henry.
Hartman, Daniel, volunteered at Fort Meigs, fifteen days.
Pierson, Thomas.
Knap, Daniel.
Joyce, William.
West, William.
Kimber, Predy, volunteered at Fort Meigs, fifteen days.
Miller, Robert.
Stewart, Charles.
Walker, Francis, discharged November 23, 1812.
Rails, William.
Winder, John, died at Fort Meigs, after expiration of tour.
Misser, Job.
Parker, John L.
Misser, Joshua, discharged December 22; allowed fourteen days home.
Moss, John.
Laughlin, Hugh, volunteered at Fort Meigs, fifteen days.
Nose, Robertson, volunteered at Fort Meigs, fifteen days.

Higinbothom, George.
Burnet, Edward.
Donilson, James.
Bivins, Robert, volunteered at Fort Meigs, fifteen days.
Anderson, Richard.
Coon, John.
Rodgers, John.
Lewis, David, discharged December 15; allowed fourteen days home.
Doyle, John.
Whipple, Joseph.
Reese, Philip.
Peters, David.
Moore, Anthony.
Walters, Peter.
Rodgers, Jesse.
Irons, John.
Vickers, Able.
Clerk, James.
Crider, John.
Fogle, Peter.
Carson, Thomas, discharged previous to first muster.
Cook, John.
Murdock, Thomas, discharged previous to first muster.
Rees, James.

I certify, on honor, that the within is a just statement of Capt. Joseph Wadsworth's company, and that roll is correct.

THOMAS GALLAHER,
First Sergeant.

ROLL OF CAPT. THOMAS WALKER'S COMPANY.

Muster-roll of Capt. Thomas Walker's company in the First regiment, First brigade, Pennsylvania militia, under command of Col. Maxwell Kennedy, at York, Pennsylvania. In service from August 29, 1814, to March 5, 1815, from Dauphin county.

Captain.

Walker, Thomas.

Lieutenant.

Still, Charles.

Ensign.

Gleim, Christian.

Sergeants.

Roberts, John.
Allison, William.

Beatty, George.
Frazier, John.

Corporals.

Fisher, John.
Bryan, William.
Adams, Richard.
Boyer, George.

Drummer.

Dubbs, Jacob.

Fifer.

Holman, Samuel.

Privates.

Ackerman, George.
Anderson, Alexander.
Antes, Henry.
Aul, Jacob.
Ball, Austine.
Baughman, Jacob.
Carson, Charles.
Cole, George.
Cowhick, William.
Crabb, Plunket.
Dearmond, Andrew.
Deemer, John.
Dickey, Robert.
Durang, Charles.
Durang, Ferdinand.
Elder, Joshua,
Fields, Michael.
Fulton, William.
Funk, Abraham.
Gleason, Alexander.
Good, Martin.
Harper, William.
Harris, David.
Heichal, Christian.
Heisley, George.
Hemmebright, Samuel.
Henry, Samuel.
Hinckley, Charles.
Hyneman, Grederick.
Jackson, Alexander I. W.
Jackson, James.
Jackson, Joseph.
Jontz, John.

Kehler, George.
Kroberger, John.
Kuhn, Jacob.
Kunkle, John.
Loyes, Philip.
Maguire, Isaac.
Martin, John.
McBay, William.
McElwain, Hugh.
McKinny, Henry.
Meek, Jacob.
Miller, Daniel.
Mintchel, Thomas.
Mitchel, James.
Montgomery, James.
Moyer, George.
Officer, James.
Rahm, Jacob.
Rissing, Lewis.
Rupley, Mitchel.
Sample, John.
Schott, John.
Sheffey, John.
Shellcott, Ezekiel.
Skinner, Robert, Jr.
Slough, Jacob.
Smith, Samuel.
Stahl, John.
Steinman, Jacob.
Stephenson, Robert.
Stepley, John A.
Straman, Joseph.
Updegraff, Ellis.
Updegraff, Isaac.
Wallis, John L.
Williams, John E.
William, Michael.
Wilkins, ———.
Wilson, Henry.
Winagle, ———.
Wounder, Samuel.
Wright, John.
Young, John.
Zearing, John.
Zimmerman, Frederick.
Zollinger, ———.

ROLL OF CAPT. JOHN WALLACE'S COMPANY.

A pay-roll of Capt. John Wallace's company of Pennsylvania volunteers, attached to the First regiment, Second detachment, Pennsylvania militia, under the command of Brig. Gen. Richard Crooks, in the service of the United States. Commencement of service, October 2, 1812; expiration of service, April 2, 1813.

Captain.

Wallace, John.

Lieutenant.

McCormick, John, volunteered fifteen days.

Ensign.

Stewart, James.

Sergeants.

Maybin, George.
Williams, Benoni.
Hopkins, William.
Brady, John.

Corporals.

Evans, William.
Persain, Amour.
Merideth, Thomas.
Wilson, Lewis.

Privates.

Wilson, William, volunteered fifteen days.
Wilson, George.
Stephens, Thomas.
Girt, John.
McLain, Jacob.
Phillips, David.
McCollough, William.
McKee, William.
Ray, Joshua.
Talkingtine, Stephen.
Fiscus, Jacob.
Lenningten, Isaac.
Painter, John, Jr.
Mires, Phillip.
Luke, James.
Hyme, George.
Millagen, James.
Keers, Andrew.

Ghaster, Stephen.
Bell, William.
McAnulty, Patrick.
Guthrey, James.
Jones, John.
Titus, George.
Foreman, Charles.
Mortimore, Daniel.
McKibens, David.
Barnet, Peter.
Latshaw, Peter.
Stephinson, James.
Findley, James.
Fulloen, John.
Williams, James.
Callon, David.
Evins, James.
Grayham, Henry.
Guthrey, Alexander.
Wilson, John.
Colpattrick, James.
Smith, Abraham.
Stout, Joel.
Man, John.
Evert, Peter.
Jack, John.
Shields, Joseph.
Kinter, Henry.
Redding, Samuel.
Alison, Robert.
Painter, John, Sr.
Simpson, Isaac.
Thompson, Thomas.
Nulph, Henary, left sick at Mansfield about the 1st of January, 1813.
Polyard, Nicholas, sick as above.
Fidler, Peter, sick as above.
Carr, Joseph, sick as above.
Lydick, James, sick as above.
McDowel, John, left sick at Canton, Ohio.
Weeks, Elijah, sick as above.
Dip, Peter, left sick at Lisbon.
Guthrey, Thomas, left in hospital at Mansfield; and I understand that there was not any of them fit for duty until the end of the tour.

I, John Wallace, do certify, on honor, that the within pay-roll is just and correct, and that remarks on the sick therein made are also just and correct, together with all the remarks therein made. Witness my hand, at Indiana, September 30, 1813.

JOHN WALLACE,
Captain.

ROLL OF LIEUT. THOMAS WARREN'S COMPANY.

Pay-roll of Lieut. Thomas Warren's company of Light Dragoons, of the First regiment, Second brigade, Pennsylvania militia, commanded by Brig. Gen. Richard Crocks, in the service of the United States on the 29th day of March, 1813, in the Northwestern Army, under Gen. William H. Harrison. Served from October 2, 1812, to April 2, 1813.

Lieutenant.

Warren, Thomas.

Cornet.

Grier, George.

Sergeants.

Fleming, Samuel.
Job, George.

Corporals.

Muse, Fantly.
Wilson, John.

Privates.

Finny, John.
Wadle, Joseph.
Duglas, John.
McAfee, James.
Duglas, William.
Penny, William.
Henderson, Robert.
Forsythe, James.
Sill, Jessy.
Forsythe, John.
Pierce, Elisha.
Greer, James, Jr.
Johnson, Joseph.
Greer, James.
Howel, Philip.
Murphy, Samuel.
Weycoff, Samuel.

Wilson, John.
Irwen, Joseph.
Dickson, John.
Hargrove, Wilson.
Wilson, Samuel.

ROLL OF CAPT. JACOB WENTZ'S COMPANY.

List of non-commissioned officers and privates in the Third company, commanded by Capt. Jacob Wentz, of the Fifty-second regiment, First brigade, Second division, Pennsylvania militia, now encamped at Marcus Hook, under command of Lieut. Col. Conrad Krickbaum.

Sergeants.

Choyce, William.
Ellicott, George.
Kimble, Isaac B.
Snyder, Jacob.
Morris, Abel.

Corporals.

Gunsinhouser, Abraham.
Williams, David.
Slack, Jacob.
Ashton, Joseph.

Privates.

Wilson, Henry.
Hammer, Charles.
Burney, William.
Deddier, Jacob.
Dyer, James.
Rynear, Joseph.
Brand, Jacob.
Engle, Jacob.
Bisbing, John.
Yerkes, Samuel.
Ramsey, Jesse.
McCoon, Edward.
Donley, Jesse.
Barnes, John.
Kreer, Andrew.
Gilbert, Israel.
Walton, Gilbert.
Yerkes, George S.

Carmon, Elon.
Linn, William.
Henry, John.
Miller, Henry.
Johnston, Jesse.
Drake, Richard.
Johnston, William.
Harr, John.
Trexler, John.
Gilkeson, Elias.
Washborn, John.
Redheifer, Jacob.
Getman, John.
Wright, Samuel.
Cope, Abner.
Smith, Philip.
Kreer, John.
Wentz, James.
Sweeny, Edward.
Shull, Tobias.
Gilbert, Jesse.
West, Thomas.
Smith, Jacob.
Burns, Christian.
Forker, John.
Weeks, John.
Roberts, William.
Yerkes, Benjamin.
Kreer, Henry.
Mann, William.
Davis, Samuel.
Roberts, Andrew.
Search, Charles.
Yerkes, Benjamin, Jr.
Larkins, Jacob.
Harsh, Elias.
Cooker, John.
Cammel, Jacob.
Henry, John.
Foust, Henry.
Hurlougher, Michael.
Shade, George.
Reed, George.
Daywalt, Philip.
Jacob, George.
Crouse, Jacob.

Bry, Daniel.
Thomas, Israel.
Daring, Jacob.
Stetler, John.
Root, Isaac.
Sherer, John.
Thacher, Samuel.
Tomlinson, Francis.
Reed, John.
Lessig, Samuel.
Ettinger, Joseph.
Bighoard, John.
Sholler, George.
Wambold, David.
Whitman, John.
Haring, John.
Kolb, Peter.
Showeck, Matthias.
Morty, John.
Zeiber, Henry.
Bender, Conrad.
Long, Christian.
Kelly, James.
Valentine, Benjamin.
Grub, Henry, entered into service October 8.
Croson, Edward.
Land, Jacob.

I certify, upon honor, that the foregoing is a correct list of non-commissioned officers and privates under my command.

JACOB WENTZ,
Captain.

CAMP MARCUS HOOK, *October 10, 1814.*

I certify, upon honor, that this muster-roll exhibits a true statement of a company of the Montgomery County militia, of the State of Pennsylvania, now in the service of the United States. The remarks set opposite the names of the men are accurate and just. I believe the annexed to be a correct muster and pay-roll.

EDWARD JOHNSON,
First Lieutenant.
CONRAD KRICKBAUM,
Lieutenant Colonel.

I certify that the company commanded by Capt. Jacob Wentz is in the service of the United States, under orders of the general commanding the Fourth military district.

SAMUEL SMITH,
Brigadier General.

CAMP MARCUS HOOK.

ROLL OF CAPT. JOHN G. WERSLER'S COMPANY.

Muster-roll of Capt. Wersler's company, in the Second regiment, Pennsylvania volunteer Light Infantry, in the service of the State of Pennsylvania for three months, from the 27th day of August last, attached to the First brigade, Second division, Pennsylvania militia, at Camp Marcus Hook, commanded by Brig. Gen. Samuel Smith.

November 29, 1814.

Captain.

Wersler, John G.

Lieutenant.

Watson, James.

Sergeants.

Kelley, Richard.
Griffith, John.
McWilliams, Robert.
Kelley, William.

Corporal.

Laur, Henry.

Fifer.

Dunlap, George.

Drummer.

Williams, Samuel.

Privates.

Bispham, Benjamin.
Peck, Charles.
Ford, Caleb.
Fritz, Christian.
McCoy, Dennis.
Burns, Eleazer.
Griffith, Elijah.
Richardson, Ezekiel
Pearce, Edward K.
King, George.
Reese, John.
Rinker, Jacob.
Watson, Joseph.
Vanleer, Isaac.
Rickman, John.
Ryder, John.
Kelley, James.

Heck, Jacob.
Whisler, John.
Watson, John.
Ivester, Jesse.
Hipple, John.
McGraw, Lewis.
Williams, Martin.
Davis, Nicholas S.
Clarkson, Samuel.
Bane, Samuel.
Smiley, Stephen.
Hall, Jarvis.
Caldwell, Thomas.
Richardson, William.
Bowen, William.
Stout, Charles.
Parker, Henry.
Potter, Joseph.
Quarll, John.
Davis, Jonathan.
McMinn, Alben.
Dhile, Joseph.
Watson, Elijah.
Brewer, John.
Markley, Nathaniel.
Rowland, John.

We do certify, on honor, that the above muster-roll exhibits a just and true statement of the above mentioned company.

JOHN G. WERSLER,
Captain.
LOUIS BACHE,
Colonel Second Regiment Penn'a Vol. Lt. Inf.

ROLL OF LIEUT. CHARLES WESTPHAL'S COMPANY.

Return of the men belonging to Lieut. Charles W. Westphal's company of militia Infantry, In the Second brigade, of the First division, of Pennsylvania detailed militia, including those who have died, deserted, or have been discharged, in the campaign of 1814, from September 14, that year, to January 4, 1815, being the time they were in the service of the United States, and mustered, inspected, and discharged on this last date.

Captain.

Painter, William, resigned November 21, 1814.

First Lieutenant.

Westphal, Charles W.

Second Lieutenant.

Evans, John.

Ensign.

Elbing, Daniel E.

Orderly Sergeant.

Miller, Jacob.

Sergeants.

Nice, Frederick.
Vantine, Joseph.
Thompson, William, appointed December 11, 1814, in place of W. Quinlin.
Gable, John.

Corporals.

Hubbert, Benjamin.
Warten, Isaiah.
Buchanan, Alexander, appointed December 2, 1814, in place of James Deboufre.
Hollowell, John.

Drummer.

Sneck, Jacob.

Privates.

Wolf, Alexander.
Henry, Annadecon.
Bosick, Henry.
Bartle, George.
Barris, Thomas.
Blecker, Jacob.
Bailey, John.
Beverlin, James,
Buck, Frederick G.
Bates, Isaiah.
Burch, David.
Baker, Frederick.
Barnholt, John.
Bentley, John.
Britton, Edward.
Clymer, George.
Cooper, James.
Cryser, Samuel.
Cox, Merrion K.

Cake, Matthias.
Duncan, Nathaniel.
Deboufre, James, acted as corporal till December 2, and then degraded.
Emery, Henry.
English, Michael.
Eyus, Joseph.
Fox, Samuel.
Fox, Anthony.
Franks, Henry.
Gawn, George, discharged.
Goldsmith, Jeremiah.
Harman, John.
Hillman, Oliver.
Howard, Richard.
Hughes, William.
Hoover, David.
Hamilton, John, substitute for Peter Walter; deserted from his post.
Haines, Robert.
Heartley, Charles.
Hemphill, Adam.
Hargrove, William, unfit for duty, account of old age.
Higgins, Frederick.
Hollingsworth, John.
Jaggers, Jonathan.
Jackson, Benjamin.
Johnston, Daniel.
Koch, Joachim.
Kessler, Martin.
Kerum, Thomas.
Lowe, Thomas.
Ludlow, Isaac.
Loche, Nathaniel.
Moxley, John.
Montgomery, Robert.
Miller, William.
Murphy, Arthur.
Morgan, Nicholas.
Nace, Jacob.
Pool, John.
Parker, Nathaniel.
Quinler, William, sergeant till December 11, 1814, and then degraded.
Rudy, Jacob.
Riter, John.
Ruckstool, or Rookstall, Jacob.

Seybert, William.
Stout, Jacob.
Steiner, Adam.
Stell, Thomas.
Smith, Henry.
Stevenson, Dennison.
Smith, Philip.
Stone, John.
Smith, Christian.
Thomas, Jacob.
Trexler, Jonathan.
Thompson, Robert.
Thompson, Constant.
Thomas, William.
Thomas, Israel.
Ulrich, Frederick.
Ulrick, Henry.
Worman, Samuel.
Weaver, John.
Watson, Christian.
Younker, Jacob.
Young, John.

PHILADELHIA, *May 10, 1816.*
I do certify the above return or muster-roll to be correct.
CARL W. WESTPHAL,
JOHN THOMPSON,
Colonel.

ROLL OF CAPT. BENJAMIN WETHERBY'S COMPANY.

A pay-roll for the non-commissioned officers and privates ―――― company of drafted militia, commanded by Capt. Wetherby, Sixty-fifth regiment, Pennsylvania militia, who entered into the service of the United States on the 20th day of September, A. D. 1814; now encamped at Marcus Hook.

Sergeants.

McGuigan, James.
Taylor, John.
Peters, George.
Ash, Thomas.
McGuigan, Patrick.

Corporals.

Roberts, Samuel.
McGuigan, Barney.
Yarnall, Benjamin.

Privates.

Bittle, Samuel.
Rauzel, or Raugel, William.
Steel, Robert.
Rattew, Eli.
Cornog, or Cornig, David.
Brown, Thomas.
Mitchell, James.
Valentine, Robert.
Hodge, James.
Davis, William.
Graff, William.
Hine, George.
Huff, James.
Russell, George.
Smith, Peter.
Griffith, Jehu.
Close, or Chase, Frederick.
Burit, or Burnet, John.
Henthorn, or Hanthorn, John.
Barlow, Curtis.
Murphy, Joseph.
Gorby, John.
Wright, Cornelius.
Young, Jacob.
Bail, or Beale, Aaron.
Ottenhamer, or Odenheimer, William.
Dick, Valentine.
Burns, Giliad.
Weare, William.
Jay, David.
McLaughlin, William, Sr.
Price, John R.
Smedly, Abel.
Stewart, Jacob.
Daugherty, Archibald.
Travis, John S.
Varly, or Vailey, John.
Smith, William.
Warnick, Richard.
Marshall, Thomas.
Rizer, Jacob.
Wheeling, John.
Smith, Aaron.
McCrackin, William.
Mase, or Mace, William.

Taylor, James.
Davis, John.
Bernard, Levan.
Hoops, John.
Turner, William.
Black, Andrew.
Fields, Felix.
Kelly, John.
Weare, James.
Collins, Henry.
Burnet, Samuel.
Russel, Samuel.
Esworthy, Joseph.
Green, Jesse.
Smith, Charles.
Hopkins, Matthew.
McCoy, James.
Mercer, Thomas.
Weare, James, Jr.
Griffith, Joseph.
Allison, Benjamin.
Parks, Alexander.
Bean, Henry.
Tompkins, Isaac.
Weaver, Baldwin.
McKinster, or McKinstry, Jesse.
Clayton, Richard.
Jones, Thomas.
Hampton, Woodward.
Lawrence, Aaron.
Sill, Anthony, N.
Marrow, Nicholas.
Dutton, Jeremiah.
Hunter, Andrew.
Likens, Daniel.
Smith, John.
Miles, Reuben.
McBride, George.
McGlaughlin, William.
Hook, John.
Stimel, Frederick.
Torton, David.
Gibason, or Gibson, Jonathan.
Torbert, Alexander.
Craig, John H.
King, John.

Harper, Peter.
Barlow, John.
Scott, Joel.
Baker, Richard.
Jester, Vincent.
Baker, Nehemiah.
Green, Abel.
McGarraty, Charles.
Bromell, Daniel.
Harbinson, or Harbison, Francis.
Alcot, John.
Pyle, John.
Hannum, John S.

CAMP SNYDER, *October 17, 1812.*

We certify, on honor, that this muster-roll exhibits a true state of the Fourth company of drafted militia from the Fourty-fourth and One Hundredth regiments of the Pennsylvania militia, attached to the Sixty-fifth regiment, Pennsylvania militia, now in the service of the United States, and the remarks set opposite the names of the men are accurate and just.

BENJAMIN WETHERBY.
Captain.

I believe the above to be a correct muster or pay-roll.

J. L. PEARSON,
Colonel.

I do certify that the Fourth company of drafted militia, commanded by Capt. Wetherby, attached to the Sixty-fifth regiment, Pennsylvania militia, in the service of the United States, under the orders of the general commanding the Fourth military district. By order of the general.

WILLIAM C. ROGERS.
Brigade Major.

CAMP SNYDER, *October 18, 1814.*

ROLL OF CAPT. JAMES WHALEY'S COMPANY.

Pay-roll of Capt. James Whaley's company of drafted militia, attached to the Second regiment, commanded by Col. Robert Patterson, in the service of the United States, from the State of Pennsylvania, Brig. Gen. Richard Crooks, commanding. Commencing the 2d October, 1812, ending the 2d April, 1813.

Captain.

Whaley, James.

Lieutenant.

Huey, George.

Ensign.

Ray, Hugh.

Sergeants.

Adair, Patrick.
Rea, Andrew.
Jones, Henry.
Killpatrick, Abraham.

Corporals.

Agan, Aaron.
Sprenger, Crawford.
Darrahan, Mathew.
Wallis, Nicholas.

Musicians.

Robbins, John.
Biddele, George.

Privates.

Regan, James.
Ragan, Weldon.
Blake, John.
Miller, John.
Mathew, Thomas.
Walker, Joseph.
Moody, Silas.
Hazleton, Henry.
Davis, Hugh.
Mader, Daniel.
Skinner, Reuben.
Keffer, Peter.
Summers, Jacob.
Eurely, George.
Asbat, John.
McCullogh, Thomas.
Durbin, Thomas.
Lynch William, volunteered fifteen days.
Obryen, Daniel.
Latta, James.
Lair, Peter.
Farshelman, George.
Murphy, Christian.
Stimmel, Jacob.
Kirkwood, ——, died since discharge.
Coughanow, Amos, volunteered fifteen days; since died.
Tharpe, Ichabud, volunteered fifteen days; since died.
Hill, Charles, volunteered fifteen days; since died.
Fleed, Abraham.
Giger, William.

Marpel, John.
Huffhane, Jacob.
Haines, Joseph.
Donales, Amos.
Ruffcorn, Simon, discharged December 28, 1812.
Ruffcorn, Lewis.
Walker, Andrew.
Boweres, Cunrad.
Stewarte, Robert.
Ebart, Levi.
Artes, John.
Martin, John, discharged December 24, 1812.
Varner, Philip, discharged December 24, 1812.
Doube, Martin.
Wentling, Henry.
Smiley, Robert, discharged December 4, 1812.
Atkines, Benjamin, discharged December 9, 1812.
Rush, William, discharged October 20, 1812.
Hisonngle, Jacob, discharged December 1, 1812.
Spencer, Michael.
Haines, William.
Shaffer, Peter, discharged December 24, 1812.
Martin, Josiah.
Turke, Ephraim.
Weatherow, James.
McGloghlin, Robert.
Gollaher, Anthony.
Quigley, James.
Bucke, David, enlisted since he was discharged.
Baysinger, William.
Irons, John.
Stansbery, Samuel S.
Harod, George.

I do certify, upon honor, that this pay-roll exhibits a true statement of ——— company of the Second regiment of Pennsylvania militia, for the period therein mentioned, and that the remarks set opposite the names of men are accurate and just.

JAMES WHALEY,
Captain.

September 20, 1813.

LIST OF CAPT. SAMUEL WHITE'S COMPANY.

Role-list of Capt. White's company, of the Ninety-third regiment of Pennsylvania militia, commanded by Maj. Gallaway.

Captain.

White, Samuel.

Lieutenant.

Gardner, John.

Ensign.

Graft, John.

Musicians.

Armer, Thomas.
Tag, Mathew.

Privates.

Spangler, Joseph.
Delap, John.
Eyers, John.
Wireman, James.
Grupe, Phillip.
Funt, George.
Proctor, Richard.
Rex, Henry.
Kennedy, William.
Taylor, John.
Mortorff, George.
Anthoney, Nicholas.
Ross, John.

Rifle Corps.

Plowman, William.
Sanders, Jacob.
Wiley, Robert.
Snider, George.
Brandon, Thomas.
Repirton, Michael.
Proctor, William.
Fickle, John.
Davis, Samuel.
Barnhart, Peter.
Gilliland, Samuel.
Hays, Samuel.
Benner, John.

Benner, Daniel.
Knop, Peter.
Echard, Henry.
Stalsmith, Daniel.
Waker, William.
Shefer, John.
Moore, James.
Bush, John.
Knaus, Conrod.
Griner, Jacob.
Boyd, William.
Kennedy, Hugh.
McGrew, William.
McGrew, John.
Hoober, Jones.
Swoveland, Jacob.
Murrey, Jacob.
Blankley, William.
Murvitz, Michael.
King, Hugh.
Miller, John.
Essick, Jacob.
Miller, Jacob.
Delap, Leonard.
Row, Michael.
Piper, George.
Fips, Samuel.
Gardner, Benjamin.
Hutton, Joseph.
Moyer, John D.
West, William.
Middleton, James.
Speer, David.
Whitford, Cornelius.
Bricker, Henry.
Snider, George.
Chambers, Robert.
Godfrey, Thomas.
Moyer, George.
George, Robert.
Sheriff, George.
Zigler, David.
Ross, Joseph.
Gross, Philip.
Caldwell, George.
Strausbaugh, Abraham.
    33—Vol. XII.

Baulsley, John.
Stokes, James.
Nicholason, John.
Clark, William.
Collins, John.
Sellers, George.
Butts, Capt.
Stumph, William.
Miller, John.
Boke, James.
Essick, John.
Hawn, John.
West, John.
McDonald, James.
McFaden, Michael.
Derr, Henry.
McAfee, John.
James, Oen.
Gold, John.
Stickle, John.
White, Caleb.
Steel, John.
Hummal, George.
Wilson, Christopher.
Kennedy, John.
Minor, John.
Heiges, William.
Dill, George.
Hughs, John.
Smith, Joseph.
Halfarty, Arthur.
Dierdorff, Joseph.
Bowsen, Mathias.
Greeniwalt, Jacob.
Reaser, David.
Alexander, Francis.

 I do certify that the above and foregoing is a correct roll or list of men in my company, ordered on a tour of duty to Erie, agreeably to a requisition of the President of the United States, and general orders of the Governor of the Commonwealth of Pennsylvania. Given under my hand the 9th day of March, 1814.

        SAMUEL WHITE,
           Captain.
       G. WELP,
         Brigade Inspector.
      SAMUEL GALLOWAY,
           Major.

ROLL OF CAPT. C. WIGTON'S COMPANY.

CAMP DUPONT, *November 13, 1814.*

A true list of Capt. C. Wigton's company, of the Eighteenth section of Riflemen, commanded by Col. Thomas Humphrey.

Sergeants.

Trueman, David.
Clingan, William.
Hollis, Thomas.
Stott, David.

Corporals.

Piersol, John.
Rankin, John.
Mann, Ezekiel.
Humphrey, Joshua.

Bugler.

Hope, Robert.

Privates.

Wilson, John.
Parke, William.
Davis, Thomas.
Fleming, Joseph.
Haslet, James.
Cochran, Robert.
Mann, Samuel.
Grier, John E.
Witherow, William.
Welch, William.
Mann, Eli.
Whitelock, James.
Wallace, Arthur.
Cunningham, Robert.
Stott, Jesse.
Cochran, David.
Harry, Benejah.
Hope. Heslip.
Parke, David.
Moore, David.
Wilson, Boyd.
Cowan, Jacob.
Davis, Nathaniel.
McGinnis, William.
McKim, David.

Jones, Richard.
Bryan, John.
Smith, Joseph.
Glasgow, Samuel.
Eifort, Charles.
Parke, John.
Richmond, Joseph.
Scott, Thomas.
Hoover, John.
Date, George.
Hanley, James.
Gibson, Samuel C.
McWilliams, Robert.
Little, Patrick.
Lasly, John.
Way, Jacob.
Hayburn, William.
Thompson, Jacob.
Gibson, Andrew.
Moore, Eli.
Fleming, John S.
Ogelsby, Jonah.

I do certify that the within list is a true statement, on honor, this 13th day of November, 1814.

CHPR. WIGTON,
Captain.

THOMAS HUMPHREY,
Colonel First R. P. V. R.

I do certify, on honor, that the company commanded by Capt. Charles Wigton, is in the service of the United States, under the command of the general commanding the Fourth military district.

THOS. CADWALADER,
Brigadier General Commanding Advance Light Brigade.

CAMP DUPONT, *November 26, 1814.*

ROLL OF CAPT. JOHN WILLIAMSON'S COMPANY.

Pay-roll of a company of Infantry, commanded by Capt. John Williamson, in the service of the United States, from the 2d of October, 1812, until the 2d of April 1813. Second regiment, Second brigade, Pennsylvania militia, commanded by Brig. Gen. Richard Crooks.

Captain.

Williamson, John.

WAR OF 1812-14.

Lieutenant.
Taylor, John, volunteered fifteen days.

Ensign.
Horrel, John.

Sergeants.
Jamison, Robert.
Larimer, David.
Patterson, James.
Wierman, Samuel.

Corporals.
Parr, James.
Doty, John.
Baird, John.
Wallace, Hugh.

Drummer.
Pihel, Christopher.

Fifer.
Salden, Benjamin.

Privates.
McFarland, Alexander.
Rose, Allen.
Gregg, Andrew.
Gross, Adam.
Burk, Andrew.
Swain, Benjamin.
Bovard, Charles.
McCee, Charlton.
Stiffey, Daniel, discharged November.
Linsebigler, Daniel.
Baker, Daniel.
Kerby, Dinnes.
Therns, Edward.
Smitly, Fredrick.
Dibler, Fredrick.
Sheffer, Fredrick.
Clyne, George.
Arrit, George.
Beaty, Hammilton.
Eagin, John, discharged at Mansfield, December 9.
Jamison, James.
Furry, Jacob.
Mygrants, Jacob.
Craig, John.
McFaddin, James.
King, John.
Henry, James.

WAR OF 1812-14.

McGill, James.
Simpson, James.
McCally, John.
Limbright, John.
Immel, John.
Therns, John.
Thethly, Jacob.
Altman, John.
Linsebigler, John.
Smelser, Jacob.
Rosensteel, Jacob.
Soash, Isaac.
Christman, Jacob.
Ditman, Jacob.
Baker, Nicholas.
Baker, Peter.
Osborne, Robert.
McGuire, Robert.
Monroe, Robert.
Stephenson, Robert.
Low, Samuel.
Larimon, Robert.
Hoops, Thomas.
Latta, William, discharged at Sandusky, January 29.
Weaver, William.
Barnet, William, discharged at Pittsburgh
McCormick, William.
Brown, William.
Churchfield, William.
Black, Peter.

I certify, on honor, that the above return is accurate and just.

JOHN WILLIAMSON,
Captain.

ROLL OF CAPT. HENRY WILLOZ'S COMPANY.

Muster-roll of Capt. Henry Willoz's company, in the First regiment, Second brigade, Pennsylvania militia, under command of Lieut. Col. Jeremiah Shappel, at York, Pa. In service from August 28, 1814, to (not mentioned,) from Berks county.

Captain.

Willoz, Henry.

First Lieutenant.

Harman, William.

WAR OF 1812–14.

Ensign.

Herberling, John.

Sergeants.

Cunnius, Ye John.
Moyer, Jonathan.
Evans, Samuel.
Houder, Solomon.
Miller, Daniel.

Corporals.

Kremer, John.
Hoyer, Daniel.
Wingert, Jacob.
Benton, Samuel.
Hacket, Daniel.

Musicians.

Rader, Conrad.
Rader, Casper.

Privates.

Ahman, Frederick.
Bast, Dewalt.
Boyer, Samuel.
Briton, Joseph.
Bushe, Joseph.
Clouser, George.
Coffee, James.
Eberly, Samuel.
Eck, John.
Feather, Daniel.
Featherolf, Benjamin.
Foust, John.
Hamerstine, Nicholas.
Haub, Daniel.
Heister, Isaac.
Heister, John.
Heister, William.
Heller, Isaac.
Heller, Jacob.
Hosler, George.
Krich, Francis.
Lash, Samuel.
Learch, John.
Louch, Michael.
Lupt, John.
Maidenport, Nicholas.
Malone, George.

McCoy, William.
McCurdy, James.
McMickins, Andrew.
Messersmith, Jacob.
Miller, Jacob.
Miller, Peter.
Neadrow, Jacob.
Nuss, Michael.
Philips, James R.
Raber, Benjamin.
Raber, George.
Reifsnyder, Jacob.
Reifsnyder, John.
Rhine, Bernard.
Rockefeller, Peter.
Rollman, John.
Rothermal, John.
Ruth, Daniel.
Ruth, Philip.
Ruth, William.
Sassaman, Henry.
Seiler, Godfrey.
Shell, Jacob.
Shell, William.
Shlegel, Samuel.
Smeek, Daniel.
Snyder, Henry.
Snyder, Isaac.
Snyder, Samuel.
Spoon, Henry.
Star, George.
Strunk, John.
Wagner, George.
Wagner, Isaac.
Wanner, Jacob.
White, Henry.
Wolfinger, Philip.
Zweidzig, Jacob.

ROLL OF CAPT. ROBERT WILSON'S COMPANY.

Pay-roll of a company of militia commanded by Capt. Robert Wilson, of the Fifth battalion, Second brigade, performing a tour of duty under the command of Major McFarland, who rendezvoused at York, under general order of the Governor dated 26th August, 1814. Commencement of service, September 8, 1814.

Captain.

Wilson, Robert.

Lieutenant.

Williamson, David.

Ensign.

Miller, or Milard, Joseph.

Sergeants.

Lockhart, Jesse.
Simpson, James.
Antricon, or Entrekin, George.
Moore, James.

Corporals.

Ogelsby, John.
Baum, Jacob.
Redheifer, or Redopher, Andrew.
Carr, or Kerr, John.

Privates.

Balentine, Hamilton.
Millegan, James.
Owens, Morris.
Mawrey, or Maurer, Joseph.
Criley, Peter.
Bellows, or Bellis, Thomas.
Sims, Joseph.
Benner, David.
Allen, Isaac.
McDerment, or McDermott, Peter.
Bathurst, John.
Krider, Daniel.
Haus, Daniel.
Sims, William.
Grubb, Abram.
Parker, William.
Worts, Peter.
Wilson, William.
Packingham, Samuel.

Miller, William.
Wever, or Weber, John.
Waddel, Henry.
Bellows, or Bellis, Hiram.
Griffith, Amos.
Miller, Daniel.
Hendrickson, Jacob.
Colwell, Andrew.
Riley, William.
Uble, Frederick.
Miligan, or Millican, John.
Talbot, Caleb.
Carson, William.
Smith, Henry.
Atchless, Charles.
Irvin, or Irwin, Jonathan.
Miller, John.
Graham, James.
Manely, Hugh.
Cofroad, Jacob.
McKinley, Thomas.
Stapleton, Samuel.
Williams, William.
Powel, Daniel.
White, John.
Guay, or Guy, George.
Brown, Benjamin.
Widner, Peter.
Stanford, James B.
Darland, Samuel.
McKinley, Samuel.
Lockhart, William.
Pierce, Richard.
Guay, or Guy, John.
Gribben, James.
Irvin, or Erwin, John.
Fleck, Samuel.
Richards, Samuel.
Allison, Thomas.
Keely, Matthias.
Essick, Bolser.
Beagle, Henry.
Johnson, Barnard.
Phillips, Josiah, Jr.
Clevestin, or Clevenstine, Henry.
Widner, Jacob.

Bumbaugh, James.
Christy, Samuel.
Whitaker, Peter.
Cogell, Arnell.
Danelson, Griffith.
Griffey, David.
Buller, Cyrus.
Sherer, William.
Harley, Benjamin.
McGinn, or McGim, Peter.
Reed, Joseph.
Snyder, John.
Lamey, Edward.
Allison, William.

I certify the foregoing to be a correct roll of my company.

ROBERT WILSON,
Captain.

Test: WILLIAM McFARLAN,
Major.

ROLL OF CAPT. SAMUEL WILSON'S COMPANY.

October 13, 1814.

Copy of Capt. Wilson's company of militia, from Bucks county. Entered September 16, 1814.

Captain.

Wilson, Samuel.

First Lieutenant.

Pecker, William.

Second Lieutenant.

Donel, John.

Ensign.

Bisphan, John H.

Sergeants.

Kohl, Jacob, Nicholas Kohl, substitute.
Rodebough, John.
Cochran, Alexander.
Sekefoos, or Sigafoos, Jacob, Henry Sigafoos, substitute.

Corporals.

Rasoner, Joseph, Frederick Troutt, substitute.
Shaver, Paul.

Rasoner, John.
Carver, James, Jacob Boughen, substitute.

Musician.

Gordon, Emanuel.

Privates.

Armstrong, Jesse.
Roof, Jacob.
Ulmer, Jacob.
O'Daniel, Dennis.
Wimer, Daniel.
Rasoner, Simon.
Strouse, Jacob.
Miller, John.
Strouse, Philip.
Ulmer, Henry.
Bugher, or Boocher, Conrad.
Miller, George.
Mills, George.
Lompin, Nicholas.
Bugher, or Boocher, Andrew.
Frauger, Abraham.
Lefever, Jacob.
Morris, William.
Hammerstone, Philip.
McCarty, Thomas.
Mills, Jacob.
Regle, Jacob.
Yonken, Abraham.
Hager, John.
Mills, John.
Melone, John.
Kohle, Joseph.
McRoy, Thomas, John Ruth, substitute
Headman, Andrew.
Selner, Peter.
Whitsel, Adam.
Grove, Henry.
Miers, Samuel.
Herron, John.
Getman, Samuel
Long, George.
Shelly, Samuel.
Barret, George, John Stevenson, substitute
Harr, George.
Loyster, Abraham.

Rodenbush, Daniel.
Wolf, Jacob.
McNely, James, Jonathan Oren, substitute.
Swope, John.
Snyder, Barnet.
Leer, Joseph.
Willduner, or Wildonyer, John.
Snyder, Daniel.
Calvin, Joshua B.
Clawson, Malon.
Holcomb, John.
Ruth, Andrew.
Opdyke, Jonathan.
Housworth, Isaac.
Hany, Jacob.
Samsel, Peter.
Warner, Jacob.
Wimer, John.
Knight, Jacob.
Young, Martin.
Barron, Philip.
Christine, Peter.
Sellers, Isaac.
Hempt, Jacob.
Wikel, Samuel.
Pearson, Henry.
Sterner, Joseph.
Heft, Joseph.
Trough, Henry.
Crimer, Samuel.
Barron, Isaac.
Long, Lewderick.
Shoemaker, Jacob.
Losey, Jacob.
Dillon, Daniel.
Warner, John.
Boucher, Moses.
Grube, George.
Stroup, John.
McPeack, James.
Good, Henry.
Mills, George.
Mougel, Henry, Peter Maugle, substitute.
Wolfinger, John, John Mills, substitute.
Yonkin, Nicholas, Michael Youngkin, substitute.
Plots, Philip.

Barron, Michael.
O'Danel, Allen.
Sign, William.
Walter, Andrew.
Lewis, Jacob.
Bennet, Isaac.
McEntire, John.
Stone, Henry.
Swope, William.
Gilmer, Henry, discharged.
Dixon, John, discharged.
Whitsal, Isaac, discharged.
Rapp, George, discharged.
Buck, John.
Dixon, Thomas.

CAMP MARCUS HOOK, *October 18, 1814.*

I do hereby certify, upon honor, this muster-roll exhibits a true statement of a company of militia, from Bucks county, now in the service of the United States, and the remarks set opposite the names are accurate and just.

SAMUEL WILSON,
Captain.

I believe the annexed to be a correct muster and pay-roll.

ANDREW GILKYSON,
Lieutenant Colonel.

I do hereby certify that the company commanded by Capt. Samuel Wilson, of Bucks county militia, now in the service of the United States, under the orders of the general commanding the Fourth militia district.

By order,

W. C. ROGERS,
Brigade Major.

CAMP MARCUS HOOK, *October 18, 1814.*

ROLL OF CAPT. GEORGE ZIEBER'S COMPANY.

Muster-roll of Capt. George Zeiber's company in the First regiment, Second brigade, under the command of Lieut. Col. Jeremiah Shappel at York, Pennsylvania. In service from September 1, 1814, to December 4, 1814, from Berks county.

Captain.

Zieber, George.

First Lieutenant.

Gaessimer, Isaac C.

WAR OF 1812–14.

Second Lieutenant.

Welman, Charles.

Ensign.

Fuhrman, Jacob.

Sergeants.

Epley, John.
Goodman, Samuel.
May, Thomas.
Wahman, Solomon.

Corporals.

Armprister, Matthias.
Perry, Caleb.
Linderman, John.
Drumheller, William.

Privates.

Ache, Andrew.
Albright, Jacob.
Bechtel, George.
Boyer, John.
Davidhiser, John.
Deetrich, George.
Dessower, Ernst.
Dickinson, Isaac.
Dodinger, Abram.
Emore, Henry.
Epler, George.
Gable, Henry.
Gillams, Aaron.
Glenser, John.
Glouser, John.
Goodman, John.
Hamelton, John.
Hoch, Jacob.
Hoffman, John.
Hoster, William.
Hughes, Stephen.
Kebach, John.
Keiner, Jacob.
Keller, Jacob.
Keplinger, George.
Kepner, John.
Kessler, John.
Levengood, Adam.
Long, Christian.
Mackefer, David.

Moore, Henry.
Moore, Jacob.
Moyer, Andrew.
Moyer, George.
Neiman, John.
Noll, John.
Petre, Jacob.
Rapp, Henry.
Reifsnyder, George.
Richards, Caleb.
Roades, George.
Schrader, Anthony.
Schrader, Jacob.
Schwenk, George.
Shaeffer, John.
Shaeffer, Philip.
Shatz, Abram.
Silliman, Thomas.
Snyder, John.
Spies, Daniel.
Spotts, Andrew.
Springer, William.
Statler, Peter.
Stout, George.
Stout, Matthias.
Wamser, Samuel.
Wenrick, Valentine.
Wice, Conrad.
Wolf, Michael.
Womsher, David.
Womsher, George.
Zeller, Samuel.
Zerby, Joseph.
Zerby, Samuel.
Zeigler, Valentine.

www.ingramcontent.com/pod-product-compliance
Lightning Source LLC
Chambersburg PA
CBHW030537080526
44585CB00012B/185